Millennial Literatures of the Americas, 1492–2002

Imagining the Americas

Caroline F. Levander and Anthony B. Pinn, Series Editors

Imagining the Americas is a new interdisciplinary series that explores the cross-fertilization among cultures and forms in the American hemisphere. The series targets the intersections between literary, religious, and cultural studies that materialize once the idea of nation is understood as fluid and multiform. Extending from the northernmost regions of Canada to Cape Horn, books in this series move beyond a simple extension of U.S.-based American studies approaches and engage the American hemisphere directly.

Millennial Literatures of the Americas, 1492–2002

THOMAS O. BEEBEE

OXFORD
UNIVERSITY PRESS
2009

OXFORD
UNIVERSITY PRESS

Oxford University Press, Inc., publishes works that further
Oxford University's objective of excellence
in research, scholarship, and education.

Oxford   New York
Auckland   Cape Town   Dar es Salaam   Hong Kong   Karachi
Kuala Lumpur   Madrid   Melbourne   Mexico City   Nairobi
New Delhi   Shanghai   Taipei   Toronto

With offices in
Argentina   Austria   Brazil   Chile   Czech Republic   France   Greece
Guatemala   Hungary   Italy   Japan   Poland   Portugal   Singapore
South Korea   Switzerland   Thailand   Turkey   Ukraine   Vietnam

Published by Oxford University Press, Inc.
198 Madison Avenue, New York, New York 10016

www.oup.com

Oxford is a registered trademark of Oxford University Press

Library of Congress Cataloging-in-Publication Data

Beebee, Thomas O.
Millennial literatures of the Americas, 1492–2002 / by Thomas O. Beebee.
  p. cm.
Includes bibliographical references.
ISBN 978-0-19-533938-3
1. America—Literatures—History and criticism.   I. Title.
PN843. B44 2008
809′.897—dc22   2008006016

9 8 7 6 5 4 3 2 1

Printed in the United States of America
on acid-free paper

A
Nossa Senhora da Conceição Aparecida,
Notre Dame de Lourdes,
Nuestra Señora de Guadalupe,
Kannon Bosatsu,
All one and the same idea,
In whom the world does not end but exists for endless compassion
And comparison . . .

ACKNOWLEDGMENTS

I wish to acknowledge first of all the financial support provided by the Institute for the Arts and Humanities and the Departments of Comparative Literature and Germanic and Slavic Languages and Literatures at Penn State, without which the research for this book could not have been completed. Nathan Devir, Monika Giacoppe, Meghan Gibbons, Justin Halverson, Quentin Youngberg, Lori Ween, and Maria Luján Tubio provided invaluable research assistance. I am grateful to Richard Landes for his enthusiastic leadership in the field of millennial studies and for his hosting of conferences at Boston University, where I was able to test my own ideas and learn from the interesting work of other scholars, many of whom are cited in this volume. Thanks to Djelal Kadir, Sophia McClennen, and Aldon Nielsen for similar probation and for inspiring me with their leadership in international American studies. Thanks, as always, to Oleone Coelho Fontes and Wilton de Carvalho for initiating me into the mysteries of Canudos. Two anonymous readers for Oxford University Press gave invaluable critiques of the whole manuscript. I extend my gratitude to Shannon McLachlan for believing in my project and to Chrissy Gibson, Brian Desmond, and Brendan O'Neill for guiding it to completion and for catching all but my most elusive errors. And to Stephen Belcher and Rosa Eberle for the many informal chats *à propos* . . .

Special thanks and acknowledgment to Chester Brown and to Drawn and Quarterly Publications for permission to use images from Brown's *Louis Riel: A Comic Strip Biography.*

CONTENTS

A NOTE ON TRANSLATION

For literary texts in languages other than English, I have supplied a published translation where this was available, with the reference given in parentheses. Important words and phrases of the original are shown in square brackets. Where not otherwise noted, the translation is mine, and the reference is to the original.

Millennial Literatures of the Americas, 1492–2002

Eschatechnologies of the Americas

[Americans] live only for salvation, the Second Coming,
the reward of Rapture. They believe in Jesus, UFOs,
decency, honest banking, and their right to buy assault
weapons.

—Andrei Codrescu, *Messiah*

Rayford had cast his lot with God *and* the miracle of
technology.

—LaHaye and Jenkins, *Desecration* (emphasis added)

In the first epigraph, Andrei Codrescu humorously defines the subject of this book, which I call eschatechnology, by juxtaposing three concepts: technological devices (UFOs, assault weapons); a disciplinary regime or "technology of the self" (decency, honest banking, the "right to buy"); and divine intervention in the form of the end of the world (Rapture, the Second Coming). Codrescu constructs a list from these three categories that characterizes a peculiarly American, millennialist view of the world that is the subject of this study. (Though Codrescu is referring to U.S. citizens, "American" throughout this book refers to both North and South America and to cultures on these continents where the dominant language may be English, French, Portuguese, or Spanish.) Anyone who has read the *Left Behind* series, on the other hand, knows that the authors of that millennial magnum opus take the link between God, technology, and the end of the world literally and seriously. It seems that more than half of the main Christian characters are jet pilots; the co-op that sustains Christian underground life around the planet arranges trades through digital communication; Tribulation Force reconnoiters the Antichrist by hacking into his computers; the true prophet, Tsion Ben-Judah, delivers his message via the Internet; cell phones are ubiquitous, and so forth.

This book compares literary eschatechnologies produced in a wide spectrum of communities across the Americas, from their colonial (and, as recorded in European languages, pre-Columbian) origins to the present, from the letters of Columbus to the *Left Behind* series of dispensationalist novels. The goal is to recover and to better understand a theme that has defined the Americas since the arrival of Europeans as a "technology of the self" that both furthers national and imperial agendas, but serves as a discourse of resistance for populations for whom a transvaluation of all values becomes the only means of survival. Historical, literary, and ethnographic records converge on the fact that the repeated irruptions of millennial conflict have been acts of resistance to the eradication of traditional ways of life in the process of nationalization and globalization, as well as important resources in the search for origins and foundations. Americans in particular tend to understand their origins by narrating their end. In the Americas, dominant societies depend upon an erasure of the cultures of conquered indigenous peoples and of the histories of slaves and slavery and hence a denial of our own roots. In traditional cultures, people belong to the land, yet the first act of conquest has always been to seize the land and claim its ownership. That the European conquerors of the Americas started from the viewpoint of land possession guaranteed the absence of origins other than those provided by eschatechnology itself. Since this end is always imagined rather than experienced, the *logos* of fiction and literature became instrumental in its propagation.

First Things about Last Things

The term *eschatechnology* combines "technology" with the Greek *to eschaton*, an adjectival noun that means "the last," "final," or "ultimate." Here it refers to the last stages of a particular race, culture, or social system, where the existing conditions are swept away by miraculous intervention, and a new community of freedom, justice, and dignity is established in their place. A common word for this new creation is "millennium," from a passage in Revelation 20 that describes the binding of Satan and a reign of Christ for one thousand years:

> And I saw an angel come down from heaven, having the key of the bottomless pit and a great chain in his hand. And he laid hold on the dragon, that old serpent, which is the Devil, and Satan, and bound him a thousand years, and cast him into the bottomless pit, and shut him up, and set a seal upon him, that he should deceive the nations no more, till the thousand years should be fulfilled: and after that he must be loosed a little season. (Revelation 20:1–3)

This binding of Satan follows a narrative of repeated suffering, death, and destruction meant to symbolize the martyrdom of early Christians. Thus, a scenario of global destruction is frequently called an "apocalypse," from the Greek title of Revelation. Apocalypse and millennialism are distinct but interconnected phenomena. In fact, they need each other: Apocalypse is, in David B. Batstone's formulation, "a cosmic vision of reality that announces a divine plan for creation's deliverance from bondage. [It is] a 'disclosure' or 'revelation' first witnessed by an announcing prophet . . . which is, at the present moment, bringing human history to the threshold of a great reversal. It therefore delegitimizes the present superior position of those groups in opposition to the envisioned divine purpose" (1992, 385). "Apocalyptic" is sometimes used as a noun to refer to a text such as Daniel or Revelation or to a corpus of such texts. In this book, "apocalypse" refers to a vision that falls within Batstone's definition, while "apocalyptic" is used as an adjective to describe writing that conveys such a vision. The goal of the vision, namely the renewal of the world and deliverance from bondage, is called "millennium."

Millennium, which is an apocalyptic vision of collective destiny, was an important tool used for the establishment of neo-European culture in the Americas. The term *eschatechnology* in my title refers both to the use of this tool and to the general role of technology in millennial visions. This role appears in the epigraphs to this introduction, but it goes back perhaps to the creatures seen by Ezekiel in the Old Testament—"like burning coals of fire or like torches [speeding] back and forth like flashes of lightning" (1:13–14)—that represent the wrath of God and the spirit of prophecy. The frequent importance of "hard" technology for a thinking that is in many ways conservative represents a paradox to be explored in the course of this book.

If the conjunction of divinely inspired millennium and technology seems surprising, given the supposed displacement of religion by science in modernity, David Noble has demonstrated that it has been a constant since the Middle Ages, when a renewed interest in millennium among religious orders led to their increasing appreciation of manual arts. Important Enlightenment figures, such as Francis Bacon and Isaac Newton, were as interested in apocalypse as they were in science. Or, to put it in Noble's terms, their interest in one depended upon their interest in the other. The combined concerns were also operative in the Age of Discovery and in the voyages of Christopher Columbus, leading to the importation and flourishing of eschatechnologies in the New World. In David Nye's (2003) reading, the operation of European technologies such as the axe on frontier environments went hand in hand with the textually derived imagery of the "Second Creation," in a process that was repeated over four centuries. In short, "[M]odern technology and religion have evolved together and . . . as a result, the technological enterprise has been and remains suffused with religious belief. In America as nowhere else before or since, the useful arts became wedded to Adamic myths and millenarian dreams" (Noble 1999, 5, 88).[1] Indeed, as Martin Heidegger puts it, "technology is a way of revealing" (1977, 12).

Technology's revelation, like John the Divine's, has negative, as well as positive, connotations. The immense and complex web of interlinked technological devices, imbricated in bureaucracies of control, can appear as a demonized form of the human, as Fredric Jameson points out:

> [T]echnology may well serve as adequate shorthand to designate that enormous properly human and anti-natural power of dead human labor stored up in our machinery—an alienated power, what Sartre calls the counterfinality of the practico-inert, which turns back on and against us in unrecognizable forms and seems to constitute the massive dystopian horizon of our collective as well as our individual praxis. (1991, 35)

Even Jameson's language of Marxist analysis contains some of the symbolism—antinatural, dead—that recalls prophetic discourse. In any case, technology increasingly obscures its human roots and applications, and its antinatural quality quickly becomes supernatural: Various technologies are read as vials poured out on the earth, and the void of agency is filled by the Antichrist.

On the one hand, in the course of this book I show several instances of hard-core technologies, such as those referred to in the epigraphs. On the other hand, my use of "technology" also owes something to Michel Foucault's "technologies of the self" and to its several avatars, such as that of Naoki Sakai, who distinguishes between objective and subjective technologies (1997, 24–25), and of Shu-mei Shih, who has introduced the notion of "technologies of recognition" (2004, *passim*). In our daily use of the term, we nearly always link technology with "hard" devices of some kind and with a "magic" that the ordinary person cannot use or understand. The word derives from the Greek *techné*, which simply means skill or art. A technology may also be thought of as a rationalization procedure for carrying out a particular task or for making a certain product—such as a self. In the collection of essays that bears the title *Technologies of the Self*, Foucault and other contributors employ synonyms such as "technique" or the original Greek term (Martin and Hutton 1988). Foucault lists four types of technologies: technologies of production; technologies of sign systems; technologies of power; and technologies of the self (ibid., 18). Eschatechnologies embrace the latter three categories.

Perry Miller (1964) and Sacvan Bercovich (1978) have published influential studies of the Puritan contribution to the eschatological sign system of the Americas, and Ernest Tuveson's 1968 work remains a touchstone. However, the impression left by *Errand into the Wilderness*, *The American Jeremiad*, and *Redeemer Nation*, respectively, which focus on communities that have contributed heavily to dominant viewpoints, is that only fundamentalist Protestants are capable of converting eschatological scripts into political realities and institutions. There is much to be gained from a broader vision of the topic and some truth, for example, to Jorge Cañizares-Esguerra's attempt in *Puritan Conquistadors* to unveil the contributions of Iberian eschatechnologies with claims such as the following: " 'Americans' need to look to Mexico for the true ancestors of the doctrine of Manifest Destiny" (2006, 80). Along with Cañizares-Esguerra's work, two other comparative studies are most relevant to my own. Frank Graziano's *Millennial New World* (1999) provides a sweeping and much-needed documentation of millennial thought and discourse in Ibero-America. However, Graziano spends very little time on literary texts, whose function as eschatechnologies is the topic of this book. Lois Zamora's *Writing the Apocalypse* (1987) analyzes literary texts but is true to its title in focusing on authorial visions of time and history: Not every apocalypse is an eschatology.[2] Because I wish to combine the historical approach and millennialist focus of Graziano with the concern for literary texts found in Zamora, I choose texts that do not just contain history but are themselves historical. The myths and poems of Louis Riel, for example, a great and tragic visionary of the waning of Catholicism and its rebirth in Canada, are a part of the political and social ideology he represented and died for, as are the reggae lyrics of Robert Nesta Marley. Riel and Marley are comparable in terms of the central role that poetry and myth played in their conveyance of millennial visions with pragmatic political consequences. It is to this role of literature in the unfolding of history that we now turn.

The End of the World Is Always a Fiction

Typology, as I use the term here, was developed by Saint Paul (who first applied the Greek *typos* to this phenomenon in 1 Corinthians 10:1–4) as a way of bringing Judaism and Christianity together as two interrelated dispensations of a single God. In his letter to the Hebrews (10:1), Paul writes that "the [Jewish] law is only a shadow of the good things that are coming." The law is not to be taken literally but only as a shadowing forth of a new covenant. In Protestant allegory, which of course is crucial for understanding Puritan perspectives on their mission in North America, types "are one of the two central methods by which the Old and New Testaments are related. Hebrew prophecy is the second. . . . Prophecy implies future fulfillment; typology asserts that the consummation has occurred" (Thomas Davis 1972, 43). By the time Samuel Mather had written his influential study (1683), this shadow had come to be called a "type," and the "good thing to come" its "antitype": "[T]he other [type] is the Shadow, this [antitype is] the Substance: the *Type* is the Shell, this [is] the Kernel; the *Type* is the Letter, this [is] the Spirit and Mystery of the *Type*" (66). Literature unveils the types upon which readers may base their own antitypical behaviors, thus becoming a technology of the self. In the case of millennialism, literature projects its shadow into history.

The emphasis on futurity and mystery in typology makes it an early form of what today is called "possible-worlds" literary theory. The possible-worlds approach sees literary texts as "a set of instructions for the reader, according to which the world reconstruction proceeds. . . . Having reconstructed the fictional world as a mental image, the reader can ponder it and make it a part of her experience, just as she experientially appropriates the actual world. The appropriation, which ranges from enjoyment through knowledge acquisition to following it as a script, integrates fictional worlds into the reader's reality" (Dolezel 1998, 21). John wrote the New Jerusalem into existence as a possible world to be contrasted with the actual Jerusalem under Roman occupation, thus as a type that his readers could learn from and perhaps use as a script. The ways in which millennial texts encourage or discourage their readers' specific appropriations is an important topic in this book.

As the most extensive, complex, and interpretable records we possess of how people have thought and felt in any historical period, products of a technology for recording and producing "structures of feeling," literary texts provide the primary study examples for this book. I use Raymond Williams's term "structure of feeling" to identify a residue of the organization of the lived experience of a community over and above society's institutional and ideological organization (see Fekete 1994, 733). As noted earlier, millennial communities are organized according to typologies that make literary texts (types) the basis for experience (antitypes). In such cases, literature goes beyond mere expression of a structure of feeling: The former becomes nearly coterminous with the latter. I have chosen texts that emphasize literature's intervention in historical events; literature, in other words, is one of the earliest and most pervasive eschatechnologies. Examples include the influence of the Millerite movement on the work of Nathaniel Hawthorne and Herman Melville; the relationship between Ernesto Cardenal's work as a Nicaraguan minister of culture and his millennial view of Native American cultures; the foreshadowing of Mario Vargas Llosa's political agenda as a Peruvian presidential candidate in his novel of the Canudos war; the terrorism of Timothy McVeigh as a condensation of the real events of the Waco massacre with the fictional ones of William Pierce's racial apocalypse, *The Turner Diaries*; and the performance of Rastafarian millennialism through the lyrics and music of Bob Marley and other reggae poets. On the other hand, literature has also been the primary vehicle for "reflective dissonance," a process by which millennial scenarios are negated and ironized, thereby enabling an examination of key issues such as disappointment (when millennial predictions do not come true), which by definition must be repressed in millennial discourse per se.

For the purposes of this book, "literature" is roughly synonymous with "fiction," texts with recognizable characters and plot events that occur not in the real world but that represent possible worlds in readers' minds. Literature, of course, profits greatly from the use of millennial plotlines, which are primordial examples of the battle between good and evil, white hats and black hats. The relationship between artistic forms and millennium itself is complex and varied. Indeed, sorting out the various stances writers may take toward eschatology is a contribution this book makes with regard to our understanding of the phenomenon.

To begin, let us consider a very simple continuum from prophecy to parody, with the titles of some literary examples on top (figure 1.1).

The two stories from which the epigraphs are drawn, *Messiah* and *Left Behind*, differ greatly from each other in their approach to millennium: *Left Behind* is a Christian self-help series (coauthor LaHaye also publishes "straight" dispensationalist interpretations of Revelation), while *Messiah* uses the eschaton as a metaphor for the postmodern, multicultural, Southern gothic decadence of New Orleans. Literary texts, of course, are multidimensional, so this one-dimensional arrangement severely reduces the complex relations such texts may have with history, with present realities, and with each other. Nor does the graph take account of the polysemy and heteroglossia of many texts. Vargas Llosa's *War of the End of the World* is listed as neutral because it counterpoints voices from each end of the spectrum of belief against each other, while *Handmaid's Tale* is right-shifted due to its placement within a frame that negates the viability of the millennial community depicted with stunning seriousness in the narration. My figure is intended merely to show that the engagement of literature with millennial communities runs a gamut from full participation in the feedback loop on the left-hand side—the book of Revelation has been the basis for the formation of a number of millennial communities, including David Koresh's Branch Davidians (see Koresh and Sevenseals.com)—to full disengagement from it on the right. The opposition is not between texts that "start" millennial movements and those that stop them but rather between texts that are fully engaged in bringing millennium about and those that break the feedback loop by taking a distanced, reportorial, parodic, or skeptical approach, or one that I call "reflective dissonance."

All of the literary texts listed on the continuum (plus many others) are treated in the course of this study, beginning with Revelation. Different chapters deal with different ends of the scale. The left-hand side is addressed by chapter one, whose center is the *Conquista espiritual* (1892) of Ruiz de Montoya, one of the leading

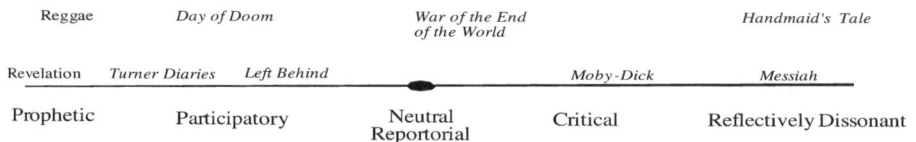

Reggae		*Day of Doom*		*War of the End of the World*			*Handmaid's Tale*
Revelation	*Turner Diaries*	*Left Behind*			*Moby-Dick*		*Messiah*
Prophetic		Participatory	Neutral Reportorial		Critical		Reflectively Dissonant

FIGURE 1.1 Millennial literature from prophecy to dissonance.

Jesuit proselytizers in the Paraguayan missions; chapter two, which discusses hybridity as a charismatic element of American messiahs; chapter three, which compares millennial communities of the late nineteenth century in Canada, the United States, and Brazil; and chapter seven, which examines the racialization of the eschaton in American fictions. The right-hand side is represented primarily by chapter four, which compares the varieties of reflective dissonance encountered in literary texts. Chapters six and seven deal with two poets of the Americas, Ernesto Cardenal and Bob Dylan. The allusiveness and intertextuality of their poems makes them hard to "rate" on the scale; my main concern is to show the influence of historical events and developing technologies on their expression of millennial themes.

In some sense, then, this study examines the way the same story gets told over and over again in the Americas. It is a "theme and variations" approach: The master narrative of millennium appears differently in the micronarratives embedded in a variety of experiences and points of view that have occurred over the history of the Americas. It is, of course, literary rather than "hard" history, and the master narrative is of what should or will happen rather than of what has already happened; however, it will become clear that representations of millennium are frequently grounded in political and social realities of the times and places they are written, and in order to foreground such historical contexts I use a wide variety of written (con)texts.

Some Eschatechnologies

Since its probable origins in the Middle East thousands of years ago, thinking about last things has facilitated our ability to conceive a future radically different from the present. Future-oriented thinking permeates Western society and distinguishes it from traditional cultures, where cycles and repetition provide the framework for time schemes. Jacques Derrida, among others, has stated that this constant (re)thinking of the "last things" in various forms, both secular and religious, has constituted one of the most powerful programs for Western thought over the centuries:

> the West has been dominated by a powerful program that was also an untransgressible contract among discourses of the end. . . . I tell you this in truth; this is not only the end of this here but also and first of that there, the end of history, the end of the class struggle, the end of philosophy, the death of God, the end of religions, the end of Christianity and morals . . . the end of the subject, the end of man, the end of the West, the end of Oedipus the end of the earth. . . . Isn't the voice always that of the last man? (1982, 80–81)

We see in this quote how a simple change in framework in our view of time and history has helped produce a vocabulary and interpretive schema for dealing with the world. Moreover, the Book of Revelation, an apocalyptic text written in Greek in the late first century AD to shore up belief in the face of the destruction of Jerusalem and subsequently canonized as the last book of the New Testament, has furnished its own symbolic vocabulary—the breaking of seals, the pouring out of vials, the binding and loosing of Satan, the Beast, the Whore of Babylon, the Four Horsemen, Armageddon, the New Jerusalem—which has been recycled by Western writers and which we will encounter in the specific analyses of this book. As a wise priest once told me, Revelation is the only single book of the Bible that people consider sufficient for founding their own separate church. Most of us have seen movie clips of machines that take on a life of their own, such as the magically reproducing brooms in the "Sorcerer's Apprentice" sequence of *Fantasia*. Such has been the book of Revelation, an image machine that produces meanings far removed from its original contexts.

Increasingly in the modern world, West has met East, and one can now find significant millennial discourse on every continent. David Cook has written on the millennial literature of modern Islam, Robert Jay Lifton on the infamous Aum Shinrikyo of Japan (1999), Nils Bubandt on "millenarian modernity" in eastern Indonesia, and Robert Edgar and Hilary Sapire on an example of "African apocalypse." I would argue, however, that the Americas present a special case whose uniqueness can best be defined through the breadth and interconnectedness of the many examples given in this study. In the Americas, eschatechnologies are foundational to modern civilizations and imbue the literatures of these continents with millennial dreams. In the Americas, the use of millennial vocabulary by the powerful to manipulate the disempowered goes back to 1492 (the next chapter briefly examines its usage by Columbus), from which point eschatechnology has been a tool for motivating settlers, missionaries, and their newfound subjects. Eschatechnology inhabits both sides of the fence, so to speak. The eschatechnology that Europeans brought to the New World represented "a vanishing-point symbolic technology, making over an otherness that disappears into the discourse of the Old—an otherness, a culture, or many cultures whose meanings Columbus couldn't know and Vespucci couldn't see and that the New Englanders could not possibly admit—and providing a purchase on narration of the New World for the European knowledge that completes the act of possession" (Washington 1992, 104). Like most technologies, however, those that eschatechnology is meant to control can seize, hybridize, and use it against its inventors.

There are many different ways that eschatechnology can produce, modify, or deconstruct an individual's conception of self, and the emphasis I place on literary works provides an excellent platform from which to view the dialectic between individual and collective awareness. Many may think of millennial movements as the very abnegation of self in view of the fact that individuals surrender their wills and identities to a single charismatic leader—an Ahab, a Koresh, or a Counselor—with results like the mass suicides of Jonestown and Heaven's Gate or the selfless courage displayed by the fighters of the Canudos and Contestado conflicts in Brazil. Frequently, however, extinction of the worldly self occurs within a vision of another, eternal self achieved through this sacrifice. Millennialists become martyrs in order to be counted among the blessed.

Again, Revelation provides a script, for example when one of the twenty-four elders enthroned near God explains the presence of 144,000 sealed descendents of the tribes of Israel: "These are they which came out of great tribulation, and have washed their robes, and made them white in the blood of the Lamb. Therefore are they before the throne of God, and serve him day and night in his temple: and he that sitteth on the throne shall dwell among them" (7:14–16). To "come out of tribulation" does not necessarily mean to survive it physically but rather to preserve one's faith in the face of it. There is of course one other type of self that I should mention, and that is the Messiah. By this I mean merely the leader of a revitalization movement, no matter what its religious orientation. Such individuals in the Americas, from Louis Riel of Manitoba, to the *Conselheiro* [Counselor] of Canudos, Bahia, to Wovoka of Nevada and Smohalla of Washington, to Ahab of the *Pequod*, seem at first glance to represent self-aggrandizement rather than self-abnegation. However, their power has been given to them by the collective as though in an energy transfer. The question of what kind of self messiahhood makes possible is explored in chapter two, "Hybrid Messiahs."

The Insistence of the Eschaton in the American (Un)Conscious

This study does not cover the European millennial movements and texts that preceded and helped shape American millennial expectations. These have been thoroughly studied by Michael Barkun, Norman Cohn, Richard Landes, Bernard McGinn, and others. However, the general background of the texts brought to the New World is important. Essentially, there are three strands: Old Testament prophecy, for which the central text is the book of Daniel; New Testament apocalyptic, for which the central text is the book of Revelation; and localized legend, such as the Portuguese one of the founding of the nation and the disappearance of Dom Sebastião. The syncretic interweaving of these texts becomes further differentiated in the New World, where they combine with indigenous stories of the end.

A typical example of eschatechnological discourse in the Americas is Albert J. Beveridge's prophecy to the United State Senate in 1900 that "God has . . . been preparing the English-speaking and Teutonic peoples for a thousand years to become master organizers of the world to establish system where chaos reign[s. . . . O]f all our race He has marked the American people as His chosen nation to finally lead in the redemption of the world" (1908, 84–85). Beveridge used this language in order to convince his colleagues to annex the Philippines. He uses the language of so-called postmillennialism, that is, the belief that progress and order are being established on the earth under a divine plan that will culminate in the New Jerusalem. (The final vision of Revelation is of a New Jerusalem "coming down out of heaven from God" [21:10].) As a historian, he was well aware that the organization had begun at home with events like the Mexican War and the appropriation of "chaotic" Indian lands for organized white settlement.[3]

A central thesis of this study maintains that part of the organization Beveridge speaks of is narrative itself. In his view, history can be told only of a system, not of chaos, and not in myths told by non-English speakers and hence history must exclude tens of thousands of years of pre-Columbian life. Self-referentially, the metanarrative Beveridge provides is itself the prime example of organization—the millennium of Revelation. That the slave trade's depopulation of Africa might have caused rather than diminished chaos does not occur to Beveridge. That the establishment of system might cause human suffering need not be addressed because the rhetorical focus is on a messianic, redemptive future. Pre-Columbian civilization, slavery, resistance, and of course the millennial dreams of the oppressed are then categorized as what Michael Barkun has termed "stigmatized knowledge" (2003,

15–38), which in turn calls forth conspiracy theories—for which Revelation serves as a type or template—as a kind of reaction-formation. Beveridge may be a chestnut, but one goal of this study is to pay more attention to how comparable thought has affected other cultures of the Americas. We can draw parallels not only with Lord Durham's remark about *Canadiens*—that they were "a people with no history, and no literature" (1963, 38)—and with the Brazilian positivist outlook that helped fuel the Canudos war of 1897–1898. Ernest Tuveson's classic study, *Redeemer Nation* (1968), which takes its title from Beveridge's statement, documents the different ways and forms in which the idea has manifested itself in U.S. history but pays too little attention both to the narratological and psychodynamic aspects of millennial thought, which converge on the need for a narrative to endow our actual, chaotic history and existence with the beauty and logic of system, and to the appropria- tion of this eschatechnology by the victims of that actual history and existence. For the latter aspect we may turn to Vittorio Lanternari, Bryan Wilson, and others, but their recounting of numerous hybrid messianic outbreaks in the Americas and in the world becomes an iterative listing that lacks any metanarrative framework. Some millennial thought of the New World hybridizes native with European millennial scripts. (On the notion of hybridity see chapter two.[4]) Situations of hybridization and syncretism are addressed primarily in the next two chapters, the first on the earliest European colonization and conversion, the second on messiah/Antichrist figures. All of them, I would argue, arise out of the confrontation with eschatech- nologies imported from the Old World and inevitably altered in the New.

The present study works comparatively throughout the Americas, analyzing ex- amples drawn from all four dominant language areas of the two continents. Though it cannot be exhaustive, my approach is comprehensive, moving through history from Columbus to the early twenty-first century as indicated in the dates of the title of this book. Since I am writing in English, my readers may already be familiar with the use of eschatechnology in U.S. culture from John Winthrop's invocations of the Puritans as a "community in perill" and his vision of a "citty upon a hill" to the selection of the eagle for the great seal (in allusion to Revelations 12:14, where the woman who repre- sents the church is given the wings of the eagle so that she can fly into the wilderness), through Beveridge's notion of "manifest destiny," all the way to the quasi-official des- ignation of September 11, 2001, as "the day the world changed." They may even be aware that the first North American bestseller was an eschatological narrative poem titled "Day of Doom" and published in 1662 by a Puritan pastor, Michael Wiggles- worth. Those Americans who are aware of this millennial heritage (rather than merely unconsciously using its rhetoric and succumbing to its imagery) might not realize the connections it shares with the history of other countries in the Americas.

There are, of course, substantial differences between millennial representa- tion in the various American languages and cultures as well. The most obvious is the official opposition to prophecy by the Catholic Church, historically dominant in much of Latin America and in French-speaking Canada, which means that mil- lennial discourse in Catholic countries of the Americas remains oppositional rather than dominant. Nevertheless, the last Brazilian president of the twentieth century and the first of the twenty-first century both launched their campaigns from beneath the huge statue of Padre Cícero, leader of a popular movement in northeastern Brazil with millennial tendencies. Another difference involves the relative incorporation of native peoples into the eschaton: "[W]hereas the progress and demise of the Indian church in America is an integral part of the ecclesiastic histories of New Spain, in New England's most prominent ecclesiastic history Native Americans remain outside the cultural boundaries of the new English nation" (Bauer 2001, 43).

However, a great many of the colonists and missionaries from whatever European country shared a late medieval mindset in which millennium remained a more or less unquestioned (or at least publicly uncontested) article of faith. Perry Miller paints a particularly lively portrait of everyday life in a millennial mindset, which once again brings science and technology into the picture:

> We find it hard to comprehend how men in medieval towns could go cheerfully, as evidently they did, about their daily business when constantly before their eyes, sculptured on the fronts of their churches and cathedrals, were extended terrifying realistic scenes of the last judgment. Still harder to comprehend is that they could live, as certainly they did, with any degree of cheer when they all, learned or unlearned, could see no scientific reason why the awful blow should not fall at any moment. In their physics, the universe was not self-sustaining. Motion was given by God and all movement was propelled by Him, so that clearly He might at any moment call a halt. Then the trumpet would sound, motion would cease, the moon turn to blood, the stars fall like withered leaves, and the earth would burn. (1964, 217–18)

Miller concludes—much in the tenor of my own study—that the beauty and moral symmetry of the vision of the Last Judgment provoked an aesthetic thrall that tempered the sublimity of its horror. In any case, Miller raises an interesting contrast between a scientific view of the universe, in which ultimate catastrophe seems more improbable, and the God-centered view, where it is always already part of the plan. The question then becomes, why does eschatechnology continue to shape language, power, and the self long after scientific views of the universe have supposedly become normative and "God is dead"?

One answer is that the same science that explained nature gave rise to the technologies that now threaten to destroy it. The sometimes lethal combination of science, technology, and biopolitics enables radically different but no less terrifying scenarios of ultimate destruction, whether those be the nuclear deserts of Walter Miller's *Canticle for Leibowitz* (1960) or the superflu of Stephen King's *The Stand* (1978). The characters of Pat Robertson's *End of an Age* (1995) do the math for us. As he waits for an asteroid to hit the earth and cause massive destruction, Charley hypothesizes that the various vials have already been poured out upon the earth in the course of the twentieth century, and he recounts for Carl the many millions of deaths in world wars and various holocausts:

> Carl stirred restlessly in his seat. "Charley, is that true? The last century was the worst in history? I mean, worse even than Rome or Greece or the Dark Ages?"
> "It's a simple matter of technology, Carl. It would have been impossible to kill so many people at any other time in history. The Romans had swords. They didn't have guns or bombs. It took two thousand years of science to give mankind the expertise to wipe out millions of people in such a short period of time." (ibid., 68)

In discussions of this type, the problem of free will is framed as one of technology even though the disaster that ends humankind as we know it in this novel is a comet that evades all technological safeguards. Unlike the *Left Behind* series, which openly embraces technology—including its weaponry—as capable of being used against the Antichrist, Robertson's novel makes it responsible for the eschaton. However, this is not the whole story either. The approaching comet does hit the earth and cause volcanic eruptions, earthquakes, and tsunamis that leave the world in a shambles appropriate for manipulation by the Antichrist. The believers end up winning through advanced weaponry, including some Pershing missiles.

Let us take as another example the cover story of the *Newsweek* issue for June 2, 1997, whose title was "The Day the World Crashes." In the venerable spirit of millennial predictions, the exact date of the crash had supposedly been made manifest to the writers (Steven Levy and Katie Hafner): January 1, 2000. Persons not living in the cyberneticized sections of U.S. society might have taken this to be a religious story. The rest of us knew that it was about the programming bug that would not allow many larger computers to "understand" the year 2000 (not knowing that "00" follows "99" since programmers tended to use two digits to designate a year, as for college class years). The cover page for the story depicts a catastrophic explosion: A computer screen bursts; dollars, microchips, diskettes, and tax forms fly through the air; scientists, secretaries, and businessmen run, while an air traffic controller throws up his hands to ward off the evil as his planes fall from the sky. Three questions introduce the article: "Will power plants shut down and your phone go out?"; "Will your Social Security checks disappear into cyberspace?"; and "Will your bank account vanish?" The answer to all three questions, it turned out, was "No," but you had to buy the magazine to find this out.

As in 1999, newspapers in 1844 (the year William Miller predicted for the Second Coming) sold more copies by suggesting the imminence of apocalypse than by denying it. The Y2K bug appeared to resolve the issue of whether the new millennium would begin in the year 2000 or, as is more mathematically precise, in the year 2001 in favor of the former—until 9/11/2001, that is. Besides newspapers and software companies, the Great Expectation was also a boon to the survivalists, who, in imitation of their archetype, Noah, stocked up on food and ammunition to last through the long winter of social breakdown that was to magically occur at the stroke of midnight. Ed Yourdon, coauthor with his daughter Jennifer of *Time Bomb 2000*, who had spent thirty-five years in the computer field, the past twenty as a consultant to Fortune 500 companies and government agencies, moved from New York City to Taos, a change of address partly based on his Y2k concerns. "There's enough of a chance that the disruptions might make major cities like New York totally unlivable for a year that I would plan accordingly," he said ("Survivalist Plans Built around Y2K," 7B). In 1999, newspaper accounts such as that about Karl Hanel, pastor of Embassy Baptist Church in Donaldson, Illinois, were in abundant circulation:

> "Within two weeks at the very most the cities will be in total chaos." Cold, desperate people roam the countryside in search of food and shelter, forcing rural folks like him to take up arms to protect themselves and their families. . . . Especially vulnerable, [Hanel] thinks, will be the middle class and lower middle class—the people to

whom he ministers. "Ultimately, the balloon is going to burst." He doesn't wish for that day, he says. But it will be a great chance to minister. "There are going to be a lot of needy people. People are going to have to start taking care of other people again." (Theobald 1999, A01)

Although 2000 turned into yet another great disappointment, the events of September 11, 2001, convinced many that, although the calendar was off by a bit, the end of the world had nevertheless arrived, and the whole well-oiled eschatechnological machinery of the Americas was now to be activated. The shift from grayscale to black-and-white visions of the world evident in post-9/11 rhetoric (just when many were enjoying some relief from it with the end of the Cold War) draws its sustenance from apocalyptic thinking and may be considered a subspecies of the shift from everyday notions of gradualism to extraordinary and cataclysmic situations of suddenism.

Causalities

When one traces the way the Cold War gave way to Y2K, which gave way to the post-9/11 syndrome, the hypothesis suggests itself that these are merely different labels and contingencies, different antitypes used to fill out a script to figure forth a shadow whose basic plotline and elements are unchanging, and that American societies have a deep and abiding need to fit events into this story. Aside from the particular eschatechnology chosen, recurrent visions of millennium have seemed largely independent of the material advances of society and of the supposedly all-encompassing advance of rationality. Let us examine a few explanations for this repetition-compulsion.

Speaking broadly, there have been three dominant paradigms in the interpretation of millennial communities: psychological, sociological, and rhetorical. The first paradigm views millennial belief as a form of psychic disturbance. It tends to view the messiah figure of the community as psychotic and the followers as either brainwashed or otherwise incapable of rational thought. A prime example of such an interpretation, which we might call the "Ahab complex," is Euclides da Cunha's analysis of the Canudos rebellion, *Os sertões* (1902; Rebellion in the Backlands), examined in chapters two and four. A perhaps unwitting modern contributor to the theory is an art catalog titled *The End Is Near!* (1998), the nucleus of which comes from the collections of the American Visionary Art Museum in Baltimore, Maryland. Whether intended or not, the "millennium equals madness" equation is present throughout. While the foreword by Rebecca Alban Hoffberger (ibid., 6) emphasizes the social aspects of end-of-the-world thinking (she recalls, as I also do, the duck-and-cover drills practiced in 1960s' schoolrooms against potential nuclear catastrophe), the brief biographies of many of the visionary artists emphasize mental instability. One such artist named Von Strӧpp describes his childhood as "grey, overcast, an eternal hangover" (ibid., 12); Tom Carapic experienced hallucinatory visions that explained his repeated failures to obtain a degree (ibid., 20); Joe Coleman's paintings are implicitly linked to his "complex and troubled childhood" (ibid., 41). Several pieces were created by patients in psychiatric institutions of Europe. Of course, while none of these artists also led millennial movements—language being the chosen medium of political leaders, as we shall see—the catalog as a whole reinforces not only the hyperromantic idea of the artist as eccentric but, more important, the hypothesis that millennial visions derive from mental aberrations and extreme suffering as well. The main challenge to this theory lies in moving from the single, mentally unstable leader to the multitude of followers. Notions of collective insanity nearly always run counter to direct observation of the participants' general mental health. From the Millerites to Canudos to Jonestown, the large numbers of communitarians demonstrate plenty of rational and pragmatic thinking.

The second paradigm, associated with the work of Wilson and Anthony Wallace and of Maria de Queiróz, is frequently called a "relative deprivation" theory. It views millennialism as a particular type of what Wallace has dubbed a "revitalization movement," called forth when a culture's values are severely challenged by defeat in war or by contact with a vastly superior technology. The eschaton becomes a symbol of the culture's need to renew itself and to re-create its values. This theory is nearly unavoidable when dealing with aboriginal cultures of the Americas. It is implicit in my comparative treatment (see chapter four) of millennial texts of the last quarter of the nineteenth century on the basis of similar economic and political developments in various parts of the Americas. Millennial communities can arise anywhere in the world when a culture realizes its inadequacies and subsequently envisions a "great reversal" based on supernatural elements. All cultures revitalize themselves over time but usually slowly and piecemeal. A distinctive feature of a revitalization movement is that this change is speeded up; the projected transformation of society is to take place within a generation—in many cases, within the lifetime of the movement's prophet or messiah.

Apocalypse reveals, first to the prophet and through that person to the individuals of a society, an alternative "mazeway" (i.e., an individual's script for negotiating society's lifeways). The Americas have seen millennial communities that offer mazeways derived exclusively from nativist traditions (e.g., the Taqi Oncoy movement in Peru) and at the other end those derived from non-Christian sources such as science or pseudoscience (e.g., Heaven's Gate and other UFO cults). More frequently, however, the vision is either hybrid, as in the case of Wovoka and the Ghost Dance, or based on biblical scripts, primarily Daniel and Revelation. The main drawback of this second hypothesis is its determinism: Millennial communities are created by historical forces rather than by individual choices.

Finally, rhetorical theories, as their name implies, locate the appeal of millennium in language, rhetoric, and mimesis. Millennial discourses function as metalanguages of faith and belief. They correspond to the future tense in grammars: a useful tool for people to create possible worlds that connect the today they are living with an uncertain tomorrow. My overall hypothesis that Americans are seeking in the eschaton a narrative of their origins belongs to this category, narrative being both a topic in rhetoric and a form of metalanguage.

Stephen O'Leary has noted the failures and inconsistencies of all three types of explanation of the persistence of millennial thought:

It comes as no surprise that sociologists and historians, lacking the perspective of rhetorical studies, should expend so much energy in trying to explain the appeal of apocalyptic discourse by discovering audience predispositions based in conditions of social and economic class, in experience of calamity, or in psychological *anomie*. It is curious, however, that even those rhetorical scholars who attempt to account for the appeal of apocalyptic never seriously entertain the hypothesis that people are actually persuaded by apocalyptic arguments; that is, that the nature of apocalyptic's appeal should be sought in transactions of texts and audiences. (1994, 11)

In particular, and in line with my own argument in this book, there is a logic to apocalyptic narrative that complements the laws of reason: "From the perspective of 'pure reason,' eschatology is an arbitrary and not a necessary idea. But from the perspective of narrative rationality . . . the idea of an ending is logically implied by the idea of beginning. . . . The cosmogonic narrative of Genesis thus implies the eschatological resolution of Revelation" (ibid., 28). In other words, the logic of narrative itself—"the sense of an ending," to use Frank Kermode's phrase—accounts for much of the continued popularity of millennial dreams. In upstate New York in the 1840s, William Miller's biblical studies allowed him to construct a timeline for the eschaton, a "possible world" into which he could precisely place his present age, thereby creating a script for action. A similar crossover occurs between the fantastic fiction of the *Left Behind* series and the genuine millennial beliefs of many of its readers—to the extent that there is some controversy about the degree to which its authors are assuming the role of prophets. In this book I move back and forth between historical instances and literary treatments of this logic.

In what we might call the rhetoric of numbers we see a small example of how technology itself, here in the form of mathematics, can persuade. The apocalyptic thinking of mathematically oriented people, including great names such as Isaac Newton and John Napier, alerts us to the fact that a certain pararationality is at work. Numbers can be manipulated to predict the end of the world or to locate the Antichrist. Michael Stifel fell under the sway of Martin Luther in the early sixteenth century and managed to prove mathematically that Pope Leo Decimus was the Beast 666. Stifel simply took the Roman numerals present in "DeCIMVs," dropped the "M," which stands for "mystery," added an "X" for Leo X, and rearranged the rest to form the number DCLXVI, or 666.

A bit later, John Napier, one of the foremost mathematicians of his day, developed the concept of logarithms in spare time stolen from his real work at the crux of politics and religion. In 1611 Napier published his *Plaine discovery of the whole Revelation of St. John*, an anti-Catholic work that analyzed the book of Revelation and concluded (again) that the pope was the Antichrist and that the world would end in either 1688 or 1700. Cotton Mather was among the most chronometrically oriented of the early Puritans, at one time setting the date of the eschaton at 1697, only to later accept William Whiston's calculation of 1716 (see Stein 1984, 277–78). William Miller's calculations done in the 1830s involved fixing the year of Nebuchadnezzar's dream in the year 457 BC and then adding the 2,300 "days" (traditionally interpreted as years) the text of Daniel itself states as the period of the four empires: "[I]f 2300 days is the length of the vision, and 490 days of that vision were fulfilled in 490 years ending with Christ's death, so must 1810 days end the vision, which, upon precisely the same rule, will be fulfilled in 1810 years after Christ's death [in 33 CE], or in 1843 after his birth, which is the same thing" (1842, 7). Another Napier avatar was NASA rocket engineer Edgar C. Whisenant, who wrote the book *On Borrowed Time: 88 Reasons Why the Rapture Will Be in 1988* (1988). Obviously but seemingly irrelevantly, Napier, Miller, Whisenant, and all of the other calculators missed.

While numerology of this kind may appear puerile or aberrant, Kenelm Burridge's placement of millennial thinking in the overall context of human evolution helps explain why numbers and calculation play such an important symbolic role in eschatology:

> Essentially, millennial activities repeat in a variety of idioms the process whereby an animal became man, a moral being aware of his morality. They recapitulate the neolithic revolution, they trace the pattern of all those revolutions by which one kind of human condition, one mode of measuring the moral stature of man, is replaced by another in more complex circumstances. The main theme is moral regeneration: the generation of new moralities, the creation of a new man defined in relation to more highly differentiated criteria. (1969, 141)

Human development, Burridge argues here implicitly, does not follow the path of gradualism but is rather composed of a series of apocalypses, in which a power beyond the group's understanding is revealed and a new order of values is promulgated to replace the old one. Examples he gives include when a system of factorial differentiation replaces a simpler one of binary differentiation and when number replaces quality. Of course, gradualism is always at work, but not in the realm of values, which can be transformed only wholesale. Gradual changes build up like water behind a dam until they gather enough force to break the barrier and completely transvalue the community's values. At such times, groups must look to their past in order to forge a vision of the future, often combining their own beliefs and values with those imported from elsewhere.

Burridge identifies four primary situations that contribute to constructing millennial movements: (1) manifestation of a power outside current comprehensions; (2) questions of the proper measurement of humankind, often related to the use of money; (3) competition for power; and (4) complete physical defeat of one culture by another. The last factor is found, for example, in the Ghost Dance, where Native American cultures sought to revive themselves by synthesizing some of their own beliefs and practices with those of Christian eschatology. Ignatius Donnelly's *Caesar's Column* (1890), on the other hand, presents a vision of the end of the world that represents an extreme form of Midwestern American populism, where the factor of money predominates. In Donnelly's vision, money and the control of money have come to dominate the world so much that they have depraved humankind and prepared it for the final conflagration that will purify the world.

For many, the combination of the term *reality* with the announcement of a divine plan represents a contradiction that moves us into the realm of literature as a discourse that transforms reality into a possible world. The core of that message, as I have already noted, has remained remarkably stable through the centuries and across cultures. Let us now examine the component parts of this menagerie of types.

Elements of the Eschaton

As the preceding section explains, the term *millennium* derives from a period speci-fied in Revelation. Millennialism in the narrow sense is thus the Christian belief in the return of Christ *to earth* to resurrect the saints and to fight a battle with the forces of evil, at the conclusion of which his thousand-year reign on earth (the millennium) will begin. But millennial movements can happen in most religious contexts, not just Christian ones. This book emphasizes the hybrid nature of such movements in the Americas, and we will see everything from a reliance on African *loas* as a resistance to Christianity to a hope that the papacy will relocate to the Americas and usher in a new era.

Millennial narratives, according to Norman Cohn, always contain five elements. They picture salvation as collective, terrestrial, imminent, utterly transformative, and miraculous (1970, 13). All of the apocalyptic texts dealt with in this book share the same basic plotline or plot background: "The world is dominated by an evil, tyran-nous power of boundless destructiveness—a power moreover which is imagined not as simply human but as demonic. The tyranny of that power will become more and more outrageous, the sufferings of its victims more and more intolerable—until sud-denly the hour will strike when the Saints of God are able to rise up and overthrow it" (ibid., 21). Cohn derives his constituent elements empirically from actual millennial movements mostly in European history. They have been confirmed by social science and psychology, the findings of which are summarized in Michael Barkun's *Disaster and the Millennium* (1974). In Barkun's view, millennialism responds to "disaster," a natural or social change that threatens the whole of a traditional way of life. Earth-quakes, hurricanes, drought, and other natural disasters have caused the individual and communal stress that finds its outlet in alternative worldviews and have served as signs for the text of Apocalypse. However, somewhere in the nineteenth cen-tury, Michael Barkun claims, "the waning destructive capacity of nature was more than matched by the rising destructive capacity of human beings" (1986, 142). As technological and social advances helped minimize the effects of natural disasters, the same technology unleashed ever greater, more powerful, and more comprehen-sive wars and catastrophically degraded the environment.

Perhaps more important, the increasing complexity and power of human so-cieties that allow them better to cope with natural disaster also gives them the ap-pearance of the Leviathan: monstrous, inhuman, and devouring. This was how the Christians of the late first century viewed the Roman Empire, which was persecuting them, and their fears were the ones John of Patmos spoke to in the text of Revelation when he told them not to worship the Beast, namely Rome. Today the same power that provides police protection and flood relief can be used for compulsory school education and invasion of privacy. Government intervention is a two-edged sword: Welfare or farm relief is not seen as making free but as creating dependency.

The utter transformation of the world that forms the goal of millennial move-ments is thus conservative in nature; it is "re-volutionary," a turning back, which how-ever always incorporates elements of the new. Thus, millennial movements always look forward and backward at the same time. The millennial community of Canudos, Brazil, for example, was founded on the most basic teachings of Christ and hence appealed to the traditional, conservative Catholicism of the Bahian backlands. In put-ting Christ's teachings into direct practice, however, the community circumvented the latifundarian landholding structure as it had been in northeastern Brazil and brought about an empowerment of the common people a century ahead of its time. The miracu-lousness of millennial movements can be explained by the breakdown in traditional structures of authority, leaving a power vacuum that can be filled only by charismatic leadership (Barkun 1974, 86–89). Chapter two examines a number of charismatic lead-ers of millennial movements of the Americas and shows how their charisma reflects the cultural or racial divide that helped cause the breakdown to begin with.

In one sense, literary versions of apocalypse rewrite a story that has circulated in the West since the Hellenistic period. Antiochus IV, a Seleucid emperor who controlled Israel and Jerusalem, attempted to hellenize the Jews and to forbid their religious practices during the mid-second century BCE. The response was not only rebellion but also a text, the Book of Daniel, which provided fictional historical ex-amples of a Jew remaining steadfast in his faith in the face of persecution during the Babylonian captivity and a vision of the end of the present persecutions and the triumph of the righteous. Daniel's vision brings together in a single narrative a num-ber of images that are taken up in later apocalypses, including Revelation. One is the use of animals to portray empires. Daniel dreams of four beasts: a lion with eagle's wings, representing the Babylonians; a bear; a leopard with wings; and a fourth beast with ten horns. A little horn, with "eyes like the eyes of a man, and a mouth speaking great things" (Daniel 7:8), grows from among the others. The terrible beast is Alex-ander the Great, and the horns are the kingdoms of his decayed empire, including the Seleucid, which arose after his death. Thus, the little horn represents Antiochus, speaking blasphemies against God. Daniel observes how this horn "made war with the saints, and prevailed over them, until the Ancient of Days came, and judgment was given for the saints of the Most High, and the time came when the saints received the kingdom" (Daniel 7:21–22). This is the basic scenario that is repeated in the book of Revelation. There, too, a heavenly figure sits in judgment of earthly events, a Beast represents present earthly power and empire (this time Rome), and the scenario is one of initial persecution but eventual triumph for the "saints." In Revelation, Christians replace Jews, and Nero replaces Antiochus as the blasphemer.

Daniel is mentioned by Jesus in the so-called Little Apocalypse found in the Gos-pel of Matthew (parallel to a briefer one in Mark 13). Jesus tells his apostles, "When you, therefore, see the desolating abomination mentioned by the Prophet Daniel, set up in the holy place . . . then those in Judea should flee to the mountains" (Matthew 24:15–16). The "desolating abomination" refers to a persecuting leader (which in modern apocalypses becomes a repressive government, a cabal of industrialists, or an evil "system"). Jesus goes on to describe natural signs that will portend the coming of the Son of Man: "Right after the tribulation of those days, the sun will be darkened and the moon will not shed her light; the stars will fall from the sky and the forces of heaven will be shaken. Then will the sign of the Son of Man be shown in the sky, and all the tribes of earth will mourn" (24:29–30). For better or worse, Jesus provided in this speech (or the Evangelist attributed to him) a whole repertoire of signs by which people may know His Second Coming. A meteor shower, for example, could (and has) set off a panic concerning the end of the world. The natural disasters in Pat Robertson's novel, described earlier, are intended to fulfill this prophecy.

Placed last in the New Testament, Revelation was written by John of Patmos (probably not the same as the Evangelist, though some traditions equate the two) near the end of the first century CE. Its purpose was to encourage Christians (still a small and persecuted community) to persist in their faith in the face of danger and overwhelming odds. It is unique among New Testament texts in not containing any straightforward doctrinal statements. It presents instead the vision of John, a series of images and memorable characters put together in a somewhat loose and repetitive narrative. As we meet their modern antitypes, we will explore particular images and phrases further.

Apocalytic communities live almost by definition "in peril." They have a sectlike status and reject the religion of the status quo and any sense of a historical dimension to revealed truth. God usually speaks directly to a prophet-messiah, who then assembles the community and acts as its center. The millennial community retreats to a special place, founds a refuge, as in the Rancho Apocalypse near Waco, a city, as in Canudos, Brazil, and at times an even larger area, such as the Contestado region of southern Brazil. The normal pace of life is changed as suddenism replaces gradualism. Thus, science fiction often has the feel of millennial texts because it seeks the Rip Van Winkle effect: that we have fallen asleep for a hundred years and are now awaking to find things utterly different from our own circumstances.[5] The concentration into a single instant of historical change that normally takes decades or centuries corresponds to the concentration of ethical and moral complexity into a single battle between good and evil.

Varieties of Millennium

It is useful to keep in mind the following triangle: premillennialism, postmillennialism, and utopian community (see figure 1.2).

Anyone studying millennium quickly learns the difference between pre- and postmillennialism. At the top of the triangle, transformation has the attributes Cohn mentions, salvation being miraculous and sudden. Postmillennials believe in gradualism—that is, that we are already living in the end time but that human effort and individual spiritual transformation will at some point bring about the utter transformation of the world into the "immanent space" of a New Jerusalem. Utopians return to the idea of collective salvation but attempt to realize it only within their limited community, which may or may not be miraculous in origin.

The "post" in postmillennialism refers to the belief that Christ's reign has already begun and that we are located historically somewhere in the millennium. In such a scheme, God and people share the responsibility for constructing the final earthly paradise, which can be carried out without necessary reversion to violence. A version

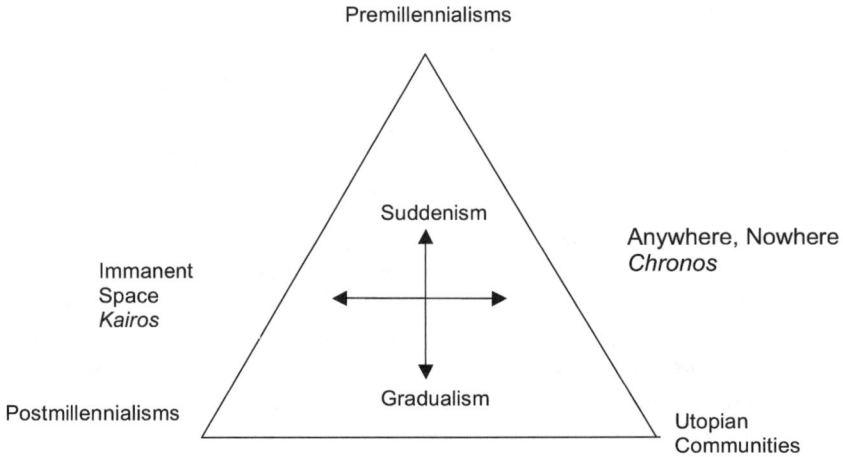

FIGURE 1.2 Premillennialism, postmillennialism, and utopianism.

of the folk hymn "Walk in Jerusalem," sung by the Blind Boys of Alabama, gives a typically postmillenialist scenario (italicized lines are repeated in each verse):

> Oh, John said the city was just foursquare,
> *walk in Jerusalem just like John*
> and I won't be content 'til I get there.
> *walk in Jerusalem just like John.*
>
> John said the city was four squares wide
> I'm gonna meet King Jesus on the other side.
>
> Well, my God told me just what to do:
> "If you make one step, I'll make two."
>
> What do you reckon He said to me?
> "If you make two steps, I'll make three."
>
> Well, He spoke again, and His voice did roar:
> "If you make three steps, I'll make four."
>
> Behold, behold, He's still alive!
> "If you make four steps, I'll make five."
>
> ("Walk in Jerusalem")

And so on. God and humans share the work, naturally with God providing a bit more under the terms of the covenant. This lyric is the epitome of gradualism, step after step, with no hint of confrontation but only of constant improvement. As Benjamin McArthur points out, postmillennialism has been the standard American approach to the riddle of apocalypse: "The American millennialist tradition . . . has meant less a dramatic apocalypticism than the 'imminent and immanent' appearance of God's kingdom that his people can help effect. The importance of such postmillennialism for nineteenth-century reform need hardly be reminded" (1996, 378). Postmillenni-alism shares its gradualist approach with utopianism but maintains Leonard Sweet's distinction (which I have used as a filter for selecting texts and movements for treat-ment in this study) between all millennialisms, "wherein space is immanent some-where and time is *kairos*, of imminent historical impingement)," and utopianism, wherein "space is anywhere or nowhere and time is *chronos* if not inconsequential" (Sweet 1979, 520). Utopian communities abound in the Americas. An example was George Ripley's Brook Farm at Roxbury, Massachusetts, which combined the ideas of Fourier with New England notions of propriety. It proposed, in the words of a contemporary, the "reorganization of society itself, on those very principles of Love to God and Love to Man, which Jesus Christ realized in his own daily life" (Peabody 1841, 214). This was the community Nathaniel Hawthorne participated in for a time before writing about it in a reflectively dissonant way in "The Celestial Rail-road" and other stories and sketches analyzed in chapter three.

Beyond my desire to select study examples that are millennial rather than uto-pian, however, I am less interested in maintaining or troubling these classic distinc-tions than in introducing ones that involve literature, such as its capacity for reflective dissonance and its depictions of racialized millennium in the texts discussed in chap-ter seven. My focus on literature and culture brings with it a tendency towards pre-millennial scenarios, which are far more conformable to plot structure, especially of the kind that appeals to modern readers and viewers. In particular, premillennial schemes are far more prone to disaster and catastrophe, which, beyond the vicarious emotionality they provide, also have a didactic impact.

Three chapters—on hybrid messiahs, reflective dissonance, and racialized millennium—address themes that persist across chronological boundaries. The re-maining chapters are arranged chronologically. We begin the next chapter, then, at the beginning, at least with regard to the historical record and the production of lit-erary texts, with Columbus's arrival and the "spiritual conquest" of the Americas.

The New Jerusalem:
Land without Evil

Of the New Heaven and of the new Earth, which our Lord
made, as St. John writes in the Apocalypse, after He had
spoken of it by the mouth of Isaiah, He made me the messenger and showed me where to go.

—Christopher Columbus, letter to Juana de la Torre,
Select Letters

From the beginning of its discovery by Europeans in 1492, the New World equaled
the end of the world. The man who ushered in the modern era with his discovery of
what would later be known as the Americas was at heart a mystic and millennialist.
Not his superior sailing and navigation skills, he claimed, had allowed him to make
his discovery but the Hand of God. Similarly, Columbus's apocalyptic has nothing
to do with the postmillennialist social movements of the eighteenth and nineteenth
centuries, which attempted to perfect humankind. Instead, the New Jerusalem had
always existed: Columbus's task was merely to take advantage of *kairos* and to find
Cipango and use its wealth to furnish knights and arms to liberate the old Jerusalem.
Martín Martínez de Ampiés, a Castilian like the royalty that commissioned Columbus's voyage, began his *Libro del anticristo* in 1493 as if the book were to be a
guidebook for eschatechnologizing the New World. Europe's prophetic tradition was
brought to the New World as a "vanishing-point technology" and, in Djelal Kadir's
phrase, as a "conquering ideology."[1] In another time and language and in one of the
interconnections between English and Iberian typologies that Cañizares-Esguerra
has documented in *Puritan Conquistadors* (2006), the Puritan Samuel Sewall (1652–
1730) considered Columbus's landing the antitype of Revelations 10:1–2: "And I saw
another mighty angel come down from heaven, clothed with a cloud: and a rainbow
was upon his head, and his face was as it were the sun, and his feet as pillars of fire:
And he had in his hand a little book open: and he set his right foot upon the sea, and
his left foot on the earth." In this reading the angel is Christ, born to the New World
by the self-proclaimed "bearer of Christ" (the literal translation of "Cristoforo") to
begin the end (see Stein 1984, 281).

Columbus's letters from the New World (the one quoted earlier is from the third voyage of 1500) describe not what he actually saw but the marvelous and paradisical, which certain narratives of the Old World had prepared him to experience. Most of the other discoverers and *conquistadores* who arrived in the New World described their experiences through the framework of Old World narratives, the most important of which were of Eden or the Golden Age (thoroughly documented by Sérgio Buarque de Holanda in *Visão do Paraíso* [1959]) and of Apocalypse. Both the conquistadores and the friars who followed in their wake brought with them to Latin America a medieval repertory of apocalyptic tropes and a religious reading of political events that have survived into the present. In both cases, through an act of "translation"—reflected in this chapter's double title—the Europeans were able to achieve resonance between their own myths and those that the inhabitants seemed to communicate to them. "The reports of the natives were constantly interpreted through the medium of such archetypal motifs" (ibid., 78). At the same time, Native Americans were absorbing the Europeans' stories and religion and using them to modify their own worldview.

In Catherine Keller's interpretation, Columbus:

> collapsed the expectation of the new creation into the tradition of the leftover paradise, the garden east of Eden denied to humanity since the fall. In this temporal inversion, the symbolic future has been remade as a literal past. A new approach to space became possible: the symbolic place of the new heaven and the new earth now reduces to a geographic literalism. . . . Surely this move expedited the "discover and acquire" project. (1997, 51–52)

If Columbus felt that his millennial mission could be fulfilled with the extraction of riches for the Christian nations to reconquer the Holy Land and rebuild the temple, the religious orders that followed him into the New World—Franciscans, Dominicans, Augustinians, Jesuits, and others—concentrated on the conversion and education of the human wealth that remained behind.

Within a few decades of the Spanish and Portuguese arrival on the mainland of the Americas, a process of mutual translation of millennial expectations was at work. Such revitalization was clearly needed by the defeated Native Americans, whose values and beliefs had been shattered by military defeat. Jacques Lafaye states that "The Indians had just suffered a total military and political defeat; their idols had been routed, their priests persecuted, they faced a void. They could only recover their full human condition by conversion to the faith of the conquerors, but they could more easily internalize that faith if some sign in their past linked them to the new religion; that sign was the pristine evangelization by Saint Thomas" (1976, 186). However, Lafaye reminds us that simply winning the "ground war" in the New World was not sufficient for the Europeans, who still needed to account for the apparent absence of the American continents and cultures from the biblical narratives that had sustained their civilization for centuries: "As for the Spaniards, their world system, founded on revelation, and their very religion would collapse if the Bible had lied or simply omitted mention of America; ignorance, forgetfulness, and injustice on the part of God were all equally untenable. If there existed a positive truth independent of revealed truth, all European thought, from Saint Augustine to Suárez, must go out the window" (ibid.).

Hence, the two sides held complementary ends of the *tesseron* of millennial expectations. For the Indians, the eschaton was something recently experienced; for the Europeans, it was something prophesied. The process of joining the two ends of this tesseron through a mutual belief in the end of the world is reflected in the double title of this chapter, where the New Jerusalem is posited as the translation for the Guaraní "Land without Evil." My goal in this chapter is to follow this process through its many twists and turns in the early colonial period, including the reimportation of American millennium into Europe.

Like Columbus, these orders also saw their mission in apocalyptic terms, adding to the premillenial notions of preexisting paradise the postmillenial ones of conversion of the heathen. This is not to say that the points of view of friar and conquistador converged exactly; for example, the religious orders presented one of the few obstacles to complete enslavement or extermination of the native peoples. But like a common language or currency that removes the friction of trade and commerce, millenarian expectations were a common frame of thought that enabled conquest and conversion to work hand in hand.

The Observant Franciscans active in Mexico in the sixteenth century revived the order's long tradition of attention to the prophecies of Joachim of Fiore, whose schema of three ages lies at the base of the millennial distinction drawn between Old World and New World and which was easily synthesized with ideas of a golden age or an Adamic man. Franciscans steeped in the Joachamite tradition "thought that the rapid completion of their missionary task would accelerate the coming of eschatological times: from this point of view, they saw armed conquest as a providential instrument that had eliminated the obstacles to evangelization" (Milhou 1987, 309). In this interpretation, Hernán Cortés, the conqueror of Mexico, was both a new Moses and an antitype of the archangel Michael, who had slain the Beast of Revelation. Satan had picked the Aztecs to recapitulate every aspect of the Israelites' history, up to and including the Eucharist in the form of human sacrifice and cannibalism (Cañizares-Esguerra 2006, 19). As Francisco de Los Angeles sent his twelve fellow Franciscan friars off to convert the recently conquered Aztecs, he cited the parable of the eleventh hour from the "little Apocalypse" of Matthew, chapters 20–24: "The day of the world is already reaching the eleventh hour; you of the Father of the family are called to go to the vineyard, not for wages as some do, but as true sons of your so great Father" (Wadding 1931, 184; cited in Phelan 1970, 24). The architecture of the missions, conversion centers, cities, and theatrical productions created by the Franciscans, as Jaime Lara has shown in his beautifully illustrated *City, Temple, Stage* (2004), was modeled on the "foursquare" city of Revelation 21–22 and on the vision of the postexilic Jewish temple in Ezekiel 40–48.

The Franciscans who came to the New World over the ocean pathways made familiar by Columbus's voyages had a tradition of conversion missions, for example, to the Mongols and other peoples of Asia in the thirteenth century. The Indians' apparent poverty seemed especially promising to the Franciscans as one of the foundational attitudes of their order. "The Amerindian becomes, authentically, that absolute Other who is the instrument of salvation of the Old World, blinded by its sins and deafened by the tumults of the new Babylons. . . . A crucial ethnic and figurative alterity distinguished by its humility, meekness, infantile availability, would therefore permit the Amerindians to fulfill a decisive role in the end of universal history, beyond historical times" (Baudot 1992, 390). Without believing in direct descent, Gerónimo de Mendieta made extensive parallels between the Indians of the New World and the Jews of the Old Testament. Cortés was a new Moses who would lead the Indians out of their Egyptian idolatry. There followed a golden age and then a Babylonian captivity, during which the Indians were dying of epidemics and subject to the slavery of *repartamiento*.

Near the end of his *Historia eclesiástica indiana*, which describes the ruthless increases in tribute demanded by the Spanish colonial government, Mendieta writes of the "Great evil, evil of evils, which are numberless, and one cannot describe them. And all this proceeds from having allowed the wild beast of avarice, who like the beast of the Apocalypse has made himself adored as the lord of the whole world, to ravish and to destroy the vineyard" (Mendieta 1945, vol. 3, 292). The vineyard is also a sheepfold; the Indians are the martyrs, suffering tortures on earth in order to appear by the side of Christ in heaven, sanctified by being washed in the very blood extracted from them. The tribulations and the apparent failure of the New Jerusalem are thus transformed into the promise of millennium. Mendieta, "the province's Cicero," also contributed with a wealth of opinions, among which was the supposition that God had chosen the Spanish people to impose their Catholicism. "Curiously, at the same time [Mendieta] maintained that Europe was unredeemed: the Old World corresponded to the Earthly City, while America would be the Heavenly City. But more importantly, [the] millennial Kingdom had begun: it was the lapse between the arrival of the "Twelve" to Mexico and the unknown night of the Final Judgment" (Fernández 1992, 70). At the end of his long career, Mendieta found it hard to reconcile reality with this vision of the kingdom. Each viceroy increased the latitude for the Spaniards to use forced Indian labor. Above all, Philip II did not possess the same fervor for conversion as had Charles V.

Toribio Motolinía (d. 1568) was the longest lived of Mendieta's chosen. In his memoirs of Franciscan priesthood, Motolinía compares Mexico to Egypt and elaborates the ten plagues: The plague of flies becomes the introduction of Africans through slavery; the seventh becomes the construction of Tenochtitlán. On top of this, however, comes the pouring out of vials: "And thus, since there was in this land of Mexico a great deal of cruelty and bloodshed offered to the demon, angel of Satan, for this reason the second angel poured out his vial over this land . . . and it was made ocean, that is, like the blood of a dead man" (1970, 11). This passage rewrites Revelation 16:3: "And the second angel poured out his vial upon the sea; and it became as the blood of a dead man: and every living soul died in the sea."

Continuing in the same chapter, Motolinía relates Revelation 16:19 to the Aztec capital of Tenochtitlán: "And the great city was divided into three parts, and the cities of the nations fell: and great Babylon came in remembrance before God, to give unto her the cup of the wine of the fierceness of his wrath." He interprets the three parts as follows: "[T]he first part is fornication [codicia de la carne]; the second, lusting with the eyes [codicia de los ojos]; the third is pride" (ibid., 14). Moving farther south, he compares the volcanoes of Nicaragua with the lake of fire in Revelation 19:20: "It looks like the place where Saint John tells us in his Apocalypse that the Antichrist will be thrown together with his allies" (ibid., 120). Actually, it is the Beast with his false prophet, often interpreted as Antichrist, who will be thrown into the fire. Considered together, these passages make it clear that the geography of the New World appeared to Motolinía as reserved for the events described in Revelation. This earliest of ethnographic histories of the Americas contains a rhetorical dualism typical of prophetic typology. In Ralph Bauer's assessment, "The projection of Aztec anti-types onto Biblical types transculturated the Spanish sense of identity in the specific geo-cultural context of the New World while rationalizing the displacement or subordination of the other heir of that past—the colonial Indian" (2001, 39).

Within this framework, Spanish discovery and conquest are seen as signs of the approaching end times. Motolinía is considered the founder of the city of Puebla. There, in the convent of the Assumption of Our Lady in Tecamachalco, the Indian Juan Gersón painted scenes from Revelation. Gersón, named after the chancellor of the University of Paris, was a *tlacuilo*, or "principal Indian" of the town. The paintings are done on fiber made from the bark of a fig tree, and comparison with European iconography shows that the artist worked from models. There are seven scenes from the Old Testament—Noah's ark, Cain slaying Abel, and other scenes of sin and retribution—and fifteen from Revelation. There is nothing in between, as though the book of Revelation contained the whole of the Christian message. According to María Elena Landa Ábrego, the choice of Revelation as subject matter showed that the Franciscans were bringing a message of hope to the Indians. Evil was earthly power such as had been shown to them in the *conquista*. Significantly, in the painting of the four horsemen the viewer's attention is drawn first to a rider in a suit of armor such as that worn by Cortés and his knights, except that its color is blue. Blue is, so to speak, the wrong color for the second horseman of the Apocalypse, unto whom "power was given . . . to take peace from the earth, and that they should kill one another: and there was given unto him a great sword," since in the symbolism of the book and the paintings it represents the divine—the New Jerusalem is also depicted in blue. Thus, the conquistador horseman represents contradictory messages: war and hope. Against the destruction of a civilization and a worldview, a new faith brought the hope of redemption and peace in the New Jerusalem depicted in one of the paintings.

Cultural translation of this kind extended to the way local saints were adopted. The Nahua of Mexico tended to adopt Christianity by choosing a local saint whose name replaced that of one of the specialized gods of the native pantheon (see Lockhart 1992). Landa Ábrego hypothesizes that apocalyptic literature and Náhuatl religion had much in common: esoteric messages, numerology, visions, voices, and apparitions (1992, 24). An *auto sacramental* called The Final Judgment (*El juicio final*), written in Náhuatl by Andres de Olmos, had been presented in the chapel of San José de los Naturales in the presence of the first viceroy and first archbishop of New Spain between 1531 and 1535. According to Adam Versényi, it was "a huge theatrical spectacle involving Christ, the Antichrist, and various devils and angels, that emphasizes the importance of marriage through the punishment of an adulterous woman named Lucia on the Day of Judgment" (1999, 28). Unfortunately, the script has been lost, and we are left to speculate on the millennial message that it might have contained. In Miguel Fernández's opinion, the performance "must have represented one of the transcendental moments in the history of civilization: Christ speaking in Náhuatl while the Indians lectured on the fall of Babylon" (1992, 137).

Through these various media, then, the millennial message underwent a process of translation that brought about its transformation in the context of the Americas. The Indians were Westernized, but at the same time "European friars learned to 'Indianize' themselves, that is, they had to interest themselves in the native cultures and begin to study the variables of American pluralism so that from there they could reach the desired planetary dimensions for their new Jerusalem" (ibid., 217–18). Motolinía represents this process, as he took his last name from a Náhuatl word for "poverty," thereby reflecting the Indians' amazement that the armored Cortés would kneel to the simply clothed friars.

To the south, Brazil, which has probably seen more distinct messianic movements than any other country of South America, was founded "by soldier conquerors . . . . with the ideological mission of creating a heaven on earth in the name of the 'divine' Portuguese regent" (Pessar, 1980, 101). René Ribeiro distinguishes between three types of messianic movements: those that rest on native mythologies, especially of the Tupi-Guarani; revitalization movements and cargo cults in the face of the extinction of native cultures, which may have syncretistic elements; and movements on the part of "neo-Brazilians," which rest primarily on Judeo-Christian messianism, along with its specifically Portuguese variant, Sebastianism, namely the belief that Dom Sebastião of Portugal, killed in the battle of Alcácer-Quibir in 1578 though his cadaver was never definitely identified, would return as a messiah to save the Portuguese empire). While Ribeiro emphasizes the distinctiveness of the three types, it is also important to consider the translation and borrowing that occur between them. We have already seen this in the Europeans' use of natural and cultural phenomena of the New World in order to rescript the millennial plotline.

As in Mexico, along with the soldier-conquerors came the religious orders, such as the Jesuits, some of whose publications claim that Brazil is the "paraíso na terra" [paradise on earth]. One of these treatises, published in 1663 in the *Crônica da companhia de Jesus*, drew the attention of the Inquisition, which confiscated the book (Chacon 1990, 31–32). The most formidable exponent of Jesuit messianism was Antônio Vieira (1608–1697). Born in Lisbon, Vieira began his Jesuit education in Salvador, Brazil, at the age of six. He entered the Society of Jesus in 1623 and was ordained in 1635. Returning to Lisbon in 1641, he became a favorite of King João IV, whom he in turn saw as the messiah of the Portuguese empire, and was subsequently made both preacher of the Royal Chapel and ambassador to various European countries. Following in the footsteps of fathers José de Anchieta and Manuel da Nóbrega, Vieira fulfilled a mission to the Tupi-Guarani of Maranhão and Amazonas from 1651 to 1661, during which he attempted to preserve their human and property rights against the Portuguese. King João died in 1656, thus leaving Vieira exposed to the intrigues of the settlers in Maranhão, who resented Vieira's interference in their government and his defense of the Indians against enslavement and had him returned to Portugal in 1661. Vieira penned his volume "The Fifth World Empire, Hopes of Portugal" (*Quinta impéria do mundo, esperanças de Portugal*) during that voyage. The Inquisition condemned his writings, and his magnum opus, the "History of the Future" (*História do futuro*), could be published only posthumously. In Portugal he was further subject to the Inquisition (a tool used by his enemies) until a stay in Rome brought him papal immunity. In 1681 he returned to Bahia and worked on his final book of prophecy, *Clavis prophetarum*, which remained incomplete at his death. (For an overview of Vieira's messianism see Thomas Cohen [1991].)

Vieira's thought combined a native Portuguese messianic strain dating from the late Middle Ages with prophetic clues perceived in Brazil. In a letter to a fellow Jesuit, the archbishop of Japan, André Fernandes, Vieira argued the following syllogism: "Bandarra is a true prophet; Bandarra prophesied that Dom João IV will perform many deeds he has not yet performed, nor can perform unless resurrected. Therefore, Dom João IV will be resurrected" (Vieira, 1659, vol. 1, 488). In the "Sermão de São Sebastião," preached in 1634, Vieira explicates this same syllogism over the course of many pages. He identifies with certainty his friend João IV as the "hidden king" prophesied by the poet Bandarra. Bandarra, born as Gonçalo Anes, a humble shoemaker, had circulated *Trovas* that predicted a messiah who would return from death or disappearance and put an end to injustice and inequality. In 1540 the Inquisition had forbidden any further prophecy by Bandarra: The Holy Office found the messianic strain in his poems to be Judaic. However, the disappearance of Dom Sebastião at the battle of Alcázar-Quibir in 1578 gave the people a perfect example of an antitype for Bandarra's type of hidden or missing messiah, all the more so since the disappearance unleashed a succession struggle that culminated in a Spanish regency of Portugal from 1580 to 1640. Portugal needed a messiah that would enable it to throw off its chains and live up to its seeming destiny as an empire by virtue of its superior sailing and navigation technologies. Vieira believed in the cumulative effect (or in the historical fine-tuning) of prophecy: He was living closer to the end times than Bandarra and could see that Dom João was the antitype of Sebastião, especially since it was João who had restored the Portuguese throne in 1640.

Vieira's advocacy of Bandarra is thus poised between elitism and democracy. Popular prophetic voices "constituted a kind of warehouse or stock of prophetic revelation, and [Vieira] maintained this democratic view of the prophetic gift as a critique of the more restrictive official position of the Church" (Jordán 2003, 50). Vieira's power of prophecy derived from the typical layering of history on the pattern of apocalypse: "[A] large part of our [Portuguese] history . . . is that of Apocalypse" (1982, 87–88). Christ had visited Affonso Henriques on the eve of battle and promised him not only the victory but also that the "fifth empire" would spring from his loins: "I am the creator and destroyer of kingdoms and empires, and in you and your descendants I want to found an Empire for me, to carry my name to foreign nations" (ibid., 130). The idea of empire derives from the book of Daniel and is paralleled in the conception of the so-called Fifth Monarchy men concerning England. In each case, Portugal and England, the global military and commercial expansion associated with colonization provided evidence for the greatest empire in history. (Indeed, as we saw earlier, Columbus had predicted the same for Spain.) The victory over the Moors marked the beginning of the second epoch of Portuguese history, when Portugal would move from a position of defeat to one of resuscitation that bordered on a "future of glory" (ibid., 41). The sign of this glory was the stream of voyages and conquests in Africa, the New

World, and Asia, which rival those of Alexander: "Who doubts that the conquests of the Portuguese in India have been more extensive and glorious than those of Alexander the Great?" (ibid., 79). The technologies of navigation and armaments are in Vieira's view eschatechnologies for Portugal's moving the world closer to its end times.

Besides Revelation and Daniel, Vieira also used the text of Isaiah 18 to prove Portugal's predestined glory, incorporating some specifics of the American situation. Indeed, he declares straightforwardly that the prophecy refers to Brazil and, amazingly, to the part of Brazil whose Indians he defended for a decade, Maranhão and the southern Amazon. In choosing to cite Isaiah, Vieira nuances a Jesuit practice that had long interpreted that text as predictive of the Jesuit missions to Asia. Such interpretations began with Jean-Frederick Lumnius's *De extremo Dei iudicio et indorum vocatione* (1569). That author's assumption that the Jesuits are the angels announced in the passage appears in practically every publication of Jesuit deeds (Haubert 1969, 122–23). Isaiah 18 reads as follows in the King James Bible:

Prophecy concerning Ethiopia
1 Woe to the land shadowing with wings, which is beyond the rivers of Ethiopia:
2 that sendeth ambassadors by the sea, even in vessels of bulrushes upon the waters, saying, Go, ye swift messengers, to a nation scattered and peeled, to a people terrible from their beginning hitherto; a nation meted out and trodden down, whose land the rivers have spoiled!
3 All ye inhabitants of the world, and dwellers on the earth, see ye, when he lifteth up an ensign on the mountains; and when he bloweth a trumpet, hear ye.

Vieira finds five Brazilian antitypes for the images of the passage: (1) Brazil lies "beyond Ethiopia"; (2) the native population of Brazil is "terrible" (e.g., cannibalistic); (3) the floodwaters of the Amazon "spoil" the region's land; (4) its people were scattered by the Portuguese conquerors; and (5) the ambiguity of a word between "bell" and "vessel" in the Hebrew (resolved as "vessel" in the King James Version; modern versions render the word as "insect") is resolved in the language of the Maranhão Indians. They use *maracás* as bells and call their boats *maracatim* [bells with beaks] due to the racket they make when tied up (Vieira 1982, 209–18).

The mountains, on the other hand, are part of the Old World, archetypes for Sinai, where Moses received the covenant. The trumpet imagery reappears in Revelation, where the angel who commands John the Divine to write speaks in a "great voice as of a trumpet" (Revelation 1:10, KJV). Arguably, the trumpet here summons to the last judgment. By populating Isaiah's allegory with historical details from Brazil, then, Vieira has constructed the following narrative: Brazil is the most downtrodden, barbarous place on earth. Following Jesus's millennial vision that "Many that are first shall be last; and the last shall be first" (Matthew 19:30; cf. also Mark 9:35), Brazil will become first and will lift Portugal with it into its destined leadership role in the construction of the new millennium. We see that the Indians play an important role in Vieira's prophecy, but he gives no details on their conversion to Christianity. For those, let us turn yet farther southward, to the Paraguayan missions and the writings of their superior, Antonio Ruiz de Montoya.

Millennium in Paraguay

Starting in 1610 and ending with their expulsion from Spanish dominions in 1768, the Jesuits built more than thirty missions or "reductions" (*reducciones*, signifying not a "diminishment" but a "bringing together" of people) in the territory of present-day Paraguay, Argentina, and Brazil. The purpose was the conversion of the native populations to Christianity. Like their predecessors, the Franciscans, the Jesuits undertook such conversions within the framework of millennial expectations. On the pragmatic level, the reductions were designed for the betterment of life through the elimination of intertribal war and polygamy. Nonetheless, an undercurrent of millennial thinking lay beneath the surface of the Jesuits' undertaking. Christians and Guaranis came to understand each other through their mutual expectations of the end of the world. The padres could be said to be constructing millennium as they fulfilled the role of *pajé* (the Guarani word for "shaman") and attempted to find concordances between Guarani belief and their own.

On January 13, 1750, Spain and Portugal signed a secret treaty that recognized the century and a half of de facto Portuguese expansion westward of Brazil's borders. The only cession Spain made of further territory was seven Jesuit missions in present-day Paraguay. Spain thereby sold out the Christian Indian army that had been instrumental in limiting Portuguese expansionism in the region and set about the enormous task of persuading the Indians to move. When the Spanish-Portuguese military surveying party arrived at San Miguel, they were met by the town's military commander, Sepé, who refused to allow the hated Portuguese to pass. The Spanish "repeated the Royal command but failed to impress Sepé; the King had been misinformed, the Portuguese were the Indians' archenemy since the time of their ancestors; this land was given to them by God and the Archangel Saint Michael and they would defend it to the last drop of their blood" (Reiter 1995, 164). The reference to Michael provides one of the few surviving, ambiguous clues for the presence of millennial thought in the missions. Michael is the most worshiped of all of the Christian angels, the most militant and powerful of them. It is he who throws the great dragon Satan down to earth in Revelation 12. In L. G. Barbour's *End of Time* (1892), an apocalyptic poem written at the end of the nineteenth century, Michael is shown as the angel militant:

> Sheathed is my sword, for the battle is o'er; the warfare accomplished.
> Satan is vanquished again, his hosts are sunk in Gehenna.
> So be it, God of Right; may Thy foes thus perish for ever,
> Angels or men that dare to upraise a hand 'gainst Jerusalem. (185)

From the historical incident recounted above, it would seem that in the Jesuits' teaching to the Indians Michael also assumed the role of the angel who shows John the New Jerusalem in Revelation 21:9–12. (The angel is not named as Michael in the text, but in the tradition surrounding the book Michael is the angel most associated with this vision.) Michael was not able to save his chosen people, the Guarani, who were later set upon by a large force of soldiers and massacred, and the survivors expelled from the towns until the treaty was later revoked. In 1768 the Jesuits were driven out of Spain, and the period of the missions definitely came to an end. Let us now look at how they began.

The writings of Antonio Ruiz de Montoya (1583–1653), one of the most important and prolific Jesuits active in Paraguay, provide interesting clues as to the millennial expectations of those involved in the missions. Born in Lima, Peru, Ruiz entered the Society of Jesus in 1606. Following his novitiate in Córdoba, Argentina, he was ordained in 1610 and immediately departed for the Paraguay missions. He became superior of the same from 1623 to 1637, traveling to Spain and Lima in order to receive and implement royal ordinances related to self-defense. It was within this context and to impress a Spanish audience with the progress of missionary work in Paraguay that Ruiz wrote his "Spiritual Conquest" (*Conquista espiritual*). Upon his death Ruiz, according to the wishes of his testament, was buried in the churchyard of the Loreto mission.

To begin our listing of millennial elements found in the *Conquista espiritual* and other writings, Ruiz, like the North American John Eliot, apostle to the Algonquins and author of an *Indian Grammar*, consistently found elements of Hebrew in the Guarani language. Traditionally, in Europe, the Jews had been a sign to be watched: A significant number of conversions to Christianity would signal the Second Coming. The textual basis for this expectation was Romans 11: "Just as you once disobeyed God but have now received mercy because of [the Jews'] disobedience, so they have now disobeyed in order that, by virtue of the mercy shown to you, they too may receive mercy" (11:30–31). With the discovery of the New World, the Indians became a new sign, and there was a strong motivation for reading them as translations (literally "carried" from the Old World to the new) of the old sign of the coming kingdom. Such a translation occurred when Antonio de Montezinos, a Portuguese Jew living in Peru, encountered an unknown tribe of Indians who spoke to him in what he perceived as Hebrew. The tale was published in the 1648 book "Hope of Israel" (*Ezperanza de Israel*) by Manasseh ben Israel, leader of the Amsterdam Jewish community and a noted Old Testament scholar, and soon passed into the English millennial orbit with Thomas Thorowgood's *Jews in America*, or, *Probabilities that those Indians are Judaical* (1650). Cotton Mather put Eliot's theory that Algonquin and related indigenous tongues were corrupted forms of Hebrew to the test at an exorcism: After using Latin, Greek, and Hebrew to address the demons (all of which languages they understood), he then tried Algonquin to no avail (1703, vol. 3, 193).

Ruiz de Montoya does not pretend to hear the actual sounds of Hebrew; instead, he comments on similarities in grammar that reveal a common theology with the Old World: "[The Guarani] knew that God existed, and to a certain extent his being One, and from the name they gave him, *tupán*, the first word, *tú*, signifies admiration; the second, ¿*pan*? is interrogation, and thus it corresponds to the Hebrew vocabulary *manhun, quid est hoc*, in the singular" (1892, 50). In other words, the Guarani are monotheistic and hence readily convertible to Christianity. Furthermore, for Ruiz de Montoya, neither monotheism nor the traces of Hebrew are accidental but rather a result of the preaching of Saint Thomas in the New World. In fact, the passage of centuries has erased all memory of the Christian doctrine Thomas had once delivered, except for monotheism: "[O]nly this they had retained of the preaching of the Apostle Saint Thomas, who as we shall see announced to them the divine mysteries" (ibid.).

Ruiz de Montoya and other Jesuits heard from the Tupi-Guarani tales of their culture hero, Pay Zumé. This sounded close enough to "Padre Thomas," who would have been the natural apostle for export to the Indians since Christ had given him the task of preaching to the "most abject [abatida] peoples in the whole world, to Blacks and Indians" (ibid., 104). The most frequently invoked sign of Thomas is his sandals, whether as relics or impressed into solid rock in various parts of South America. In Peru, for example, "Today there can be seen a large stone slab, and impressed into it the feet of a man of great stature, and some characters in a language that must be Greek or Hebrew, because no one who has seen them has been able to decipher them" (ibid., 103). Ruiz de Montoya does not speculate on how Saint Thomas arrived in the New World, but his fellow Jesuit, Antônio Vieira, has no problem explaining: "Saint Thomas, who brought the Gospel to India from Brazil, when there was no commercial traffic, had to walk on the top of the waves (as tradition has it)" (1982, 322).[2]

The approximation of Pay Zumé to Saint Thomas provides a clear example of the process of translation and of the colonizer's ability to build on and modify native beliefs and customs rather than suppressing or supplanting them. In reading Ruiz de Montoya, one is drawn into a perspective that makes the approximation instructive for Christians by filling in a missing chapter in the life of Saint Thomas, who becomes the archetype of the missionaries to the New World. This perspective obscures the more relevant historical workings of the translation, which revealed to the Guarani that their cultural hero had actually been the ultimate prophet of their doom. The Jesuits' revelation to the Guarani that Pay Zumé was really a European Christian—and it would be interesting to have some of the details of how this explanation was carried out—became, in Maxime Haubert's words, "the myth's realization. And, paradoxically, it is the Jesuits, the strangers, who end up imposing themselves as the true inheritors of the mythical ancestor. It is the Jesuits who are supposed to save the Guarani from the metaphysical cataclysm that conquest by the Europeans has brought down on their heads" (1990, 169). Only by entering the missions and becoming Christians and by renaming Pay Zumé as Saint Thomas can the Guarani escape the enslavement that the profane colonizers seek to impose on them.

The chief impediment to conversion of the Guaraní is Satan's active opposition and interference. The impression given by the *Conquista espiritual* is that the whole of South America is the realm of Satan and that Ruiz de Montoya is the champion of Saint Michael entering the lists against him. Satan comes in three forms: in that of the traditional Guarani prophets, called *karai*; in illusory (what we would call "virtual") shapes and personages, often of priests; and in the Portuguese who invade and destroy the reductions.

In terms of the first, Ruiz de Montoya's anodyne translation of *karai* is revealing: "persevering, astute. A word with which [the Guarani] universally honor their wizards: and thus they apply it also to Spaniards, and very improperly to the Christian name and to holy things, and we do not use it in those senses" (1639, 90). Indirectly, Ruiz de Montoya's comments suggest the translation process by which the Guarani used their own term for their prophets to designate a number of different cultural figures among the Spanish. Ruiz de Montoya uses the general term "Spaniards," but there is evidence that the Guaraní reserved the term for the European clergy who evangelized them and who bore resemblance to their own shamans in terms of their celibacy, abstinence, special clothing, use of ritual objects, and control of language. The conversion of the Guaraní often came down to a war between shamans to see which was more powerful. The *demonio* [Devil] also repeatedly appears in the form of a priest to tempt the Indians for brief periods.

Third, Ruiz de Montoya calls the invasion of the reductions by the Portuguese the Last Judgment (*juicio final*) and relates them to the forces of Antichrist:

> It is not unusual for God to give signs and demonstrations of serious and important things to come. . . . And in his Gospel, Christ our Lord gives the signs of the An-techrist [*sic*], and foretells the loss of many. . . . The foresight that God's majesty had more than twenty years earlier in sending subjects to the province of Guaira to harvest the predestined, before the Antechrist came to upset them. . . . The demons that Christ mentioned in verse 16 signified [the Antichrist], showing themselves to be in their appearance similar to those of São Paulo and the coast of Brazil, revealing themselves in their faces with their muskets and arms, and they even said that they were [the Antichrist's] friends. (1892, 274–75)

"Verse 16" appears to refer to Matthew, where Christ compares the meteorological signs to those of the coming kingdom, which, significantly, the last sentence of that verse prophesies: "I guarantee that some of you living now will see the Son of Man returning at the head of his kingdom." Yet there is no mention of demons in this verse. Antichrist, on the other hand, does not appear by name in the gospels, but the figure receives definition in Jesus's warning to the disciples concerning false messiahs: "Then if any man shall say unto you, Lo, here is Christ, or there; believe it not. For there shall arise false Christs, and false prophets, and shall shew great signs and wonders; insomuch that, if it were possible, they shall deceive the very elect" (Matthew 24:23–24). The first use of the actual term *antikristos* occurs in the first letter of John: "Little children, it is the last time: and as ye have heard that antichrist shall come, even now are there many antichrists; whereby we know that it is the last time. They went out from us, but they were not of us; for if they had been of us, they would no doubt have continued with us: but they went out, that they might be made manifest that they were not all of us" (I John 2:18–19).

Expanding on Christ's warning in Matthew, John sees the appearance of anti-christs as a sign that the final days are at hand. He makes explicit something implicit in Jesus's words: The antichrist comes not as something foreign, alien, and terrible to afflict the faithful. Rather, he is produced by a schism among the faithful them-selves, or—and this is the key to his portrayal in Christian art in the centuries to come—his "appearance" is merely the revelation that some who were thought to be believers have been faking it. The Antichrist does not enter the picture from outside but appears as a change of perspective, as when we look at a drawing that can be a rabbit or a duck, an urn or two faces, but not both at the same time. Who was seen as a prophet or a messiah suddenly becomes an Antichrist. As Bernard McGinn sum-marizes, "Christianity was—and is—founded upon the Christ whose nemesis seems required by both doctrinal and symbolic symmetry" (1994, 113).

The creation of Antichrist out of Christians completes a process of mitosis that perhaps goes back as far as the origins of language. First, evil is conceived as different from good, then Satan rebels against God and becomes something different. Norman Cohn credits the Babylonian Zoroaster (ca. 600 BC) with the first breakthrough connecting this dialectic to a vision that the world was not balanced and cyclical but tending toward an end: "In Zoroaster's view the world was not static, nor would it always be troubled. Even now the world was moving, through incessant conflict, towards a conflictless state. The time would come when, in a prodigious final battle, the supreme god and his supernatural allies would defeat the forces of chaos and their human allies and eliminate them once and for all" (1993, 227). While other traditions recognize the constructed nature of these oppositions between order and chaos, good and evil and attempt to reconcile them or maintain deities who carry contradictory aspects, in the West these notions became reified and differentiated on an absolute scale, while at the same time not losing their spectral qualities. The Antichrist appears not as something absolutely alien but as a doubling or reproduction of Christ in which something has gone horribly wrong.

As stated above, Martín Martínez de Ampiés's *Libro del anticristo* was published just one year after Columbus's discovery. The long wars of reconquest against the Muslim parts of Spain, just concluded, had certainly sharpened the Spanish perception of the world as divided between good and evil and given them Mohammed as a principal figure of the Antichrist. Ampiés was a *hidalgo* of Aragón and a soldier (against the French). What is striking, then, is that this treatise on Antichrist is not the work of a professional theologian but of a scholar who has read widely in the literature of apocalypse and Antichrist by authors such as Adso de Montier-en-Der and Lactantius.

The work is divided into forty-five chapters, each with a woodcut illustration and each confined to a particular aspect of Antichrist, a "sign" by which he may be known. The first chapter has Jacob predicting Antichrist, using Genesis 49:17: "Dan will be a serpent by the roadside." The author then names some evils of Antichrist: knowledge and persuasion; false miracles; gifts of money and riches [dádivas de thesoros y riquezas]; and the torment of the faithful [tormentando con diversas maneras de martirios a los constantes en la fe de Cristo] (66–67). The following chapters describe an aspect of Antichrist not found in most other "biographies": He is a product of incest between father and daughter and is born in Babylon. These characteristics invert those of Christ: virgin birth (also, in a sense, the product of father and daughter) in humble and provincial Bethlehem. Numerous chapters depict the miracles performed by Antichrist, which again parallel those of Christ: He roils the seas and moves the winds; he practices alchemy; he makes dead plants bloom again; he conjures a knight out of an eggshell and hangs a castle from a thread. He has the old books of the law and the prophets burned and substitutes his own doctrine (unfortunately but understandably not discussed in detail) for these. The Jews believe he is their promised Messiah and rebuild their temple.

Several chapters are devoted to the preaching of Elias and Enoch described in Revelation 11: "I [Jesus] will give power to my two witnesses, and they will prophesy for 1,260 days, clothed in sackcloth." At the end of that time they are killed by Antichrist (in Revelation, by the beast) but are resurrected and ascend to heaven. Antichrist places his sign on the hands and foreheads of his adepts and sends them out into the world, where they preach to the kings of Egypt, Libya, Ethiopia, and

Amazonas. Ampiés implies that the Muslim faith of the first two of these kings contributes to their reception of Antichrist's teachings. The king of Libya believes only when Antichrist kills and then resurrects him. True believers are captured, tortured, and executed. They hide in caves and abysses. Antichrist pretends to die and resuscitates himself on the third day—to prove that he is the true messiah, a plotline adapted by the *Left Behind* series as well. Finally, the angel Michael kills Antichrist. Elias and Enoch return and convert the world [convertir el mundo] (ibid., 182).

As mentioned, Antichrist is not directly named in Revelation, and his life story told here bears a somewhat oblique relationship to John's narrative. Important elements that have been retained include the two preachers, the tribulation, and the mark. Just as important are the things that have been left out: the woman pursued by the dragon; the New Jerusalem; and the role of John himself in Revelation. The story of Antichrist is, then, a composite cobbled together from a variety of sources. Besides the thrilling plot of the story itself, each episode serves as a negative example to drive home the lesson of how true Christians ought to conduct their lives. In other words, the Antichrist story is the original Christian self-help book, an aspect that has carried through to the best-selling *Left Behind* series initiated at the end of the twentieth century. Undoubtedly, this use of Antichrist as the anti-Christian is one reason for the generic qualities of his physical appearance in the woodcuts. Mediocrity, rather than evil, shows in his face; the demonic is reserved for the accompanying devil figure—a presentation of evil not accounted for by the text of Revelation itself.

Bernard McGinn has correlated the decline in Antichrist belief with a narrowing of the mutivalence of the figure. Antichrist could come either from outside as a pagan persecutor, a Jewish pseudomessiah, the dangerous Turk, or the American Indian, or from inside as a false believer or corrupt priest. Martin Luther consistently identified Antichrist with the papacy, and that interpretation seemed to mark a limitation of the figure's symbolic variance. In Catholic Latin America, on the other hand, Martin Luther could function as the Antichrist. Gerónimo de Mendieta (1525–1604), a Franciscan living in Mexico and whose "Ecclesiastical History of the Indies" (*Historia eclesiástica Indiana*) was thoroughly imbued with apocalypse, emphasized the parallels between Hernán Cortés and Martin Luther, claiming that they had been born in the same year. (Luther, born in 1483, was in fact older by two years.) Cortés's "liberation" of the Aztecs from the sin of idolatry occurred in the same year as Luther's debate with Johann Eck and his subsequent identification of the pope with the Antichrist. For Mendieta, the Old World was passing away under Lutheran rebellion, while Cortés was building the New Jerusalem in Mexico.

This reification of the identity of Antichrist contrasts sharply with the constant multiplying of Antichrists out of once solidarian communities throughout Christian history. The early years of the Americas were still able to witness this process. The Lutheran interpretation largely guided the thinking of dissenting ministers such as John Robinson, whose church founded Plymouth Colony. For them, "the Church of England . . . was an offshoot of the Church of Rome and the Roman Church had never been a true church freely gathered. To be true, saints had lived in Rome during Christ's time, and true churches had also maintained themselves. The Antichrist, or the Church of Rome, made his appearance long after the Apostle's time. The Antichrist existed 'as an embryo in the womb,' the Pope was its head, the hierarchy, his body. The Antichrist grew in size until he dispossessed Christ of his leadership of the Church in the world" (Middlekauff 1971, 39–40). Removal to the New World was originally undertaken as a tactic for defeating Antichrist and beaming the triumph of a true church back to England and Europe. Yet once the church was established in the New World, its conflicts with the Church of England were minimized, while other potential Antichrists arose from both within and without. During the French and Indian Wars, for example, the French were associated with the Antichrist, while during the Revolution it was George III.

Roger Williams believed that "the desolation of the Antichrist through the ages had destroyed all true religion, even though from time to time small bands of Christians had witnessed against the beast. . . . He contended that the churches had become so tainted by antichristian influences that they no longer had authority to convert the Indians, or any one else for that matter" (Stein 1984, 270–71).

And what of the native peoples? "It is important to remember that Mather, Edwards, and their contemporaries took for granted the Protestant axiom that the pope was the Antichrist. They were, therefore, reluctant to affix this term to those who currently occupied the wilderness that they coveted for themselves. Yet insofar as the term antichrist designates the forms and personages through whom Satan operates in this world, it is clear that the early settlers regarded the Native Americans in the symbolic universe as closely linked with the Antichrist tradition" (Fuller 1966, 47). In both North and South America, the wilderness was the Antichrist's domain. In particular, their shamans were his tools. This is what we see in Ruiz de Montoya's comment.

Seizing Eschatechnology

Ruiz de Montoya's references to the Antichrist come not only from typology but also from local history. From before the time of the Jesuits, Christians in Paraguay had been aware of the antichristical colorings of various Guaraní rebellions. The Indian leader Oberá, who led a messianic rebellion in the sixteenth century, had been baptized as a Christian and deliberately assumed and inverted central symbols of the faith: virgin birth with God as father, baptism, and the founding of a church with a pope. His rebellion was the subject of perhaps the earliest Spanish-language apocalyptic—or at least antichristological—poetry of the New World, the twentieth canto of the epic, *Argentina, or the Conquest of Rio de la Plata* (*La Argentina o la conquista del Rio de la Plata*; 1836), by Martín del Barco Centenera (1535–1603). The rebellion of Oberá figures as an obstacle to this spiritual and political conquest of the New World by the Spaniards. It is described in the twentieth canto: "Of how an Indian named Oberá gave himself the title of Son of God, and to one of his sons the title of Pope, and to another that of Emperor" (ibid., 215). We have only del Barco's account of the rebellion, which makes Oberá and his minions seem villainous and irresponsible and sets the incident as a playing out of the typology of Antichrist. However, we may use later, better-documented millennial movements as a reference point to read between the lines of del Barco's condemnation to construct a more complex picture.

Moreover, del Barco notes that the name "Obará" itself means "splendor," leaving his reaers to wonder whether it too is not an assumed name alluding to the transfiguration of Christ. He writes of Obará:

> [H]e had been baptized as a Christian,
> but did not keep the promised faith,
> the tyrant said with bestial cunning
> that he was the son of God, and conceived
> of a virgin, and that a virgin had borne him.
>
> [El bautismo tenia de cristiano:
> Mas la Fé prometida no guardaba,
> Que con bestial designo à Dios, tirano,
> Su hijo dice ser, y concebido
> De Virgen, y que Virgen lo ha parido]. (ibid., 216)

Del Barco doubtless knew the tradition of Antichrist, and it is conceivable that he had read Ampiés's primer on the topic. While Ampiés's version does not specifically mention the claim of virgin birth as one of Antichrist's blasphemies, it fits with the theme of reversal in his portrait since Antichrist is in fact born of incest between a father and his daughter. Del Barco makes it clear that Obará's rebellion could not have happened without his Christian upbringing, which endowed him with the millennial technology for controlling others. At the same time, he frees his adherents from all obligations of work and prayer imposed on them by the Europeans and orders them to sing and dance all day, "With the result that they did nothing else" (ibid., 217). Conceivably, Obará's commands derive from and are reinforced by the Guaranís' traditional "Land without Evil" concept. Another sign that the rebellion was in fact a revitalization movement lay in the rebaptizing of Indians under their own names by Obará's son:

> Obará had a son, whose name
> was Guiraró, which means "bitter stick."
> He assumed the title of pope.
> On that his father said, "I discharge
> my great obligation
> by making him pontiff."
> Guiraró it was who went around baptizing
> and changing everyone's name. [los nombres a todos trasmutando] (ibid., 218)

As Christ named Peter the first pope, so Obará the Antichrist named his own son, Guiraró, the first pope of his revitalization movement. As opposed to the solid rock represented by Petrus, however, the latter is only a "bitter stick." Under this antipope, the Christian rite of baptism becomes not the giving of grace (or of "faith," as the poem has it) but the erasure of one's own name under the generic title of a Christian saint. (Remember the process by which Pay Zumé was translated into Saint Thomas.) Guiraró carried out reverse baptisms by removing the Christian names and reestablishing Indian identity. We may compare Guiraró's actions with those of a later rebellion. In 1660 the Guarani Rodrigo led a similar movement in Arecayá, where he established himself as God, his wife as "Santa Maria la grande" (the Virgin Mary), and his daughter as "Santa Maria la pequeña" (Mary Magdalene; Mélia 1986, 36–37). These natives turned eschatechnology against itself as they refused to give up their ethnicity in favor of sublimation into Christian universalism. Instead, they modified Christian symbols and used them to place themselves back in the center of history.

Eventually del Barco enters into his own narrative as he attempts to regain the renegades for the true faith:

> One of them [the pope] was baptizing, changing
> the names that the Indians already had:
> The other [the emperor] went around
> punishing the faults they committed.
> Obirá went around preaching,
> and I saw that some mestizos were following him,
> and I became eager to get them back.
> and in the end I had to seize them by force. [Y al fin hube con maña de cojerlos]
> (1836, 229)

As a priest, del Barco does not prosecute the war against those Indians beyond the pale but instead leaves that to the secular army, which eventually intervenes and easily defeats Oberá. He is interested in recovering lost sheep from the flock; the verb *cojer*, which he uses to describe this activity, is synonymous with *reducir*, which refers to leading the Indians back into the fold, giving rise to the noun *reducción* for the missions. The passage suggests that the attraction of mestizos by the new, hybrid faith represented a turning point for the Spaniards, since this was a group that was considered to be already safely within the fold of Christianity. Symbolically, however, the invocation of mestizos points to the hybridity of the entire conversion process with its double naming and syncretistic faith.

Oberá's movement seems to fall into the second category of millennial movement in the Americas, a nativist reaction to Christianity that makes use of the dominant religion's surface features in order to reassert control. However, the available information on Oberá is limited and, as we have seen, is hardly composed from a neutral perspective. For additional understanding of Oberá, it may be useful to adduce the case recorded by Nimuendajú among the Tukuna people, who inhabit the Solimões and Marañon rivers in the eastern portion of the Brazilian state of Amazonas, southern Columbia, and western Peru. Cargo cults, in which people believe in the end of the world as represented by the arrival of a huge cargo ship with Western goods destined—in contradistinction to reality—for indigenous peoples—were first identified in Oceania, and the Tukuna represent one of the only cases of this form of millenarianism in the Americas.[3] The repeated outbreaks among the Tukuna extended over a period of more than half a century, from around 1900 through the 1960s, and recurred in several different forms, each representing the vision of a particular Tukuna, who then became the center of a cult. In one, natives gathered around the Indian outpost station at Tabatinga, where they awaited a "big boat" filled with goods that would save them from the coming flood of boiling water. Ten years later the message was repeated by a *pajé* named Ciríaco, who then became the Messiah and to whose small community dozens of families flocked.

The syncretism of the Tukuna cults derives not so much from Christianity as from the general incorporation of Western values, objects, and people into the native mythological system. The imminent arrival of the big ship is inevitably announced by a white man seen in a vision by the Indian prophet. In some of the early outbreaks, Nimuendajú—the anthropologist who recorded the events—became identified as the divine figure. In others, it was a beneficent leader of the Indian outpost, Manelão. The ship was loaded with goods from the white man's world that were accorded high value among the Indians. All of these features symbolize the identification of traditional power structures with the system imposed from outside, which has appropriated Tukuna lands and subjected them to the rewards and coercions of dominant Brazilian culture and its complex Indian policies. In a refracted and ironic mirroring and comparison of cultures, Indians dream of "becoming white" while at the same time eliminating their oppressors:

> In a kind of compensatory gesture, failed attempts at assimilation can reverse themselves and become aggressive nativism. The more the Indians are oppressed and dominated by the non-natives, the more such reversals tend to occur. Despite their wish both to enjoy the advantages of civilization and to assume the culture of civilized humans, the nativist attitude prevails. It informs even the messianic recourse to miracles. The opposition between Indians and whites should no longer be transcended, but only inverted. Then the old ethnic identity need no longer be renounced.
> . . . [The cases here] have little or nothing to do with a return to the lost paradise of the tribal culture, indeed . . . they are radically opposed to traditional institutions, due to the recognition that these stand in the way of the new ideal of culture and personality. The old institutions must be destroyed to prepare the way for the dawn of the millennium, but in the name of an Indian hero, not that of a Christian saviour. (Schaden 1971, 17–18)

We see here a particular instance of the paradox at the heart of all millennial movements: Radical change appears in the guise of extreme conservatism. In the case of the Tukuna, there was a compromise as the native culture's hero employed a white emissary.

In that context, it is interesting to note the translation problem in rendering the role of the Tukuna culture hero Dyoí, whose emissaries the white figures were thought to be:

> The *pajé* asked us [ethnographers] what Dyoí, the principal culture hero [herói civilizador] of the Tukuna, would be called in Portuguese. Then he explained his question:
> "He is 'our God,' is he not? Or is he 'he who governs us,' 'our government' [o nosso govêrno]?"
> On another occasion . . . Ponciano gave us a long list of fabrics, medicines, and tools for us to request that the "government" send soon to the Tukuna, who will be glad to receive the items. He emphasized in great detail, so as not to leave room for any doubt:
> "So that's it, give the message to Dyoí, our government."
> Clearly Ponciano was syncretizing, in a way which appears confusing to us but is not to him, the paternalistic idea of the Brazilian government with the tribal myth

of Dyoí. Thus it does not appear improbable to us that in 1946 the Tukuna had seen in Manelão a type of emissary of their immortal culture hero. (Vinhas de Queiroz 1963, 50)

In this reading, "government" takes its place as a technology alongside items such as medicine and tools, all of which the Tukuna are eager to syncretize with their existing social and economic structures. The millenarian, dreamlike aspect in which these desires are expressed reflects the hopelessness and oppression of everyday reality for the Tukuna.

Translating Millennium

If messianic rebellions occurred on the watch of Ruiz de Montoya, however, they did not find their way into his writings, where the enemy takes the forms we have seen. However, the Guaraní apparently had their own version of the end of the world. Ruiz de Montoya's vocabularies have several entries to indicate this: *Ibipapape* is "at the end of the world, and day of judgment" [en el fin del Orbe, y dia del juyzio]; *ibitorirerequaba apirey* is the "land of endless joy" [tierra de alegría sin fin] (1639, 167). None of this vocabulary appears in the translation of the Christian "end of the world" [fin del mundo], which in one place (1876, vol. 2, 1) is glossed as *ara canyramo*, while in another (1639, 107) it becomes *arapapaba*. The Guaraní notion of Land without Evil represented a translational challenge for Europeans. Apparently from prediscovery times, the Indians thought of this as a physically existent, this-worldly place where they could find their favorite fruits, good hunting and fishing, beautiful women, and so on. Every so often, a *karai* would arise who would pronounce the direction in which this earthly paradise lay, and the tribe would pick up and march in that direction until they reached an insurmountable obstacle. To Europeans, the Land without Evil seemed closest to the classical pagan notion of the Elysian Fields, except that there was no need to die in order to go there. Ruiz de Montoya translates what has become the present-day Guarani term for Land without Evil, *yvy marane'y*, simply as "virgin soil" [suelo intacto] (ibid.), which should alert us that the mystical element has been added to the term through centuries of colonial frustrations. That is, the precolonial meaning of the term pointed to an earthly paradise—what we would call a Shangri-la—that coexisted with the more familiar and painful aspects of subsistence. Colonization and enslavement by the Spaniards and Portuguese—from which the Jesuits succeeded in rescuing many Guarani—made ordinary life more like hell and may have produced the messianic impulses that appropriated the term *yvy marane'y* and brought it closer to what we would call a New Jerusalem.

That Ruiz would devote an entry to this item is itself revealing. The seemingly total this-worldliness of the Land without Evil placed it outside the realm of religion altogether, and since the Land without Evil constituted the Guaranis' central belief, their religion—which lacked places of worship, idols, and most other accoutrements of faith familiar to the Europeans—remained as invisible as the color of water to the earliest observers altogether, making them less than pagans, a people totally without religion. In fact, the Europeans' refusal to find a religion euphemistically translated something far more scandalous:

> a religion in which men themselves try to become equal to the gods, immortal like them. For what is the significance of the restlessness that compelled the Tupí-Guaraní into such a quest [of the Land without Evil], and of the affirmed hope that immortality can be reached without dying, if not to express the question of the possibility (or the impossibility) of men becoming their own gods? To what thought is such a practice related, if not to the refusal of theology: men and gods are two poles and one wants other ways to consider them than as disjunctive. (Clastres 1995, 24)

We remember that the absence of a Guarani pantheon allowed Ruiz to read Guarani monotheism, however negative its outward manifestations, as the trace of doctrine preached by Saint Thomas. Lucia Gálvez's reading of the Guaraní concept of the Land without Evil also emphasizes the similarities between Christian and pagan notions of peregrination:

> When the Guaranís told to the first Spanish missionaries their myth of the Land Without Evil that made them eternal wanderers, more than one of the Spaniards heard in the story, with great emotion, the medieval accents of their own Gonzalo de Berceo: "Todos somos romeros que de camino andamos . . ." (We are all of us pilgrims walking down the highway . . .). What better figure for explaining to the Guaranis that life was a pilgrimage towards the kingdom of God? . . . In their double role as Christians and Guaranis, the mission Indians, along with their *padres*, could feel themselves united in the search for a city "without pain or sorrow, eternal city." (Gálvez 1995, 218)

Notice the Europeans' conversion of the originally pastoral notion of the Land without Evil into an urban one, for which the New Jerusalem of Revelation is clearly the model. There are striking similarities, at least in the translated versions of this myth. Guarani myth related that the world was created two times (the first creation was destroyed by a flood). The Guaranis' cultural heroes escaped the flood through prayer and other good conduct to join the Creator in his dwelling place. The present world is held up by crossed beams; when these fall, the world will be consumed by fire. Like the cultural heroes, those alive in the present may escape the conflagration by self-purification and then travel to join the Creator in the Land without Evil (Ribeiro 1992, 71). The notion of physical wandering to find paradise is perhaps the greatest difference, though it too recalls the Jews wandering in the desert and finding Canaan.

Similarities of the notion of Land without Evil to that of the Christian New Jerusalem make it difficult to judge the degree of assimilation of the Guarani. Following Haubert, J. C. Garavaglia has speculated that the Jesuit promise of heaven seemed to the Guarani the "necessary price" of Christian baptism and adaptation to the discipline of mission life (1981, 232). On the other hand, Ganson cites a mission Guarani, Felicitas, who spoke a prophecy of doom and destruction that was widely circulated. She predicted that "her mission of La Cruz would become depopulated, and that there would be death, total destruction, and an end to everything. In her native language, she spoke of 'mbabuçu oicone,' which means that 'the great work, a great death is the fate of the missions'" (1994, 232). Yet, Felicitas was a model Catholic who went to Mass every day, took communion, and gave frequent presents of fish to the missionaries. What does "great death" mean here: a death of many people or one of great redemptive qualities, such as Christ's? This ambiguity is a typical product of the mutual translation between radically different cultures. Meanings were produced that were new to each culture and hence not fully accessible to either. The meaning of Land without Evil/New Jerusalem resided in a black box that could be estimated but not directly known. I have suggested here that millennial expectations held on both sides may have furnished part of the vast energy driving the epochal enterprise of the missions.

Translation of the New Jerusalem into Modern Terminology

The European view of the Jesuit missions that caused their expulsion and the closing of the reductions, widely known through Voltaire's depiction of them in *Candide*, is of a thoroughly profane political and economic empire, a "state within a state." Increasingly during the modern period, however, European thinkers reimported the apocalyptic *techné* exported to the New World centuries earlier. Whatever the real circumstances of their origins and daily reality, the reductions were reinterpreted as symbols in the history of utopia and dystopia. Ludovico Antonio Muratori, in his influential *Cristianesimo felice nelle missioni dei padri della compagnia de Gesù* of 1743, argued, in postmillennialist fashion, that mission life resembled that enjoyed by the first Christians: a community of belief with a minimum of coercion and hierarchy. He declared that his readers should feel glad that "the kingdom of Jesus Christ grows so considerably every day on earth" (48).

The rise of socialism made the missions a focus of controversy. Robert B. Cunninghame Graham, cofounder of the Scottish Labour Party and supposed inspiration for characters in Bernard Shaw, Joseph Conrad, and Mario Vargas Llosa, provides a good example of the socialist writers who saw in the missions a model of utopian socialist society. The title of his 1901 account, *A Vanished Arcadia*, reveals his viewpoint. The concept of a lost Arcadia is based upon the primitive communistic system of the Jesuits, which emphasized cooperation rather than competition: "The simple, ceremonious, if perhaps futile, mission-life had withered up at the first touch of vivifying competition—that competition which has made the whole world gray, reducing everything and everyone, to the most base and commonest denominator" (Cunninghame Graham 1924, 286). In a move typical of millenarian thinking, Cunninghame Graham discovers traditional values in the distant past that can be resurrected in order to counteract the present destruction of social relations. Satan is now represented by capitalism. Cunninghame Graham returned to this theme in a later work on a different millenarian scenario, Brazil's Canudos war. *A Brazilian Mystic* (1925) follows closely, indeed plagiarizes, much of *Os sertões*, the classic study of the conflict by Euclides da Cunha (1902). Viewing the two situations—which are separated by centuries—side by side, one can see the same basic scenario: A utopian theocracy is threatened and eventually crushed by capitalism.

Peruvian novelist Mario Vargas Llosa puts Cunninghame Graham and Euclides da Cunha at the center of his novel of Canudos, *The War of the End of the World* (1981; *La guerra del fin del mundo*). The latter remains nameless, referred to only as the "nearsighted journalist," thereby reflecting an inability to see millenarian movements as the complex social phenomena they inevitably are. Cunninghame Graham receives the alias of Galileo Gall, indicating his position between science and pseudoscience (that is, the phrenological theories of European scientist Franz Josef Gall), the difficulty of distinguishing between them, and Gall's devotion to the same positivist philosophy that permeated the Brazilian republic. Like Cunninghame Graham, Gall is born in Scotland, fights for the Paris Commune and other revolutionary causes and finally travels to Latin America. But Vargas Llosa lets us know that Gall stands for all of Europe: "[H]e scribbled notebooks that corroborated, and enriched with examples, the teachings of his masters: his father, Proudhon, Gall, Bakunin, Spurzheim, Cubí. He had been clapped in prison in Turkey, in Egypt, in the United States for attacking the social order and religion" (ibid., 15).

Gall is equally distanced from both sides of the Canudos conflict: The new Brazilian republic is crony capitalism at its worst; Canudos has the makings of a commune, but of course its religious atavism repels Gall. His incomprehension culminates in his rape of a peasant woman, Jurema, and his eventual murder by her husband, who fails to understand the modern principles of free love and condescends to fight with Gall over a mere "cunt." Jurema is the name of a ubiquitous plant of the backlands, and Gall's act can be interpreted as the violence committed against a part of the Americas that is beyond the Europeans' experience or comprehension. The real Cunninghame Graham, of course, did not come to such an end; rather, Vargas Llosa signals in the misadventures of Gall the Europeans' deadly misinterpretations and mistranslations of American millennialism. We have seen in this chapter how, as a technology of conversion, translation worked to confirm Europeans' millennial expectations. At the same time, mistranslation was an inevitable by-product of this translation process and gave rise to Native Americans' millennial visions of resistance. The next chapter examines some hybrid visionaries of the New World more closely.

2

Hybrid Messiahs

Long enough have we [Americans] been skeptics with regard to ourselves, and doubted whether, indeed, the political Messiah had come. But he has come in *us*.

—Herman Melville, *White-Jacket*

The Mexicans are a *hybridous race* withal. . . . Nine-tenths of the population are made up of various intermixtures formed from white, Indian and black parentage, in all its mottled varieties. Nothing possessed by such a people can stand for a moment before such a race as the American.

—Walt Whitman (1846; emphasis added)

The nineteenth century intensely debated the question of whether the offspring of different races were hybrids or "mongrels," a distinction related to questions of monogenetism vs. polygenetism and of the relative fertility of sexual intercourse between heterogeneous groups. An assumption behind the discussion was agreement about the distinct status of hybrid offspring. In other words, hybridity was seen as a deviation from, rather than the creative force behind, racial types:

In the different theoretical positions woven out of this intercourse, the races and their intermixture circulate around an ambivalent axis of desire and aversion: a structure of attraction, where people and cultures intermix and merge, transforming themselves as a result; and a structure of repulsion, where the different elements remain distinct and are set against each other dialogically. (Young 1995, 19)

The result, in Homi Bhabha's words, is that "these heterogeneous sites and circuits of power . . . must continually be re-presented in the production of terror or fear. The

---

The first epigraph to this chapter is cited in Bercovitch (1978, 177). Notice that Melville capitalizes "Messiah." In this chapter and throughout this book "Messiah" is capitalized when it refers to a specific person but more frequently appears in lowercase when it refers to the concept.

For the second epigraph I am indebted to Donald Pease.

paranoid threat from the hybrid is finally uncontainable because it breaks down the symmetry and duality of self/other, inside/outside" (1994, 116). As I point out in the first chapter, millennial discourse is an eschatechnology inherent to structures of power in the Americas. When it confronts itself in hybridized form, the breakdown in categories mentioned by Young and Bhabha and the resultant paranoia and panic are inevitable. Concomitantly, the categories of messiah and Antichrist inevitably contaminate each other. Whitman's statement is thus riven by contradictory principles, both lamenting the negativity of miscegenation and at the same time upholding the view that it is ultimately a centrifugal force for the creation of national identity (not to mention Whitman's apparent blindness, at least in this editorial, to the presence of similar racial heterogeneity in the American army.)

Renata Wasserman summarizes the particular hybridity of the Americas:

> New World populations call into question all definitions of identity that rest on clear oppositions between those recognizably like and those unlike a predefined European self. That self is shattered and combined with other fragments into identities whose heterogeneity precludes complete acceptance as well as complete rejection and who are both self and other, kin and stranger. (1993, 466)

Wasserman's words are directed specifically at the situation of Antônio Conselheiro of Brazil, one of the most dramatic historical and literary examples of messiah, whom I discuss later on. Messiahs of the New World are painfully aware of themselves as simultaneously Self and Other, as I show in this chapter, and their messianic missions involve seeking a symbolic resolution to this conflict.

If Walt Whitman's assessment of the Mexican hybrid as inferior to the Anglo-Saxon (whose hybridity is bracketed) shows the limit of the multitudes he is willing to contain, Melville's democratic pluralization of the messiah implicitly embraces America as comprising a variety of races and ethnicities. *Moby-Dick* shows this hybrid messiah most compellingly in the figure of Ahab. Not coincidentally, I argue, in his hybridity Ahab swings around into Antichrist. Many of the messiah figures of American millennialist movements, both real and fictional, have demonstrated hybridity and hence become subject to this dialectic. Since the messiah type generally combines religious with political functions, it is not immediately clear why hybridity would be so prevalent, why the parade of messiahs would not identify completely and solely with either a dominant or a dominated group. One answer lies in the very logic of prophets: The messiah must be an outsider in some way, a *homo sacer* or *pharmakeus*. Another possibility, as noted earlier, relates to the messiah's symbolic resolution, in or with the messiah's body, of the contradictions related to hybridity.

To the basic demographic meaning of hybridity we should add the more metaphorical (and affirmative) appropriations of the term in the twentieth century. Mikhail Bakhtin applies the Russian *gibrid* or *gibridizm* to language rather than to people, an idea that Homi Bhabha, Stuart Hall, and Edouard Glissant, among others, have expanded to include a variety of cultural and semiotic practices within colonial situations. Glissant prefers the term *créolité* over "hybridity," drawn from the idea of creative mixings of two or more languages to create a new creole. Thus, creolization has to do not only with the primacy of culture over raw biology, but also with the element of chaos and unpredictability that the semiotic dimension injects:

> Creolization, and not *métissage* or crossbreeding, accurately describes the process originated by the contacts and conflicts of cultures. . . . Creolization is unpredictable, whereas the immediate results of crossbreeding are more or less predictable. Furthermore, creolization opens on a radically new dimension of reality, not on a mechanical combination of components. (1995, 270)

In extending its own cultural paradigms to the colonized, the colonial power can never produce "purebreds," clones of its own citizens or subjects, but rather hybridized structures and types that belong fully neither to colonizer nor to colonized and that become challenges to either or both groups. Millennialism, many have claimed, is one such weapon, and the hybrid messiah its purveyor.

Anointed Ones

The term *messiah* comes from Hebrew and literally means "anointed one." It referred simply to the political ruler chosen by God. The Jewish high priest was also ritually anointed, thus indicating the unity of religious and political leadership. Technically, then, Melville's formulation, "political messiah," is redundant. In the Old Testament messiahs differed from prophets—John the Baptist was the prophet for Jesus the Messiah—but the distinction is often difficult to draw once we move outside the specific religious context that gave birth to these terms. For my purposes here, "messiah" simply refers to the acknowledged leader of a millennial movement, who is always perceived to possess a saving message or technology. Indeed, millennium and messiah are mutually defining: One cannot exist without the other because "[a] messiah is an individual believed to be empowered by a superhuman or divine agent to create the millennial kingdom. Both prophets and messiahs have charisma—their followers believe they have access to a divine or superhuman source of authority" (Wessinger 2000, 11–12).

Pierre Alphandéry has identified seven features of the messiah which, however, overlap with each other, so I reduce them here to just three. A messiah: (1) acts as a divine messenger who receives messages directly from God and does not work through institutions; (2) imparts to followers the appropriate means for achieving terrestrial paradise (e.g., holy war, asceticism, dancing) and himself takes actions to install the new regime; and (3) dominates the followers' lives and institutes new social relations among them (Pereira, 1972, vol. 1, 5). We can trace in these characteristics the elements of Cohn's definition of the millennium: the miraculous afflatus with God; the need for strategies, given the terrestrial nature of the paradise and the need to bring it about soon; and the collectivity forged with the strength of the leader's personality and ability to utterly transform followers' lives. In comparing the biographies of millenarian leaders of Indonesia, Burma, Africa, and New Zealand, Michael Adas has discovered certain commonalities in their biographies. Messiah figures come from a variety of backgrounds: "At one pole are indigenous authority figures whose position is threatened by changes introduced by the agents of alien civilizations" (1979, 117). At the other pole of the continuum are "men of low birth, who are exposed to a high degree to alien but dominant civilizations" (ibid., 117–18). Adas also finds a commonality among all prophetic figures of failure or physical illness that conceivably contributes to their sense of mission (ibid., 121). Illness or mutilation signals the transformation of the messiah's body into the social body as it enters the liminal space of danger.[1] The hybrid, we might say, is the messiah, whose power of prophecy derives from the knowledge of elements of the dominant culture but is delivered in creole or in the language of the native. The creolization of millennial discourse allows it to escape the orbit of control and recuperation and become a sign of danger. From the dominant point of view, then, the messiahs who deliver such messages are Antichrists.

Ahab as Type of the American Hybrid Messiah

An early, anonymous reviewer of *Moby-Dick*, writing for a religiously affiliated New York newspaper, the *Independent*, seemed already to conflate its author with the messianic type he had created. The reviewer placed Herman Melville in the camp of the Antichrist, to be thrown into the lake of fire: "The Judgment day will hold him liable for not turning his talents to better account. . . . The book-maker and the book-publisher had better do their work with a view to the trial it must undergo at the bar of God" ("Judgment Day" 1992, 57). Since their revaluation of the novel in the early twentieth century, scholars of *Moby-Dick* have recognized the narrative as an original statement both on American politics and American religion; however, they differ substantially as to what that statement might actually be. For Marcus Sheffield, Melville is the "last great Puritan" (2000, 114), and *Moby-Dick* in particular is a "Puritan jeremiad concerning the pathway to American salvation" (ibid., 110). Yet it is hard to find much salvation, either national or personal, in the Romantic catastrophe of shipwreck that ends the novel. Leo Marx bases his political analysis on that catastrophe and on the failure of Ishmael or Starbuck to stand up to Ahab, whom Marx compares to the U.S. government as an elite utilizer of millenarian discourse:

> Both [Ahab and the U.S. government] seemed to be animated by a concept of manifest destiny, a fatalistically and potentially self-destructive aggressiveness. Both also embodied the racial bias whereby white Americans used their "brains" to organize non-whites to accomplish their physical ends. . . . Ishmael's mode is comparable to the opposition of the dropout culture of the sixties and its emphasis on private salvation. In the case of opposition to the war, too, no organized movement aimed at changing the underlying structure of power emerged. Our individualistic responses to power are politically ineffectual, and they tend, as in *Moby-Dick*, to lend credence to an apocalyptic view of the nation's destiny. (1976, 3)

If Melville's use of typology is to have consistency (a big "if," admittedly) then the shipwreck must be considered an inverted baptism into the demonic, as the *Pequod* is an inverted antitype of Noah's ark (Berkeley 1973, 121). The title of T. Walter Herbert's

Moby-Dick and Calvinism: A World Dismantled (1977) encapsulates Herbert's thesis that Melville wished to reproduce the conflict between Unitarian and Calvinist religious positions, as shown in the "notable resemblance between Captain Ahab and the liberal heretic that Calvinist rhetoric depicts" (40). Charles Olson (1947), on the other hand, in an influential reading, felt that Melville was striving in *Moby-Dick* to throw off the husk of institutional American religion and create his own. On the political side, readings tend to sort out according to the perceived unity of purpose between the Anglo Ahab and his racially diverse crew. Furthermore, C. L. R. James has argued that Ahab represents the rise of totalitarian dictatorship exploiting the courage and craftsmanship of the colored harpooneers. "It is the biography of the last days of Adolf Hitler" (1985, 68). Timothy Powell (2000), on the other hand, sees Ahab and the harpooneers as united in a common campaign of "ruthless democracy" against the monocultural whiteness represented by the whale. Common to both readings, however, is the assumption that Ahab cannot be considered independently from the multiracial crew, whose fate he has linked to his own. Ahab as a character, on the other hand, and his fate, as well as that of the *Pequod* crew, are filtered for us by the narrator, Ishmael. Ahab's duality is reflected in his inseparability from Ishmael, whose own name reflects that of a more favored other, Isaac, as well as the parlous duality of curse (to be always less than brother Isaac) and blessing (when God saves Ishmael and his mother, Hagar, in the desert in Genesis 21: 15–21). Hence, the polar oppositions of these critical readings can be explained through the hypothesis that *Moby-Dick* was Melville's working out of the American hybrid messiah: the messiah that has come in *us*, plural. The pluralities of the American messiah are multitudinous and self-contradictory.

The Millerite movement of 1843–1844 peaked just as Melville returned from his sojourn at sea. His friend Nathaniel Hawthorne was content to parody its ideas in writings such as "Earth's Holocaust" (discussed in chapter four). Melville, perhaps associating Millerite disappointment with the descent of his own patrician family, signaled by the financial ruin and early death of his father, seemed to sense that the separation of millennial aspirations from mainstream religion would mean the rise of countless splinter religions or cults, some numbering no more, say, than the crew of a whaling ship. *Moby-Dick* contains all of the necessary elements of apocalyptic community. Ahab is the prophet figure, whose will is absolute and who is obeyed in all things. The crew fails to understand his purpose or share his heretical views but obey him nonetheless. Though nominally a Quaker, Ahab will have nothing to do with established creeds and instead invents his own improvisational, pantheistic religion as he goes. At one point, for example, Ishmael writes of

> that intangible malignity which has been from the beginning; to whose dominion even the modern Christians ascribe one-half of the worlds; which the ancient Ophites of the east reverenced in their statue devil;—Ahab did not fall down and worship it like them; but deliriously transferring its idea to the abhorred White Whale, he pitted himself, all mutilated, against it. (1851, 185)

Ishmael appears to present Manicheism—the idea that the world is divided between good and evil forces—as an orthodox belief of Christianity, when in fact it is one of its most prominent and contested heresies. He presents Ahab's quest of the white whale as different and more holy than the standard economic whaling venture. Life's purpose is to be poured into the single moment of battle against Moby-Dick. The community is of course hermetic and isolated, alone on the ocean in a ship. The view of Ahab as a madman corresponds with the prevalent views of apocalyptic messiahs—William Miller, the Counselor, David Koresh—by "normal" people, established religion, and secular authorities.

Consider the parallels between Ahab and Jim Jones, leader of the People's Temple and founder of Jonestown: Both fought what they considered to be the ultimate evil (for Jones it was capitalism, opposed by Divine Socialism in the place of Christ) and forged alliances with darker races than themselves—hybridized themselves—in order to carry out the war. Jones's faith healing is echoed in Ahab's magic tricks with the compass and the corposants (it has parallels in Wovoka's "hand magic" as well). Both of them offered bodily sacrifice to this hatred (Jones would claim numerous serious medical conditions, such as cancer and a fungus in his lungs, none of which appeared in his autopsy, drug consumption being his single greatest debilitator). Both were willing to die in defiance of their Antichrists and could not bear the thought of their flock falling into the Beast's hands (flukes), so they took everyone down with them and earned the name of Antichrist themselves. Jonestown and the *Pequod* both "float" as alien, manmade bodies on a sea of green (jungle vs. water), allowing their multicultural, millenarian communities to develop in splendid isolation. For each messiah, utopia comes to equal a state of permanent exile. Jones chose Guyana as the best location to survive nuclear Armageddon, after which the People's Temple would provide the new Adam and Eve.

Ahab chooses to "hoop" himself with the dark harpooners and with Fedallah. Jim Jones transculturated himself at an early age, claiming that he was African American. He thereby reversed the stigmata of hypodescent and hybridity, which he emphasized by claiming that his genealogy included a king of England. In a rhetorical inversion symbolic of the seizure of dominant discourse by the dominated, Jones embraced the word "nigger." The goal of the People's Temple would be to "niggerize" its congregation, to make them aware "of being cheated, persecuted, oppressed, and subclassified by the prevailing network of social relations in America" (Chidester 1988, 71), as the impoverished Jones had been in his early years. If "money whitens," then "poverty blackens." Ahab is hybridous in a number of different ways. He is, as noted earlier, a creation of Ishmael. That is, the legitimate heir of the Hebrews (albeit a wicked king) is immortalized by the illegitimate son of an Egyptian. Recall that some theories of the origins of the Native Americans made them Abraham's progeny, a theme we revisit with Louis Riel. So, too, Ahab's messiah status is confirmed not only by Elijah, the crazed sailor, but also by "the old squaw Tistig, at Gay-Head, [who] said that [Ahab's] name would somehow prove prophetic" (Melville 1983, 93). (Elijah is the prophet of the Messiah and a type for John the Baptist.) As a machine, Ahab is intimately connected with the East Indians he brings on board the *Pequod*. In the end, he is not just Ishmael's creation but that of his entire hybridous crew.

Such is one interpretation of Ahab as the hybridized other. From another perspective, he is a conquistador or a U.S. president leading men into war. The *Pequod* is a war machine that Ahab commandeers in conformity with his vision. As an American leader, Ahab is the type of those from Beveridge to Bush the Second who claim to have a "personal relationship" with God, who gives them the knowledge of good and evil. No one has caught this better than Peruvian playwright Rodolfo Hinostroza in his adaptation of Shakespeare's *Midsummer Night's Dream*, *Apocalipsis de una noche de verano* (1988). Replacing Bottom and company in the woods of Athens are U.S. soldiers in Central America, which the United States has just invaded, apparently tired of using proxies like the contras and provoking first a Cuban, then a Soviet response and the start of nuclear war. (The date of the play, 1988, is revealing. One year later and the Cold War premise would no longer have resonance.) The soldiers put on a propaganda play for the peasants, *Moby-Dick* rather than "Pyramus and Thisbe." Significantly, the white whale is now the red whale, and Ishmael is revealed for what he always was, a hybrid: "SOLDIER 4: I am Ishmael Ochoa, chicano from San Diego. What's up, man?" (ibid., 66). Several political cartoons of the period use Ahab as a type in a similar way. One shows Cold Warrior Ronald Reagan dressed up as the captain.

Like the mutually assured destruction (MAD) of the nuclear arms race, Ahab harnesses and fine-tunes dominant technology to the purpose of bringing about the eschaton. As Leo Marx has noted and as the examples of Isaac Newton and others in the introduction to this study show, technology is not opposed to "wild, metaphysical purpose" (1976, 299) but becomes its greatest ally:

> A whaling captain's life, as Ishmael sees it, is peculiarly conducive to illusions of Promethean power. Ahab's vocation endows him with mastery of what Carlyle had called the "machinery' of the age"—in both senses of the word. As captain he is, of course, master of an intricate piece of machinery in the literal sense. More important, however, is the mechanistic habit of mind, which Carlyle had attributed to modern man and which enables Ahab to control the consciousness of his men. . . . As the *Pequod* approaches the white whale, Ahab's preoccupation with power becomes obsessive. Images of machinery, iron, forges, wheels, fire, and smoke fill his speech. . . . The shattering fact is that his madness fits the needs of this technically proficient society. (ibid., 298–99)

As messiah, Ahab overtly rejects the institution that Ishmael subsumes under the heading of "joint-stock" company. He advertises the pursuit of Moby-Dick not as a personal vendetta but an eradication of evil from the world that will enrich the lives of all of the sailors, not to mention the whole world. There exists, then, a dialectic between the leader and the community, who together engage in "joint-stock" millennialism with the aid of eschatechnology. James Tabor and Eugene Gallagher responded to the media's Ahabization of David Koresh with the following message: "Followers play a crucial role in constructing and maintaining any leader's charisma. To a significant degree the followers actually make the leader. The Seventh-Day Adventists who made up most of the population of the Mount Carmel center had long been prepared by both tradition and personal experience to expect a living prophet among them" (1995, 143). The messiah always comes *in us*.

Evaluations of Ahab coalesce around a vision of him as an anti-Jonah, who, in contradistinction to Father Mapple's advice, chooses to obey himself rather than God. Ahab is, in Daniel Hoffman's words, an "unrepentant Jonah" and hence an Antichrist (1970, 259). In creating an anti-Jonah, Melville was able, in T. Walter Herbert's words, to "challenge the theocentric scheme [of the early nineteenth century] within its own terms" (1977, 9). From the heart of Puritan New England arises an individual whose religious obsession is so great that he turns away from the unfathomable qualities of redemption in the New Testament Father and passes through the Old Testament Jehovah of wrath to something more elemental and unconscious—the white whale. The mission to kill Moby-Dick, the ceremony of the harpoons, the incidents of the corposants and the turned compass needle are all animistic, "heathen" in nature.

Sacvan Bercovitch sees Ahab as a culmination of the tension inherited from the Puritans between a view of the sacred as utterly divorced from the profane and the view of political projects as leading to a divine millennium. (To some extent, this distinction maps onto that between premillennial and postmillennial thinking.):

> If Ahab is a distortion of the "political Messiah" celebrated in *White-Jacket* [see the chapter epigraph], that may be because the messianic promise, the dream of knowledge, power, and the spirit, is itself a distortion. If Ahab proves false to Father Mapple's vision of the "anointed pilot-prophet" who "ever stands forth his own inexorable self," it may be not Ahab who fails, but a certain vision of selfhood. . . . Ishmael embodies Melville's quarrel with America, Ahab his quarrel with what America symbolically represents. (1978, 192–93)

Charles Olson posits that Ahab is self-made God, a necessary supplement to Melville's wanderings among the deserts of theology in search of the proof of divine providence: "Melville could not rest without a belief, he had to have a god. In Moby-Dick he had one. I called him the Ancient of Days. The job was a giant's, to make a new god. To do it, it was necessary for Melville, because Christianity surrounded him as it surrounds us, to be as Anti-Christ as Ahab was. When he denied Ahab, he lost the Ancient. And Christianity closed in. But he had done his job" (1947, 102). Olson frantically mixes two different concepts in his assessment. The Ancient of Days is described in Daniel 7:

> Thrones were set up
> and the Ancient One took his throne.
> His clothing was snow bright,
> and the hair on his head as white as wool;
> His throne was flames of fire,
> with wheels of burning fire.
> A surging stream of fire
> flowed out from where he sat;
> Thousands upon thousands were ministering to him,
> and myriads upon myriads attended him. (Daniel 7:9–10)

Olson implies that this figure represents an entity different from the Elohim, Yahweh, and so forth. The name is unusual in the Old Testament, and the representation of God more visual than most. (Rastafari, the Bible-based religion originating in Jamaica, claims that this description of God with hair like wool reveals that He is Black and is hence more original and authentic than most other descriptions in the Bible that have systematically edited Africans out of a narrative that is largely theirs).

While describing Ahab's "special lunacy," Ishmael suddenly breaks into a long description of another Ancient—the Anti-Ancient, as it were:

> Far beneath the fantastic towers of man's upper earth, his root of grandeur, his whole awful essence sits in bearded state; an antique buried beneath antiquities, and throned on torsoes! So with a broken throne, the great gods mock that captive king; so like a Caryatid, he patient sits upholding on his frozen brow the piled entablatures of ages. Wind ye down there, ye prouder, sadder souls! question that proud, sad king! A family likeness! aye, he did beget ye, ye young exiled royalties; and from your grim sire only will the old State-secret come. (Melville, 1983, ch. 41, 187)

This Ancient may represent the original Zoroastrian principle that posits the universe as shaped by an eternal battle between good and evil. The positing of evil forces divides and mutilates the self since one can recognize evil only from within. No one attends this Ancient, darkness rather than fire surrounds him, and he is located far beneath the earth rather than in the heavens. He represents the root of what we are instead of its culmination, our origins rather than our messianic end. It is as though Melville wished to represent the unconscious or the whole biological basis of being human, the "lower layer" behind the pasteboard mask.

Biology makes its appearance in the physical suffering Ahab must undergo in order to achieve his vision. There is, of course, the loss of his leg, which becomes a hole in his soul to be filled with a divine or demonic plan of vengeance. From another perspective, the intense pain, fever, and near-death experience open a portal into the dream world, where such plans reside and can be revealed:

> for long months of days and weeks, Ahab and anguish lay stretched together in one hammock, rounding in mid winter that dreary, howling Patagonian Cape; then it was, that his torn body and gashed soul bled into one another, and so interfusing, made him mad. That it was only then, on the homeward voyage after the encounter, that the final monomania seized him, seems all but certain from the fact that, at intervals during the passage, he was a raving lunatic, and though unlimbed of a leg, yet such vital strength yet lurked in his Egyptian chest, and was moreover intensified by his delirium, that his mates were forced to lace him fast, even there, as he sailed, raving in his hammock. (ibid., ch. 41, 186)

With the hermetic adjective "Egyptian," Ishmael once again points to Ahab as his twin since the narrator's own name makes him the son of Hagar and thus half-Egyptian. The fever and delirium finally leave Ahab, and he is able to assume his captaincy again. Yet now, Ahab, "in his hidden self, raved on" (ibid.).

Ahab's "spirit sickness," his visit to the spirit world and return with a message for his fellow mortals, belongs to the type of the messiah. The symbolism of such sickness is clear enough: The old self that was in collusion with the Beast must be rooted out to make room for a new, revitalized self. One historical example would be Jemima Wilkinson, who fell critically ill after being expelled by the Quakers and had a vision of two archangels bringing a sealed pardon for sin. Their trumpets announced not disaster, as in John's text, but "Room, room, room" for everyone in the Lord's house with many mansions. When Jemima awoke she believed that she had died and literally been reborn with a new spirit. She never referred to herself as Jemima Wilkinson again but only as "The Universal Publick Friend." The Friend founded a community called New Jerusalem in New York state.[2]

Skolaskin, dreamer-prophet of the Sanpoil tribe on the Columbia plateau, provides another parallel to Ahab. From the time of his ascendancy following the great earthquake of 1872 to his imprisonment in 1889, Skolaskin urged his small band to resist the incarnation of evil, his Moby-Dick, the white man. The Sanpoils resisted reservation life, farming, white religion, and other aspects of white culture. When still quite young, Skolaskin fell ill and was crippled. Accounts of his crippling vary: It may have been caused by a fall from a horse; maiming by vengeful husbands whose wives he had seduced; or an illness such as polio. Again typically, the malady caused his removal from society for some time, perhaps two years. He turned the disability to his advantage as he told his people that he had visited heaven during his illness and was returning with a dream to lead them (Ruby and Brown 1989, 135–37). One of his commandments was to build an ark in which the people could ride out the last flood, which would eliminate all of the white people from the face of the earth.

A similar debility also leads to vision in the historical case of Wovoka, the prophet of the Ghost Dance movement who caused its popularity throughout the West in the 1880s. Wovoka described his experience to ethnologist James Mooney:

> [H]e fell asleep in the daytime and was taken up to the other world. Here he saw God, with all the people who had died long ago engaged in their oldtime sports and occupations, all happy and forever young. It was a pleasant land and full of game. After showing him all, God told him he must go back and tell his people they must be good and love one another, have no quarreling, and live in peace with the whites; that they must work, and not lie or steal; that they must put away all the old practices that savored of war; that if they faithfully obeyed his instructions they would at last be reunited with their friends in this other world, where there would be no more death or sickness or old age. He was then given the dance which he was commanded to bring back to his people. . . . He then returned to earth and began to preach as he was directed, convincing the people by exercising the wonderful powers that had been given him. (1970, 13–14)

Just as Skolaskin and Wovoka provided ceremonial frameworks for their followers, so Ahab sets up the theater of the harpoons and the doubloon. Both used magic tricks to control their followers, as Ahab uses electricity. Skolaskin placed burned glass into the hollow stem of an anise plant. When he held it to the sun, the "magic tube" showed a kaleidoscopic light that he claimed represented God (Ruby and Brown 1989, 149). Wovoka made ice fall from the sky and had a relative shoot a gun at him to show his invulnerability. A Cheyenne and an Arapaho both witnessed one of Wovoka's magic tricks. The first saw only something black being drawn out of a hat, while the latter saw "the whole world" in the hat. "From my knowledge of the men, I believe both were honest in their statements," adds Mooney (1970, 18). Such are the eschatechnologies of the hybrid messiah.

Nat Turner: Millennial Recovery Project

Nat Turner, who led a bloody slave rebellion in Virginia in 1831 and was hanged in the same year, cannot simply be contrasted with Ahab either as a "real" person with a "fictional" one or even as an antitype to Ahab's type. Virtually every historical document we would need in order to reconstruct Turner's historical, individual personhood is missing. Instead, we must contrast the performative utterances of the Southampton court that synopsized his trial with the constative language of the considerable body of fiction and drama that has attempted to draw his portrait and determine his motives. The earliest of these, the *Confessions*, published by white lawyer Thomas Gray (1831), supposedly based upon interviews with Turner in prison, derived those motives from a hybridized, racialized apocalyptic. A more recent but equally notorious version of the *Confessions*, by novelist William Styron (1967), displaced Turner's vision of the Day of Judgment (in true D. H. Lawrence style) onto his imagined sexual hang-ups, thus provoking a storm of protest from black intellectuals who wanted us to see Turner's millennialism—if at all—as rooted in his desperate circumstances. So great is the desire for a "genuine," undialogized Turner that Daniel Panger based his novel *Ol' Prophet Nat* (1967) on the apocryphal discovery of an autobiography written by the title character. The insertion of Turner into this comparative study implicitly argues for considering his rhetoric as a product of American millennialism.

I need not recount Turner's textual history, for it has been done at least twice—by Albert E. Stone (1992) and by Mary Kemp Davis (1999). The key fact is the coconstruction of Turner's life, starting with his interviews by Thomas Gray. The problems and paradoxes of Gray's *Confessions of Nat Turner*, reminiscent of the "Ishmael-Ahab perplex," are reproduced in the history of further mimesis, so that one of the most written-about New World messiahs appears as an irredeemably hybrid, mythic figure.

There are, moreover, not one but several layers to this hybridity, beginning with the African Christian. Donald G. Mathews refers, for example, to the voice that Turner hears when he has his vision that leads to rebellion: "Such is your luck, such you are called to see, and let it come rough or smooth, you must surely bare it [*sic*]" (Turner and Gray 1831, 46). Mathews comments on this passage:

> [T]he words came not only from God, but from Africa, whose western nations believed that every man had a unique destiny ordained for him from before his birth. This destiny was made known to him, as it had been to Turner, upon his initiation into manhood; and from that time forward he was subject to this personal benevolence or destiny, or as it is best translated into English, "Luck." And if Turner has no "good destiny shrine" as had his ancestors in Africa, by the time of this vision (1825), the whole universe seemed to the sensitive man to have enshrined his "luck." (1977, 234)

Gray himself seems to recognize or fear the Africanness of Turner's apocalypse or at least its non-Christian aspect, for when Turner mentions the spirit speaking to him, Gray asks, "What do you mean by the Spirit?" (Turner and Gray 1831, 46). Turner does not immediately say in response, "the Holy Ghost," although he does so on the next page, but rather answers, "the Spirit that spoke to the prophets in former days" (ibid.). Which prophets? At least some of them might be African. Turner's sense of destiny had already manifested itself in childhood when his parents told him he was "intended for some great purpose, which they had always thought from certain marks on my head and breast" (ibid., 44). Gray parenthesizes that these are mere "excrescences," hence removing them from biblical tradition. That this art of reading the body is African in origin seems likely, given that Turner's mother had been brought to Virginia from Africa only five years before his birth.

Furthermore, Nat's preaching is not welcomed by the local Christians, so he founds a new religion: "[W]hen the white people would not let us be baptised by the church, we went down to the water together, in the sight of many who reviled us, and were baptised by the Spirit" (ibid., 47). This baptism is apparently into either no particular church or a newly created church, a millennial African church, in the face of those "who reviled us." Not coincidentally, a short while later Nat hears a loud noise in the heavens, and the Spirit appears to him and gives him the mission of fighting against "the Serpent" reminiscent of St. George. The modern avatars of such practices include Jim Jones's People's Temple, for whom the Serpent was a capitalism that "niggerized" most of the world's population.

On the other hand, Turner's spirit speaks to him through the Bible, and his assumption of the role of prophet is similar to that of Anne Hutchinson, the Universal Publick Friend, and others. In particular, Richard Brodhead has noted both the similarity and contemporaneity of Turner's reception of the spirit of prophecy with that of Joseph Smith, the founder of the Church of Latter Day Saints (Mormons):

> Turner, like Smith a farm laborer and worker in others' fields, like Smith propels himself towards an encounter with the sacred through a prior act of a biblical fixation, a mounting obsession in which he finds or is found by a scriptural verse that promises to open the kingdom if he will seek. Turner's obsessional text is Luke 12:31: "Seek ye the kingdom of Heaven"; Smith's was the closely related James 1:5, "If any of you lack wisdom, let him ask of God . . . and it shall be given him. . . . [A] burst of spiritual elation moved [Smith] to baptize Cowdery in the Susquehanna River. In a strikingly parallel event, Nat Turner gives expression to the joy of this vision by reinstituting, on his own inspired authority, the sacrament of baptism. . . . [T]he millennialism of Nat Turner's visions was . . . an American commonplace. (2002, 222–25)

The African connection provides only the deepest layer of hybridity in the textual construction of Nat Turner. It is difficult to say whether Thomas Gray—whose motives in publishing the account and sympathies or antipathies toward other forms of millennialism remain unclarified—has exacerbated or attenuated these Africanisms. What seems beyond doubt is Gray's Ishmael-like stylistic reshaping of Turner's very language. Rather than a stenographic account, the *Confessions* are a ghostwritten autobiography. Scholars point to sentences such as the following that, in both its diction and hypotaxis, seem unlikely to have escaped from a slave's mouth: "In my childhood a circumstance occurred which made an indelible impression on my mind, and laid the ground work of that enthusiasm, which has terminated so fatally to many, both white and black, and for which I am about to atone at the gallows" (Turner and Gray 1831, 44).

Yet the Turner/Gray recounting of Turner's visions also contains highly original vocabulary that seems unlikely to have stemmed from the white. For example, the text reads that "the Serpent has been loosened, and Christ had laid down the yoke he had borne for the sins of men" (ibid., 47). This is not the exact language of Revelation, eliding the millennium itself, which is the period before the unbinding of Satan. Nor is there mention of Christ laying down the yoke (nor of his blood returning to earth as dew, another of Turner's images), nor is it exactly clear what this means. Here, it would seem, Gray was attentive to what Turner actually said rather than layering it over with his own hypercorrections. Nor, when Turner compares himself to Christ in responding to Gray's question as to whether his prophecy was mistaken, does Gray hesitate to print the apostasy. While one might argue that its radical nature contributes to the literary impression Gray wishes to leave of Turner as a fiend and fanatic, that is not what Turner's rhetorical question, "Was not Christ crucified?" (ibid., 48) has come to mean in its effective history. It has been interpreted instead as the first assumption by Africans of human dignity within the white world they were forced to inhabit and as the origin of Afro-American self-interpretations as the tribe of Hebrews to be freed from the Egyptian or Babylonian yoke. Gray must explain Turner in language either that gives his subject a voice that renders his language ambiguous and interpretable or that draws the reader's attention to gaps and contradictions of the text that point to alternative histories. In Eric Sundquist's terms, "Gray's rhetoric . . . is in contest with, and parasitically bound to, Nat's, as masters and slaves were bound in a game of cunning" (1993, 50). The cunning of history.

This contest continues in the literary appropriations of Nat Turner. The many fictions based on the rebellion divide according to the degree of authentic millennialism they are willing to accord its leader. Styron infamously interpreted Turner's visions as a sublimation of sexual desire for a young white woman whom he ended up killing. Styron had seized on a peculiarity of Gray/Turner's *Confessions*: Margaret Whitehead was the only white Turner confessed to killing with his own hands. Just before his execution, Styron's Turner has a vision not of the New Jerusalem but of finally consummating his desire for the woman he has killed:

> And now beyond my fear, beyond my dread and emptiness, I feel the warmth flow into my loins and my legs tingle with desire. I tremble and I search for her face in my mind, seek her young body, yearning for her suddenly with a rage that racks me with a craving beyond pain; with tender stoking motions I pour out my love within her; pulsing flood; she arches against me, cries out, and the twain—black and white—are one. . . . I recall a meadow, June, the voice a whisper: *Is it not true, Nat? Did He not say, I am the root and the offspring of David, and the bright and morning star?* (1967, 426)
>
> *I would have destroyed them all. . . . Yet I would have spared her that showed me Him whose presence I had not fathomed or maybe even known.* (ibid., 428)

Turner quotes Revelation 22:16: "I Jesus have sent mine angel to testify unto you these things in the churches. I am the root and the offspring of David, and the bright and morning star." The Revelator takes up a traditional symbol of the Jewish Messiah. In fact, Nat's last words are "Oh how bright and fair the morning star" (1967, 428). While Styron's imaginative reconstruction of Turner outraged many because it seemed to rob the hero of dignity and sincerity and to reproduce stereotypes of African lust, I am more interested here in how Styron's Nat Turner parallels treatments of the other hybrid messiahs of this chapter. Once again, a "dismasted" Ahab can be seen as a type for the compensatory aspect of millennial dreams: The symbolism of his being shy a leg is unavoidable. In terms of their sexuality, messiahs seem to have two choices: celibacy vs. the appropriation of all women in the group. Skolaskin, Jim Jones, and David Koresh represent the latter extreme, Turner, along with Ahab and the Counselor, the former.

Since underindulgence vs. overindulgence in sex conforms to the messiah/ Antichrist divide, authors frequently deliberately "get it wrong" in recounting this aspect of their subjects' lives. In *La bourrasque* (1925), the first novel to feature Louis Riel as its unsavory protagonist, Maurice Constantin-Weyer makes him a philanderer of the first order despite the historical record (including Riel's own poetry), which shows Riel falling in love with at least two women from afar and marrying a third after more than a year of living together. Riel's only true love in *La bourrasque*, à la Turner, is for a white woman whose first words to him are "I hate you" (ibid., 71; "je vous déteste"), supposedly referring to his mixed racial origins, but who is nevertheless sexually attracted to him in the familiar pattern of desire and aversion. So famous was the Counselor for asceticism and celibacy, on the other hand, that writers on Canudos displace the sexual predations onto his lieutenants, typically João Abade (Abbot John). Manoel Benício portrays Abade as a sexual predator who abuses his power in order to coerce as many women into his bed as possible. The narrator of the novel *João Abade* notes that in Canudos "there wasn't a virgin left older than eleven or twelve" (dos Santos 1958, 64; "não se achava uma só virgem de mais de onze ou doze anos") due to the predations of Abade and his followers. Hence, a single story combines the two extremes of messianic sexual behavior.

The Turner/Whitehead couple (named here Dred/Nina) also structures the narrative of Harriet Beecher Stowe's adaptation of the Denmark Vesey rebellion, *Dred: A Tale of the Great Dismal Swamp* (1856), although the two never meet. Nina Gordon, mistress of a plantation, follows the path of Christian meekness and humility, communicating Christianity to the slaves, seeing that their legal causes are furthered, and ministering to the sick. Dred, whose first appearance occurs two-thirds of the way through the first volume, is the "wild old warrior prophet of the heroic ages" (ibid., vol. 1, 241), theeing and thouing his interlocutors like an Ahab. Dred maintains a maroon community while awaiting a sign from God to lead the slave insurrection. Nina dies of cholera contracted from her patients; Dred of a gunshot wound while rescuing a maroon.

Stowe, a daughter, sister, and wife of ministers, had used prophetic discourse before, notably in the death of Little Eva in *Uncle Tom's Cabin*. However, that language was produced by the narrator, whereas in *Dred* Stowe sought to create a hybrid messiah in the crucible of history, literature, and her own imagination. Stowe says as much in her foreword to the novel. She chose the theme of slave rebellion, led by the messiah Dred, not in order to wake the nations but because the subject matter is tinged with a Romantic and feudal spirit and with a fascinating hybridity: "Two nations, the types of two exactly opposite styles of existence, are here struggling; and from the intermingling of these two a third race has arisen, and the three are interlocked in wild and singular relations, that evolve every possible combination of romance" (ibid., vol. 1, iii). Here, then, is Styron's will-to-hybridity couched in more discrete language. Stowe does not tell us why we should think of European and African as "exact opposites."

Both parts of Stowe's title are symbolic: "Dred" alludes to the dread of the non-elect before judgment; the swamp is the liminal space of untutored symbolic appropriation of the world. The swamp, by extension, represents the American petri dish in which millennial dreams may grow unchecked. Dred is a product of this swamp, which muddies the boundaries between history and fiction, messiah and Antichrist. He is the son of the historically documented Denmark Vesey, a free black who conspired to lead an insurrection and was caught and hanged. Dred's major inheritance from his father was a Bible:

> There is something there for every phase of man's nature; and hence its endless vitality and stimulating force. Dred had heard read, in the secret meetings of conspirators, the wrathful denunciations of ancient prophets against oppression and injustice. He had read of kingdoms convulsed by plagues; of tempest, and pestilence, and locusts. . . . He had heard of prophets and deliverers, armed with supernatural powers, raised up for oppressed people; had pondered on the nail of Jael, the goad of Shamgar, the pitcher and lamp of Gideon. . . . Cut off from all human companionship, often going weeks without seeing a human face, there was no recurrence of every-day and prosaic ideas to check the current of the enthusiasm thus kindled. Even in the soil of the cool Saxon heart the Bible has thrown out its roots with an all-pervading energy, so that the whole frame-work of society may be said to rest on soil held together by its fibres. Even in cold and misty England, armies have been made defiant and invincible by the incomparable force and deliberate valor which it breathes into men. But, when this oriental seed, an exotic among us, is planted back in the fiery soil of a tropical heart, it bursts forth with an incalculable ardor of growth. (ibid., vol. 1, 255–57)

The end of this quotation gives a specific example of the literary hybridity Stowe posits abstractly in her preface and metaphorically in her description of the Dismal Swamp: The oriental text of the Bible, translated by the cold English, grows luxuriously in the tropical African heart to produce a hybrid messianism. The idea of "revelation" is meant generally, as the Babel of prophetic examples demonstrates. The mention of locusts, for example, could refer either to the Egyptian plagues or to a pouring out of the vial from Revelation. While such ambiguities are intrinsic to biblical typology, in Dred's case they also indicate the intertextuality of his prophetic language. The offspring of Denmark Vesey, Dred actually mentions Nat Turner as well, and Stowe gives excerpts of the confessions in an appendix (ibid., vol. 2, 338–46), but it is clear that Dred is no Nat. The difference goes beyond the obvious failure to carry out an insurrection. As the preceding passage shows, opposed to the narrow range of New Testament (mostly the gospels and Revelation) that forms the basis of Nat's vision, Dred, as we have seen, creates a farrago out of Old and New Testament language. Furthermore, he is described variously as a "sleep-walker in a somnambulic dream" (ibid., vol. 1, 294) or a cataleptic (ibid., vol. 2, 90), rarely if ever as a prophet. In Mary Kemp Davis's words, Stowe shows Dred manufacturing a "call" and then answering it. God does not speak to Dred through audition, theophany, or vision, unlike the God of the Old Testament prophets who shows a wonderful inventiveness in speaking directly to men and women. Burning bushes, talking asses—any media will do. By leaving the "call" undramatized, however, Stowe creates the impression that Dred's "call" is his own creation, that it has welled up from the depths of his own tortured being. . . . But if Dred is not a prophet, what is he? (1999, 125–26)

One answer, of course, is that he is Antichrist (though again, one more intertextually than divinely engendered), and as we have seen, the fact that he is portrayed with some degree of sympathy does not stand in the way of Stowe's repetition of the typical pattern of desire and aversion toward messiah/Antichrist. In almost Darwinian fashion, her novel depicts the inevitability of the emergence of a messiah from the "third race," nemesis of the slavocracy, a race whose untutored hybridity is nevertheless so painful and dreadful that she must kill him off before he achieves his goal. Stowe is one of the few American authors to play both sides of the divide between controlling and rebellious millennial discourses. From her white, high-church background she understands the healing, postmillennial discourse of progress and conversion embodied in Nina. Her abolitionist ideology and reading of history brought her into contact with the premillennial discourse of Nat Turner, which she could comprehend as a true judgment on the Serpent of slavocracy. The ambivalence of Dred's prophecy mirrors Stowe's own.

Wovoka/Jack Wilson

The hybrid nature of Wovoka's teachings is shown first of all in his double name.[3] Paradoxically, the prophet's "Indian" name, a corruption of the Paiute "Wy kothyi," meaning a cutting or chopping instrument, first appeared in a newspaper account of 1894, after the high point of the Ghost Dance had passed. It is not clear where it came from. Paiutes interviewed after Wovoka's death remembered him only as Jack Wilson. Says one relative, "You know I never heard that name Wovoka until 1938, when we first moved up here [Campbell Ranch]. Jack, Jack Wilson, that's how they speak about him all the time" (Hittman 1990, 341). That was also the name given in the early newspaper accounts. The Wilsons were white ranchers who took Jack into their home and introduced him to fairly rigorous Christian piety, such as prayers before meals and Scripture readings, and to the telling of stories from the Bible. *Ghost Dance Messiah* is a "faction" about Wovoka by novelist/historian Paul Bailey. By "faction" I mean a writing in which fact alternates with fiction and which undertakes the presentation of history, contemporary events, or biography within a fictional framework. In Richard Johnstone's definition, "faction" combines fiction with nonfiction, presenting itself "now as one thing, now as the other. It derives part of its strength from being seen as fictional—literary, invented—and part from being seen, paradoxically, as fact" (1985, 5). Bailey invents the Paiute's undergoing the ceremony of blood brotherhood with a young Bill Wilson, who later helps him with his magic tricks. Bill hopefully trusts that the white blood has made Wovoka "all the same white man" (1986, 32; pidgin for "just the same as a white man"), and Wovoka extends the complementary wish that Bill now be Paiute. However, it is not blood but social practice that sorts the races in Bailey's fiction:

> When young Bill Wilson started mixing at dances and socials, and playing closer heed to the girls growing up in other white families, the inclination to show off his more swarthy brother as true and presentable kin, began speedily to diminish. A few times Jack Wilson sat with the family at the Valley's Protestant church, and heard Christ-preachings with fire and eloquence, but his sensitive nature was already warning of white antipathy toward smelly Paiutes in their midst. Interesting as was the story of Christ and the prophets, it was definitely appearing improper for him to share a listening with the whites. . . .
>
> Regrettable as it was to Wovoka, time itself was turning him back to an Indian. (ibid., 33)

Bailey follows Wovoka in his migrant work to California, Oregon, and Washington, where he absorbs the Shaker ceremonies of John Slocum, and then to his taking up of the Ghost Dance upon his achieving the status of shaman after making ice appear in summer and undergoing the "deep sleep." Eventually he calls himself the "Paiute Jesus." In fact, the variety of terms Bailey uses for Wovoka's function—dreamer, wizard, messiah, and prophet are others—provide another sign of the hybrid nature of his undertaking.

In Bailey's novelized version of the story, Wovoka is driven by the contradictory forces of wanting to be white and being deeply aware of his Indianness and all it implies. His calling to prophecy is as politically motivated as it is a personal wish for power and prestige. When the Mormons appear to preach their religion to Wovoka, with the claim that the Indians will someday turn white, he responds, "When Paiute turn white—then I join [the Mormon church]. . . . It would be good to be a white man. Maybe I wanta be a white man" (ibid., 83). The Mormons surface again and again in Bailey's novelized account, hybridizing Wovoka's Ghost Dance to the extent of giving him the idea of the ghost shirt, which was supposed to protect against bullets. Mooney had already circulated the idea that the ghost shirt was adopted from the Mormon temple garment; Bailey invents for it a comical scene in which Wovoka virtually strips a Mormon elder to see his underwear and, unable or unwilling to understand that the clothing is suitable only for the religiously indoctrinated, orders two pairs from him. When his request is rejected, Wovoka asks his uncle to get him two pairs even if he has to "skin 'em off" (ibid., 150). With the resulting two pairs (probably stolen off clotheslines) Wovoka begins the manufacture of ghost shirts.

In reality, the ghost shirt probably derived from a variety of sources. The interaction between the Latter Day Saints and the Ghost Dancers went beyond the appropriation of clothing items, however. Mormon theology had identified the Indians as "Lamanites," descendants of Hebrews who had emigrated to the Americas and undergone a complex series of wars and tribulations that are recounted in the Book of Mormon. Native Americans were thus seen as the Jews, whose conversion was thought to trigger the end times. The news of an Indian messiah, while never officially recognized, aroused a great deal of excitement among Mormons, to the extent that church officials felt compelled to give lectures to discredit the identification of Wovoka with Jesus. In 1890 President Wilford Woodruff, fourth president of the Mormon church, advised the community that the person visiting the Lamanites in Nevada was not the Risen Lord but rather one of the Three Nephites (Barney 1986, 169–70).

Bailey's account ends with the Wounded Knee massacre of 1891 and the subsequent collapse of the Ghost Dance movement. Wovoka fears white reprisals for the violence and confronts the death of his dream: "His mistake was one the good and more enduring prophets had never been guilty of—he had named the date. And because of it, time itself was now his enemy" (1986, 205). These enduring prophets are not named, but in the Americas many have indeed fixed the date and brought about disaster. The ending is optimistic, as Wovoka counts his blessings—among them the continued friendship of the Wilson family—while his wife, Mary, pledges her continued loyalty.

Bailey's Wovoka is ambivalent, equal parts true messiah and Antichrist, a politically self-conscious Indian who yearns to be white. Not surprisingly, Wovoka's descendants (some of whom Bailey interviewed for the novel) have bitterly contested the book's accuracy, fitting it into a long line of betrayal of the Indians and Wovoka/Jack Wilson into a long line of martyred Native American prophets: "If Jesus walked the streets today, He would be treated in no different terms than Paul Bailey did to Jack Wilson. Because they just don't understand him" (Hittman 1990, 348). Bailey's account of Wovoka undoubtedly abounds with inaccuracies and wild guesses—most of the incidents I have mentioned are historically undocumented—and seems written to debunk not just the Ghost Dance but also religion in general. More interesting from the point of view of this chapter, however, is Bailey's insistence on the hybridity of Wovoka's messianic mission. The double-edged nature of Wovoka's message is well known: on the one hand, peace with the whites; on the other, divine intervention that will reunite the living with the dead and return the world to a pristine state. Bailey ruthlessly invents subterranean underpinnings for the hybridity of this stance, from blood brotherhood to the use of white technologies for magic tricks to the Mormon origins of the ghost shirt. He insists that Wovoka's campaign was a search for a self that could not be whole. Bailey finds his "facts" in the shadow of the hybrid messiah.

Louis Riel Exovide

Nat Turner, Ahab, Jim Jones, Skolaskin, and Wovoka are all "purebreds"—African, European, and Native American—who sought the path of power and salvation through creolized prophetic discourse. Louis Riel (1844–1885), leader of two (1869 and 1884) rebellions by the Métis of central Canada against the government, was biologically hybridous. (The rebellions are described in their political context in chapter six; my emphasis here is on the figure of Riel himself). In Canada the word "Métis" refers to descendents of unions between Europeans and Indians. Riel himself was one-eighth Chippeweyan. Métis could be either French speaking, like Riel, or English speaking. The former group—"Les Métis canadiens français," in Riel's terminology—generally resisted the integration of Manitoba into Canada, whereas the latter group approved and furthered it. In a country without a pantheon of founding figures, Louis Riel, representative of its multicultural origins, could have served but instead remains, in true messiah/Antichrist fashion, an ambiguous figure in Canadian artistic and literary representations: "To mention only the most prominent roles attributed to him, Riel is simultaneously a sage and a madman; a Catholic mystic and an Anabaptist visionary; an Aboriginal leader and a puppet of white forces; a cultural mediator and a promoter of racial warfare; a Prairie maverick and a pan-Canadian patriot" (Braz 2003, 191). Most historical figures are intangible and provoke contradictory interpretations, but in Riel's case the contradictions are intensified by his bridging of several Canadian cultures and languages.

Riel took the name "David" for himself, referred to himself as the "president" of the Métis nation, and also coined a unique title, "exovide," from the Latin "ex-" plus "ovis," meaning "sheep" (meant here in the collective sense of a flock, a common metaphor for a religious congregation). The term is ambiguous in that it refers both to Riel's goal of establishing a new Catholic church out of the old and also to himself as standing apart from the flock of his fellow Métis as a *perdu* and *aliené* and of course as the sacrificial lamb who will undergo sacrifice and *sparagmos*. Jean Morisset's explanation of the term's oxymoronic qualities is eloquent:

> Ex-ovidate. This name that Riel gave himself in order to compensate his belonging [*appartenance*] to a universe that in every sense condemned him to non-belonging [*désappartenance*] marks with emphasis the stigma of the Métis in a society that wants to be absolutely white and free of every alloy. Though in actuality *métissage* is the constitutive principle of the nations of the New World, Riel is born in one of the few corners of the continent officially founded on the prohibition of *métissage*: Britannic America. This prohibition will always give Canada regrets for being impure, degenerate, and *métis*. (1992, 398)

Morisset's remarks preface the question of why Riel's writings, in a diversity of genres, have never appeared in any anthologies of Canadian writing in French. Riel was "ex" everything, Canada's "marginal man," as Wolfgang Klooss (1989, 79) calls him, rejected in equal parts by the English-speaking dominant culture and the French-speaking *Québecois*. Nor was he a typical Métis: His family followed a more sedentary way of life, and Louis was chosen to become the first Métis priest of the Red River area and sent to study in Montreal. Riel quit school due, among other things, to his love for a young woman whose family rejected him as not racially pure enough (see the epigraph to chapter eight and the following discussion).

Significantly, Riel's call to prophecy and his name change occurred as he lived in exile between the two rebellions, in a period of political stagnation during which the Métis were attempting to negotiate the best political solution for themselves and to hold on to the land they were due in consequence of their Indian blood; however, they received little attention from Ottawa. Riel was elected to parliament from Red River but, as a result of his role in the execution of Thomas Scott in 1869, was not allowed to take his seat. Even more significantly, Riel's burning-bush experience occurred near Washington, D.C., where he was staying in 1874 as a political fugitive while lobbying congress and President U. S. Grant for support of his cause. He reported the moment in an interview with the *Montreal Daily Star*:

> On 18 December 1874, while alone on the summit of a mountain near Washington, D.C., the same spirit that had appeared to Moses amidst flaming clouds appeared to me in like fashion. I was astounded. I was stupified [*sic*]. It said unto me: "Get up, Louis David Riel, you have a mission to accomplish for the benefit of humanity." (cited in Martel 1984, 151)

There are no true mountains in the vicinity of Washington, D.C., so one wonders whether Riel meant one of the ridges across the Potomac or instead imagined the scenario in order to establish the mythic connection between physical heights and the presence of God. Similarly, one finds alternative explanations of the assumption of the name David, such as for purposes of alias to disguise the wanted man.

Like Ezekiel, Daniel, or John, Riel reported a number of visions full of symbolic objects: He learned of the Hebrew origins of the American Indians; he saw the "two gloves," the "tortoise," and the statue of Italian nationalist Camillo Benso di Cavour. Riel's perception of his mission coincided with his increasing alienation from his fellow human beings. "Aliené" is a French term for insane, and Riel was eventually pronounced "aliené" and spent nearly two years in the asylums of la Longue-Pointe and later Beauport. Significantly, one of his repeated "crazy" actions—besides declaring himself to be a prophet—was to remove all of his clothing; at times he ripped his own clothes and bedclothes to shreds, making himself into the "bare forked creature" who could be transculturated and born again into a New Heaven and New Earth. Chester Brown allows the imagery of hands, arms, and absence to dominate over words in depicting the "black hole" and *désappartenance* of the messiah's alienated existence (Brown 2003, 113–14). In figures 2.1 and 2.2 Riel's disembodied hands and arm, which seem to be acting of their own will, symbolize the schizophrenia of his personal and political situations and foreshadow the *sparagmos* his body will undergo as a sacrifice for the Métis and, in some interpretations, for Canada.

The calculated rhythms of Brown's panels signal the ebb and flow of Riel's mental state and millennial aspirations. At the time of his discharge from the Beauport asylum, Riel made the following statement to the doctor:

> I had come to believe myself a prophet or something similar. . . . However, one day, tired of remonstrances and objections, I asked myself if perhaps I was wrong and everyone else was right. From that moment light dawned in my mind.
> Today I feel better, I even laugh at the proud hallucinations of my brain. My mind is clear; but when one speaks of the *Métis*, of those poor people pursued by Orange fanaticism . . . Oh! then my blood boils, my head swirls, and . . . it is better that I talk about something else. (Flanagan 1996, 78)

From 1878 to 1884 a chastened Riel eked out his existence as a schoolteacher in Montana. A bit to the north, his native Manitoba was experiencing a flood of Anglo settlers, overwhelming the Métis of all origins and placing French speakers in the minority. He communicated with those Indians, such as the Sioux, ready to fight for

FIGURE 2.1 Chester Brown, *Louis Riel* (113–14).

FIGURE 2.2

their territory, hoping that they could become allies of the Métis, and a few hundred Cree under Poundmaker did join the 1884 uprising. After his trial and condemnation, the *Montreal Star* reported the words of an Indian who promised an uprising if Riel were hanged (August 31, 1884). (One could also note, however, all of the tribes who chose not to take part in the rebellion.) Riel also developed his plans for the Canadian cosmic race, which would be constructed from pluralistic, Catholic *métissage*. The Italians were to come and found New Italy, the Bavarians New Bavaria, the Irish New Ireland, and the Poles New Poland as states of western Canada, all by intermarrying with the Indians occupying the land. They would join together in a kind of superrace fit to house the Exovedate of the Catholic Church, whose time in Rome had ended in 1870 with the invasion of church lands by Italian troops.

Riel embraced his Indian blood in poems such as "Le sang sauvage en moi rayonne" (Riel 1993, 58–59; "Indian blood shines forth in me") while at the same time connecting it with the narrative of redemption brought from Europe by insisting that Native Americans descended from Hebrews. In all of Riel's voluminous writings about "la race sauvage," one finds very little specifically about the components of Indian "race" or culture that would make them a desirable component of the New World. Riel's one and only justification for his Indian blood was to make it Jewish and thus to link Métis history to the millennial master-narrative brought from Europe. As seen in the last chapter, such linkages had been attempted from the earliest periods of European settlement.

Riel thus laid out a mythological story that proved that the Indians were descended from the Hebrews. In the novel *The Scorched-wood People* (1977), Rudy Wiebe summarizes the vision Riel needed in order to show that the blood of David ran in his veins:

> The Holy Spirit has revealed to me, Monseigneur, that the savages of North America are Jews of the purest blood of Abraham with the exception of the Eskimos, who come from Morocco. For while Moses was exposed on the waters of the Nile in order to save him, an Egyptian boat containing twenty-seven Egyptians and seventeen Jews was lost at sea. This ship was tossed about for months, and they abandoned all hope until one evening the four-year-old daughter of Agareon the Jew, who had been praying to the God of his Fathers, took him gently by the hand. My father, she said, you are still looking for the land of the Egyptians. And pointing to the sun which just then touched the horizon, she said, Let us reach that fire there. Then the father knew that God was speaking to him; the ship's company had faith in him, and so they changed direction. And, though they experienced great storms, eventually islands did appear, the strait between Haiti and Cuba, and finally the mainland of Mexico. Nineteen days after the vision, on the thirteenth day of April in the year after the birth of Moses they reached the happy shore, found through the faith of a virgin. The Egyptians went south into Mexico, the Jews north. (1977, 159)

In John Phelan's formulation, "the idea of Jewish descent of the North American Indians is the point where the Apocalypse of the Protestants meets the Apocalypse of the Age of Discovery" (1970, 26). It also meets the Apocalypse of a Catholic Church in exile. Like Father Miller, Riel took 457 bce, when Ezra arrived in Jerusalem to take religious control of the Jews, symbolizing the rebirth of Judaism, as his starting point. Adding up the numbers in various parts of the Old Testament, Riel arrived at two periods of 2,333 years, each composed of 457 plus 1,876 years. The first 457 years had led to Christ's birth and then to Riel's discovery of himself as a prophet. In 2333 ce the papacy would be transferred to French Canada. Another 1,876 years after that, in 4209 ce Christ would return.

Certainly there was megalomania involved in Riel's undertaking. which Gilles Martel sees as compensatory, an argument we will also see made in the case of the Counselor: "After having been humiliated, persecuted as a murderer, condemned to political inaction, exiled from his country, and fallen ill in an asylum, Riel seems to accumulate the most exalted titles for himself in a process of psychological compensation: priest; king; pontiff; prophet" (1984, 165). Riel's poem "Alexandre-le-grand" [Alexander the Great], written for Alexandre Taché, bishop of Saint Boniface, allows some of the greatness applied to the religious leader to reflect on Riel, his prophet: "Listen, my mouth has been transformed. / I am President Riel. / Listen to me, this is a prophet / Who will translate Ezekiel" (Riel 1993, 74). In his writings, Riel rarely, if ever, used biblical quotation, preferring instead to develop his own, original mythology and prophetic visions within a general framework of analogy and allegory. David Day makes the point that Riel's verse "belongs to the tired European poetry of the time" (Riel 1997, 11).[4] Day proposes that Riel's true poetic gifts were poured into his speeches and his diaries, where he combined the prophetic tradition of the Hebrew Bible with the shamans of the Great Plains.

The earliest scholarly attempts at explaining millennial movements focused on the messiahs' supposedly aberrant psychographs, for which the case of Louis Riel provided abundant material, particularly at his trial for treason. An equal number of expert witnesses were called for each side and provided contradictory opinions. In the end, the jury agreed with the Crown that Riel was a "malingerer" who faked insanity in order to manipulate his followers. So clearly delineated were the conflicts in this trial that it furnished the basis for two plays by John Coulter and Frederick Walsh, based almost entirely on the testimony. Both authors reproduce the climactic moment when Riel attempts to speak for himself and reveals the dilemma of his trial:

riel: Your Honour, this case comes to be extraordinary. The Crown are trying to show that I am guilty. It is their duty. My Counsel, my good friends and lawyers whom I respect, are trying to show I am insane. It is their line of defence. I reject it. I indignantly deny that I am insane.

DEFENCE: (Trying to break in): Your Honour . . .

RIEL: (Not giving way) I am not insane! I declare that in rousing and leading my people against cynical disregard and neglect by Ottawa . . .

JUDGE: Stop! You must stop! . . .

RIEL: (Rising again) I cannot abandon my dignity. Here I have to defend myself against the accusation of high treason, or allow the plea that I am insane and consent to the animal life of an asylum. I don't care much about animal life in or out of an asylum, if

it does not carry with it the moral existence of an intellectual
being in full and sane possession of his faculties.

JUDGE: Stop now! No more! Stop!

(Coulter 1968, 36–37)

While the dramatic structure of Coulter and Walsh reproduces the agonistic aspects
of Riel's struggle, it also eliminates his supporting cast and hypostatizes political,
cultural, and linguistic antagonisms that were far more fluid and complex. It is possible for an insane person to deny being insane, as Riel does in the preceding passage, and both authors depend upon their readers to become part of the jury trying
Riel, aided by historical distance. In *The Scorched-wood People*, on the other hand,
novelist Rudy Wiebe attempts a "thick description" of the rebellions that reconnects
Riel with his followers. Wiebe also uses complex narrative layers—the most comprehensive of which is that the entire English text must be read as a "translation"
of a narrative spoken or thought in French—that problematize interpretation. For
example, Pierre Falcon, the Métis bard who narrates the novel, omnisciently sees into
the asylum doctor's thoughts. (Falcon is a historical personage who died shortly after
the first rebellion and did not write about Riel.) Wiebe, too, holds to the ambiguous
vision of millennial movements. The doctor's diagnosis is countered by a believing
Métis consciousness, for whom Riel's behavior makes sense:

> The doctor was suddenly overwhelmed with tenderness. Such a clear case of mega-
> lomania, of messianic paranoia; overheated on Bible-reading and persecution, the
> world in the clutch of evil, take the flaming sword of God and destroy it in judgment.
> Father Bolduc saw too much religious problem here; Riel's political ambitions on
> earth finished forever, and now clearly he was making himself a role so unreal that
> actual events would never prove him wrong; destroy Protestant London, papal Rome.
> Oh, poor Louis! Lachapelle placed his arm carefully around his patient's shoulder; a
> brilliant mind, a charismatic personality destroyed, destroyed. The doctor could have
> wept, if that would have helped; but never believed the way we would. (ibid., 166)

That "role so unreal" may be played by messiahs but rarely by novelists, who factor
millennial disappointment into their texts. Wiebe structures his novel around the contrast between Riel and Gabriel Dumont, the latter a large, energetic, unwashed, and
unlettered Métis. Wiebe has Gabriel come to Riel to convince him to return and lead
the rebellion. Gabriel's formulation of Riel's necessity to the rebellion opposes the
doctor's: "'You have a vision here bigger than at Red River. Heaven and earth—show
us, help us to see!'" (ibid., 215). The Métis need to place their own exigencies and
concerns within a wider context linking them to world events, and only Riel is capable of doing that—at the price of his own sanity and mental integrity.

The Counselor versus the Law of the Beast

The Canudos war of 1893–1897, fought in the backlands of Bahia, Brazil, remains
the millennial conflict with the most documented casualties (conservatively, ten
thousand dead) of any in the Americas. I reserve the details and a comparison of

fictional treatments for the next chapter. For now I wish to concentrate on Brazilian writers' treatment of the leader of the so-called rebellion, Antônio Conselheiro, or the Counselor, including a comparison with another Brazilian messiah, José Maria.

Antônio Vicente Mendes Maciel, who founded Canudos, was born in 1830 and became famous in the backlands of Bahia, Sergipe, and Ceará—an area of precarious economic existence, landless peasantry, and consequent crises of morality and faith—as a *beato*, or itinerant lay priest. Such figures were not unusual in the backlands, where most dioceses lacked a resident priest, and his title of *conselheiro*, or counselor, was also a standard term of respect. His large following and efforts to help local landowners and priests eventually made him a man to be reckoned with in the region and an object of official concern. In June of 1876 his arrest was ordered from Salvador on the charge that he had murdered both his mother and his ex-wife. Arrested and taken to Salvador, his long hair was shorn, and he was beaten, led through the jeering crowds, and put on a boat for Ceará. In his hometown no one would appear against him, and it was admitted that his mother had died when he was three and that his wife was living as a prostitute. Antônio was freed and returned immediately to meet his followers. Their Jonah had been freed from the belly of the beast.

Antônio Conselheiro's own stated objective was to construct churches and cemeteries and to provide analogous foundational support for Catholics. The declaration of the republic in 1889 gave the authorities grounds for moving against the Conselheiro, for he could now be labeled a monarchist and an enemy of the republic. Police forces were sent against the *conselheiristas* on at least four occasions, the last and most violent in Masseté, where deaths occurred. Conselheiro and his followers realized that they would have greater security from the incessant attacks and harassment if they could found a permanent community in a defensible position. In 1893 Belo Monte—the "city upon a hill" for the world to wonder at—was founded on the site of a ranch called Canudos, and it quickly grew to be, according to some estimates, the second-largest town of the state of Bahia.

It is not necessary to agree with the arguments of João Arruda, Edmundo Moniz, and others who, influenced by Brazilian leftist politics of the 1960s and 1970s, claimed that Belo Monte was a utopian, egalitarian New Jerusalem with communal ownership of goods. The preponderance of evidence shows that the town had its share of social hierarchies and rivalries for power. Canudos was radical enough in providing free land to all who came, in welcoming all, including freedmen and Indians, in relative racial equality, and in the prohibition of corrosive factors such as alcohol and prostitution.

The Counselor was "O Bom Jesus" for his followers, and the government forces he preached against became the Antichrist:

> The Anti-Christ was born
> To govern Brazil
> But the Counselor is here
> To free us from him.

> We will be visited
> By our King, Don Sebastian

> Woe to the poor fellow
> Who lives under the law of the Beast! [na lei do cão!] (da Cunha 1944, 139)

The agonistic drama of apocalypse inheres in these simple verses. The second stanza reproduces the situation of the first: The Counselor is a representative or an incarnation of Don Sebastian, and the Antichrist is assimilated to the beast. The phrase "lei do cão" [law of the Beast] was a play on the letters of the word "eleição" [election]. Voting, a principle aspect of the recently founded republic, was anathema to the Counselor since it substituted the Brazilian emperor, whom God had chosen, with a mortal chosen by mere humans. Another hated "lei do cão," however, was taxation. The leader of the third expedition, Colonel Moreira César, became particularly associated with the figure of Antichrist. His popular nickname, "O Treme-Terra" [Earthshaker], perhaps recalls the pouring out of the sixth vial, which causes earthquake (Rev. 6:12).

In his masterpiece, *Os sertões*, meaning roughly "the backlands" in Portuguese, published in 1902, after the corner of millennium had safely been rounded, Euclides da Cunha found the necessary texts to link this movement of the 1890s with the magic 00 date. Supposedly the mysterious Counselor who founded and ruled Canudos had made this prophecy, which enters into the accepted apocalyptic norm of a countdown to millennium:

> In 1896 a thousand flocks shall run from the seacoast to the backlands; and then the backlands will turn into seacoast and the seacoast into backlands.
> In 1897 there will be much pasturage and few trails, and one shepherd and one flock only.
> In 1898 there will be many hats and few heads.
> In 1899 the waters shall turn to blood, and the planet shall appear in the east with the sun's ray, the bough shall find itself on the earth, and the earth some place shall find itself in heaven.
> There shall be a great rain of stars, and that will be the end of the world. In 1900 the lights shall be put out. (1944, 135)

This passage is footnoted with its source: notebooks found in the houses of Canudos during the war. It is important to note, however, that these are popular verses and phrases rather than words of the supposed messiah himself. Though nearly every fictional portrayal of Antônio Conselheiro—from Manoel Benício to Mario Vargas Llosa—depicts him as preaching the eschaton, no eyewitness familiar with the Counselor's preaching attributed any such apocalyptic thinking to him, nor does it appear in the two sets of his sermons that were preserved (cf. Maciel 1978). Even topics such as Noah, which would naturally give occasion for thoughts on the end times, occasioned no end-time harangues. On the other hand, the Counselor's documented antirepublican stance may have been, as Valdemar Valente (1963) has argued, a transfiguration of the theme of national redemption found in Portuguese Sebastianism into the context of Brazilian politics.

The two manuscripts found in Canudos after its destruction, which contain the Counselor's semioriginal thoughts and meditations on a variety of subjects, are drawn in part from the *Missão abreviada* and other sources. Indeed, a great deal of the second manuscript consists of the four gospels, the Acts of the Apostles, and some of Paul's letters, copied word for word out of a Bible lent to the Counselor by a sympathetic priest. The copied books of the New Testament do not include Revelation. Parts of the Old Testament are also retold, and when the Counselor recounts the story of Noah, he passes up an excellent chance to present it as a type for divine punishment and constitution of the New Jerusalem. The remaining scripts in the notebook are completely orthodox. The Counselor's thought, as expressed in sermons such as "On Attending Mass" and "On Confession" and a long series of pictures of Mary's sufferings for her son, Jesus Christ, are purely devotional. The Counselor's religious thought, as revealed in his literary testament, was absolutely orthodox. His view of the world was chiliastic but pragmatically postmillennial rather than apocalyptic, bent on construction rather than destruction. In this sense, the Counselor was the puppet whom Euclides da Cunha describes as a creation of the folk Catholicism from which he emerged and of the armed attacks against him that inevitably appeared to originate from a single, Satanic source.

The Counselor found his Ishmael in Euclides da Cunha, who observed part of the war as a journalist; however, da Cunha became determined to write an account of the war that went beyond journalism. Inspired by Spencerian Darwinism and other deterministic and positivist philosophies prevalent in the late nineteenth century, da Cunha advanced the thesis that the Canudos struggle was a "clash of civilizations" between Europeanized and hybridized Brazilians and that the latter "subraces" are "short-lived, destined soon to disappear before the growing exigencies of civilization and the intensive material competition offered by the stream of immigrants that is already beginning to invade our land with profound effect" (1944, xxix [ix]). The "races" he refers to carry untranslatable names such as *caboclo, cafuso, curiboca, mulato*, and *tabaréo*, all of which indicate some mixture of African, European, and Native American blood. And indeed, all of these groups were present in the population of Canudos under the Counselor's leadership, as were full-blooded Africans and Indians. (Most were present in the government forces sent against Canudos as well.) On the cultural level, da Cunha theorized that the medieval mindset of the original Portuguese settlers of the *sertão* had been held in its sixteenth-century place by the hybridization of African fetishism, Indian mysticism, and Portuguese medieval piety. Supporting this atavism was the physical environment that isolated the population and, in the struggle for survival, allowed a warrior ethos to dominate all of their affairs. Nearly one hundred years later Patricia Pessar makes a similar assessment, though without the negative valuation—indeed, with apparent praise for the creativity of hybrid religions:

> The absence of clergy provided fertile ground for the maintenance of traditional Catholic beliefs and practices—as well as syncretic, folk Portuguese, indigenous, and African elements—which were passed on orally and were managed by local *irmandades* and lay ritual specialists. Folk Catholicism emerged, then, as a site of cultural creativity and hybridity. It has also been a site in which, from the time of conquest to this day, subaltern actors (indigenous peoples, Afro-Brazilians, and poor mestiço *sertanejos*) have struggled against elite state and church projects intent on eradicating alternative and often highly localized understandings of identity, place, belonging, power, and destiny. (2004, 20)

Da Cunha's negative attitude towards hybridity was typical of his generation and inti-mately tied to the ideology of Brazilian nationalism, which, as Thomas E. Skidmore (1993) has shown, in general saw the only hope for progress as a "whitening" of the population. What distinguished da Cunha's writing was its recognition that scientific racism conflicted with environmental explanations of behavior and that the tragic dimensions of the Brazilian problem outlined earlier exceeded the meliorist and positivist narratives meant to control it. Finally, he took into account actual events of the Canudos war, from the brilliant defense carried out by the *jagunços* (i.e., the mixed-race inhabitants of Canudos) to the army's barbaric acts, which called into question the binary structure he had started with. Skidmore sees the contradictions of *Os sertões* as benefiting its reception and attributes the book's instant popularity on publication to its ability to "touch the raw nerve of the elite's guilt about the gap between their ideal of nationality and the actual condition of their country, without making . . . readers uncomfortable by questioning all their basic social assumptions" (ibid., 109).

According to this determinist thesis, one must view the Counselor himself as a product of his hybrid environment, one who produced paradoxes such as that in the following pronouncement:

> And so the evangelist [the Counselor] arose, a monstrous being, but an automaton.
> This man who swayed the masses was but a puppet [Aquelle dominador foi um titere]. He acted passively, like a shadow. But this shadow condensed the obscuran-tism of three races.
> And it grew large enough that it was projected into History. (da Cunha 1944, 129) [163][5]

With this quote, da Cunha appears to be writing against occupants of the region who saw Canudos as a conspiracy of newly freed slaves and army deserters, which precisely lacked "projection." A letter from Antero de Cirqueira Galo to the Baron of Canudos, written while the conflict was unfolding, shows the widespread fear of the acephalous, "colored" masses, whose leaders lack "projection":

> In Canudos, the figures that are developing the revolt are the Counselor with his fol-lowers, including deserters from various states and a lot of freedmen [13 de maio], the latter of which in fact forms the majority; let me tell you further that there are few white people there, not to mention those of some stature [que ocupam certa projeção]! (Cirqueira Galo 1999, 160)

Both the popular press and government propaganda had vilified the Counselor as a lunatic. Da Cunha preserves this opprobrious judgment but negates its moral dimen-sion by placing it into a larger context of determinism. The messiah becomes a pup-pet ventriloquized by the masses.

The further reduction of the Counselor to a shadow, without specifying the solid form that throws it, suggests multiple interpretations, all of which contrast with the positivism suggested by the sentence at first glance. The first would, in consonance with the theme of this study, recognize the puppet-master as the type of the messiah. On da Cunha's interpretation, the Counselor was forced into certain actions, words, and attitudes in his efforts to conform to the types of messiah and prophet. As Walnice Nogueira Galvão points out, an inverted typology provides the structure and the hermeneutic framework for the Euclidean interpretation of the insurrection:

> To confer unity on his material, the author relies on an eschatological view borrowed from the millennialists and messianists who gathered in Canudos, their Promised Land. . . . By so doing, da Cunha shows how it is possible, by a demonic inversion of the Biblical imagery of a salvationist myth, to get a glimpse of the insurrectionists' own viewpoint. Their world had become disenchanted. "Belo Monte"—"Mount Beautiful" . . . their New Jerusalem—had been changed into its opposite: Hell. The river of the City of God, the river of eternal life, was embodied in the dry bed of the Vaza-Barris. The gold walls promised to the just are made of mud and twigs. The luxuriant vegetation of the Garden of Delights they long for decays into the dry and bare *caatinga*. And so on.
>   In this way, through mimesis of the great syntagmatic narrative of the Bible, which begins with Genesis and ends with the Apocalypse, *Os sertões* covers the full span of the story of Canudos, from the foundation of the town to its destruction by fire, in accordance with Biblical prophecy. (Nogueira Galvão 2001, 156)

Along with all of the other inversions, the *beato* Antônio Maciel must be viewed as the Antichrist, the shadow of the genuine Christ, to be exposed and denounced. As a result, the best generic designation for *Os sertões*, despite all its use of scientific discourse, is "jeremiad," targeting equally the profane, quotidian world of the Brazilian republic and the anagogic hell of Belo Monte.

A second reading of the quotation would discern the Romantic doppelgänger motif and its psychological theorization by Carl Gustav Jung. The "shadow" is Jung's version of the unconscious, "the primitive and inferior man with his desires and emotions" (1966, 93) whom we carry within us and which the conscious mind rejects or denies; unlike the Freudian id, however, our shadow contains more than drives and appears to us not only in dreams, slips of the tongue, and literary works. Saint Paul fights directly with his shadow, which he calls "sin" or "the flesh," in Romans: "I do not understand what I do. For what I want to do I do not do, but what I hate I do" (7:15). In generalizing humans' repression of our shadow selves, Jung, writing in the 1930s, moves to an analysis of society strikingly similar to da Cunha's "two Brazils" thesis:

> [The shadow] even contains inferior, childish or primitive qualities which would in a way vitalize and embellish human existence, but "it is not done." The educated public, the flower of our actual civilization, has lifted itself up from its roots and is about to lose its connection with the earth. There is no civilized country nowadays where the lower strata of the population are not in a state of unrest and dissent. . . . One set of people identifies itself with the superior man and cannot descend, and the other set identifies itself with the inferior man and wants to reach the surface. (1966, 95)

One could debate whether Jung's application of the term "shadow" to social groups takes on a racist tone. In any case, when applied to the Americas, the division Jung describes becomes racialized. The former set, in da Cunha's analysis, consists of littoral Brazilians with strong ties to Europe and to republican values, while the latter set consists of racially and culturally hybrid *sertanejos* (backlanders), who maintain loyalty to folk Catholicism, the Brazilian monarchy, and the Antichrist.

Yet a third context of "shadow" leads us back to Plato's cave, where perception or everyday reality is analogized to shadows projected—through the back illumination of various puppets—onto a wall. Plato would agree, of course, that such shadows project themselves into history as humans act and deal on the basis of perceptions rather than on any higher insight or abstraction from brute facticity. Socrates' argument against literature is that it is a reflection of a shadow and thus even further removed from reality. It is tempting to read the last line of da Cunha as referring not only to the Counselor—who, after all, has been reduced to a shadow—but also to literature that projects itself into history. Only fragments of Revelation became part of the Counselor's vocabulary; rather, the narratives of the *Horas marianas* and the legends of Sebastian and Charlemagne were the texts that projected themselves through him into history, producing the conflagration of Canudos, which revealed Brazil's deep division between shadow and substance.

Da Cunha closes *Os sertões* with the note that the Counselor's head, as was proper for a "criminal type," was cut off and sent to Salvador for positivist medical examination:

> They took it to the seaboard, where it was greeted by delirious multitudes with carnival joy. Let science here have the last word. Standing out in bold relief from all the significant circumvolutions were the essential outlines of crime and madness.
> VII
> TWO LINES
> The trouble is that we do not have today a Maudsley for acts of madness and crimes on the part of nations. (1944, 613–14)

The "circumvolutions" are the folds of the cerebral cortex, which, in the positivist atmosphere of the late nineteenth century ("let science have the last word"), were thought to provide material indicators of mental aberration. However, da Cunha then places a hiatus, a pregnant pause enforced by a chapter division ("VII") and a notice to the reader that the rest is only a matter of two lines, before taking it all back by referring instead to the madness of crowds and nations. (Henry Maudsley was one of the earliest psychologists to attempt scientific definitions of the "criminal mind.") Group behavior cannot be explained as a simple effect of the charisma of a single individual, and messiahs are as much a creation of their movements—and of the authors who describe them—as the reverse. It is difficult to explain in English the irony of the subjunctive of reported discourse for the verb "dizer" [to say] as it is used in "Que a sciencia dissesse a ultima palavra." The English gives the impression that da Cunha himself feels that science can have the last word—supplementing with its technologies of the self, of course, the inferior *logos* of prophecy. The Portuguese in fact conveys the opposite impression, confounding once and for all the generic placement of *Os sertões* as a scientific treatise as opposed to a jeremiad. Finally, if the assignment of *logos*, the ultimate word, to science is not by Euclides da Cunha, then who is its enunciator? Presumably a "nation," whose insanity itself confounds scientific measurement.

Antônio Conselheiro has often been seen as sublimating a series of personal humiliations, as well as carrying out his family's desire for revenge on a different plane from the bloody feuds that it had been subjected to. Manoel Benício's novel, *O rei dos jagunços* (1899), which preceded da Cunha's book by three years, begins with a detailed recounting of the family feud between the Araújos and the Macieis, which began generations before Antônio Maciel's birth. The Counselor's messianism is thus explained less in terms of psychosis than of sublimation, in which passivity substitutes violent revenge but in which such Christian passivity, when practiced on the grand scale of a Canudos, returns to its violent origins and vendetta mentality of human injustice and fatal misfortune. Added to this background is the Counselor's personal history, which included failed business ventures and an adulterous wife whom he abandoned.

Da Cunha relied on Benício's and on other novels to develop his portrait of a "dismasted" Counselor whose messianism was compensatory for his reduction in circumstances. Yet the truly apocalyptic thinker of Canudos was Euclides da Cunha, who saw its clash of civilizations as the end of postmillennial republican possibilities of "order and progress" in Brazil, and it was da Cunha's *Os sertões* that projected Canudos as an apocalyptic event in the Brazilian imaginary. What appeared as fanaticism and abnormality to those outside the community of Canudos and culture of the backlands appeared entirely normal to those within it: "After a review of the few existing interviews with Canudos survivors, one message becomes clear: the followers thought of Antônio Conselheiro as a good man doing good religious works. He promised nothing more than to construct churches and cemeteries in this life, and promised salvation for the righteous in the afterlife" (Madden 1993, 12).

Canudos Redux

Brazil did not learn a lesson from Canudos. Rather, it lurched from one crisis into the next, from north to south. The Contestado rebellion lasted four years, from 1912 to 1916. It began with the completion of a railroad line and readings from a romance. José Maria (Miguel Lucena Boaventura) seems to embody many of the same qualities as the Counselor. Followed by some three hundred apostles, he wandered the region of Santa Catarina known as the "Contestado," curing people with herbs and the laying on of hands, preaching against the republic, and pleading for a return to the monarchy. At night he would read to his followers from one of the classics of Brazilian folk belief, *A História do Imperador Carlos Magno e os doze Pares da França* [The Story of the Emperor Charlemagne and the Twelve Peers of France].

No activity could be considered more banal than this in the *sertão*, north or south, for no book was more widely read than that of *Charlemagne and the Twelve Peers of France*. Noted Brazilian folklorist Luís da Câmara Cascudo calls it "the book best known by Brazilians of the *sertão* . . . being at times the only existing printed volume in a home. . . . No *sertanejo* was unaware of the deeds of the Peers or of the life of the Emperor with the flowing beard" (Câmara Cascudo 1953, 441). Passages dealing with the masters' loving treatment of their vassals were probably read, in which Charlemagne "rested for a number of years in a profound spiritual retreat, dealing only with issues related to the well-being of his vassals, who loved him because of the care he took to see that they were treated in a just fashion" (Diacon 1990, 511). Such "possible worlds" substituted the dire reality of peasants in an isolated region who were seeing the disappearance of their traditional systems of support and hierarchy. The railroad brought with it new forms of work, such as on the railroad itself, and a capitalization of the surrounding lands, whose timber could be exploited with relative ease for the first time. Landowners who had previously stood in a signorial relationship to the people who worked their farms were converted into labor bosses. In the former system, elites had been connected to each other through complex obligations symbolically expressed in the practice of godparenting (*padrinagem*). The labor boss, on the other hand, sold his godson's labor to strangers as Joseph was sold into slavery by his brothers, threatening an entire ethos. Landowners who perceived the threat to their way of life posed by the contract system of labor conceived sympathies with the messianically inspired, while those who persisted in the lucrative practice became, along with the railroad and the towns, the main targets of the rebels, the very symbol of the Antichrist.

Far less is known about José Maria's life than about the Counselor's, though we have photographs and a physical description: "part-Indian, dark-skinned, with small brown eyes, long straight hair, untrimmed and unkempt beard, nearly toothless, of medium height and stout, and thick, short neck" ("O Contestado," November 19, 1972, folio 7). Like the Counselor, José Maria had failed at a previous occupation—he was an army deserter and was imprisoned by the authorities, who soon released him at the demands of the local populace. José Maria founded the holy city of Taquaraçu, where he named twenty-four people as the twelve peers of France. In Portuguese, the word "par" can refer to a "pair," as well as a "peer." Confusing the two, José Maria picked twelve pairs of men as the knights of his realm, and this feature of the rebel organization remained intact throughout the war. The adoption of medieval European literature as a model for behavior was inspired by the relationship between the perceived knightly qualities of medieval Europe and the preoccupations of backlands society: "Valor, loyalty, courage, arrogance, violence, such is the axis of values that runs through the life of the *sertanejo* of this area. . . . The organizational principles created by the holy brotherhoods of the Contestado region, including its elite corps, drew their inspiration from this medieval tradition" (Peixoto 1995, vol. 1, 13).

In the familiar Canudos scenario, a small detachment of one hundred soldiers was sent against José Maria and his three hundred followers. Though the rebels defeated the soldiers, the latter managed to kill José Maria. The rumor soon spread that José Maria and those slain in that first battle would soon return and form the army of San Sebastian in order to prepare for the thousand-year war of Charlemagne. The confusion of terms indicates the hybridization of millennial numerology, romance values, literature, and folk belief. The rebels began to speak of a "holy war" (*guerra santa*) and to perform military exercises based on the chivalric codes of the literature they were reading. However, no actual violence occurred until the government troops arrived with their cannons and bombarded Taquaraçu, killing mainly women and children. This incident made the hypothetical holy war into a real one. The rebels ranged freely within an area of twenty-eight thousand square kilometers, attacked farms and ranches, and destroyed three offices of the U.S.-owned Brazil Railway

Company. General Fernando Setembrino de Carvalho, fresh from fighting the fanatics of Padre Cicero not far from Canudos, was brought south to deal with the rebels. He fought a war of attrition that eventually holed up the most devout fanatics in the redoubt of Santa Maria. After a siege of nearly two months, the city was penetrated, and its five thousand houses burned to the ground in April 1915.

As Todd Diacon's full-length study reveals, in the Contestado "subsistence peasantry, joined by a few landowners, fought back against public and private land grabs and against what they correctly perceived as a threat to their life-style" (1991, 115). The monarchy was seen as god-given because it had (supposedly) always protected the peasants against such wholesale transformations in their way of life. Eventually the monarchy would be given up, and new ideas of unionism and political parties as expressions of popular sentiment imported from Europe and North America. The "union movement in the countryside will come to take up a large part of the space formerly occupied by messianism and banditism—but even today, it does not cover the whole space" (Souza Martins 1981, 69).

The stories of the Contestado and Canudos capture in its essence the destruction of traditional societies by the capitalist world-system. They thus serve as a prolegomenon for the next chapter, which returns to three incidents reported here through the lives of their leaders—the Métis rebellion, Wounded Knee, and Canudos—to view them as part of a generalized tribulation of the late nineteenth century and as imbricated in the new technologies and social organizations of the period.

Tribulations of the Late Nineteenth Century

As the cult of Nature captured what we may call the higher
levels of the American mind, an image of infinite progress
bit by bit blotted out the ancient expectation [of millennium].
Reinforced in the second half of the century by Darwinism—
or rather, by what optimistic and liberal theologians made out
of The Origin of Species—the dominant Protestant mind so
yielded itself to the vision of an unchecked progress which
was, of itself, to bring about the Kingdom of Christ on earth,
that eschatology became virtually a lost art.

—Perry Miller, *Errand into the Wilderness*

In Perry Miller's (not related to William) view, after the Great Disappointment of 1844, "regular" technology and its benefits increasingly replaced eschatechnology in the "dominant Protestant mind." In other vocabulary, a kinder, gentler postmillennial thought increasingly replaced premillennial expectations. Other scholars, however, point to a revival in premillennial fervor from about 1875 to the beginning of World War I. Starting in the late 1850s, John Nelson Darby made a series of lecture tours to the United States, where he planted the seeds of dispensationalism, a premillennial belief different enough from Millerism for those who condemned the latter to nevertheless be able to adhere to the former (for a discussion see chapter seven). Above all, in the cruel logic of premillennialism, the progress of the end of the century was a sure sign of the Antichrist, "the devil's cunning scheme for bringing in a mock millennium without Christ" (Ironside 1919, 103; cited in Boyer 1992, 96). For the more radical premillennialists, "[i]t was as though God had wound up a cosmic clock: until the Devil's time ran out, the world was his to do with as he pleased. Christians who had been called out of the world were best advised to keep completely out of the entire sordid affair" (Timothy Weber 1987, 93).

Certainly, millennialists of any stripe were in the minority in the 1890s, and yet they brought about events of extraordinary moment up and down the Americas in both Protestant and Catholic cultures. On the upscale side of things, premillennialist William Blackstone wrote an 1891 memorial urging President Benjamin Harrison to support a Jewish homeland in Palestine—not, of course, out of humane sympathy or geopolitical prescience but because the dispensationalist script required a state of Israel to be warred upon and then made peace with. Cyrus McCormick, J. P. Morgan, and John D. Rockefeller were signers. Among the hybridous abject, the 1891 document was prepared after the Wounded Knee massacre had curtailed the millennial Ghost Dance of Native Americans west of the Mississippi. A bit farther north, Louis Riel gave himself the name "David" as he led the Métis in two rebellions that shaped the relation of Manitoba and Saskatchewan to the rest of Canada, while in the backlands of Brazil the Counselor founded and defended his mud-hut Jerusalem of Canudos.

This chapter examines the way in which, in the last quarter of the nineteenth century, premillennial thought shifted from the "dominant Protestant (or reform Catholic) mind" to the "dominated hybrid mind." The "infinite progress" (or Crystal Palace), as we now realize all too well, was achieved at the expense of the closing of frontiers, the destruction of traditional values and social structures, and the final capitulation of governments to the interests of capitalist multinational industry in a collusion that persists to this day. Angel Rama summarizes the process of "littorization" and "capitalization" as it occurred in Latin America:

> From 1870 to the beginning of the 20th century, a popular cry [clamor] recurs throughout Latin America, testifying in a pathetic, desperate tone, to the appalling sufferings of those who have come to realize that there will be no salvation for them, that their fate—to be crushed and exterminated—is already sealed. These are the years of order and progress, of the economic rebirth of the continent, of the first flowering after an entire century (from the Bourbon reform of the second half of the 18th century) of stagnation and regression.
>
> This story is told us by a written history that reviewed these decades, because, significantly, documented testimony—not to mention literature—is lacking for the events of this period. This lack can be explained: the cry proceeds mostly from rural, non-literate communities, which begin to be rapidly alienated from the capital cities that are growing [by] leaps and bounds, and which thus are losing the intellectuals who might have translated their concerns into writing.
>
> In 1870, the year the German army defeated France and the German Empire was constituted, the peasant rebellion in Uruguay could be called the "revolution of the lances," because the rural troops fought with these against an army that used the Remington rifle to defeat them. National unification, the imposition of national capitals on the vast hinterland, the suppression of separatist tendencies, the pauperization of the rural communities that still held the majority of the population, the increased productivity of export economies, all this was called positivist progress, the enemies of which were the Church and the Indians. (1982, 619–21)

It is interesting to note how the eschatological vocabulary of salvation, the seal, and the *vox clamantis* of prophecy invade Rama's secularized account. The campaigns of the 1870s, 1880s, and 1890s, then, against Indians, sertanejos, and Métis of North and South America were all wars of extermination against a side of the American self that had been deemed too weak to survive.

This chapter deals with the period from 1869 (the time of the first Red River rebellion in present-day Manitoba) to 1897, the year of the Canudos war, as well as with the literary testimonials to these events. Within this period fall terrible droughts, starting in 1877 in Brazil and 1887 in North America, and a worldwide economic recession. In 1881 Charles Giteau received a vision of his mission similar to Nat Turner's and gunned down President James Garfield. An economic downturn started in England in September 1890 and hit its trough in 1895. (Millennial fiction of the English depression includes William Morris's *News from Nowhere* [1890] and R. Jefferies's *After London* [1885].) The full cycle lasted ten years. There were variations in timing and in the frequency of minicycles from country to country (see Charles Hoffmann 1970).

One of the period's unusual features was the simultaneous occurrence of significant millennial movements in North and South America: Just a few years after the end of the Red River rebellion, led by Louis Riel, and while the Counselor was preaching the end of the world in the backlands of Bahia, Brazil, Wovoka began (re)delivering the message of the Ghost Dance in Nevada. In all three cases, the racial makeup of the population, which distanced them from the dominant culture and made them victims of progress, was a contributing factor. Hybridity played a role as Christianity was combined with native elements and endowed with messianic capabilities. These movements were in the end contained by the respective dominant culture through violent confrontations in which superior technology played a key role in the victory, and each was accompanied by an outpouring of literary texts that reflected the apocalyptic mood of the times.

The dangers of selecting a particular historical period as more disruptive of traditional ways of life than others are well known. Notable, however, is the coincidence between the closing off of the U.S. frontier during this period through a practice of total war against aboriginal peoples, the rise of monopoly capitalism with the prominence of magnates Andrew Carnegie, Jay Gould, J. D. Rockefeller, and J. P. Morgan, and the resultant rise of Populism and the presidential candidacy of William Jennings Bryan in 1896. Technological advances had produced firms and economies that for the first time dwarfed humans, as shown in the triumph of the *société anonyme* (i.e., the corporation), an entity that divorces responsibility of every kind from the individual and places it in a calculating machine. "Manifest Destiny," as we have seen, is a term that transforms millennial impulses into military victory and the absorption of territory. It was to this project that post–Civil War America turned. Millennial fervor dissipated in the gray politics of Reconstruction. It was to revive again several decades later with the closing of the frontier and the perception that American exceptionalism was threatened by international capitalism.

Some of the factors that led to a crisis of confidence in the cultures of the United States were: the rise of wage labor and the subsequent decline in self-employment; the greater disparity of wealth brought on by industrialization; fear of immigration (by 1900 forty percent of the population of the twelve largest U.S. cities was foreign born); and unease with the entry of women into the workforce (Moorehead 1999, 79–85). These are mostly urban phenomena, but the crisis was not confined to the city:

> Cycles of boom and bust affected more people than ever before. Skilled craftsmen were forced to sell their labor and became slaves of the wage system. Farmers lost control over their own produce to railroaders and middlemen. Unskilled laborers worked unbelievably long hours for incredibly low wages. . . . As a result, many

people felt that something solid had gone out of American life. The old unity, if it had ever really existed, seemed gone forever. . . . A growing number of people honestly believed that things were not going to get any better and probably were going to get a lot worse. (Timothy Weber 1987, 85)

The rise of Populism among the agrarian population had much to do with the perceived oppression of farmers by international capital and the gold standard. Partly as a result of changes in the world economic system, the other large slaveholding country of the Americas, Brazil, abolished slavery in 1887 and became a republic in 1888, setting off a chain of responses that resulted in millennial movements in Bahia and Paraná/Santa Catarina.

There also appear to have been the inevitable countdowns to the turn of the century, coupled with the prediction of utter transformation, as we have seen was the case with Y2K a century later. One would expect a cluster of millennial fictions to be published near the end of the century, and there were two subjects for authors in the United States to depict: the Nat Turner slave rebellion of 1831 and the Millerite movement of the 1840s. Normally, centennials are events that bring forth renewed interest in an author or a historical event, and so it is not surprising to find several novels and stage productions devoted to Turner in the 1930s: Frances Gaither's *The Red Cock Crows* (1934); Arna Bontemps's *Black Thunder* (1936); and Randolph Edmonds's *Nat Turner* (1934). The year 1899, on the other hand, brought forth two novels, Mary Johnston's *Prisoners of Hope* (1898) and Pauline Bouvé's *The Shadows Before* (1899), which came a year before a scholarly monograph, William S. Drewry's *Southampton Insurrection* (1900). These had been preceded by a spate of fictionalized treatments of the Millerites: Edward Eggleston's *End of the World* (1872); Jane Marsh Parker's *Midnight Cry* (1886); and Mary E. Wilkins's "New England Prophet" (1894). (For a discussion of the Miller fictions see Scharnhorst 1980 *passim*.)

Yet the feeling of the age's dark side was best summarized in an 1890 eschatological novel based on an entirely imagined plot, Ignatius Donnelly's *Caesar's Column*. Just as *Moby-Dick* furnished a type for comparing and understanding historical messiahs, so too will this novel serve as an introduction to the eschatechnologies of the last quarter of the nineteenth century. I then revisit the three movements in chronological order, reading the fictions generated out of them against the historical record.

The Shadow People

We meet in the midst of a nation brought to the verge of moral, political and material ruin. Corruption dominates the ballot box, the legislatures, the Congress, and touches even the ermine of the bench. The people are demoralized. . . . The newspapers are subsidized or muzzled; public opinion silenced; business prostrate, our homes covered with mortgages, labor impoverished, and the land concentrating in the hands of capitalists. The urban workmen are denied the right of organization for self-protection; imported pauperized labor beats down their wages; a hireling standing army, unrecognized by our laws, is established to shoot them down, and they are rapidly disintegrating to European conditions.

Thus spake Ignatius Donnelly at the People's Party convention in Saint Louis in 1892. The speech revisits a scene he had already presented as a "possible world" in his novel, *Caesar's Column*, published two years earlier. It is meant to invoke, as through a glass darkly, that other possible world, a pastoral one, that has disappeared under the corrosive force of capitalism. In dealing with the future rather than the present, the novel spoke to rural America's

> dim perception that realistic fiction denied that the home-bred moral sense was invulnerable to social change. If there was a connection between the daily toil of the farmer who produced all the soil would yield him and the steady decline of prices for his crop, surely the fault couldn't lie with the man who honestly went about earning his bread by the sweat of his brow. This behavior should result in an Eden regained, and, if it did not, something other than the concept of godly toil was at fault. (Ziff 1966, 84–85)

Donnelly, a Minnesota farmer and politician, was an important leader of the People's Party and eventually ran for vice president in the election of 1900. He started composing *Caesar's Column* in 1888, after being defeated in a U.S. Senate race he felt he could not win because it was dominated by the money of big business. *Caesar's Column* is consequently the first millennial fiction of the Americas to depict money as a transformative power. Money does not carry with it simply, like all forms of wealth, the possibility of corruption. Rather, when it becomes the center of an economy, it makes all people theoretically equal. People are no longer distinguished qualitatively but quantitatively. Money destroys set hierarchies of value in an analogous fashion to the destruction of cosmologies through the mathematico-physical concept of the universe, in which all bodies are theoretically equal to each other and differ only according to their particular size, shape, and velocity. Kenelm Burridge writes that

> money, belonging to the highly differentiated society whose ideas on virtue, vice, right and wrong are likewise highly complex and differentiated, demands greater freedom of choice, reveals the vice in cultivated virtues, allows no vice without some virtue, concedes an element of right in wrong-doing, finds the sin of pride in an upright fellow. Just these kinds of differentiation the millenarist in a moneyed society cannot abide. The unordered emergence of just these kinds of differentiation in the non- or newly-moneyed community is what a millenarist seeks to control. . . . [B]ecause money is passive and can be used for a variety of ends, it vitiates the bundle of binary qualities on which a moral order is based. Money as an abstract, factorial, and quantitative system must be opposed to the qualities that measure the stature of man. Yet it also evokes the individual in whom, ultimately, the highest qualities of being human are reckoned. (1969, 149)

Caesar's Column (Donnelly 1890) charts the course of civilization in the United States as capitalism continues its relentless march to monopolization. This novel stands at the threshold of a period of American self-questioning in the face of industrialization, which often resulted in the scapegoating of immigrants, African Americans, and Jews as the virus that had killed the "American way of life." Donnelly was concerned with Midwestern farmers like the novel's title figure, Caesar Lomelli, but not with the Native Americans living in the same territory, who, like Caesar, had recently lost their land to the unscrupulous.

Set in 1989, *Caesar's Column* is composed of a series of letters from Gabriel Weltstein in New York to his brother, Heinrich, in the state of Uganda, Africa. The brothers are Swiss and make their living by raising sheep. Donnelly's message is clear: Independent farming has become impossible in North America. Gabriel has come to New York, a city with ten million inhabitants, traveling in one of the dirigibles on steel cables that are used for transoceanic travel, in order to sell his wool outside of the monopolistic "wool ring" (in vain). His plight demonstrates the international cartel capitalism that was an object of wrath for Populists like Donnelly. The character Caesar Lomelli had farmed in Saskatchewan until the money-lenders took everything from him. As we have already seen, both Lomelli's foreign origins and his predicament reflect the very real conditions of the Midwest. Lomelli gathers a band of fellow desperadoes and leads a "bloody and incessant war on society" (ibid., 130).

Gabriel sees a beggar about to be run down by a carriage and, stopping it, whips the insolent driver. The beggar whisks him away to avoid arrest. The carriage belonged to the evil Prince Cabano, whose real name is Jacob Isaacs and who is, coincidentally, the most powerful man in the world. The beggar (really a handsome young lawyer in disguise, Max) explains that "the aristocracy of the world is now almost altogether of Hebrew origin. . . . They are the great money-getters of the world. They rose from dealers in old clothes and peddlers of hats to merchants, to bankers, to princes. They were as merciless to the Christian as the Christian had been to them" (ibid., 36). Here is Donnelly's first departure from the religious millennial script, which has a large number (144,000 in Rev. 7) of Jews converting to Christianity. In *Caesar's Column*, on the other hand, no Jew converts (partly because Christianity has lost all traces of its evangelism). At these two poles are the equally racialist positions vis-à-vis the Jews, both of which turn them into objects, one to be used, the other disposed of. There seems little doubt that the author's attitude can be traced to a deep-rooted anti-Semitism in American culture that was exacerbated in the period by the perception that the banks and lending companies foreclosing on Midwestern farmers were owned by Jews who lived in Eastern cities.

Max and Gabriel prevent miscegenation by rescuing Estella Washington, who has been sold into slavery to Prince Cabano. They eventually succeed through Gabriel's spying on a meeting of Cabano's council, and Gabriel abducts Estella and marries her. (Part of the book's artistic weakness is the shallowness of Estella's characterization.) After the revolution Isaacs disappears: "It is rumored that he has gone to Judea; that he proposes to make himself King in Jerusalem, and, with his vast wealth, reestablish the glories of Solomon, and revive the ancient splendors of the Jewish race" (ibid., 288). Since the story's heroes escape to a purportedly Edenic setting far from civilization, it seems clear that the world will continue to be ruled by this Antichrist figure and will wear the mark of the Beast. Donnelly is working out a theory of cyclical emergence, growth, and decay, as David D. Anderson explains:

> Prince Cabano—an aristocrat rather than a simple carpenter—is the last symbolic and actual ruler of a cycle that had begun in Judea two millennia before, and the

nameless renegade escapes to Jerusalem in a mad effort to begin the same pattern once more. . . . The role of the Jew as the founder of the age-old tradition of which we are the heirs is paralleled by the perverted role of the Jew in the destruction of that tradition, and one more phase of the human story has come full circle. (1980, 79)

Anderson also believes that this cyclical theory accounts for the anti-Semitic diatribes of *Caesar's Column*, though few readers will be sophisticated enough to read the text in this way.

Everyone not in the cabal belongs to the proletariat in the great division into just two classes predicted by Marx and Engels. The ablest of the proletariat join the Brotherhood, which plots revolution. This group has its own weaponry, the "newest improved magazine rifles" (Donnelly 1890, 73), manufactured in its own armory in the wildest and most mountainous part of Tennessee. "Every able-bodied man in the whole vast Brotherhood, in America and Europe, has been supplied with his weapon and a full accompaniment of ammunition" (ibid.). Armaments are often hidden by burial, a practice described in detail in the opening pages of William Pierce's *Turner Diaries* a century later. The brotherhood is led by: Max, whose father was ruined by the perjury of a plutocrat; by Caesar Lomelli, who was a farmer in Saskatchewan until storm and crop failure caused his eternal indebtedness to the bank and a lawyer seduced his daughter, after which he took to the hills to form a *posse comitatus*; and by a Russian Jew who has a handicap. These three incorporate the different aspects of revolution: intellectual, military, and mystical. Max is the only one to articulate precise goals for the transformation of society. Unsurprisingly, these sound like the platform of Donnelly's People's Party: Do away with all interest on money; repeal all laws that give one class advantage over another; limit wealth and land ownership; go off the gold standard and start using paper money. Gabriel witnesses a meeting of the conspirators where the gigantic form of Caesar and the defective one of the mystic are present: "At the end [of the room], on a sort of dais, or raised platform, was a man of gigantic stature, masked and shrouded. Below him . . . sat another, whose head, I noticed even then, was crooked to one side. . . . Every man present wore a black mask and a long cloak of dark material" (ibid., 151). Gabriel reports on a spy whom he had identified at the meeting, and the undercover agent is executed on the spot.

The most formidable obstacle to revolution comes in the form of dirigible airships, called "Demons," that drop deadly bombs of poisonous gas. They are both a prophecy of coming air power and its use in terrorizing civilian populations and the antitype of the angels of Revelation, who pour out the vials of wormwood, among other things, onto the earth. Donnelly arranges the conflict as an interaction among three of the four elements: The airships throw firebombs onto the earth below. The absence of the fourth element, water, indicates the petrified wasteland of the modern city. The commander of the Demons is brought before the brotherhood and sells out for fifty million dollars. Max has only loathing for the traitor who will help the Brotherhood, but the end justifies the means: "It was noble [Max said] to crush a rotten world for revenge, or for justice's sake; but to sell out a trust, for fifty millions of the first plunder, was execrable—it was damnable . . . Yet there was one consolation—the end was coming! Glory be to God! The end was coming!" (ibid., 160). Here, as with the imagery of the wandering Jew and the demons, the archetypal religious language breaks through into a text that otherwise appears thoroughly secularized. Gabriel attends a worker's meeting and proposes a Brotherhood of Justice, which is rejected as too gradualist. The preferred Brotherhood of Destruction expresses itself in the language of a Zephaniah or other Old Testament prophet: "One hundred years ago a gigantic effort, of all the good men of the world, might have saved society. Now the fire pours through every door, and window and crevice; the roof crackles; the walls totter; the heat of hell rages within the edifice; it is doomed" (ibid., 178). Donnelly compares the coming conflagration and the capitalists' fin de siècle nonchalance with the attitudes of Southerners before the civil war: "But a day came when there was a corpse at every fire-side. And not the corpse of the black stranger—the African—the slave; but the corpses of fair, bright-faced men, their cultured, their noble, their best beloved" (ibid., 265).

The language in these passages shows that, in *Caesar's Column*, religious fervor and apocalyptic expectation have become politicized. When Gabriel goes to a church service, Donnelly offers a prediction of the religion of the future that shows why this is so. The church is built like the Crystal Palace, with no images of devotion. Gabriel notes the aggressivity of the glances from women. The preacher talks not of theology but only of love, including the most venal kind. "I could not help but think by what slow stages, through many generations, a people calling themselves Christians could have been brought to this curious commingling of intellectuality and bestiality" (ibid., 188). (In *Islands in the Net* [1989], Bruce Sterling predicts a similar path for religion, where by 2025 the Church of Ishtar, whose priestesses are prostitutes, seems to be the only established religion left in the United States.)

Gabriel had already been brought to reflect on the absence of God in this hyper-technologized world. Shown a communal air-conditioner, which works by drawing down cold air from several miles above the earth and letting hot air rise, Gabriel responds, "I could not help but think that there was need that some man should open connection with the upper regions of God's charity, and bring down the pure beneficent spirit of brotherly love to this afflicted earth, that it might spread through all the tainted hospitals of corruption for the heal ing of the hearts and souls of the people" (Donnelly 1890, 19). A central type for such communication between earth and heaven is the ladder that Jacob, in a dream, saw angels using in order both to ascend into heaven and to come down to earth (Genesis 28:11–22). The human replacement, however, is literally empty, and Gabriel sees only air. New technology reveals only the gap between scientific perfection and the soul's imperfections, a theme Donnelly might have derived from Nathaniel Hawthorne's story "Earth's Holocaust" (1844), discussed in the next chapter.

At midnight of the appointed day, barricades are erected, and banks blown open to obtain the fifty million. A Demon flies through the air and retrieves the money, then more airships come and kill the soldiers. After the army is destroyed, the proletariat goes on the rampage. "The rude and begrimed insurgents are raised by their terrible purposes to a certain dignity. They are the avengers of time—the God-sent—the righters of the world's wrongs—the punishers of the ineffably wicked. They do not mean to destroy the world; they will reform it—redeem it" (Donnelly 1890, 263). There follows an orgy of blood worthy of the grapes-of-wrath passage of Revelation:

"Now and then some poor wretch, whose sole offense was that he was well dressed, would take fright and start to run, and then, like hounds after a rabbit, they would follow in full cry; and when he was caught a hundred men would struggle to strike him, and he would disappear in a vortex of arms, clubs, and bayonets, literally torn to pieces" (ibid., 261). At the end, in New York there are 250,000 bodies, and Caesar's Column is made by pouring cement over them. Its plaque reads:

This Great Monument	The Brotherhood of Destruction
is	in
Erected by	Commemoration of
Caesar Lomellini	The Death and Burial of
Commanding General of	Modern Civilization (ibid., 287)

Caesar himself is killed by the mob, and his head put up on a pole. Max tries to restore order but cannot. As the mob comes to kill him, Max, Gabriel, and Estella escape in a Demon toward Africa. Max prophesies that after three-quarters of humanity have died of hunger, the rest will form squads, or gangs. Each will elect a chief, and "the history of the world will be slowly repeated" (ibid., 296). They return to Africa and build a wall worthy of the New Jerusalem, thirty feet high and fifty feet broad, to keep chaos out. "And the wolves [capitalists] have disappeared; and our little world is a garden of peace and beauty, musical with laughter" (ibid., 318). Donnelly here takes up the New Adam and New Eve typology and also steps into the controversy about the placement of the New Jerusalem, eschewing both the United States and the Middle East in favor of Africa.

The name "Caesar" invokes a purely secular idea of power, which Donnelly shows to unleash forces it cannot control. Neither mysticism nor latitudinarianism can channel the destructive side of humans. Thus, while *Caesar's Column* does not follow any particular millennial script to the letter, employing instead typology and biblical language on the most general level, that very lack of a plan can be seen as a failure to listen to the word of God: "God wipes out injustice with suffering; wrong with blood; sin with death. You can no more get beyond the reach of his hand than you can escape from the planet" (ibid., 265). It would be interesting to determine, among the readers of this novel when it appeared in 1890, how many agreed with this central role of God in the unfolding of history.

The Scorched-Wood People

Louis Riel's myth of the origins of the Métis from the Hebrews (see chapter two) places in that story a revelation of God's response to nineteenth-century technology:

God said unto me: "I am now revealing the greatness and simplicity of my economy [mon économie]. During this century when men boast [se vantent] of having stolen the sky's fire and of using it through the low valleys of the ocean to communicate from one continent to another within minutes, I, too, wish to develop my resources. The world accuses my church of being an obstacle to progress. I am giving my knowledge [donner mes lumières] to my infallible church who is my sole bride. I will go up against impiety [Je veux rivaliser avec l'impie]." (Riel to Ignace Bourget, May 1, 1876; Riel, 1985, vol. 1, 44)

Since the Tower of Babel story of Genesis, human technology and development had been seen as attempts at rivaling God. Here as in that story, humans boast of their technological prowess in using electricity and telegraphy. Riel refers here to the transatlantic cable, which had been laid in 1858 and then again more successfully in 1866. For Donnelly, this undersea cable, which carried electrical impulses, may have inspired not only the sky cables that carry dirigibles but also Gabriel's feeling of the absence of an analogous pathway for communicating with God. Rather than wishing to destroy these developments, however, as in the Tower of Babel story, God wishes to assemble an arsenal and, above all, to enlighten and technologize the church ("donner mes lumières," literally, "give my lights").

By inserting this divine prophecy into the story of the Métis, Riel displaces the threat to Métis culture from the more immediate issues of land ownership and economics onto the larger scheme of a battle between the Métis in a state of nature and the more technologized Anglo culture of Canada. God will come to the aid of the Catholic Church in its fight against overwhelming technology. The adjective "infallible" used by Riel no doubt refers to the doctrine of papal infallibility introduced in 1870 as a response to the loss of church territories and the papacy's final eclipse as an independent political unit among the Italian states.

We could even view the undersea cable as a displaced image of the true threat to the Métis, the "land cable" of the railroad. So crucial did Robert de Roquebrune consider the railroad in the provocation and termination of the rebellion that he titled his 1924 novel of the troubles, *D'un océan à l'autre*, which could be translated "From sea to shining sea." Riel plays only a minor role in this novel, whose heroes are a Québec father-son team of ethnologists and Father Albert Lacombe, who is credited both with keeping most of the Indian peoples out of the conflict and with convincing them to allow the Canadian Pacific Railway to cross their lands. The novel ends with the younger ethnologist marrying a white woman of Red River in a Canadian Pacific car. Missing is the railroad's role in transporting soldiers—and their Gatling guns—to quell the conflict.

In his graphic novel recounting the Riel story, Chester Brown places the railroad, capitalism, and technology front and center. Despite its title, *Louis Riel* (2003) begins not with Riel himself but with maps of North America and then of the French- and English-speaking parishes in the Red River settlement. The first scene takes place in London, where the first prime minister of Canada, John MacDonald (1815–1891) finalizes the transfer of Rupert's Territory from the Hudson's Bay Company to Canada. As Brown points out, MacDonald did not in fact travel to England for the deal. The purpose in placing him there is to emphasize the cartel manipulations that will eventually cause a millennial outbreak in central Canada. The transfer of Hudson's Bay Company lands to the Dominion of Canada sets up the surveying issue that eventually leads to the Red River rebellion.

The central government drew up square townships that violated the traditional Métis configuration of narrow strips moving from a river to the backlands. In 1869 the Métis seized Fort Garry (Winnipeg) and, with Riel's permission, executed an Irish settler. For this crime Riel had to flee to the United States, where he was hospitalized for a time with religious delusions, as recounted in chapter two. In 1884 the Métis sought him out to lead resistance against white settlers' encroachments. Upon his return to Canada, he preached to Anglos and Métis of his divine purpose, using a solar eclipse to convince nonbelievers. He renamed the days of the week, claimed Saturday as the Sabbath, rejected the rule of Rome, and predicted the movement of the papacy to Saint Boniface and the foundation of a truly American Catholic church. As the Métis ransacked stores to obtain weapons, Riel proclaimed that "Rome had fallen" and that Father Bourget of Montréal was now pope. The Métis army was easily defeated, and Riel was hanged after a trial in Ottawa.

As Catholics and speakers of French, the Métis experienced disenfranchisement and accompanying confinement to rural identity as the French "lost" Canada to the English in "la cession." The Red River rebellion in some sense continues that of Lower Canada in 1837. As the mobility of Métis life was threatened, they moved farther inland. The Catholic church's importance in life was increased by a lack of town organization. The fervor of Riel's prayers, meditations, and religious poetry thus acquire a political dimension even when no explicit program is mentioned.

MacDonald becomes Riel's nemesis (as Riel himself considered the prime minister to be for not granting him amnesty) throughout Brown's version of the story. MacDonald, however, has no personal interest in Riel, whom he has never met; his only concern is to maintain power. Brown uses a dramatically lit, late-night confabulation between MacDonald and George Stephen, president of the Canadian Pacific Railway. Brown has MacDonald hatch a Machiavellian scheme:

> [MACDONALD:] The half-breeds in the North-West are close to rebelling—Riel is leading them now, and I'm sure he'll get them to take over a fort or something soon. When they do that, we'll send soldiers out on your trains. The soldiers will easily defeat the half-breeds, and the whole nation will cheer. But the people won't just be cheering for the brave Canadian soldiers—They'll also be cheering for the railway that enables the Canadian government to bring law and order to a remote part of the country. Parliament will then gladly give you all the money you need to finish your railway.
>
> [STEPHEN:] You devious bastard. . . . Are the half-breeds really headed for rebellion?
>
> [MACDONALD:] I'll do everything I can to make sure they are. (Brown 2003, 136–37)

In his footnotes to these panels, Brown admits that the actual evidence for this conspiracy is lacking. In Riel's own viewpoint, of course, the railroad, another form of cable bringing fire, would be part of a greater conspiracy, another branch of that "progress" that disturbs God. Brown manipulates his plot so that technology directly causes its millenarian reaction.

Riel combined his religious vision with a political notion of the Métis and Indians as the original landholders of central Canada, thus fueling their objections to the redrawing of boundaries as an impingement on their way of life. Riel was hailed by most of the rebels and formed them into a religious government called the Exovedate. Polygamy and incest were political doctrines of this new regime, though it did not last long enough to see them put into practice. Riel spoke of himself in the most exalted terms as Prophet of the New World:

> "Where am I today? At the altar. Who has brought me here? The Good Lord. Who speaks through my mouth when I speak to you? It's God." . . . While he sang, his followers danced around him emitting cries of joy. He imparted the Holy Spirit to his men by breathing strongly upon them. He repeated that the pope was no longer their master. (Flanagan 1996, 151)

It is difficult to measure the extent to which other participants in the uprising shared a belief in Riel as their religious prophet. The central aim of most rebels was to force Ottawa to negotiate and respect their land claims, not to found an exovedate. After the swift military defeat of the innumerous and poorly armed rebels, Riel took the familiar path of reinterpretation as a way of explanation by beginning to emphasize elements that spoke not just to the Métis or the French Canadians but also to the Protestant majority. No matter, he was put on trial in 1885 and condemned to death.

While the Métis rebellions failed utterly in their military and millennial objectives and Riel was hanged for treason, they were a founding moment for the Canadian province of Manitoba, for French exceptionalism within Canadian history, and for Canadian federalism. The initial treatments of Riel and his Métis as traitors have gradually given way to treatments such as Brown's, where the treachery is by politicians and financiers.

Ghost Dance and Populism

Shortly after Riel's death, the Great Plains states of the United States were hard hit by recession and crop failure. Dakota's drought started in 1887 and continued for several years. Starving farmers commingled with defeated Sioux, who depended on the U.S. government for their beef supply, and with millennially oriented Mormons. The result was a potent mix:

> The backbone of Dakota was its farm families: poor people, some American, but mostly European peasants who had come straight from their homelands to this widely advertised land of plenty, bringing very little with them beyond their strong bodies and stout hearts. They had now lost everything from drought and were worse off than Sioux Indians, who were assured of food, clothing, and other needs through their treaties with the government. Where the Sioux complained of short rations, many of the white settlers were face to face with downright starvation. (Hyde 1956, 233)

Nor could these farmers just pick up and leave: their wagons and horses had been mortgaged to the same banks that dispossessed Caesar Lomelli in Donnelly's fiction.

One Native American response to their victimization was the Ghost Dance of 1888–1892, which promised a return of the way of life that neo-European culture had systematically destroyed. The doctrine of the Ghost Dance reflects this basis of millennial thinking in its simplicity: "The time will come when the whole Indian race, living and dead, will be reunited upon a regenerated earth, to live a life of aboriginal happiness, forever free from death, disease, and misery" (Mooney 1970, 19). The technique for bringing this about was to perform the dance, a traditional one among all of the peoples who practiced it, and named differently (Round Dance, Dragging Dance, Clasped-hands Dance) in different languages. The goal was to dance long and hard enough that the dancer entered a trance state, where visions of dead relatives or of the messiah, or indeed of everyday items were seen and reported to the hopeful living. Alongside descriptions of being reunited with one's departed family members were visions of new bed coverings, fresh meat, or dice games. All of these activities occur in a natural environment of plenitude—for the Sioux, for example, the buffalo have returned.

John Kucich notes this "everydayness" of so many Ghost Dance visions and hypothesizes that they represent a significant change from former interactions with spirits:

> Such specific descriptions of the spirit land contrast sharply with the more traditional visionary experiences of the western Indian nations, in which contact with spirits was marked by strangeness. . . . Indeed, the Ghost Dance inverted the traditional Indian cosmology. Whereas contact with the spirit world had previously given a numinous charge to the ordinary world, in the Ghost Dance, people turned from a physical world grown alien and strange to find, in the spirit world, the familiar environs of home. In the Ghost Dance, the visionary becomes nostalgic. Rather than mystify ordinary social relations, the visionary nostalgia of the Ghost Dance songs helped preserve threatened traditions. Ghost dancers journeyed to heaven to save the earth they once knew. (2004, 108–109)

The "possible world" constructed in the Ghost Dance, then, was not of the future but of the past.

Occasionally, travel to the spirit world resulted in hybridized doctrinal revelations, as in the report made by Little Horse of his vision:

> Two holy eagles transported me to the Happy Hunting Grounds. They showed me the Great Messiah there, and as I looked upon his fair countenance I wept, for there were nail-prints in his hands and feet where the cruel whites had once fastened him to a large cross. There was a small wound in his side also, but he kept himself covered with a beautiful mantle of feathers that only could be seen when he shifted his blanket. He insisted that we continue the dance, and promised me that no whites should enter his city nor partake of the good things he had prepared for the Indians. The earth, he said, was now worn out and it should be repeopled. (Boyd 1891, 193–94)

As with Gray's version of Nat Turner, one can sense the interventions of a white English transcriber in this account, injecting precious phrases such as "fair countenance" and the rather technical term "repeopled," which had probably not occurred to Little Horse. A different balance of hybridity inhabits the language of the so-called Messiah Letter, which purports to be the words of Wovoka himself and exists in various versions, each in a pidgin or creole English, for example, in this Arapaho version:

> No hurt anybody. No fight, good behave always, it will give you satisfaction, this young man, he is a good Father and mother, dont tell no white man. Juesses was on ground, he just like cloud. Every body is alive again, I dont know when they will [be] here, may be this fall or in spring. Every never get sick, be young again—(if young fellow no sick any more), work for white men never trouble with him until you leave, when it shake the earth don't be afraid no harm any body. (Mooney 1970, 780)

The outline of the millennial story is recognizable: At the sign of a great conflagration or natural disaster ("shake the earth") Jesus ("Juesses") appears on earth ("on ground"), revives the dead, heals the sick, and makes the living young again.

Leslie Marmon Silko frames her novel *Gardens in the Dunes* (1999), a book about the painful separation and eventual reuniting of a family, within a scene of Paiutes in the area around Needles, California, thus participating in Wovoka's vision. Though they supposedly await the Messiah, their vision is less about the reconstitution of the earth or of society than it is about reunion. As in the historical documents quoted earlier, the Jesus seen by Native Americans, the Lord of the Dance, differs in appearance and message from the one the Europeans brought: "Jesus wore a white coat with bright red stripes; he wore moccasins on his feet. His face was dark and handsome, his eyes black and shining. . . . He told them all Indians must dance, everywhere, and keep on dancing. If they danced the dance, then they would be able to visit their dear ones and beloved ancestors" (ibid, 25). The breaking up of the ceremony by Indian policemen foreshadows the separation of the two sisters, Indigo and Sister Salt, who become the novel's main protagonists. Each travels a roundabout and painful journey, made more difficult by the white world they are forced to interact with, until they are reunited at the end of the novel to await the Messiah's return.[1]

Millennial doctrines similar to Wovoka's had been preached by Smohalla and John Slocum in the Northwest, and it is no accident that the Ghost Dance did not catch on in that region as it did with most tribes west of the Mississippi. Wovoka's version of the dance did not differ significantly from that of Wodziwob, who had introduced it in the 1870s, and it would seem logical to conclude that the deeper impact of Wovoka's version was directly proportional to the greater desperation of First Nations in the 1890s. By simply removing the whites from the picture, the Ghost Dance seems to magically restore the status quo of a time before the European invasion. Yet, its ecumenical vision of harmony among all Indians is paradoxically made possible only by the Indians' defeat and the influx of Christian universality. Indeed, basic technology itself played a role in the spread of the practice, and advances in technology may also help explain the different reception in 1890 of essentially the same practice introduced in 1870:

> Innovations of modern American civilization spread the news from tribe to tribe faster and farther than was possible in an earlier generation. Some of the methods designed by assimilationists to obliterate Indian cultures served to spread a religion dedicated to cultural rebirth. Concentration of tribes on reservations made them more accessible to one another. . . . Mass communication, represented by

an expanding postal service and the telegraph, hastened the flow of information between reservations. Indians trained in eastern boarding schools became tribal scribes and communicated with other tribes through the common language of English. Finally, railroads carried tribal delegates to Nevada, where they learned from [Wovoka] himself and became his apostles to the unconverted. (Moses and Szasz 1984, 10)

Another technological development played a crucial role in ending the Ghost Dance story. Hotchkiss guns, an early form of the machine gun, were part of the Seventh Cavalry's armament and deployed in the Wounded Knee massacre of December 1890, where they killed hundreds of Ghost Dancers, along with several troopers in "friendly fire." The question of who fired first at Wounded Knee has not been resolved; however, the intentions behind the placement of weapons of mass destruction make the first shot almost an irrelevant question. The manufacturer was no doubt pleased that its cutting-edge technology had performed to satisfaction.

As the introduction points out, millennial dreams can affect any stratum of the population in the Americas, and they fuel the dialectic between the use of millennial rhetoric and ideology by the dominant structures of societies founded on such dreams, such as that of the United States and the appearance of alternative visions in the disenfranchised. The emphasis in this chapter has been on groups in the Americas that suffered under a variety of political and economic developments in the late nineteenth century. However, one can also find traces of millenarianism in the discourse of nonvictims. It is tempting to speak of postmillennial fervor among the latter as opposed to premillennial attitudes among the oppressed. Social Darwinism and positivism are two worldviews strongly associated with this period that can be incorporated into postmillennial viewpoints and were certainly held with as much tenacity and blind faith as anything in the Bible. James P. Boyd, whose *Recent Indian Wars* appeared already in 1891 as one of the first book-length interpretations of the Ghost Dance, opined that "The Indians are . . . a doomed race, and none realize it better than themselves" (289). The parallel with the Métis and the sertanejos is patent. At least some Christian missionaries saw the massacre at Wounded Knee as a sign of providence. One sees this, for example, in an article published in the *Word Carrier* of January 1891: "There is a providential aspect [to the massacre] which demands notice. . . . It was needful that these people should feel in some sharp terrible way the just consequences of their actions, and be held in wholesome fear from further folly" (cited in DeMallie 1982, 397). Robert O. Pugh, the issue clerk at Pine Ridge and eyewitness to the disturbances, saw the conflict as a clash of messianisms:

> Commissioner Morgan was a Baptist preacher, filled with more religious zeal than sound judgment. He did not realize the importance of creature comforts as a foundation of religious conversion. . . . He was zealous for God, expecting the Indian to take care of his own stomach before the time of enthrallment. . . . It seemed as though the devil had come, in capricious mood to do all the wickedness he could invent. (Danker 1981, 226)

Though he plays down the messianic aspect of the Ghost Dance in his drama of the same title, Derek Walcott also makes the whites as zealous and irrational as the

Native Americans. He has Catherine Weldon, the "strong independent widow type" reminiscent of John Ford films, emphasize the movement's messianic aspects as essentially Christian:

> But [the Ghost Dancers] are Christians, Sergeant Donnelly. We made them.
> First, we preach the Resurrection and the life,
> of a Second Coming, of a pale-faced Messiah,
> whom we have crucified so He can redeem us,
> whom we must first murder to receive His pardon.
> That must be baffling enough to those savages
> who dare not presume to torture their gods.
> When they go a little further, as all converts do,
> of bringing heaven within their actual reach,
> you turn and call them crazy. But they believed us.
> They believed with us. Now what do you say?
> You tell these converts that they believe too much.
> That they exaggerate, they take belief too far.
> That they misunderstood us or they're too immoderate.
> When once you said that their doubt was indecent
> and their gods were smoke.
> *You* made the Ghost Dance. (2002, 226; emphasis added)

Walcott's invention of Weldon's testimony conforms to what we know of the historical person. Abandoning Brooklyn after the death of her husband, Weldon saw her role as that of a mediator or translator between Indians and whites. Famously, she lived in Sitting Bull's encampment for a number of years (Walcott invents the beginning of their friendship as happening through Buffalo Bill Cody's Wild West Show). Weldon was disappointed with the Ghost Dance in much the terms we see above, failing to recognize its native characteristics and seeing it as a capitulation to white messianic technology. She exchanged letters with the Indian agent for Standing Rock, James McGloughlin, another main character of Walcott's play. McGloughlin styled himself as a friend to the Indians but insisted on converting the Sioux to sedentary agriculture, the failure of which helped fuel the anger in the Sioux version of the Ghost Dance. Walcott centers the play on a fictional brief affair between Weldon and McGloughlin, which leads to McGloughlin revealing to Catherine the army's plans for conflict, which she communicates to Sitting Bull. That this is Catherine Weldon's play is evident in the fact that Walcott also devotes a section of his earlier poem, *Omeros*, to her. Weldon is Walcott's Ahab or Riel: the mediator of cultures whose attempt to control events ends in tragedy.

Weldon's own loss is perhaps the greatest of any character of the play, as her son dies of typhoid fever, though this loss competes with the suicide of Swift Running Deer, who had converted to Christianity and become engaged to a soldier, only to be shunned by the whites. She dances the Ghost Dance and then hangs herself from a tree. She had been humiliated by Sergeant Donnelly, who forced her to "dance Indian" at a white social, essentially denying her own attempt at transculturation, which balances Weldon's. Donnelly's version of failed hybridity is that of the aggressive "tourist" who understands everything from its exterior. In an early scene he sells ghost shirts to the troops: "Yer looking at a chance to be invisible! I've worn it meself and survived many a battle. . . . So I've got some on order that were captured from the enemy" (ibid., 134). The audience is left uncertain as to whether to judge Donnelly as a superstitious retrograde, a mocker, or a shrewd businessman willing to sell products he himself does not believe in. In addition, the cognoscenti are left uncertain as to whether, with the sergeant's name, Walcott may be alluding to Ignatius Donnelly, whose novel was published in the same year as the Wounded Knee massacre.

Canudos 1893–1897

The role of arms in proving the superiority of a "stronger" over a "weaker" race by simply eliminating the latter was also apparent to the Brazilian Euclides da Cunha, who described the Brazilian army, equipped with German Mannlicher rifles and Krupp cannons, in the following terms: "[W]e, the sons of the same soil . . . being ethnologically undefined, without uniform national traditions, living parasitically on the brink of the Atlantic in accordance with those principles of civilization which have been elaborated in Europe, and fitted out by German industry, we played in this action the singular role of unconscious mercenaries" (1944, xxix–xxx [xxix]). The arms race symbolized for da Cunha what the Canudos conflict had been at its core: telluric Brazilian interior vs. Europeanized littoral cultures. In the case of Canudos, these fundamental differences had been obscured by another, less fundamental opposition: monarchist vs. republican. The essential impetus for the millennialism of Canudos was given by the disruption of traditional ideologies through the declaration of a republic.

Unlike Louis Riel, who wished to found a specifically American Catholicism, the prophet of Canudos had nothing to say against Rome. He had everything to say, however, against the deposition of a monarch whom God had chosen to lead Brazil. If Riel opposed his concept of *Métis-français-canadien* to the emerging nation of Canada, the Counselor could not conceive of living under any other national arrangement than that of an "archaic" Brazil still ruled by an emperor. The monarchist-republican controversy that sealed the fate of Canudos would be unthinkable in any other American nation of the period. One feature that distinguishes Brazil from its neighbors in the Americas is that it is the only country to have been the capital of an empire—in Portuguese, "o império." The *translatio* had occurred in the first decade of the 19th century when Napoleon invaded Portugal.

In 1888 abolition marked the end of the sugar oligarchies of the northeast, which had been the backbone of the Brazilian monarchy, and its overthrow in favor of a republic soon followed. The armed forces fomented the coup of September 7, 1889, which sent Emperor Dom Pedro II into exile and installed a republic that lacked popular civilian support. The government's precariousness led to a climate of suspicion, fear, and repression that made Canudos, a relatively insignificant town lost in the wasteland of a region few cared about, appear to threaten the stability of the whole republic.

While the embers of Canudos were still aglow after the city's destruction by government forces in 1897, Brazilian authors were already setting pen to paper in an effort to recount and explain the most significant millenarian event of Brazil and possibly of the Americas (cf. Levine 1992, 217–45). The significance of Canudos was a product of its reception and rescripting in the Brazilian imaginary. During the war, Canudos—founded in 1893, when the republic was only four years old—was interpreted contradictorily as both a redoubt of primitive religious fanatics and bandits and a counterrevolutionary state-within-a-state, financed by the substantial number of monarchists who remained in Brazil and by their sympathizers abroad. Canudos is not just an event that happened but also a literary topos that has been treated from a variety of ideological and aesthetic perspectives. The war of bullets produced a war of words in which basic concepts of *brasileiridade* (Brazilianness), modernity, and social justice have been debated under the pretext of getting the Canudos story "right."

The messianism of the Counselor has found an echo in the single-minded mission of finding the ultimate truth of Canudos. Lori Madden accurately expresses the trajectory and interests of Canudos historiography when she writes that the Canudos conflict:

> has stimulated the imagination of diverse writers of alternative points of view since it affords evidence to be viewed as a political rebellion, a civil war, a problem of ethnicity, a messianic movement, a social movement, and other phenomena. It has become a mirror to the manipulations of its interpreters to such a degree that Canudos historiography, studied over time, tells a story of the evolution of ideas. (1993, 6)

Madden traces some of this history of the history of Canudos. However, though she invokes "imagination" in the preceding passage, she does not consider a group of early monographs on the war that take the form of "faction." (See my explanation of this term in chapter two.) One reason for the prevalence of faction in the early history of Canudos is the authors' urge to present both sides of the story as a counterbalance to propagandistic government and journalistic accounts. Official and journalistic accounts of the conflict showed the viewpoint of the republican side almost exclusively. The one-sidedness went beyond the old adage that "history is written by the victors"; in this case, writing and recording were exclusively associated with the government forces. Survivors of the conflict, many of them illiterate, were persecuted, went into hiding, and were reluctant to give interviews until many years later. The Counselor's sermons were published only in 1978.

For decades after the war, the only possibility for telling the sertanejos' story was to resort to fiction. Each author I consider here used faction to construct "his" Canudos as a historical entity rather than a possible world. Two of these factions predate da Cunha's *Os sertões* of 1902: Afonso Arinos's *Os jagunços* (1898) and Manoel Benício's *Rei dos jagunços* (1899). The third, *Accidentes* [*sic*] *da guerra* (1905), by Egmydio Dantas Barreto, postdates da Cunha's masterpiece but is based on Dantas's own *Última expedição a Canudos*, a memoir published in 1898. Indeed, one could almost say that these factions are the earliest monographs to attempt a holistic explanation for the Canudos event. While da Cunha's masterpiece is known to every student of Brazilian literature or history, those of Arinos, Benício, and Dantas Barreto are known almost exclusively to Canudos specialists and, when known, are more mentioned than read (although Benício's narrative provided much of the basis for a 1997 film, *Guerra de Canudos*, in which he appears as the character of the reporter).

Afonso Arinos (1868–1916) was the only one of the three authors considered here who did not travel to Canudos during the war. His novel thus combines the greatest sympathy for and nuancing of the Canudos rebellion with rather gross errors of fact. Arinos had pronounced monarchist sentiments and a profound interest in the culture and geography of the *sertão*. He published his faction, *Os jagunços*, under the pseudonym of Olivio de Barros in order to avoid the possible repercussions that had led to lynching and exile for certain monarchists during the Canudos conflict. This disinheriting of his own work by a future member of the Brazilian Academy of Letters began the long process of its forgetting.

Arinos interprets the decision to found Canudos as messianic. In his account, the Counselor has a vision several years before founding his City of God, called Belo Monte, which is revealed in an interior monolog:

> That land could only be the new Canaan. This people had been called to realize the divine task. And he would call them, reveal to them the grand destiny God had in mind for them. He would lead them to erect the holy city. . . . The missionary's face had been transfigured. Grandiose and sublime ideas fermented in his brain illumined by the divine ray. A vision of the future passed before his eyes that were full of fire. (1898, 50)

Is there really a divine ray, and is the Counselor's face really transfigured? Or is Arinos using free indirect discourse to filter the Counselor's own thoughts through the narrator's language, as da Cunha will do with the discourse of his fellow Brazilians at the end of *Os sertões*? In any case, in this novel the Counselor deliberately plans Belo Monte as a refuge for his abused followers and as a challenge to the impiety of the republic. As though Arinos had read Louis Riel's writings and applied them to the Brazilian circumstances, he chooses the Hebrews as a perfect analogy for the sufferings and neglect of the sertanejos. Their history tells the Counselor that the latter, too, are a put-upon but "chosen race" destined to fulfill a divine plan: "God had told him that he, the humble one, the stranger, poor as he was, he the *sertanejo* with no education would be assigned the great mission of redeeming the rights of all men of the *sertão*; he was to be the avenging arm for the affront suffered by the Emperor" (171). There is, however, no evidence in any of the writing Maciel left behind that he thought in this way. His opposition to the republic was based upon the objection to God's law being replaced by human law, as well as to some pragmatic considerations such as the new taxes the republic imposed.

Arinos's fiction begins a long line of interpretations of Conselheiro as a religious fanatic and madman obsessed by a monomaniacal vision. Modern historical interpretations have corrected this view. Marco Antônio Villa, Robert Levine, and others have argued that the decision to found Belo Monte was part of a nondivine and far less grandiose plan based on the Counselor's advancing age and the need for a permanent defensive position against attack. Arinos chooses to jump from the Counselor's early career (1877) to the eve of the government's attacks on Belo Monte in 1897, thus relieving himself of the need—and the opportunity—to portray the move to Canudos as a response to escalating violence. Arinos is correct, however, in leaving Sebastianism out of the picture, in assigning Genesis a greater part than Revelation in the symbolism of the Counselor's undertaking—his was not a vision of the eschaton—and perhaps in making his mission that of founding a new race, the *sertanejo*.

The erection of a permanent settlement intensified rather than diminished conflicts with the authorities since Belo Monte as a town acquired its own police force, paid no taxes, accepted no republican money, and conducted no civil marriages. Prostitution and alcohol, both endemic to the ordinary life of the *sertanejo*, were forbidden in Canudos. Most irritating of all, Belo Monte was a free city, whereas every other town of the interior was ruled directly or indirectly by the large landowners, called *coronéis*. The necessary detonation device did not take long to appear. The *Conselheiristas* had bought wood in Juazeiro, and when delivery was delayed, the Counselor sent word that his men would come and get it. The deputy then sent telegrams to the governor of Bahia predicting that the city would soon be invaded. The governor, in order not to acquire the reputation of being a cryptomonarchist, acceded to the demand and dispatched a command of 116 men to protect Juazeiro in November 1896.

When the predicted attack did not materialize, the force proceeded to the town of Uauá, where a force of Conselheiristas attacked them in the early morning. Oddly, and as a sign of how far removed he was from events, Arinos places the battle outside the town of Uauá rather than within it. The soldiers have left the town and are heading for Canudos when they see the jagunços and fire on them. In relocating the battle and the combatants' movements, Arinos has removed any doubt that the army initiated the conflict by having them approach the jagunços rather than vice versa as in most accounts. The battle left eight soldiers dead, along with about 150 jagunços, who fought with scythes, clubs, and blunderbusses. Despite their superior results, the soldiers retreated to Juazeiro. The battle hardened positions on both sides of the conflict. The backlanders had won their first real victory against constituted power. Converts streamed into Canudos.

A second expedition of six hundred soldiers and a third of twelve hundred men were defeated in January and March of 1897, respectively. The death of the commander of the third expedition, Colonel Moreira César, made Canudos a national concern, a threat to the entire republic. The city's extraordinary armaments, the only apparent explanation for its amazing resistance, were rumored to have come from foreign powers. Monarchist newspapers were destroyed, and angry mobs as far away as Rio de Janeiro and São Paulo lynched monarchist sympathizers. The fourth expedition, which eventually involved half of the Brazilian army, could not fail. Five times as large as any of the previous expeditions, it besieged Canudos from late June to October 5, 1897, when the last defender was killed and the city razed.

Although Arinos's knowledge of the *sertão* of Minas Gerais was extensive, he had never seen the area surrounding Canudos in Bahia and hence had to rely on newspaper and other accounts of the war for his descriptions. Arinos follows a tried-and-true mimetic strategy by inventing a fictitious *jagunço*, Luís Pachola, whom the narrative follows as he becomes a convert to the Counselor's campaign, settles in Canudos, and fights the war to its end. This strategy allows Arinos to make full use of his knowledge of *sertanejo* culture and psychology despite his lack of direct knowledge of the area. It also allows him to recount his story "from the inside outward," the opposite direction from Euclides da Cunha, from whose dispatches Arinos may have borrowed.[2] Arinos's story of the war is told almost entirely from the perspective of the *jagunços*, while for da Cunha the *jagunço* is a foreigner within Brazil, a "shadow," as chapter two explains, and an object of study to be viewed from the outside.

Less intuitive than the creation of a fictional character to support the narrative is Arinos's setting for the opening of the novel in 1877, sixteen years before the founding of Canudos, and in Periperi, located in a region Arinos was familiar with but which was not one of the Counselor's more usual haunts. At one of the region's large ranches, Pachola attends a festival (Festa do Divino) where the Counselor is also present. Another cowboy, jealous of the young girl Conceição's attentions to Pachola, attempts to eliminate his rival but kills the girl instead. Her death marks Pachola for the rest of his life with sadness and a sense of mission. When he encounters the body of his rival hanging from a tree, an apparent suicide, Pachola decides that "his life, then, should take a different path, or, even more, should begin again from the point of Conceição's death" (1898, 114). These two sacrificial deaths, one recalling Christ, the other Judas, symbolize the sacrificial victims Arinos sees in the dead of Canudos. Pachola is meant to represent the typical man of the *sertão*, particularly in his religious faith, which lacks a sophisticated theology but has an extensive inventory of prayers, images, and fetishes. "The prayers he knew were means as certain to deliver him from evil or danger, as his poncho was to protect him from the rain" (ibid., 98).

In an "epilogue" published in his newspaper, *O Comércio de São Paulo*, Arinos wrote the following: "The *jagunços* received the splendid and mysterious baptism of blood, and, wrapped in its purple, opened the doors of Brazilian nationality [nacionalidade brasileira] for their brother sertanejos" (1969, 646). Arinos's phrasing synthesizes the Christian motif of baptism with classical ones of mourning purple and of the glory of self-sacrifice for one's country. In Arinos's cadences, as in the seemingly digressive events of *Os jagunços*, Canudos ceases to be a historical accident or a politically motivated revolt and instead assumes the dimensions of a sacrificial rite that, in the words of Leopoldo Bernucci, contains "the Christian redemptive dimension that allows the death of a few to become the salvation of many" (1995, 70). In effect, with Pachola's story Arinos has sublimated the divisive political language of monarchist-republican with an inclusive one of redemption; he has substituted a matrix of Christian love and sacrifice for the violent archetype of Apocalypse, with which Canudos had been marked by the press, and he has turned the Counselor from Antichrist into Christ.

On the other hand, Arinos portrays Canudos as neither an agglomeration of fanatics nor a solidarian, utopian community but more as a Spartan dictatorship that combined unity of purpose with repressive mechanisms. For example, Arinos depicts the flogging of women who were thought not to mourn sufficiently for their husbands killed in battle. Arinos's Canudos is schizophrenic, dominated in equal parts by profound religious idealism, pragmatic defense of a viable way of life, and the mechanisms of petty personal rivalry evident in the earlier examples. As an illustration of the first instance, Carlota, the wife of one of the secondary characters, Pedro Espia, at one point expresses her horror at the bloodshed and her presentiment that "neither we nor our children will survive this war" (ibid., 267), to which her husband responds, "So what? At least we will have our sins purged and we will not have to suffer as much in the fires of purgatory" (ibid.). This passage shows not so much an eschatological vision of the inhabitants as one derived from crusader mentality that explains the presence of so many former bandits in Canudos: One is forced to lead a violent life that loads one down with sin; it is therefore necessary to engage fully in a struggle against the infidels in order to achieve redemption. This redemption is not collective but depends upon individual commitment and performance. In passages such as these, Arinos acquaints his readers with the Canudos war from its victims' point of view. The narration never shifts to the army ranks or the halls of power, to the governor's palace in Salvador, or to the urban centers of Brazil. It remains with the *jagunços*, giving their perspective on the conflict and their reasons for fighting.

As the war ends, Arinos allows Pachola and a few others to escape through underground tunnels to the river, and the novel's last sentence, in a continuation of the governing Old Testament intertext, equates this escape to the flight from Egypt and subsequent wandering of the Israelites: "And the tribe marched into the desert" (ibid., 319). This sentence implies that the culture of the long-suffering *jagunços* will be sublimated in the future of Brazil, just as the Hebrews' culture was taken up into Christianity. Arinos's fiction is participatory in asking its readers to convert the premillennial violence of Canudos into the postmillennial project of constructing Brazil.

At the far end of the spectrum from Arinos's sympathetic account is Dantas Barreto's *Accidentes da Guerra*. Dantas Barreto took part in the fourth expedition against Canudos as a lieutenant colonel of the Third Brigade. His memoir, *Última expedição a Canudos*, is unrelenting in its vituperation of the "fanatics" and "subversives" of Canudos, who needed to disappear "in the name of order, of civilization, and of morality in Brazil" (1898, 233), and unwavering in both its support of army strategy and its praise of the common soldier's bravery and patriotism. The author does at times show admiration for the *jagunços'* courage, as well as sympathy for their plight. Canudos was literally infernal: "Every torture of Dante's Inferno was reproduced there!" (ibid., 225).

Dantas Barreto carries this essential antipathy toward the *jagunços* over into his faction, *Accidentes da guerra*, which the author himself terms "a novelized episode [um episódio romantisado]" (1905, 7). The episode involves two residents of Monte Santo, the nearest large town to Canudos. Alberto becomes a soldier, while Germana, his childhood sweetheart, follows her parents to Canudos. The clearest distaste is shown in the novel's final event, when the two lovers are killed by *jagunços*: Alberto is killed by sniper fire, and then "five disgusting men, bandit types [typos de salteadores], each with the face of a murderer" (ibid., 275), emerge from hiding and carry off Germana. When she resists rape, they stab her to death. Alberto and Germana's romance had been destroyed by their families' different social standings. "It's that my region has a history full of accidents" (ibid., 16), as Albert explains earlier to his curious friends. Germana's father had been a debt peon on land owned by Alberto's father, Coronel Nogueira, making marriage between the two unthinkable. When the troops arrive in Monte Santo, Alberto learns that Germana's family has moved to Canudos.

Until Alberto discovers Germana near the end, narrative suspense revolves around the possibility that he will either unknowingly kill her and her family or else be able to liberate her. Alberto is obsessed by the thought that "he had been in the citadel [Canudos] perhaps a few paces from Germana" (165–66). With this simple plot device, Dantas Barreto dramatizes the very real social differences and economic devastation that gave rise to the Canudos movement. The mimetic device of frustrated romance indirectly demonstrates more comprehension for the motivations behind the rise of Canudos than does the author's straightforward labeling of the *jagunços* as monarchists and fanatics. Indeed, the story of how Germana got to Canudos shows little religious motivation or belief in the eschaton.

If the literary model for Arinos was the Bible and for Dantas Barreto *Dante's Inferno*, for Manoel Benício it is Don Quixote: The Counselor has a noble and understandable purpose that has no chance of succeeding in the real world. An army colonel, Benício accompanied the fourth expedition as a reporter for the *Jornal do Comércio* and was nearly executed for his severe criticisms of the army's actions. Benício's faction, *O rei dos jagunços* [King of the Jagunços] (1899), moves between several genres. For example, historical records are interlaced with the fictions recounted below. Febrônio de Brito's published account of the second expedition he commanded against Canudos is simply inserted whole into the narrative, as is an exchange between ecclesiastical and civil authorities concerning the danger the Counselor represents, as well as other documents.

The *coronelismo* and clan politics that gave rise to bloody vendettas such as the one that decimated the Counselor's clan were logical results of the isolation of the *sertão* from the stabilizing structures of church and state, which remained confined to the littoral region (the capital of every northeastern state of Brazil is located on the coast). However, vendettas clearly undermine *coronelismo*'s attempts at regulating society and introduce a further destabilizing factor into the backlands. The messianism of a Conselheiro or a Padre Cícero, as Maria Isaura Pereira de Queiroz points out, is the common solution of a traditional society for resolving such crises of organization, whether caused by the vendetta or, as in the case of Canudos, by economic blight and the change in larger political structures exemplified by the fall of the monarchy. The messianic leader either substitutes the figure of the landowner, as in the case of Antônio Conselheiro, or allies himself with one of them to eliminate rivals and reestablish order (1972, 12, ch. 5).

Benício initially focuses his narrative on one such *coronel*, the owner of a ranch where the Counselor stops to preach in 1888. The rancher, João Thomé, hopes that the pilgrim will exhort his followers to construct a reservoir, which will benefit his ranching activities. Benício thus provides an example of the complex relations between the Counselor and the backlands power structures, which historian Ralph Della Cava has summarized thus:

> [T]he capacity of Conselheiro . . . to attract "pilgrims" to the labor-shy regions
> of Bahia and Ceará (where they remained as workers) was tantamount to political

power. . . . Conselheiro was an asset to both curates and *coronéis* of the Bahian backlands. There is strong evidence that in addition to rendering services to the church he
often assisted the local colonels. They appreciated the dams and roads that the *beato*
constructed for them, and above all, the free labor provided by workers whom the
Counselor kept well disciplined. (Della Cava 1968, 411)

The novelistic focus of this long section is on the amorous involvements of
Thomé's three daughters and especially those of the youngest, Benta, who ends up
among the Counselor's followers. Benício depicts the three daughters as noble savages, raised by a careless father far from civilizing influences and without a thought
of marriage. The arrival of the Counselor's following at the farm wreaks rapid
changes in the girls' disposition: by the end of the chapter all three have eloped with
their lovers. Benta is depicted not as a religious fanatic but as someone who joins
the pilgrims because she has no future and no fixed place in the social order. She
is besieged by the unwanted attentions of Candinho, a former slave and her "irmão
de leite" (i.e., Candinho's mother was Benta's wet nurse). Benta detests Candinho,
but when she takes the step of running away, following the trail of her sisters (who
have both eloped), the ex-slave abducts her. They take to wandering the countryside
and sleeping in abandoned houses, following the Counselor's trail. One night they
are surprised by a *capitão de mato*, or bounty hunter. The bounty hunter, who is described as a *caboclo*, or mixture of Indian and African, later kills Candinho, marries
Benta for her inheritance, and returns her to her father's farm.

The incident is less marginally related to the Counselor and to the question of
Canudos than it may seem. The numerous freedmen among the Counselor's followers
became a subject of discussion in the period, and the emancipation of 1888 created
a whole new class of individuals without employment or place in society, which
increased the need for a free city like Canudos. Benício's faction shows this quite
clearly: Ex-slave and unmarried woman together have no place in society. Benta's
journey eventually returns her to the ranch from which she had started. Her aversion to Candinho's advances, as well as the bounty hunter's racist statements, reflect
the landed class's distrust of blacks as free laborers, which led to the importation
of workers from the Mediterranean to take their place. Benício faults the leading
classes for this and baldly states the link with Canudos: "Unhappy [desventurada]
Bahia that had to witness the brutal slaughter of her sons and will have later to pass
over so many of the living with national blood in favor of Calabrian lives that will
cost rivers of money at the least! . . . (1899, 216). Beyond the economic requirements
of conformity to a world system and not only the importation of armaments from
France and Germany, the international labor market and chance for using immigrants
as cheap, reliable labor also helped shape the Canudos conflict. The elites of "des-
venturada" Bahia are as much to blame for the war as the *malaventurados* [wretched]
of Canudos.

The end of Canudos is represented in the surrender of Beatinho and the immediate decapitation of his prisoners. After the slaughter, Vilanova digs up the treasure and
disappears with it. The last scene is of Jararaca, a former incestuous father whom the
Counselor caused to reform, riding his burro through the desert: "[H]e appeared like
some Quixotic or fantastic being!" (ibid., 220). This image of picaresque wandering

seems to echo ironically Arinos's solemn biblical allusions. Unlike Arinos, Benício has no destination in mind for the survivors of Canudos except the chimerical ones invented by a Don Quixote.

Benício's narrative not only probes the background of the conflict but also emphasizes the backlanders' ignorance, the vices of some members of the Canudos community, such as Vilanova and João Abade, and the Counselor's mental aberrations. Yet Benício concludes that the Counselor, as a bad Catholic, was also a true martyr who died, like Jesus, for his faith. His followers, moreover, were defending their faith, their possessions, and their honor. The government of Bahia comes off no better in his account. Whereas Arinos attempted to understand the *jagunço* from the inside, as it were, Benício seems to satirize him, while also exposing the massacres and other vices of the army and the government to a much greater extent than had Arinos, who perhaps feared repercussions from such a stance.

Canudos at One Hundred

Undoubtedly inspired by the 1993–1997 centennial of Canudos, José J. Veiga, José de Oliveira Falcón, Edmundo Guedes, Ayrton Marcondes, and Eldon Canário are among the Brazilian authors who have produced fictions or factions about Canudos, not to mention the Peruvian Mario Vargas Llosa, whose earlier *La guerra del fin del mundo* helped raise Canudos to the status of world event. Bahian writer Oleone Coelho Fontes's *A quinta expedição* [The Fifth Expedition] (2002) is the most recent example of the power of Canudos to explode the restrictions of genre and compel its authors to tell its story through the imaginative form of faction.

Let us consider one example of the way modern Brazil looks back at Canudos. Edmundo Guedes creates a "New Antonio Conselheiro" in a novella with that title. A monk, Fabrício, becomes aware of the distance between church hierarchy and the needs of the people and, upon expressing his opinion, is defrocked. He then appears in the *sertão* and preaches from the top of Monte Santo to the people, who recognize him as an avatar of the Conselheiro. His speech to the people, reminiscent more of the language of Louis Riel than of the Counselor, takes on a decidedly apocalyptic tone, including the traditional view of the republic as Antichrist:

> Before the turn of the century, and even before the absolute chaos, the Other Brazil will come to us again, with its destructiveness, with its hatred, with its horses of iron, with its weapons of iron and with its birds of iron shooting out fire from their nostrils, eager to kill without mercy, as in Belo Monte.
>
> But, measureless is the power of God! Just as we did in the Belo Monte of Canudos, we will receive them here too with fire and steel, with determination and courage! This time, victory will be ours, despite the help, the unnatural help, which the enemy will receive from the four beasts of Satan. (1997, 51)

At this point the author inserts a footnote that explains that these four beasts are, in the "delusional idea" of the New Counselor, four powerful nations of the earth that lust after Brazil's riches.

The "other Brazil" [outro Brasil] preached against is the one called the "littoral": Europeanized, civilized, urbanized. It considers the peasants of the northeast to be subhuman, lazy, and brutalized. The adherence to da Cunha's "two Brazils" thesis provides Guedes with an interesting interpretation of the most famous prophecy of the messiah of Canudos (given in detail in chapter two): "In 1896 a thousand flocks [rebanhos] shall run from the seacoast to the backlands [sertão]; and then the backlands will turn into seacoast and the seacoast into backlands" (da Cunha 1944, 135). The "flocks" are troops of soldiers; "praia" is the littoral pseudocivilization that seeks to crush the *sertão*. The reversal occurs as the civilized carry on a brutal war that makes them identify with the savages they are to assert their superiority over. This symbolic interpretation, which makes a supposedly raving announcement seem reasonable, resembles similar interpretations of the difficult passages of Revelation. Once the text is interpreted as symbolic, the supposed divide between reason and fanaticism disappears. At the height of Fabrício's sermon, sounds of exploding bombs and helicopters are heard—it is the Brazilian army taking part in practice maneuvers, with the scenario of an occupation of a "'problematic region' in the scenario of 'serious and imminent institutional instability'" (Guedes 1997, 74). An army helicopter crashes into the Counselor's hut on the mountain, killing him. His death makes neither the regional nor the national news, impinging itself not a whit on the "other Brazil," those followers of the Beast who are busy with the trivialities technology keeps them occupied "with their soap operas and television game shows, with soccer, with bingo, with the state lotteries, and . . . oh yes, and with the Carnival that was coming up" (ibid., 77). Like Brazilian carnival, with its roots in political satire and other counternarratives of Brazil, Guedes's fantasy—typical of the centennial fiction surrounding Canudos—represents not a call to take sides like the earliest fictions but a parodic distancing from *both* sides of the *jagunço*-republican divide. It is thus a prime example of "reflective dissonance" in millennial fiction, which is the topic of the next chapter.

Kingdoms of This World: Millennial Literature as Reflective Dissonance

And I took the little book out of the angel's hand, and ate it up; and it was in my mouth sweet as honey: and as soon as I had eaten it, my belly was bitter.

And he said unto me, Thou must prophesy again before many peoples, and nations, and tongues, and kings.

Revelation 10

To envision millennium, John tells us, and indeed to read the literature of millennium, is at first a sweet experience, then a bitter one. We can imagine John's eating of the book (an age-old symbol for the reception of prophetic gifts) as his simultaneous identification and conflict with eschatology, and we might interpret the book's travel from the angel to his mouth to his stomach as an allegory for the trajectory of millennial movements—from enthusiasm to conflict to defeat—or for the trajectory of millennial literature from participation to reflection. One notices as well the insertion of the word "again" (Greek *palin*) to indicate that this cycle will recommence. That is, the changes eschatechnologies effect in societies are redirected, diffused, or delayed but not necessarily diminished by the failure of specific prophecy. Bryan Wilson summarizes some of these effects:

> [A] new conception of the social organization of the collectivity occurs: a glimmering sense of a different future is acquired. The idea of social change is grasped. The deities who hitherto have sanctioned custom, now—suddenly—become the initiators of change (even if that change is restoration). . . . Although millennialism is an ideology of change, the real change which it inaugurates is a latent function rather than the realization of its promise. (1973, 495)

In their perpetual defeat, eschatologies are always transformative, recombinant technologies that render reading-food both bitter and sweet. As an example of Wilson's thesis, after the Great Disappointment of 1844 Millerites were faced with two options: continue with revised premillennial expectations or channel one's energies into reform, often with a postmillennial flavor. In its concentration on signs, Millerism had focused people's attention on the evils of the age, the most prominent of which was slavery, and hence had played an indirect role in the growth of the abolitionist movement. Many free African Americans (one of whom was the future feminist abolitionist, Sojourner Truth) became associated with the movement. It was in June 1843—exactly the height of Millerism—that Isabella Baumfree took the name Sojourner Truth and lived up to her new name by forsaking a fixed abode to travel from tent meeting to tent meeting. She preached at several of these gatherings, moderating the fervor of some of the more radical speakers and not consenting to give a date for the rapture. Millerites steered her toward the utopian community of Northampton, whose people "were not second adventists; they were counting on the world to last long enough for them to cure its savagery and injustice" (Painter 1996, 88). Here Truth met abolitionists such as William Lloyd Garrison—not to mention Fredrick Douglass—and dictated her autobiography to Olive Gilbert. *The Narrative of the Life of Sojourner Truth* devotes many pages to the Millerite movement.

In Wilson's terms, the significance of social change had been grasped. Signs previously associated with the eschaton were now seen for what they were: concrete social ills to be combated directly through movements for abolition, temperance, and suffrage. This was one pole of active response; the other was the formation or increase of new religions that held to the millennial vision, such as the Adventists and the Mormons. There was also a middle ground of people who still believed in millennium and in humans' ability not to predict it but to work for it. Such was, for example, Clorinda Strong Minor, wife of a Philadelphia businessman, who established a small agricultural settlement in Palestine. Her goal, like that of hundreds of other emigrants to Palestine, was the conversion of the Jews to hasten the Second Coming, though she managed little progress toward it.

This brief history of the fallout from Millerism in the United States should demonstrate that rather than causing adherents to give up hope, the defeat of millennial prediction either redirects or redoubles their energies. Psychologist Leon Festinger developed a theory of cognitive dissonance in part to explain the persistence of belief in the face of disconfirmed prophecy. He published two books within a year of each other, one with a trade press and the other with an academic press. The former, *When Prophecy Fails* (1956), follows the fortunes of a small flying-saucer cult that predicted a cataclysm. One surprising finding of the study was that, under certain conditions, disconfirmation of prediction can intensify rather than diminish followers' commitment to a particular group. Festinger's *Theory of Cognitive Dissonance* (1957), on the other hand, is mostly theoretical and uses general and very ordinary examples. "Cognitive dissonance," besides adding another motivation to the standard repertory of psychology, became a standard term in millennial studies, essential for analyzing the continuation of millennial expectations in the face of failed prophecy.[1] I examine numerous literary examples of defeated millennium in this chapter under the lens of Festinger's theory of dissonance and supplement the notion of cognitive dissonance with what I call *reflective dissonance*, which is more appropriate to the interventions of literature in history. The issue in millennial literature is not so much defeat per se but instead the positioning of literary texts on the right-hand side of the continuum shown in the introduction, that is, an analysis of these texts' rhetoric of reflection vs. persuasion, the types of possible worlds they construct, and the contribution—positive or negative—they make to millennial discourse in the Americas.

Reflective Dissonance

Festinger defines cognition as "any knowledge, opinion, or belief about the environment, about oneself, or about one's behavior. Cognitive dissonance can be seen as an antecedent condition which leads to activity oriented toward dissonance reduction just as hunger leads to activity oriented toward hunger reduction" (1957, 3). Failed prophecy and defeated millennial movements provide prime examples of such dissonance, which, as noted earlier, can be "reduced" in a variety of ways. This chapter analyzes the theme of defeated millennium not as it has occurred in the history of the Americas but as literary texts and films have depicted it. Since Plato, Western thinking about literature has debated the relationship between mimetic treatments of reality and cognition, and, interestingly, there is still no consensus on the kind of knowledge literature conveys or on whether fiction induces opinions or beliefs about anything whatsoever.

Of course, the overlap between historical and literary defeat has been substantial: Works such as Rudy Wiebe's *Scorched-wood People*, Mario Vargas Llosa's *Guerra del fin del mundo* [War of the End of the World], or Alejo Carpentier's *El reino de este mundo* [The Kingdom of This World] recount historical millennial conflicts that took place in Canada, Brazil, and Haiti respectively. In each case, however, there is a substantial difference between historical defeat and its fictional depiction—Carpentier, for example, seems to graft millennial attitudes from his own historical situation onto a scenario where they were absent or ambiguous. Literary treatments of millennial disappointment exhibit the condition of reflective dissonance, that is, of a dissonance based not on cognition but on reflection and imagination. Immanuel Kant's aesthetic philosophy implicitly denied art's power to instill belief by differentiating reflective judgments of the beautiful and the sublime from cognitive judgments: "The beautiful and the sublime are similar in some respects. We like both for their own sake, and both presuppose that we make a judgment of reflection rather than either a judgment of sense or a logically determinative one" (1987, book 2, par. 23). Kant's highly formalistic approach to the beautiful and the sublime privileged natural objects and events and, beyond these, mostly nonnarrative forms of art, including lyric poetry.

However, Kant's definition of the dynamic and mathematical sublime as the absolutely powerful and the absolutely great (infinite), respectively, allows room for the depiction of the end of the world. Judgment of the sublime proceeds from a dissonance between faculties of the mind, as "all the might of the imagination [proves] still inadequate to reason's ideas" (ibid., par. 26). An analogous dissonance may take place in a mind reflecting on the end of the world. In the introduction to this book I contrasted the gradualism of everyday experience with the suddenism posited by the eschaton. These may be associated with Kant's reason and imagination, respectively. Even fictions based on historical instances of defeated millennium take the path of reflective dissonance structured by the disjunction between imagination and reason rather than the epistemological path of the need to reconcile brute ontological facts with prophecy. The treatment of literary texts as making aesthetic judgments of reflective dissonance on millennium differs somewhat from their treatment in previous chapters, where the mutual influences of history and literature were emphasized. This approach suggests that millennial belief is itself an aesthetic preference.

Reflective dissonance no doubt provides the "room for maneuver" that Ross Chambers has identified as enabling literature to function as oppositional:

> [O]ppositional reading, as the production of the oppositional in texts, can become an agency of change, since it changes in the first instance something in the economy of the reader's desire. In other words, the "influence" that texts can exert on the "minds" of their readers needs to be analyzed, on the one hand, as a function of the duplicity of literary discourse, its constitutively split identity implying an appeal to be read otherwise, but also, on the other hand, in terms of the vulnerability of our desires—produced as they largely are by the mediations of the system of power—to seduction. (1991, 16)

Chambers's claim for literature thus resonates with Wilson's for the latency of millennial change itself.

Foundational Texts

The first text of reflective dissonance in Western literature may be the book of Jonah in the Hebrew scriptures. That book portrays Jonah as a religious fanatic who believes in the eschaton. He refuses the Lord's command to preach to the Ninevites not out of fear or laziness but because he prefers to leave apostasy in the world so as to more quickly bring about the world's end. This is not explained at the beginning of the story but becomes clear when Jonah is sent to Nineveh a second time and announces the end: "Forty days more and Nineveh shall be destroyed" (Jonah 3:4). Everyone in Nineveh repents, and the Lord spares the city. Jonah rebukes God: " 'I beseech you, Lord,' he prayed, 'is not this what I said while I was still in my own country? This is why I fled at first to Tarshish. I knew that you are a gracious and merciful God, slow to anger, rich in clemency, loathe to punish'" (Jonah 4:2). Jonah lives in eager expectation of the destruction of the world, which will be followed by millennium. The story ends with the incident of the gourd plant, which God causes to wither and die. When Jonah complains, the comparison lies close at hand: " 'You are concerned over the plant which cost you no labor and which you did not raise; it came up in one night and in one night it perished. And should I not be concerned over Nineveh, the great city, in which there are more than a hundred and twenty thousand persons who cannot distinguish their right hand from their left, not to mention the many cattle?'" (Jonah 4:10–11).

Thus, in a strange inversion, Jonah has been treated in parallel fashion to the people he despises. As Douglas Robinson points out, "the Book of Jonah points clearly to an imagistic reversal of the apocalypse—an invocation of apocalyptic threats (structural collapse in ship and city) in order to replace the ideology of apocalypse with a 'liberal,' antiapocalyptic tolerance" (1985, 144). In the gospel of Matthew,

Jesus associates his own work and temporary death with that of Jonah and continues the story on into what will become the Christian millennium: "At the judgment,
the men of Nineveh will arise with this generation and condemn it, because they
repented at the preaching of Jonah; and there is something greater than Jonah here"
(Matthew 12:41). A similar displacement, Robinson argues, occurs in Melville's
Moby-Dick, where apocalyptic images in the *world* are mediated by the *word* (1985,
162). Yet Ahab, as Father Mapple's sermon makes clear, is an anti-Jonah, one whose
own will-to-divinity trumps both cognitive and reflective dissonance. For Robinson,
every work of literature is an act of reflective dissonance, a gourd plant or mediatory
gesture that allegorizes rather than documents.

Hence the Bible itself "authorizes" works of literature such as Mario Arregui's
"Los dos amantes del apocalipsis" ["The Two Lovers of the Apocalypse"] (1972),
whose dissonance derives from a principle of inversion similar to that of the Jonah
story. Arregui replaces the usual trigger events of Tribulation with a single, softer
one. When true love occurs, it will restore the world to Eden:

> Yes, two lovers who as such reach perfection will set off an instant apocalypse [un
> instantáneo apocalipsis], without cataclysms or oceans of blood, without horrible
> horses or mysterious animals with wings full of eyes, without swords of fire nor
> deadly abysms nor fiery rains, without trumpeting angels, without the seven cups
> of God's wrath poured out onto the earth . . . with nothing, to make a long insanity
> short, of what was plotted by the destructive delirium, the cosmic and visionary re-
> sentment of that bogey-man [tremebundista], John of Patmos. (ibid., 103–4)

Arregui's rewriting of John is direct and conflictual. John is made to play the role
of Jonah (i.e., of one who desires the destruction of humankind out of one's own
psychological makeup). Using words such as "without," Arregui performs a simple
negation on the well-known symbols of Revelation, such as the trumpet blasts and
vials of wrath: None of these will occur. This approach is of course contradictory,
acknowledging the power of John's imagery while simultaneously deflecting it.

In comparison, Nathaniel Hawthorne's "Earth's Holocaust" establishes dissonance
in a less binary fashion through hybridizing—in fact, Americanizing—millennial discourse. Hawthorne's story first appeared in *Graham's Magazine* in 1844, one year after
the collapse of the Millerite movement. Hawthorne's failed apocalypse in "Earth's
Holocaust" combines the breaking of the seventh seal, when the earth is consumed
by fire, with the Native American tradition of the "busk," described by ethnographer
William Bartram and advocated for all by Henry David Thoreau in *Walden* (Mani
1972, 163–64). Busk was a Green Corn ceremony celebrated by the Natchez, Creek,
and other southeastern Native Americans in midsummer. It was suffused with an ethos
of annual renewal in which the sacred fire was rekindled; old debts and grudges were
forgotten; and a sense of community was regenerated. Every wrongdoing, grievance,
or crime—short of murder—was forgiven. In the busk, old and useless things were
burned in order to make room for the new. Here is Bartram's description:

> When a town celebrates the busk, having previously provided themselves with new
> clothes, new pots, pans, and other household utensils and furniture, they collect all
> their worn out clothes and other despicable things, sweep and cleanse their houses,

squares, and the whole town, of their filth, which with all the remaining grain and other old provisions they cast together into one common heap, and consume it with fire. After having taken medicine, and fasted for three days, all the fire in the town is extinguished. (1791, 509)

And here is Thoreau's appreciation of this ceremony in the "Economy" chapter of *Walden* (1854):

> The customs of some savage nations might, perchance, be profitably imitated by us, for they at least go through the semblance of casting their slough annually; they have the idea of the thing, whether they have the reality or not. Would it not be well if we were to celebrate such a "busk," or "feast of first fruits," as Bartram describes to have been the custom of the Mucclasse Indians?
>
> The Mexicans also practised a similar purification at the end of every fifty-two years, in the belief that it was time for the world to come to an end.
>
> I have scarcely heard of a truer sacrament, that is, as the dictionary defines it, "outward and visible signs of an inward and spiritual grace," that is, and I have no doubt that they were originally inspired directly from Heaven to do thus, though they have no Biblical record of the revelation. (65–66)

Thoreau feels justified in equating a practice of annual renewal with one of world-ending millennium that must be revealed from Heaven. He undoubtedly also saw characteristics that fit the text of Revelation, particularly the renewal of community through destruction.

Hawthorne's busk-holocaust is a fitting image for the singularly American, syncretistic shape of his story, which sets the millennial impulses of the European tradition based on a linear progress of time within a setting derived from Native Americans. The very first sentence recalls the cyclical time typical of myth: "Once upon a time—but whether in the time past or time to come is a matter of little or no moment—this wide world had become so overburdened with an accumulation of worn-out trumpery, that the inhabitants determined to rid themselves of it by a general bonfire" (1844, 887). Reflective dissonance begins with the two ideas of time—*kairos* vs. *chronos*—suggested by the narrator's uncertainty. For "trumpery" we might read the word "technologies." The punch line of the story will involve the lack of newer and smoother technologies of the self to replace the older, worn-out ones. The uncertainty about time reflects the story's ambiguous status between satire and allegory. Events recounted in the mythic past are really ongoing or set in the future. In the *Popol Vuh*, for example, the succession of imperfect humans created by Heart of Sky out of wood and mud also represent their degeneration and forgetting of the divine that will progressively take hold of them and bring about their destruction. The story supposedly told to account for origin repeats itself as an end. Why tell the Flood myth if it has no bearing on the present?

First to be burned is all of the "rubbish of the herald's office," which causes the "plebeian spectators [to] set up a joyous shout." All ties with Europe are severed: "[S]ome rough-looking men advanced to the verge of the bonfire, and threw in, as it appeared, all the rubbish of the Herald's Office; the blazonry of coat-armor; the crests and devices of illustrious families; pedigrees that extended back, like lines of light, into the mist of the dark ages" (ibid., 888). Like the prairie, the men's rough-hewn look provides a clue to the frontier democratic forces providing the impetus for this upset. The destruction of the patents of nobility is like the sailing of the *Pequod*, a breaking of every mooring in time and history. Left unanswered is the implicit question concerning the piloting mechanism: How is the ship of state and society to be steered?

With the first jettisoning comes the first protest—from an old man with the bearing of "one who had been born to the idea of his own social superiority" (ibid., 889). A hopelessly self-interested party, then, and yet what the man has to say must give us pause: "With the nobles, too, you have cast off the poet, the painter, the sculptor—all the beautiful arts—for we were their patrons" (ibid.). When a representative of the aristocracy thus disinherited dares to protest, he is shouted down by a "rude figure" representative of the plebeian crowd, who voices the principles of possessive democratic individualism (later dubbed Social Darwinism), starting with "strength of arm." This pattern continues throughout the sketch. A set of objects is thrown on the bonfire; some individual notes that these objects will be missed, but the crowd shouts him down. In a sense, the destruction of nobility unleashes all of the other events by creating a political vacuum. David Leverenz rightly points to the "tension between entrepreneurial self-reliance and colonial accommodations" (1993, 122) in this and other texts by Hawthorne. At the same time, this American social leveling points toward the New Jerusalem, in which infirmities and other differences between individuals will be overcome. As the flames consume each layer of social order, the narrator grows increasingly uneasy but is reassured each time by an unnamed friend at his side.

In a prophetic vision of the final "triumph" of the temperance movement in the early twentieth century, Hawthorne next has Father Mathew pour out all the alcohol of the earth onto the blaze. While only topers seem to regret this loss, it is soon followed, quite logically, by other drugs: tea, coffee, and tobacco. Since there is yet to be a perfectly straight life, all readers are bound to feel that they are losing something in the elimination of "everything rich and racy" (1844, 892). At this point the general reform pauses in favor of individual unburdenings. A child throws in his playthings, a college graduate his diploma, a widow her dead husband's miniature, and so forth. A desperate girl is stopped from throwing herself into the fire since she deems herself "the most worthless thing alive or dead" (ibid., 893). She is told that only things of matter are to be disposed of. She should live for her immortal soul: "'Your day is Eternity!' 'Yes,' responds the girl, 'and the sunshine is blotted out of it!'" (ibid., 894). This incident contains a foreshadowing of the tale's ending, when it is discovered that precisely the material nature of the sacrifices that have been made ensures their futility. In moving to the level of individual desire, Hawthorne highlights the dialectic between deficiency and excess that his sketch explores. The bonfire is an inverted cargo cult, where people find salvation in ridding themselves of the objects and goods of advanced society rather than in acquiring them by magic. Not the appearance but the disappearance of a set of man-made trumperies is posited as miraculous. This is of course also the sense of the title since a holocaust is literally an offering to God. Such an inversion corresponds to that of social classes: The gathering at the bonfire does not represent an oppressed group. Although the ritual may be Native American, no Indians appear in the story—nor is slavery mentioned. Since the concrete social factors behind millennial movements are as absent as the actors in them, human desire and its boundless needs become the engine of apocalypse, to be represented at the end of the sketch in the symbol of the human heart.

Then the various war engines are thrown into the fire, followed by the instruments of capital punishment. The next stage of destruction is of all visible symbols that create obligation: Marriage certificates, paper money, ledger books, and legislation are all consigned to the flames. Finally, the works of all the authors of the earth are thrown onto the fire in a general book burning, followed by the vestments of religion and the Bible. Hawthorne comments on his own rewriting of Revelation when, in the climactic moment of the bonfire, the Bible itself is thrown onto the flames, "and then a mighty wind came roaring across the plain with a desolate howl, as if it were the angry lamentation of the earth for the loss of heaven's sunshine; and it shook the gigantic pyramid of flame and scattered the cinders of half-consumed abominations around upon the spectators" (ibid., 903–904). There is no longer any script to follow. The eschatological direction that the Bible had given to human history has given way to a cyclical, man-made pattern of destruction and renewal.

When these last items have been added to the bonfire, a bystander to whom Hawthorne expresses his dismay assures him that "there is far less, of both good and evil, in the effect of this bonfire, than the world might be willing to believe" (ibid., 904). The notions of millennium and apocalypse depend upon absolute distinctions between good and evil, as well as on the concept of the "end of history" and the possibility of stopping the changing distinctions between evil and good in order to reach a final decision. The bystander's remarks deny that distinction. In the brief responses to the conflagration (such as those the girl makes), we have seen that what was thought to be bad and useless was deemed worthy by some. At the end of the story the Devil appears and agrees with the bystander that "it will be the old world yet!" because the bonfire has not consumed "the human heart itself! And unless they hit upon some method of purifying that foul cavern, forth from it will re-issue all the shapes of wrong and misery" (ibid., 905). "Old world" refers not only to the people's accustomed way of going about their daily lives but also to their European inheritance, which they continue to carry with them as a repressed origin. Critics have tended to lambaste this ending for its cheapness or sentimentality, but I have shown here how the sketch anticipates this ending at every moment. Furthermore, by reading "Earth's Holocaust" against its millennial contexts, we can see that the image of the heart, representing human desire, genuinely confronts "conventional millennialism," to coin an oxymoronic phrase, with reflective dissonance.

As noted earlier, "Earth's Holocaust" reflects upon the historical event of Millerism. Hawthorne referred to "Father [William] Miller" repeatedly in his correspondence and sketches. In a letter to Horatio Bridge, Hawthorne jokingly cites inadequate financial responsibility as one of the "signs of the times" that might trigger the eschaton: "The system of slack payments in this country is most abominable, and ought of itself to bring upon us the destruction foretold by Father Miller" (March 25, 1843; Hawthorne 1984, 681). In "The New Adam and Eve," published during the height of Millerism, Hawthorne makes use of Miller's prophecies to pave the way for his neolapsarians:

> For instance, let us conceive good Father Miller's interpretation of the prophecies to have proved true. The Day of Doom has burst upon the globe and swept away the whole race of men. From cities and fields, sea-shore and midland mountain region, vast continents, and even the remotest islands of the ocean, each living thing is gone.

No breath of a created being disturbs this earthly atmosphere. But the abodes of man, and all that he has accomplished, the footprints of his wanderings and the results of his toil, the visible symbols of his intellectual cultivation and moral progress,—in short, everything physical that can give evidence of his present position,—shall remain untouched by the hand of destiny. (1843, 746)

Into this scene Hawthorne places the new Adam and Eve with no knowledge of their predecessors. The premise complements that of "Earth's Holocaust," where the visible signs are destroyed, but the postlapsarian despair remains unchanged.

The Millerite movement thus provides a second antitype for the happenings out on that prairie, a shadow behind the more obvious reformist movements that direct the proceedings. Readers of this tale have noted the movements themselves but not the shadow. For example, Hyatt Waggoner observes that Hawthorne's sketch

is dense with allusions to particular men and events, so much so that full explanatory notes would bulk as large as the piece itself. . . . Hawthorne's contemporaries, from Emerson and Ellery Channing to Mrs. Bloomer, and the chief reforming movements of his time, from the French Revolution to feminism and the Oneida Colony, enter the picture; but the central concern remains with the permanent nature of man and of history. (1963, 19)

In an astute article, Jonathan Cook proves that in this story, as in the other four "apocalyptic sketches" of *Mosses from an Old Manse*, premillenarianism (the supernatural bonfire and mob violence) and postmillenarianism (the idea of worldly reform) share the stage, reflecting "a basic ambivalence toward the conflicting claims of guilt and the possibilities for regeneration, an ambivalence mirroring both the dualistic universe of St. John's Revelation and America's traditional 'manic-depressive' syndrome that envisions either millennial success or doomsday failure for the culture" (1993, 238). This sharing of the stage, however, is structured in a peculiar fashion, one "inside" the other since the story shows a premillenial conflagration consuming the postmillennialists.

Hawthorne's story also rehearses Jean Baudrillard's theory of the simulacrum. This theory will not allow for an end to history because it will not allow for history itself. The last great historical event that pointed toward the end times was the squaring off of the United States and the Soviet Union in nuclear confrontation. Nuclear apocalypse became a subgenre of apocalyptic literature. Since the breaking up of the Soviet Union and the deflection of the possibility of mutually assured destruction, history seems no longer to have closure or direction, only more of the same. Consumer capitalism has triumphed but gives us no clear issues to take sides on. "Terrorism apart, is there not also a hint of this Parousiac exigency in the global fantasy of catastrophe that hovers over today's world? A demand for a violent resolution of reality, when this latter eludes our grasp in an endless hyperreality? For hyperreality rules out the very occurrence of the Last Judgment or the Apocalypse or the Revolution" (Baudrillard 1997, 255). The same contradiction inhabits apocalypse as the concept of "re-volution," which literally means a "turning back" rather than a "going forward."

As Christopher Keep points out, speed and urgency are characteristic of the apocalypse, the last words of Christ in the text of Revelation (22:20): "Surely I come quickly" is "an exhortation for *speed*" (1995, 267). Humankind's is a history of ever-increasing speed, which makes Christ's return seem ever slower, which makes space smaller and thus paradoxically leads to the claustrophobic end of history Baudrillard speaks of. His theory of inertia and hyperreality explains the almost comic nature of movements such as Heaven's Gate, in which the members of a cult took their own lives because they expected their souls to be hijacked onto a passing comet, and that of countless minor and more benign movements that link the eschaton to flying-saucer technology. It applies as well to the Branch Davidian siege, in which David Koresh's black Camaro was hauled away by an FBI truck as an act of symbolic castration and a slowing down of the movement's attempt to accelerate events toward the end of time. In a return to older varieties of millennium that took their cues from natural phenomena, Heaven's Gate pinned its hopes on a natural phenomenon rather than history or people. As the members were not crazy, deranged, or especially oppressed, their motives were not directed against people or governments but were linked to the hopelessness of hyperreality.

Fictions that pit millennial aspirations against the hyperreal tend to reveal what I call pseudomillennium: Their reflective dissonance derives from the shrinking of millennial activity down to a simulation exercise, as we have seen with Canudos fiction in the last chapter. Fictions that posit real possibilities of historical movement introduce reflective dissonance in the form of dystopia. That is, the millennial movement "succeeds," but the result is far from the joy and plenitude promised by Revelation, and its eschatechnologies are used for surveillance and control. Accounts based on historical events have the option of taking either approach to introducing reflective dissonance.

Pseudomillennium

Taken literally, Hawthorne's story presents a pseudomillennium, in which a small group of people believe that they are helping bring about the end of the world but where the larger context of the story shows how such a project must fail. In this section I treat three stories in which the "small group" consists of a single individual. The scenario of individuals believing that they are experiencing the eschaton could be portrayed as a pathology. However, these three stories emphasize the dissonance between an individual's historical and cultural situation and the circumstances within which that person's world ends.

Nowhere is this contrast more poignantly displayed than in the short story by Peruvian writer José María Arguedas (1911–1969), "La agonía de Rasu-Ñiti" [The Death of Rasu-Ñiti] (1962). A subtitle for this story might have been "The Last *Taki Onqoy* Dancer." In colonial Peru of the 1560s, the *Taki Onqoy* movement arose in the Huamanga region. The name literally means "dancing sickness." In this movement the "Andean *huacas* [gods or spirits]—no longer confined to rocks, waters, or hills—swept down on the natives, literally 'seizing' them, entering their bodies, and causing the 'possessed' to shake, tremble, fall, and dance insanely. . . . The seizure spiritually purified the possessed, who renounced Christianity and spoke for the reinvigorated native gods" (Stern 1982, 52). The conflict was symbolized through the Manichean war between the European *Dios*, a newcomer to the region, and the native *huacas*, who were seen moving through the air, starved from lack of sacrifice and destruction of their images. According to eyewitness Cristóbal Ximénez, "the basis [of the movement] was the Indians' belief that all the *huacas* of the kingdom that the Christians had burned had revived and were in two groups—some under the *huaca* Pachacama; and the others under the *huaca* Titicaca—with the purpose of giving battle to our Lord God, whom they already considered defeated" (Millones 1989, 15). The leaders of the movement prophesied the vanquishing of the Spaniards through the flooding of their cities. As Steve Stern notes, the *Taki Onqoy* represented a message that Andean society was giving itself in code: "that conflict between native *huacas* . . . and the European elements of colonial society was at once inescapable, irreconcilable, and decisive" (1982, 56). Pierre Duviols identifies it as a syncretistic movement: The one leader whose name has been preserved, Don Juan Chocne, was a Christianized *cacique* who named his two wives Maria and Magdalena (1971, 117–18).

Through a combination of reform and repression, the Spanish were able to drive the movement underground by the end of the 1560s. The founding of a true colonial society in the highlands by Francisco de Toledo, including an "Indian elite" and the adoption of Catholicism, relieved some of the tensions that had given rise to the movement. The *Taki Onqoy* survived as a "ritual of the sick." Still, the Andes remained a prime breeding ground for hybrid messiahs. In the eighteenth century, for example, Juan Santos Atahualpa (1711?–1756?) claimed to be the Holy Spirit. His theology drew parallels between two trinities: From Europe came the Father, Son, and Holy Spirit. These corresponded to the Incan positions of Sun God (Capac Inti), Huayna Capac, and Juan Santos Atahualpa. Atahualpa also saw the trinity as corresponding to three ages, perhaps showing the influence of the Franciscans' Joachimite beliefs. He claimed to be at once the son of Huayna Capac, of Christ, and of the Sun God and thus to be the "absolute God of America" (Zarzara 1994, 97).

The modern author Arguedas, a bilingual Quechua-Spanish speaker with a profound knowledge of Andean culture, ended the brief preface to a hymn of praise to the Inca god Tupac Amaru with this mysterious phrase: "Quechua is also a millennial language" (1962, 9). In part, Arguedas seems to have transferred onto the language itself his own millennial aspirations. The poem that follows speaks of the suffering of the native peoples of Peru under the "false Viracochas" of Spanish descent. ("Viracocha" was originally a Quechua term for a god, but Quechua speakers now use it to address their Spanish or mestizo masters.) His short story is an elegy for this millennial aspect. In this story, the *danzak* [dancer] Rasu-Ñiti dances the *Taki Onqoy* for himself as a death dance. He dons his outfit, which is, as Rita de Grandis points out in her reading of the story, a reminder of the syncretistic origins of the dance: "[T]he material is composed of precious Andean 'cintas elaboradas' (embroidered ribbons) and luxurious European silks and velvets, while his pants, jacket, and hat are tailored like those of a bullfighter's 'traje de luces' (sequined suit)" (1998, 59). In doing his dance, Rasu-Ñiti gradually crumples first one leg and then the other as his arms become paralyzed. Counterpointing this rhythm of progressive physical decrepitude is an increasing power of vision. As he dances, Rasu-Ñiti asks his family whether they can see what he sees: his family in the form of a condor. The condor (native to the Americas) is set in opposition to the landlord's horse (a European animal imported to the Americas). There is also a generational conflict: The *danzak*'s wife can see the condor spirit, but his daughters cannot:

> "Do you see the Wamani [god represented as a mountain] on your father's head?" the mother asked the older of her daughters.
> Silently, the three of them looked at him.
> "See it?"
> "No," said the elder.
> "You are not strong enough yet to see it. It's quiet, hearing all the heavens; seated on your father's head. Death makes it hear everything. What you have suffered; what you have danced; what you are still to suffer.
> "Do you hear a galloping of the boss's [del patrón] horse?"
> "Yes, she hears it," responded the dancer, although the girl had pronounced the words inaudibly. "Yes, she hears it! Also what the hooves of this horse have killed. The filth it has spattered you with. Listen as well to our god growing [el crecimiento de nuestro dios], who will swallow this horse's eyes. Not those of the boss. Without the horse he's just lamb dung." (ibid., 10)

Pseudomillennium is expressed most poignantly when the *danzak* puts words into his daughter's mouth and hears things that are not there to accompany his own vision. As a celebrated *danzak*, Rasu-Ñiti speaks for and sacrifices himself for his community and restores to the rite of the sick its millenarian vision of a world in which Indian values and spirituality will triumph. His wife and fellow musicians understand and are able to see the *wamani*, who is both a familiar of the dancer and a reminder of the traditional ways that the community is in the process of losing. In the dance, "the world's sacred order is . . . is restored for all Andeans. The privileged relation of the *danzak* with the *wamani* is through his dance and music rendered communitarian" (Castro-Klaren 1989, 182). Rasu-Ñiti's goal, no less than Arguedas's, is to reach the pseudomillennium of "utopía arcaica" (primitive utopia—the term is Mario Vargas Llosa's [1996], as is the revelation of the argument as chimerical), which preserves the Indians' communal values against modern society's devouring individualism.

If the background to Arguedas's pseudomillennium is a historical one of wholesale dispossession beginning with the conquest, that of Flannery O'Connor's "Judgment Day" is one of dispossession of the supposedly dominant race by the descendants of its slaves. White protagonist W. T. Tanner is forced to move into his daughter's New York City apartment when the land he was squatting on was purchased by Foley, a mixed-race doctor in Corinth, Georgia. Tanner has based his life upon his ability to handle "niggers": "He was known to have a way with niggers. There was an art to handling them" (O'Connor 1971, 536). Tanner blames his dispossession and the reversal of hierarchy on the government, presumably for its increasing enforcement of civil rights, which made the Deep South a battleground precisely in the midsixties, when this story was written. Sitting lost in his daughter's living room day after day, Tanner unleashes his *ressentiment* with visions of the eschaton, a "show" superior to what is playing on television. His daughter tries to distract him:

> "If you would let me pull your chair around to look at the TV, you would quit thinking about morbid stuff, death and hell and judgment. My Lord."

> "The Judgment is coming," he muttered. "The sheep'll be separated from the goats. Them that kept their promises from them that didn't. Them that did the best they could with what they had from them that didn't. Them that honored their father and their mother from them that cursed them." (ibid., 541)

When he tries to reestablish the accustomed social hierarchy with African American neighbors, Tanner's condescension eventually provokes a violent reaction and injury to himself. From that moment, he dreams only of getting to a boxcar and riding the train back to Corinth. Death and life mingle in his dream of return, according to his preoccupation with the resurrection of the dead for judgment. He dreams of his friends, Coleman and Hooten, receiving his coffin at the train station: "Even before [Hooten] had the upper end pried open, Coleman was jumping up and down, wheezing and panting from excitement. Tanner gave a thrust upward with both hands and sprang up in the box. 'Judgment Day! Judgment Day!' he cried. 'Don't you two fools know it's Judgment Day?'" (ibid., 546). Judgment day is the reversal of the current earthly rule by the "governmint" Antichrist and reestablishment of the patriarchal relations and supremacy of white skin Tanner had once enjoyed. His last rerun of this vision comes as he is lying upside down in the stairwell, having fallen while trying to make his getaway. He dreams of jumping out of his coffin and shouting "Judgment Day!" at his friend and servant, Coleman, but is actually gazing into the face of the same black neighbor who had previously acted aggressively toward him: " 'Judgment day,' he said in a mocking voice. 'Ain't no judgment day, old man. Cept this. Maybe this here judgment day for you'" (ibid., 549). An hour later Tanner is found dead, his arms thrust between the banister spokes and his legs dangling. The daughter ships her father's body home to Georgia, and the story ends with a reference to her resting well at night: no millennial dreams.

As the last quote indicates, this story ironizes the idea of judgment. The entire historical movement of liberation and democracy becomes a judgment on those like Tanner who have insisted on maintaining feudal relations. The parallels with the Arguedas story are remarkable, given the lack of direct influence. In both stories, the daughter is seen as the person who is to be educated in the vision of Judgment but who proves incapable of or uninterested in carrying on the tradition. In each story, the fervor and clarity of the vision are inversely proportional to the loss of physical vigor and to the accumulated dispossession of the visionary.

Like Arguedas and O'Connor, Josip Novakovich frames his story of pseudo-millennium in an act of dispossession: The aptly named hero, Daniel Marovich, persists in his Christian faith in Communist Yugoslavia and is denied employment. He emigrates to the United States and begins a long process in which his belief is chipped away, remolded, and brought to the brink of prophecy by a number of life crises over a thirty-year period. In a move distinct from the other mimeses of pseudomillennium, this contemporary book of Daniel introduces reflective dissonance as an echo of the protagonist's experienced dissonance. Significantly, one of the earliest events of the story has Daniel declining to learn English in favor of studying *koiné* Greek so that he can read the New Testament in the original. Daniel must work hard as a painter, and the noxious fumes give him dizzying headaches and kidney disease. His exhaustion causes him to stay in bed on Sundays rather than going to church. His daughter elopes and remains estranged from the family. Daniel experiences TV evangelism in the form of Reverend Schuyler of the "Hour of Power," who proclaims that with enough prayer anyone can become Miss America. "One more false prophet" (1998, 144), judges Daniel.

When war erupts between parts of the former Yugoslavia, Daniel becomes obsessed with learning the fates of his family members: "Gradually, he managed to hear from most of his relatives, but he still feared for their lives. But even more he feared for their souls; most of them were atheists" (ibid., 147). He is seduced by a woman in a house he is working on, and that night he gets drunk at a gathering ostensibly for helping Croatians under attack. The next morning, uneasy from having "so much trouble at once," Daniel reads Matthew 24, the so-called Little Apocalypse, which speaks of signs of the eschaton such as "wars and rumors of war" and nation rising against nation. Connecting this passage both with his life events and with world events, "Daniel panicked. The end of the world was coming. He did not know how fast—maybe there was a year to live. And he was not ready" (ibid., 150). Daniel discusses his vision with his wife and with a Baptist minister (twice), both of whom exhibit a Baudrillardian consumerist nonchalance regarding the topic. In the absence of spiritual guidance or confirmation of his belief by others, Daniel becomes obsessed with committing adultery once before the coming of Christ. His apocalypse is reconfirmed by a view of Cincinnati's smog and intense heat, where his shoes become stuck in the asphalt, and by the disappearance of his wife when he returns home, which seems to confirm Matthew 25:40–41: "Two women shall be grinding at the mill; the one shall be taken, and the other left." Daniel turns on CNN, expecting to see Christiana [*sic*] Amanpour reporting the second coming of Christ.

Daniel awaits the now imminent *parousia* in a park and is caught in a hailstorm, after which "[t]he air was cool now, cool and clear, as though the world was washed clean. Daniel felt a moment of sadness. He wondered whether God had changed his mind. What had happened? Like Jonah, who would have liked to see the destruction" (1998, 158). So far, Daniel follows Festinger's model—the various disconfirmatory signs and delays in the realization of his apocalypse only reconfirm his faith as he moves from New Testament signs of the end to the Old Testament story of Jonah to explain both his own frustration and God's secret plan for the earth. The final failure of prophecy, however, comes from the two women in Daniel's life. On returning home, Daniel learns that his wife has not been raptured but has left him for a coworker. When he dials the number of the woman who had seduced him, there is no answer: "Surely, she was not ascended, he thought, and the thought entertained him. As he laughed, he felt a terrible relief" (ibid., 159). Daniel's double laughter, of course, echoes that of the reader of this whimsical story as a symptom of reflective dissonance. Laughter, as Henri Bergson (1911) argues, is a corrective to deviant social behavior, which is not in this case adultery—since all of the characters are complicit in this, it becomes the norm—but Daniel's own stupidity or tunnel vision. Laughter is the explosive that collapses the prism of belief that has colored Daniel's vision of the world. Reversing the alimentary trajectory of John, the story begins bitterly and ends with a sweet taste. Its final paragraph gives Daniel/Jonah's antiapocalypse:

> He no longer believed in the end of the world and in the prophets, not even the prophets of global warming effect. He knew his reasoning was not quite right now, as it hadn't been right before, but he was sure that the granite faith of his trans-Atlantic youth was gone. The faith had through the years attenuated into a delicate crystalline structure that broke down the light—broke it down into the aura of transcendent, otherworldly, seeking and relishing extreme spectacles of collapse; and this fragile aesthetic faith crumbled in the heat, into a heap of glass dust that could no longer be resurrected into crystal, and that would be lost in the sand of the entropied world as a spittle in the ocean. (1998, 159)

Were Baudrillard to pick a mimetic text to illustrate his theory, he might well choose Novakovich's. Entropy is the randomization of energy, including in this story the energy of information. Throughout the story, images of consumerism abound of both products and, more interestingly, information. Religion appears as just another informational product for packaging and delivery, as in the reference to Schuyler and the Baptist minister who only wants to show Daniel his computer chess program. These come together in the expectation of CNN, the "always-on" news channel, reporting on the Second Coming. The last great apocalyptic scenario, the Cold War, had derandomized information so as to construct Daniel's crystalline structure, which is finally crushed by the entropy of consumerist gradualism. The date of this story, 1998, is important in this regard as it reports on the entropic 1989–2001 period—before "the day the world changed"—just as O'Connor describes the end of the Deep South in the 1960s under the influence of the Cold War, when civil rights were pushed in the United States as part of the effort to win Africa away from Communist influence.

Dystopian Millennium

Hawthorne's story falls short of being a dystopian millennium because it does not actually depict the society that results from millennial violence. However, the reflective dissonance introduced into the story in the spectators' increasingly dismayed responses prepares us for the Baudrillardian pronouncement at the end: "[I]t will be the old world yet!" It is, of course, hard to depict "more of the same" in an interesting way. Dystopian millennial fiction, then, focuses on the reflective dissonance of change and stasis, reflecting a glitch in the millennial notion of "utter transformation." Dystopian millennial fictions show profound change but with a remnant that is unchanged and becomes the focus of the fiction's conflict. A ready scenario for this is provided by the absence of gender issues in millennial discussions: The deaf shall hear and the lame shall walk; the first shall be last and the last shall be first, but women shall not be raised to equal status with men. Readers will have noted the relative paucity of women writers in this book, which perhaps reflects their relative scarcity as leaders of millennial movements (or history's obscuring their role).

Historically, besides the Publick Friend, discussed earlier, Ann Lee (who was born in England) of the Shakers would be one of the few "straight" millennialists of note.[2] Two of the three fictions that I discuss in this section make this remnant of gender inequality the basis of their dystopias.

The setting for the 1983 film *Born in Flames* is a postsocialist United States. The Revolutionary Party has triumphed in America. The party simply stands for the achievements of civil rights and other libertarian actions, which have left women's conditions largely untouched. Similarly, while the film appears to take place in the future, it uses documentary footage that is all too familiar: scenes from Harlem, demonstrations, and women's rights rallies. A terrorist martyr figure, the lesbian black feminist Adelaide Norris, struggles to change this "old world yet." Caught by the police while attempting to smuggle weapons into the United States from Africa, Norris is found dead in her prison cell the next day. In response, liberal feminists become radical feminists, and the war of the sexes begins. The film's last image is of a bomb exploding at the top of New York's World Trade Center. The bomb makes a pitifully small puff of smoke emerge from the building. By ending at this point, the film stresses not apocalypse but the immense inertia against which its protagonists are battling.

A similar background is provided in Bruce Sterling's near-future science fiction dystopia, *Islands in the Net* (1989). First published in 1988, it plays with the then up-coming 2000 milestone, making it coincide with the year that nations agreed to dismantle their nuclear weapons and armies and submit to an international police force called "Vienna," after the city where the accords were signed. The term *premillennial* in this novel designates the world we are used to, with nation-states, corporations, and wars. The millennium brings about multinationals like Rizome, which engage in corporate welfare and egalitarianism and whose associates cultivate their own fig trees. The postnational setting also raises NGOs such as the Red Cross and the successor to Interpol to equal-actor status with governments. Moreover, it pumps up the concept of data piracy, which certain postnations, such as Grenada and Singapore, engage in to raise a large part of their GNP. Predictably—too predictably—Sterling has Africa descend into a state of anarchy, out of which arises a terrorist-vigilante organization that starts a war. As in Donnelly, the major religions have lost all evangelical fervor and given in to crass sensualism. Sterling's vision is Hawthornian: Neither the abolition of weapons nor the complete internationalization of populations nor steps toward egalitarianism has done anything for peace.

Margaret Atwood's *Handmaid's Tale* (1985), however, provides a counterimage to Baudrillard's scenario of nonmovement. In this novel, set in the last decade of the twentieth century, millennium has been brought about precisely by Baudrillard's endless consumerism, which extended into pornography and the "control of one's own body." Excessive liberalism provoked an armed, ultraconservative revolt that set up a patriarchal, theocratic state dubbed Gilead. In Gilead, the handmaid-narrator, Offred, remembers items such as Pornomarts and Feels on Wheels vans for mobile prostitution. At her indoctrination center she is shown porno films as a reminder of the bad old days, as well as films of women's rallies of the seventies and eighties, with banners reading "RECAPTURE OUR BODIES" (ibid., 154). The repossessing of women's bodies by patriarchy is symbolized in the role of the handmaid, whose main function is to be fertilized by and to give birth for the elites. *Caesar's Column* contains a similar image in its prediction of millennium: "The rich man's daughters shall be their [the working classes'] hand-maidens; they will wear his purple and fine linen" (Donnelly 1890, 263). Here is a similar feeling of utter reversal based primarily in class distinctions that are present in Atwood's scenario but less emphasized than the crucial role of gender.

The commander to whom Offred is assigned gives her little gifts, among them an old copy of *Vogue*. Offred recalls the appeal of such magazines in Baudrillardian terms:

> What was in them was promise. They dealt in transformations; they suggested an endless series of possibilities, extending like the reflections in two mirrors set facing one another, stretching on, replica after replica, to the vanishing point. They suggested one adventure after another, one wardrobe after another, one improvement after another, one man after another. They suggested rejuvenation, pain overcome and transcended, endless love. The real promise in them was immortality. (Atwood 1985, 201)

The language here is apocalyptic, promising transformation, but also absurdly ironic. The phrase "replica after replica" points to the simulacrum. The immortality promised is not of salvation or awareness but of the endless repetition of the same. Furthermore, it is an apocalypse viewed from within a dystopic possible world. The promise of a future world where the lame shall walk and all participate in eternal life is recalled by someone living in a dystopic millennium, where she will be ceremonially raped and then forced to conceive and give birth.

A military coup gives the Gileadeans control of at least the northeastern part of the United States: "[T]hey shot the president and machine-gunned the Congress and the army declared a state of emergency. . . . That was when they suspended the Constitution. They said it would be temporary. There wasn't even any rioting in the streets. People stayed home at night, watching television, looking for some direction. There wasn't even an enemy you could put your finger on" (ibid., 225). The rebels, an extreme form of the religious right (Atwood took as her two main models the Puritans and the ayatollahs of the Iranian revolution), immediately institute a series of "invented traditions" combined with totalitarian control tactics designed to erase consumerism and liberalism from people's minds. From the narrator's perspective, the decisive element of the new regime is the removal of women's rights, including the right to have their own bank accounts. The emphasis on the individual body is replaced by ceremonies such as Birthings, where women give birth in front of other women and with the help of midwives, and Salvagings [*sic*], where women tear rebels and other offenders to pieces.

The word "apocalypse" occurs only once in the novel, as part of a name. Offred is watching a news report on television:

> Wooded hills, seen from above, the trees a sickly yellow. . . . The Appalachian Highlands, says the voiceover, where the Angels of the Apocalypse, Fourth Division, are smoking out a pocket of Baptist guerrillas, with air support from the

Twenty-first Battalion of the Angels of Light. We are shown two helicopters, black ones with silver wings painted on the sides. Below them, a clump of trees explodes. (ibid., 106)

The novel's reflective dissonance extends to the failed antitypes of this scene. The soldiers throwing explosives are named according to their function: the angel who blows his trumpet, for example, "and there followed hail and fire, mixed with blood, which fell on the earth; and a third of the earth was burnt up, and a third of the trees were burnt up, and all green grass was burnt up" (Rev. 8:7). It is not made clear in what way apocalypse could become a part of the official propaganda line of this regime since there seems to be no core belief to their system. Nor is it clear why Baptists would be organized to fight against the theocracy of Gilead, which is not shown to take any particular stand on theology.

This lapse of information is due in part to the apparently limited knowledge of the narrator, who may know more than she wishes to tell. Supposedly the narration is recorded onto a series of cassettes, so that there is a deliberate process of inclusion and exclusion of details and data. Offred has no interest in giving a theoretical picture of the society she lives in. Rather, her narrative alerts us to the feminist concerns that drive the story, over which the millennial references hang like so many paper moons. Atwood is not attempting to break into the masculinist business of writing the end times; au contraire, the plainness of Offred's confession and the uncertainty about her fate remind us of Susan Palmer's claim that "Apocalyptic dramas starring women have been comparatively rare and usually confined to esoteric circles" (1997, 160). Atwood is seeking to document the limited vocabulary of such narratives, which makes them hardly worth telling:

> Apocalypse always charges its batteries with sex/gender images, not originally as "essences" or "separate spheres" but as primal abhorrence: a male fantasy of a cosmic holocaust of other *males*, the oppressors, satisfyingly symbolized as Whorequeen and purged of female agency. In the lascivious sex of a powerful woman is inscribed the object of all endtime hatred. . . . Fundamentalist neo-Victorianism merely renders explicit what otherwise the social order sublimates and objectifies as its cryptoapocalypse." (Keller 1996, 253)

Indeed, "Victorian" seems exactly the right adjective for the novel's atmosphere, with quaint terms like "handmaid" and "commander."

In contradistinction to both *Born in Flames* and *Islands in the Net*, however, *The Handmaid's Tale* shares with millennial narratives a sense of utter transformation. It causes the reader to dwell on "re-volution" as a turning back. For readers at the time of the book's publication, the interest lay in the eeriness of seeing familiar landscapes with utterly changed purposes: The wall of an ivy-league school, for example (probably Harvard), is endowed with meat hooks for displaying the bodies of traitors who have been executed. A store that formerly sold lingerie now sells canned prayers, reminiscent of the medieval practice of indulgences (1985, 218).

Needless to say, there is nothing divine—only pseudodivine—about this transformation, although it is apparently sold to its victims as a "back to the Bible" movement. More interesting is the complete absence of ideology from the movement and also its ready appropriation of non-Christian traditions, if we are to judge by the scholarly paper given more than a century later by Gopal Chatterjee on "Krishna and Kali Elements in the State Religion of the Early Gilead Period" (ibid., 380). (Atwood, of course, could merely be satirizing academics' well-known tendency to see what they want to see in both texts and history.) There is in Gilead only a carefully arranged hierarchy and role-playing carried out under coercion. From Canudos to Waco, millennial movements have sprung from people's deepest desires to belong and to believe. In *Moby-Dick*, Ahab substitutes the usual flogging and physical disciplinary measures with the scene of the communion with his crew on the quarterdeck. He is, of course, the very image of a demagogue and false messiah, but he has no armed guard to enforce discipline. Over Starbuck's objections and in spite of the existence of differences among them, the crew does become attached to the purpose of killing the white whale. In *The Handmaid's Tale*, on the other hand, the extreme isolation of and separation between classes means a total lack of collectivity and communication among people. Revelation comes in the form of collective amnesia, though about different things. The commander, in giving some forbidden hand lotion to his handmaid, betrays complete ignorance of the conditions of total surveillance under which she lives:

> The trouble is, I said, I don't have anywhere to keep it.
> In your room, he said, as if it were obvious.
> They'd find it, I said. Someone would find it.
> Why? he asked, as if he really didn't know. Maybe he didn't. It wasn't the first time he gave evidence of being truly ignorant of the real conditions under which we live.
> They look, I said. They look in all our rooms.
> What for? he said. (ibid., 204)

These are the naïve questions of a commander, one of the architects of the transformed society. They are meant to show, among other things, a total gendering of the mechanism of surveillance—it is women who do the searching and enforce discipline. The narrator is, of course, equally ignorant of the commander's life and his concerns. Still a consumerist at heart, her conversations with the commander never broach the topic of the larger picture.

The narrative of *Handmaid's Tale* is set within the framework of a symposium held in 2195, several hundred years after Offred recorded her tapes. The participants' perspective on Gilead is much the same as ours, one of amusement and distaste. The analysis of Gilead clears up any doubts that it was a dystopia. Atwood has remarked that in this section she deliberately paralleled the epilog on Newspeak in George Orwell's *1984*. This epilog is hopeful because it is written in the past tense (2004, 516). Hence, the premillennial pseudohope of the Gileadeans is sublimated into a postmillennial view of a world that has gradually shifted the center of power. The symposium takes place in Nunavit, and the participants have names like Maryann Crescent Moon and Johnny Running Dog. A large part of North America, we assume (though not the Republic of Texas), has recognized its Native American status, as is foretold though not shown in Levar Burton's *Aftermath* (1997) and in Leslie Marmon Silko's *Almanac of the Dead* (1991), both discussed in chapter eight.

Defeated Millennium

As noted earlier, historical millennial fictions are for the most part restricted to depicting the exact circumstances of millennial defeat but have some choice in how they introduce reflective dissonance into their narratives. In this section I contrast two narratives in terms of their use of reflective dissonance. In depicting the Haitian revolution and its immediate aftermath, Alejo Carpentier's 1949 novel, *The Kingdom of This World*, takes the path of dystopian millennium. Mario Vargas Llosa's 1981 Canudos novel, *The War of the End of the World*, uses polyglossia and intertextuality to construct multiple pseudomillennia in its main characters.

The Haitian revolution that Cuban novelist Alejo Carpentier chose as material for his historical novel presented the opposite problem from most millennial movements: It was a military success, resulting in the independence of the island in 1803, whereas the resulting Republic of Haiti became an ongoing political disaster. The New Jerusalem as simulacrum is invoked at the end of *Kingdom of This World*. Carpentier names the hero of his novel "Ti Noël"—a name more or less equivalent to John Doe in English (though it may also indicate that he was born on Christmas)—and constructs the novel's time frame so that this character's long lifespan falls just within the conceivable. In the first three parts of the novel, Ti Noël shadows historical messianic figures of the black independence movement: Mackandal, who led a poisoning campaign against whites in the 1750s before he was caught and burned at the stake; Bouckman, who led a slave revolt in the 1790s; and Henri Cristophe, who ruled northern Haiti from 1820 until his death in 1824. This parallel composition of the novel and the gaps left in between important events contribute to an idea of cyclical history and, as Naomi B. Sokoloff puts it, "a denial of progress . . . and a stress on loss of self, that is, a presentation of characters less as individuals than as apsychological variants of one another" (1986, 145).

After Haiti's independence, Ti Noël builds his mansion from the ruins of the Mézy plantation (Mézy was Ti Noël's former owner) and from the random objects looted from Henri Cristophe's palace. He commands imaginary armies and is greeted, at least in his own mind, by the women as Christ entering Jerusalem: "When the women saw him approaching, they waved bright cloths in sign of reverence, like the palms spread before Jesus one Sunday" (ibid., 171 [183]). This vision is followed, however, by that of the land surveyors, who seek to replace Ti Noël's palimpsestic culture and hallucinatory pseudomillennium with the rational engineering of the foursquare. Fleeing mulatto rule, Ti Noël attempts to become animal but is oppressed by the ants and rejected by the clannish geese. He realizes in the end the futility of millennial hopes:

> In the Kingdom of Heaven there is no grandeur to be won, inasmuch as there all is an established hierarchy, the unknown is revealed, existence is infinite, there is no possibility of sacrifice, all is rest and joy. For this reason, bowed down by suffering and duties, beautiful in the midst of his misery, capable of loving in the face of afflictions and trials [capaz de amar en medio de las plagas], man finds his greatness, his fullest measure, only in the Kingdom of This World. (ibid., 185 [197])

The quotation reverses Revelation 11:15: "Then the seventh angel blew his trumpet, and there were loud voices in heaven, saying, 'The kingdom of the world has become the kingdom of our Lord and of his Christ, and he shall reign for ever and ever.'" The original statement gains special importance from following the seventh and last angel, who completes the process of destruction and transformation. The word "plagas" in Carpentier alludes to the vials that are poured out upon the earth, which in the context of the novel become the historical plagues of slavery, war, poverty, racism, and political oppression. At the first trumpet, hail and fire fall on the earth and burn a third of it. In Revelation, at the second trumpet, a great mountain falls into the sea and turns it to blood, killing a third of the creatures and destroying a third of the ships. By the time we get to the sixth angel, warriors are released on the earth to kill a third of its population. But the "plagas" are also the various forms of destruction, especially slavery, which man uses against man. Those in Revelation find parallels in the repeating cycle of violence in revolutionary Haiti. McKandal uses poison against the whites. Bouckman announces the armed insurrection, which takes its cue from the principles of the French Revolution. In the uprising, Ti Noël sacks his master's house and rapes and murders his wife. When the French briefly retake control of the island, they commit violence against the blacks, beheading them and feeding them to the dogs. Henri Cristophe, king of the north of Haiti after the defeat of the French army, uses violence against his own people in order to enrich himself. The response is another revolution and another sack, this time of Henri Cristophe's palace, and the coming into being of a nativist church of the savanna. Finally, the mulatto regime is established, which dispossesses Ti Noël.

Carpentier has been criticized for skewing the history of the Haitian uprising and for passing over important figures such as Toussaint l'Ouverture in favor of trivial ones such as Pauline Bonaparte. However, Carpentier's motives for this stem from his desire to place syncretistic aspects of Haitian history and culture front and center and to make events follow Revelation's cyclical patterns. There may be yet another reason: Carpentier claims to have been expecting (since his adolescence) the revolution on his own island—Cuba (1968–1969, 127). In the 1920s he had spent some days in jail for political activities against the Cuban regime. It seems logical that his interest in Haiti as a subject of fiction stems from its unique revolutionary position in the Americas: It was the second nation to achieve independence and the first to do so through a true revolution. Fidel Castro and Che Guevara wanted their revolution to have a transformative effect on their population. "The Cuban Revolution's official morality was anormalization and extension into everyday life of the virtues exemplified by the guerillas in the Sierra Maestra, including austerity, discipline, abnegation, and comradeship. . . . The emerging new society would have to 'compete fiercely' with the patterns of a corrupt past, but new generations would be born 'free of "original sin"'" (Graziano 1999, 71). While this novel predates Castro's success, it is conceivable that revelationary prophecy is revolutionary rhetoric in disguise.

One is inclined to agree with Ana Serra (1995) that history appears in this novel as a simulacrum. In his seminal study of Carpentier's work, Roberto González-Echevarría (1977) describes in minute detail the carefully planned architectonics of the novel, with carnival occurring halfway through and apocalypse at the end. The interpretation must be first of a world ruled by Satan or Antichrist but then of a Baudrillardian world in which simulacrum and pattern destroy every attempt at finding meaning:

The numerical disposition in Carpentier's text does not lead ultimately to faith, but rather to positing the existence of one of Borges's minor gods who assemble a complex and precise game of affinities only to perish in the kingdom of this world on completing their work. . . . And in fact, the one who metaphorically rules the Kingdom of This World is Satan . . . who within the text—in the web of its history—attempts to exert control over all destinies. But all these systems are simulacra, semblances of order . . . schemes that fail or are revealed as lies and imposture. (ibid., 146–47)

However, the seventh angel does not destroy but only announces the effects of the previous destruction, which has been utterly transformative. The phrase "kingdom of this world" shows the end of the process and emphasizes that God's plan is for a terrestrial paradise and not just for souls to go up into heaven. The distance between the two spheres is collapsed in the image of the New Jerusalem, which is handed down from heaven. Irlemar Chiampi argues analogously that Carpentier wishes to enact through this novel the "non-contradiction between mythology and history" (2004, 58). This noncontradiction would be a viable definition of the "real maravilloso" (marvelous real, with obvious ties to so-called magic realism) that Carpentier sought to define in a prologue to the novel and to embody in most of his later fiction. However, the novel and its title explicitly reject the mythology of Revelation as a basis for history. I wish to emphasize the telluric aspect of Carpentier's much-discussed theory. The apprehension of the marvelous real is a cognitive-sympathetic process that presupposes an openness to environment, an ability to live in "this world" rather than in a textually constructed divine plan. "This world" is opposed not only to the world beyond the eschaton but also to the New World, which creates its own telluric narratives while discarding or radically transforming the templates brought from the Old World.

Vargas Llosa for President—of Brazil!

> For me [Canudos] was like seeing in a small laboratory the pattern of something that had been happening all over Latin America since the beginning of our independence. All Latin American countries have had more or less similar situations. . . . [I]n contemporary Latin America you still have Canudos in many countries. In Peru, for instance, we have a living Canudos in the Andes.
>
> —Mario Vargas Llosa,
> *A Writer's Reality*

In 1981 Peruvian author Mario Vargas Llosa published his fifth novel, *La guerra del fin del mundo* (hereinafter *GFM*), considered by many critics as one of the finest novels ever produced in Spanish America. In 1987 he ran for the presidency of Peru but lost in a runoff to Alberto Fujimori, who would hold power for ten years before leaving in disgrace for Japan. Are these two events connected? The epigraph at the beginning of this section suggests that they are: *GFM* narrates an epochal defeat (and not just of Canudos) that Vargas Llosa then experiences in person. Of course, there are a variety of other sources beyond history and personal political views for Vargas

Llosa's own favorite among his novels, including Joanot Martorell's Catalán master-piece, *Tirant lo Blanch*. According to Franklin de Oliveira, "Vargas Llosa's known elective affinities with this chivalric romance of the waning of the Iberian middle ages assured his novelistic treatment [tratamento romanesco] of the Canudos theme, the epic of Brazilian exceptionalism" (1983, 65).

In one sense, in his presidential run Vargas Llosa was simply trying to over-come with the force of his personality the disjunction between Latin American in-tellectuals and Realpolitik. According to Vargas Llosa himself, it was Euclides da Cunha more than any other author who had opened his eyes to the origins of the problem. Da Cunha's analysis, in *Os sertões*, of the disjunction between European-ized, coastal society in Latin America and the indigenous, mestizo populations of the interior explains why the intellectuals in Latin America, no matter what the political stripe of their writings, have never been able to speak for its people. Without using it directly as a literary source, Vargas Llosa wrote around *Os sertões*, recognizing its importance and grandeur and converting da Cunha into a character—the near-sighted journalist. Despite the immense amount of specific detail that locates the novel in Brazil of 1897, Vargas Llosa wrote his novel "to present in fiction the description of a continental phenomenon" (1991, 133).

Foremost among the villains in Vargas Llosa's list of pseudoengaged intellectu-als are the Marxists, represented in the novel by the character Galileo Gall. Their application of an abstract theory developed in Europe and Asia (the infamous *Sen-dero Luminoso*, or Shining Path, guerillas of Peru are Maoists) to the heterogeneous situations of the Americas has left them out of touch with the reality of the oppressed they are supposedly trying to help. Vargas Llosa thus repudiates his own earlier writ-ings and ideology, when he supported the Cuban revolution. His bibliography reveals that he has gone from "a political and literary position [of leftist engagement] to his current standing as spokesperson for the neo-liberal right and for Flaubert's tradition of the objective, disengaged narrative" (Stiegler 1998, 168). Vargas Llosa simultane-ously admits, in a 1996 study, *La utopía arcaica* (Primitive Utopia), that José Maria Arguedas's novels are the only Peruvian narratives he feels a strong relationship to, while nevertheless rejecting, as the title suggests, Arguedas's view of the indigenous world as a paradise destroyed by Spanish conquest. Thus, we might expect the kind of structure that in fact the reader experiences in *GFM*, which simply reimagines the phenomenon of Canudos as a sequence of possible worlds seen through different lenses, without opting for any one of these in particular—or rather, by taking sides equally against all. Significantly, for example, the last words of the novel—"I saw them [Yo los vi]" (Vargas Llosa 1981, 568 [531])—are spoken by an elderly survivor of Canudos who has "seen" João Abade raptured to heaven by the archangels. Vargas Llosa—who is well aware of the traditional view of Abade as one of the most mor-ally flawed and hypocritical defenders of Canudos—throws in the reader's face an absolute epistemological divide that is in one sense the source of the conflict. The positivists can kill their opponents and assume their position of barbarism, but they are unable to make them see things differently.

Enrique Krauze agrees with Vargas Llosa that *GFM* addresses an American problem; in fact, the novel was prophetic. True to its role as prophecy, *GFM* was misunderstood by the majority of critics at the time of its appearance:

Most Latin-American intellectuals read [*GFM*] without perceiving its hidden prophecy, of the bloody appearance of university messianism, or of the messianism of the guerillas of El Salvador who during the 80s tore their country and themselves to pieces, or that of the Sandinistas who, disdainful of freedom and democracy, felt themselves to be sole possessors of Truth, morality, and History, and of the most terrible messianism of all, which murdered peasant children in order to better instruct them in the ethics of the New Man: *Sendero Luminoso*. (Krauze 1993, 19)

In his memoir, *A Fish in the Water* (1994), Vargas Llosa implicitly compares the Sendero Luminoso to the Canudenses. Several of his own campaign workers and other candidates of the United Front were assassinated by the Sendero Luminoso simply because they represented the electoral path to change. As Ilan Stavans (1993) points out in a Plutarchian comparison of parallel lives, Carlos Reynoso, the founder of Sendero Luminoso, is Vargas Llosa's shadow. The two intellectuals were born just two years apart in the town of Arequipa and attended two different branches of the same Catholic boy's school. Both attempted to control the fate of Peru, using, of course, very different means to attain this goal. They shared a common root in the writings of Mariateguí, though Vargas Llosa came to this writer through the intermediary of José María Arguedas.

Nor does *Fish in the Water* completely lack apocalypse, though, as we might expect from Vargas Llosa, it is an intertextual and ironical one. After polling only a few percentage points more than the unknown Fujimori in the first round, Vargas Llosa contemplates handing the presidency to the latter in exchange for compromise on reform issues. He receives a visit from Monsignor Vargas Alzamora, archbishop of Lima:

[H]e told me that every morning, as soon as he got up, he always read a few pages of the Bible, opened at random. What chance had placed before his eyes that morning amazed him: it seemed to be a commentary on current events in Peru. Did I have a Bible at hand? I fetched the Jerusalem version and he told me which chapter and verses he was referring to. I read them aloud and the two of us burst out laughing. Yes, it was true, the intrigues and misdeeds ablaze with the fires of hell committed by that Evil One of the holy book were reminiscent of those of yet another one, more terrestrial and closer at hand. (1994, 478)

Together, the liberal secular novelist and the Catholic patriarch engage in a typological reading of Peruvian politics. In sixteenth-century Europe, accusations of the Antichrist flew back and forth between the Catholic and Protestant churches. His type has now been summoned from the vasty deep by Peru's small evangelical churches—sects that had "become more and more deeply involved with the marginal sectors of Peruvian society, filling the vacuum left by the Catholic Church because of the scarcity of priests" (ibid.)—and placed in the person of Fujimori. These were precisely the conditions of the *sertão* that gave rise to the Counselor a century before. Furthermore, as the evangelicals lined up behind Fujimori and the Catholic Church began to react, the runoff election "came to resemble a religious war. . . . [S]ome of the evangelical organizations, above all the most bizarre of them, believed, following the success attained by their candidates for seats in Congress, that the time had come to declare open war on the 'papists'" (490–91).

In fact, the symmetrical arrangement of Sendero Luminoso and evangelical churches in their competition for Peruvian souls indicates their common origins in the messianic heritage of native peoples. Anthropologist Juan M. Ossio draws a parallel between the syncretism of both institutions and the development of so-called *chicha* music in Lima, which combines Andean melodies with tropical rhythms and electric instrumentation: "Parallel to the continuation of the myth of Inkarrí, we see today the proliferation of a nexus of religio-political movements, some peaceful and others violent, which express themselves in the language of foreign ideologies. Neither the new music nor these renewed systems of beliefs directly make use of Andean symbols. Nevertheless, one can detect that this cultural tradition is always present" (1994, 58). The myth of Inkarrí—that is, *Inca rey* or the Inca king—recounts that the Inca was a god or half-god, killed by the Spanish. His head was buried in Cuzco, and his body is growing downward from it. When it completes its growth, he will come again: "When [his body] has been reconstituted, then perhaps will the Judgment take place" ("El Mito de Inkarrí" 1956, 181). Thus, "messianic fanaticism" is certainly a key term that can be used to link Peru with Canudos, and we have seen that Vargas Llosa admired *Os sertões* for its analysis of the disconnection of intellectuals from reality, which is the topic of this chapter of *Fish*, titled "Cut-Rate Intellectuals." In fact, Vargas Llosa himself fell prey to this disconnect, as he underestimated Fujimori's appeal to the evangelicals.

How does this analysis reveal itself, then, in the structure and texture of *GFM*? The conflicts of the novel are driven by four mutually exclusive—though in certain respects comparable—worldviews: the patriarchal, represented by the Baron of Canabrava (and his godson, Rufino); the religious-millennial, represented by the Counselor and his followers; the republican, represented by the commander of the third espedition, Moreira César; and the socialist-revolutionary, represented by Galileo Gall. Of these, only the baron escapes fanatical adherence to ideas, which seem to have lodged instead in his godson and the peasant laborers. The novel's multiple points of view are shown through the fragmentation of the narrative into separate "tracks" or narrative pathways that connect with and overlap each other.

To begin with the last of these, do not Gall's words—subtracting the reference to Satan—resemble those of the Sendero? "[N]ot God but Satan—the first rebel—is the true prince of freedom, and . . . once the old order was destroyed through revolutionary action, the new society, free and just, would flower spontaneously" (Vargas Llosa 1981, 16 [26]). The reception of this foreign preaching in Salvador is not enthusiastic: "Although there were some who listened to [Gall], in general people did not appear to pay much attention to him" (ibid.). The preceding segment had described the contrasting success of the Counselor's preaching, which, like Gall's, invokes an eschaton, but one to be brought about by obedience and self-denial rather than violence. Gall brings a socialist ideology born out of European industrial conditions—he fought for the Paris Commune—to an area of Brazil still ruled by feudal conditions. He is struck by the differences between Europe and Bahia:

> [W]hat Galileo Gall was interested in was not the beauties of Bahia; it was, rather, the spectacle that had never ceased to rouse him to rebellion: injustice. Here, unlike Europe, he explained in his letters to Lyons, there were no segregated residential

districts. "The mean huts of the wretched lie side by side with the tiled palaces of the owners of sugar plantations and mills. . . . Any revolutionary whose convictions as to the necessity of a major revolution are wavering"—he wrote in one of his letters—"ought to take a look at what I am seeing in Salvador: it would put an end to all his doubts." (ibid., 33 [42–43])

To use Ossio's insight, Gall's socialism represents the importation of a European symbolic system, whose success in the New World realizes itself only in Gall's own mind. His messianism remains disconnected from millennial energies because millennial movements such as Canudos seek a restoration of values that are under attack rather than a new set of theoretically derived ones. Gall's ignominious death halfway through the narrative—he and Rufino, whose wife Gall raped, kill each other in the mud—points to the inadequacy of his conception.

Moreira César plays the patriarchal republican, the one capable of carrying out the *volonte générale* as opposed to Gall's *volonté de tous*. The Baron de Canabrava compares him to Gall as a "dreamer." When Gall takes up the thread of the conversation again, "dreamer" has been transformed into "idealist":

> "Yes, he too is a dreamer [soñador]. Though his dreams and yours don't coincide" . . .
>
> "An idealist?" Gall's voice took him by surprise. "A man reputed to have committed so many atrocities?" . . .
>
> "Does it strike you as odd that Colonel Moreira César is an idealist?" he replied, in English. "He is one, there's no doubt of that. He's not interested in money or honors, and perhaps not even in power for himself. It's abstract things that motivate him to act: an unhealthy nationalism, the worship of technical progress, the belief that only the army can impose order and save this country from chaos and corruption. An idealist of the same stamp as Robespierre." (ibid., 244, 247 [236, 240])

Moreira César plays Robespierre to Gall's Danton. Like Gall, Moreira César dies through his own fault as he leads the third expedition into a Canudos he believes to be incapable of coherent defense.

The Canudos side of the story garners sympathy today in part due to intellectuals' skepticism toward republics. Some Brazilians during the failed 1980s' presidencies of José Sarney and Fernando Collor, for example, would fondly reminisce about the days of military dictatorship (or, at times, of the empire), when corruption was supposedly less. Moreira César appears to many as a greater, more violent fanatic than the Counselor. When Moreira César describes the state of the early Brazilian republic, its fragile nature very much resembles that of Peru or the "classic" Latin American state. He accuses the monarchist Canabrava of sabotaging the republic:

> Objectively these people [of Canudos] are the instruments of those who, like yourself, have accepted the Republic the better to betray it. . . . There is now a civilian president, a party rule that divides and paralyzes the country, a parliament where every effort to change things can be delayed and distorted thanks to the ruses of which you people are past masters. . . . Well, you people are mistaken. Brazil will not go on being the fief that you have been exploiting for centuries. That's what the army is for. To bring about national unity, to bring progress, to

establish equality among all Brazilians, to create a strong, modern country. (ibid., 217 [213])

Here is an entire theory of the Latin American state, as applicable to Peru as to Brazil and expressing from the inside the aspirations of the more idealistic military leaders. Who else, besides the military, would be able to free Peru from the terror of the Sendero Luminoso, or other countries from equally fanatical leftist movements?

In order to effectively communicate the opposition between these points of view, Vargas Llosa presents an oddly utopian, anodyne picture of the Canudos community by reducing it to a single shared viewpoint. In comparing Vargas Llosa's presentation of the Canudenses to those by Brazilian authors, as explored in the previous chapter, one is struck by the relative harmony and single-mindedness of the peasant's goals and by the complete absence of hypocrisy. Even as sympathetic an author to their cause as Afonso Arinos depicts intrigues, machinations, and jealousy within the Canudos community. Not so Vargas Llosa, who refuses even to carry on the traditional depictions of João Abade's lubricity or Antônio Vilanova's cupidity. Economic motivations for the popularity of Canudos are scarcely mentioned. There are two explanations for this authorial strategy. One, the avoidance of additional complications, has been mentioned at the beginning of this paragraph. The other is Vargas Llosa's admiration for *Os sertões*, which also depicts complete harmony—that of collective insanity—within Canudos in order to build up the chiliastic vision of two worldviews in mortal combat. Vargas Llosa's highly intertextual work explores many more viewpoints, including one of literally not viewing, represented in the unnamed, nearsighted journalist. The reflective dissonance that results from the polyglossia and contradiction of this text could be seen as a response to Carpentier's collapse of history and mythology. These two monuments of Latin American possible worlds, then, *Kingdom of This World* and *War of the End of the World*, both engage in a reflective dissonance in which their respective authors see their own millennial situations mirrored in those of another land, people, and language.

Like Carpentier and Vargas Llosa, Ernesto Cardenal, one of Latin America's greatest living poets, shared an early enthusiasm for Marxism and the Cuban revolution; like those authors, Cardenal perceives the religious and millenarian dimensions of political revolution. Unlike the novelists treated in this chapter, however, Cardenal has kept his millenarian faith and written in the cause of fully participatory apocalypse, not of reflective dissonance. The next chapter examines an eschatechnological image Cardenal has found to express his own version of archaic utopia: golden flying saucers.

Golden UFOs: Ernesto Cardenal and Millennial Ufology

The Mother of Planes . . . is a small human planet made for
the purpose of destroying the present world of the enemies
of Allah. . . . The small circular-made planes called flying
saucers, which are so much talked of being seen, could be
from this Mother Plane. This is only one of the things in
store for the white man's evil world.

—Elijah Muhammad, *Message to the Blackman in America*

Before they said Ibeorgun came in a cloud of gold,
now in a flying saucer of gold.

—Ernesto Cardenal, *Golden UFOs*

E schatechnology harbors a double, self-contradictory longing: that technology can create a palpable God or bring about salvation, but also that God can somehow put a stop to a technology that serves itself rather than people or the earth. Like the surface doctrine of the separation of church and state, which only hides a deeper intertwining, so too does the supposed incompatibility of faith and science conceal the fact that "investigators may be laboring under a scientized faith with convictions that border on the millennial or chiliasm. . . . American culture is suffused with technological millennialism" (Bozeman 1997, 141, 155). While the number of core believers in eugenics, cryonics, uploading of consciousness, and space colonies as postmillennial projects may be few, their futurist concepts have broad appeal for literature and film. Millennial ufology represents a highly visible and endlessly varied secularization of eschatology.

I take here the definition of millennial ufology given in the *Encyclopedia of Millennialism and Millennial Movements* as a subculture consisting of "individuals and organizations who are focused on the phenomenon of UFOs, extraterrestrials, intergalactic civilizations, and interstellar or interdimensional travel and contact. . . . Rather than angels or the messiah emerging from the clouds to battle the Antichrist and redeem the chosen, the messiah is a benevolent interstellar space traveler, returning to Earth to rescue his space brothers from sinister 'gray' aliens and the ravages inflicted on the planet by technology and pollution" (Lamy 2000, 410). As Michael

Barkun notes, UFO narratives fit the eschatological type for the end of history: "[UFO] material combines an unprecedented event—the arrival of intelligent, non-human species—with groups that are demonically evil, made up either of human beings alone, or aliens, or some pernicious alliance between the two. Once these elements are in place, one need not engage in much elaboration to envision an end to ordinary history" (2003, 170–71).

This chapter explores the relation of technology, extraterrestrialism, and millennium as developed in the writings of Nicaraguan poet Ernesto Cardenal (1925–). Cardenal uses the UFO motif to link first with last things, alpha with omega, Indian with European. As far as I know, Catholic priest and former minister of culture Ernesto Cardenal is neither a ufologist nor someone who has been contacted by aliens or been aboard their spacecraft (the technical term for the latter is "experiencer"). If he were merely an agnostic, he would find himself in fairly good company with Carl G. Jung and John Mack; if a believer, he would join Billy Graham, Hal Lindsey, José Argüelles, and Salvador Freixedo. If an experiencer, then he could exchange notes with Elijah Muhammad and Louis Farrakhan. Cardenal is, however, perhaps the most apocalyptic poet of the Americas, and that allows him to use UFOs in the title of his 1993 poetry collection, *Los ovnis de oro* [Golden UFOs; hereinafter *Ovnis*] as symbols of the millennial changes he desires. Among those hoped-for changes is the return to the native peoples of the Americas (or to their mestizo descendents à la Riel) of their land, their cultures, and their voices. *Ovnis* supposedly empowers First Nations by merging the prophetic voice of the poet with stories out of the *Popol Vuh*, the *Chilam Balam*, the Ghost Dance, and other prophetic books and movements of the Americas. Taken theologically, Cardenal's poetry implies that Americans should seek the true religions of this continent, which have hitherto been driven underground. Catholicism must become more like ufology, that is, more hybridized and apocalyptic, if it is to respond to American concerns.

The implication of an emergent form of spirituality in Cardenal's title resonates with the development of new UFO religions, including the best-known and probably largest of these, the Raelians. The dialectic of technology is crucial here: Ufologists posit that beings with advanced, "good" technology will be able to save us from the present, "bad" technology. It is possible that the increased pace of technological development—exponentially accelerating since technological innovations are then used to create new developments, as in the classic image of robots making robots—has caused the discernible growth in UFO religions. In North America, the first great wave of UFO sightings occurred in 1896 and 1897—shortly following the defeat of millennial movements such as the Ghost Dance and Canudos—and produced no lasting religions. These dates fall, readers will notice, in the period of tribulations discussed in chapter three. A new wave of sightings began in 1947—the opening of the nuclear age can be hypothesized as a proximate cause—and continued through the 1950s, spawning groups such as the Aetherians, Unarius, and Urantia. The stage of abduction witnessing began a decade later, with John G. Fuller's *Interrupted Journey* (1966), a book that tells the story of a New Hampshire couple abducted and experimented upon by aliens. The discovery of DNA's role in the biological code seems to have furnished an explanation for what exactly the aliens wanted from us: our genes. This genetic-harvesting theme has continued with the Raelians, perhaps the largest and most newsworthy UFO religion, who made headlines starting in the late 1990s for founding Clonaid, one of the first institutes dedicated to cloning a human being. In 1997 they announced the birth of a cloned human girl, but no one from the wider public has yet seen this individual (see the institute's website at http://www.clonaid.com).

Raelian theology centers on the reinterpretation of biblical creation as a technologized cloning event. A French citizen named Claude Vorilhon was visited by the Elohim of a UFO for six consecutive days beginning on December 13, 1973. Vorilhon eventually took the prophetic name of Raël, which is the latter part of the name "Is-rael" and means "bearer of light"; thus, Raël's self-naming impulse was parallel to that of Columbus, who chose the Greek version of the term. Raël then wrote his first, foundational text, *Le livre qui dit la vérité* [The Book That Tells the Truth]. Like the Rastafarians, Raël transmits the message that the Bible gives only a confused record of reality. For Raelians, not racism but technological incompetence is the problem, as Susan Palmer summarizes:

> [T]he book of Genesis is a ship's log recounting a scientific research project that sparked a bioethical debate on the Elohim's home planet. The creation of humans and the science lessons taught to Adam and Eve were surreptitious and illegal acts, resulting in the expulsion from Eden and the Flood. Yahweh was the head scientist who created life on earth, and Lucifer was the name of the Elohim's political party that decided to give humans awareness of their artificial origins (hence the ability and responsibility of humans, in turn, to clone human beings in homo sapiens' image in the future). (2004, 35)

The Raelians participate in a number of activities, such as sex education, peace advocacy, and attempts to dismantle the Vatican, that are meant to prepare the world for the return of the Elohim in their spacecraft in 2035. Above all, to greet the aliens they raise money to build a huge embassy analogous to other groups' efforts to rebuild the temple in Jerusalem.

The intersection of ufology with themes of cloning and government conspiracy in the popular 1990s' television series *X-Files* (which coincidentally aired its last episode shortly after 9/11), should alert us to the hold these ideas have on the American imagination. Eric von Däniken had provided a holistic explanation in his best-selling *Chariots of the Gods?* (1969): UFOs were not a new development in human history, he argued but were in fact the basis for ancient religions and holy sites in the first place. Benighted humans had misidentified UFO astronauts as gods, angels, and Ezekiel's wheel. The 1970s saw the development of alien grammatology in the form of so-called crop circles that appeared in many countries. These "agriglyphs" were interpreted as indecipherable messages left for us by visitors from other planets and can be related to DNA as yet another form of alien hieratic writing.

In what follows, I explain the millenarian dimensions of ufology and then move to the texts of *Ovnis* and show how this book intersects with some of ufology's basic ideas. Textual analysis shows that Cardenal is particularly interested in cyclical notions of time that condense the eschatechnological with prophetic traditions of the last becoming first.

Ufology as Millennialism

Millennialism provides the central religious script for ufology. Daniel Wojcik notes that, like previous millenarian worldviews, "UFO traditions often provide systems of meaning for understanding human existence and promise believers that the universe is ordered, that evil and suffering will be eliminated and that an age of harmony and justice will be established through the fulfillment of a cosmic plan" (2003, 274). We recall Norman Cohn's five necessary elements in the belief structures that power millenarian movements: Salvation is to be collective, terrestrial, imminent, utterly transformative, and miraculous (1970, 13). Ufology displays all of these elements as it seeks to convince followers that an advanced civilization has arrived on earth and will utterly transform our lives with its science and technology, which in comparison with ours can only appear to be miraculous. The second main UFO doctrine, that we are either descended from aliens or will soon leave earth to join an alien civilization, is clearly an alternate, symmetrical version of the first. Humans are to be transformed through recognizing what they already are. Either version sees the utter transformation of human life as imminent and as happening in the physical world rather than in heaven or the afterlife. Notably, UFO experiences rarely interpret personal salvation into their experience; rather, they tend to emphasize its import for the larger collective. They see themselves as called on to convey a message concerning the earth's fate. Along with Raël's 2035 date, typical of millennial prophecy is the prediction by the Unarius Academy of Science for a mass starship landing in 2001 (Heard 1999, 26–27) and the automatic writings of the prophet Marian Keech, who channeled the alien Sananda and predicted a cataclysm that would submerge the West Coast of the Americas from Seattle to Chile in 1952.

The latter, together with her followers, became the subject of Leon Festinger's celebrated study, *When Prophecy Fails* (1964), discussed in chapter three. One can discern in Keech's prophetic language an attempt at both biblical formulation and poetic mysticism as she introduces new words such as "sibet" and "carting" as though untranslated from the alien tongue (approximate translations of these terms into English are shown in square brackets):

> "And the scenes of the day will be as mad. The grosser ones will be as mad. And the ones of the light will be as the sibets [students] of teachers who have drilled them for this day. . . . In the carting [plan] it is cast [prophesied] that the event will begin at dawn and end swiftly as a passing cloud—in the seen.
>
> "When the resurrected have been resurrected or taken up—it will be as a great burst of light . . . the ground in the earth to a depth of thirty feet will be bright . . . for the earth will be purified.
>
> "Yet the land will be as yet not submerged, but as a washing of the top to the sea, for the purpose of purifying it of the earthling, and the creating [of] the new order. Yet will it be of the LIGHT, for all things must first be likened unto the housecleaning, in which the chaos reigns first, second the ORDER." (ibid., 56)

Alien prophetic discourse, as conveyed by Keech, combines biblical metaphor ("swiftly as a passing cloud") with Pentecostal neologisms ("sibet," "carting") and the banal language of domestic American life ("housecleaning"). Cardenal, I would argue, presents an analogous yearning for constructing a new, heteroglossic prophetic language. He of course does not claim to channel an extraterrestrial. He reshapes long-standing traditions, both prophetic and poetic, that Keech apparently did not have access to or use for.

As Barry Brummett points out, the imminence or momentary nature of apocalypse, that it is sudden, decisive, and relatively quickly finished, cuts across all division between its types:

> For Christians, the apocalypse occurs at the Second Coming of Christ (the *parousia*). For Jews, it is the arrival of the Messiah. For New Age mystics, it is the moment in which full enlightenment and thus complete spiritual unity are achieved. For economic apocalyptists, it is when the current economic system collapses totally. For ecological apocalyptists, it is a climactic moment in which the damaged environment changes suddenly. (1991, 48)

For ufologists, one might add, it is the moment in which life on earth is transformed through confrontation with life from outside the solar system. The normal pace of life here speeds up dramatically as suddenism replaces gradualism. Humans suddenly "awaken" to find themselves confronted with higher beings. The acceleration of evolutionary process that telescopes decades and centuries into a single instant corresponds to the concentration of ethical and moral complexity into a single battle between good and evil.

The Psychology of Ufology

Harvard psychiatrist John Mack's book *Abduction* (1994) argues that, while the facts of alien abduction may or may not be true, the abduction narrative provides a positive transformation in his patients' psyches. The experiencer follows a path familiar to us from the writings of Joseph Campbell on the hero: danger; near destruction of the ego; and acceptance of mission. Moreover, C. G. Jung and Keith Thompson both note the generally religious or supernatural aspects of human encounters with space aliens. The shapes and sizes of aliens and of their craft parallel stories of elves, for example. As part of the change in consciousness that contact experiences provoke, Mack reports a frequent conversion to (perceived) Native American spirituality:

> Although they may have had no special knowledge of indigenous traditions, abduction experiencers seem to be drawn inevitably to Native American spirituality and Earth consciousness. "I've never had any interest in Indians," Karin said, but in one of our sessions, she shared an image of "really old Indians being whisked away from their connection to the Earth. They had a connection that was apparently so profound. But now so many of them have lost this connection that was such a direct line to the Earth's vibration. It's a huge wound among their people." Sue said to us, "There are so many parallels between native American spirituality and the UFO phenomenon that you would be amazed." (1999, 99–100)

The mentioned parallels derive largely from the aliens' prophecies of ecological disaster. Often the alien civilization has gone through such disaster but overcome it and is either trying to warn us humans before it is too late or, in a scenario that parallels Revelation's dark images, is preparing the Elect for transportation off the doomed planet, as in the Heaven's Gate cult. Combinations of these aspects give numerous different scenarios, but the basic paradox remains: The possessors of phenomenally advanced technology offer us salvation from technological and systemic disaster. *Similis similibus.*

In another, more overt example of the nativist aspect of ufology noted by Mack, since 1996, conferences under the name of "Star Knowledge" have explored the conjunction between Native American thought and UFO experiences. According to Ed Morningstar, an attendee at the first conference, UFO visitation merges with the teachings of pre-Columbian cultures:

> [A]s each teacher stood, their [*sic*] message was similar: We are approaching the time when open contact with the Star Nations is very close. Humanity is preparing to be a member of the Galactic Community, and before we can become responsible members of the Universe, we must become responsible members of the Earth.
>
> The red nations are now unable to uphold their care of Mother Earth because the other nations [black, white, and yellow] have forgotten their legacy. Our air is polluted, the fish are dying in the sea, and fire has become a tool of destruction. That is why the red nations have decided to come forward with their Sacred teachings at this time. (Morningstar 2002)

Here is a double revelation that bypasses dominant forms of Christianity. Salvation points in two equally uncertain directions: backward, toward the darkness of prehistory, and outward into the blackness of space. The symbols that shine forth against the darkness of each background condense into one: The advanced alien has arrived closest to the state of prehistoric or primitive human beings. We have seen this phenomenon before in the typical selectivity revitalization movements—cargo cults, for example—show for appropriating newer technologies and in the Adamic component of Messiah discourse.

Ernesto Cardenal's Apocalypses

Ernesto Cardenal was born in Nicaragua in 1925. He became involved in attempts to bring down the U.S.-supported Somoza regime, for which several of his friends were captured and executed in 1954. In 1956 he converted to Catholicism. The American poet and priest Thomas Merton helped stimulate both Cardenal's poetic ambitions and his interest in Amerindian cultures and especially in their "sabiduría milenaria," a phrase that could mean either millenarian knowledge or millennia-old knowledge (Cardenal 1999, 193). Cardenal underwent his novitiate at Merton's Trappist monastery in Gethsemani, Kentucky, from 1957 to 1959. He founded the primitive Christian community of Solentiname on an island in Lake Nicaragua in 1965. It was ravaged by government forces in 1977, at which point Cardenal "officially" joined the Sandinista insurrection. In 1979, when the Sandinistas succeeded in ousting Somoza, Cardenal was named minister of culture and continued in that post for a decade. After Rubén Darío, Cardenal is considered to be Nicaragua's most important and influential poet.

One can derive an idea of the Solentiname community from *El Evangelio en Solentiname* [The Gospel in Solentiname] (1982), four volumes of gospel readings in the form of dialogs. Much of the fourth volume deals with Matthew 24–26, where Jesus speaks of the Second Coming. Numerous interlocutors mention the many people who interpreted the Managua earthquake of 1971 as a sign of the end of the world. Cardenal consistently construes these gospel passages as political. Here, for example, is his explanation of the passage that warns against false Christs and the surprising response by one of the interlocutors:

> I [Cardenal]: It's those political leaders that make false promises of salvation that are the false Christs. And also the dictators, the ones who deceive people and exploit them.
>
> Even if they don't exploit them or deceive them, even though they do good to the people, if they want to be adored like God, they also are false Christs.
> LAUREANO: You mean Fidel Castro, because you've been reading propaganda that the Yankees are handing out. (ibid., vol. 4, 11)

Elsewhere, Cardenal shows the influence of French theologian Teilhard de Chardin, who reinterpreted prophecy in the scientific language of history and evolutionary theory. Thus, Cardenal ventures the following interpretation, reminiscent of Melville's that began chapter two, of what Christ meant by his Second Coming:

> [T]he Son of Man will not come as an individual, as he did the first time; he will be a collective Christ, he will come as a society, or rather a new species, the New Person. Father Chardin says that just as for the first coming of Christ it was necessary for the individual human being to have reached a certain degree of evolution, for his second coming it's going to be necessary for all of society to have reached a certain special degree of evolution. (ibid., 50)

Cardenal's poem "Apocalipsis" was published in 1967, and this theme has recurred throughout his work. This early poem was a fairly "conventional" rewriting of the book of Revelation as a description of nuclear war:

> AND LO,
> I beheld an angel
>   (all his cells were electronic eyes)
> and I heard a supersonic voice [una voz supersónica]
> that told me: open up your typewriter and write . . . .
> and the first angel sounded the alarm siren
> and Strontium 90 rained down from the heavens
>   Cesium 137
>   Carbon 14. (1967, 75)

In a rhetorical move as old as Western poetry itself, the poet becomes the antitype of John the Divine, whom the angel commanded to write. The "great voice as of a trumpet" (Rev. 1:10) becomes "supersonic," the typewriter replaces John's pen and parchment, radioactive materials replace the seven seals poured out on the world, and so on. This updating process contrasts with the approach taken by LaHaye and Jenkins in *Left Behind* (1995). Despite the presence of technology in both texts, the process of incorporating it into the Tribulation narratives differs radically. LaHaye and Jenkins equate the truth of Revelation and Daniel with literalness. Wormwood must be wormwood, not radioactivity, and the Four Horsemen appear literally to the believers of the series, not substituted by tanks or other war machines. Such a procedure creates a fundamental paradox, where technology seems essential to Tribulation Force's ability to fight Antichrist but can be trumped at any moment by scriptural literalness. The result is a narrative version of "creation science," where faith and natural law live in uneasy and paradoxical conjunction.

Cardenal's approach, on the other hand, is more attuned to Revelation's symbolic texture. While the text Cardenal writes clearly parallels Revelation, he also innovates and syncretizes in significant ways. For example, the many angels of Revelation are never described in terms of either cells or eyes; the line about electronic eyes alludes to the Greek mythological figure of Argus, with his thousand eyes. In giving the technical names of radioactive materials, Cardenal expresses the fear of millions who feel that nuclear weapons are indeed the stars and wormwood of Revelation and that to live in a nuclear age is to live in the end times. Cardenal can be faulted for his obsession with having the "latest technology" at every point of his rewrite: "John" now writes with a typewriter; the angel's loud voice is now "supersonic" or a siren; and these are only a few out of the poem's several hundred lines. Nevertheless, we can say that "Apocalipsis" effectively reminds its readers of how often, in literature, God's wrath at accelerating human degenerateness has unleashed itself in apocalyptic disaster by means of technology—from Ezekiel's vision of creatures with feet of bronze that speed back and forth like lightning, to the fireworks of Revelation.

While Cardenal's scenario of a nuclear end of the world is practically a topos of post-1945 poetry, an undoubted source of his particular vision is Thomas Merton's "Figures for an Apocalypse" of 1948. Merton divides this ambitious sequence into eight parts—a surprise, given the prominence of the number seven in Revelation, and seemingly an indication that Merton wishes to turn the disastrous scenarios of that text in a more positive direction to "even out" the cosmos. Indeed, the last lines show the New Jerusalem "Dressed in the glory of the Trinity, and angel-crowned / In nine white diadems of liturgy" (ibid., 148, ll. 386–87). The peace and splendor are possible because nuclear war has exhausted itself: "[T]he steel circle of time, inexorable, / Bites like a padlock shut, forever, / In the smoke of the last bomb: / And in that trap the murderers and sorcerers and / crooked leaders / Go rolling home to hell" (ibid., ll. 369–74). Merton follows the trajectory of Revelation itself in moving from images of profanity, death, and disaster to new creation. Earlier in the poem he had warned his friends that it was "the hour to fly without passports / From Judah to the mountains, / And hide while cities turn to butter / For fear of the secret bomb" (ibid., 139, ll. 128–31). Although this poem caused T. S. Eliot to remark that Merton should write less and revise more and Merton himself rated it on the low end of his lyrical work, "Figures" typified the union of poetic, religious, and political sensibilities in Merton that Cardenal admired and imitated.

Cardenal's upgrade of Revelation's trumpets into sirens, on the other hand, may allude to one of the most famous Spanish-language protest poems ever written about Central America and in fact about Cardenal's Nicaragua: Pablo Neruda's "La United

Fruit Co." Neruda begins his poem with a metaleptic citation of Revelation superimposed on Genesis:

> When the trumpet blared [Cuando sonó la trompeta] everything
> on earth was prepared
> and Jehovah distributed the world [y Jehová repartió el mundo]
> to Coca-Cola Inc., Anaconda,
> Ford Motors and other entities:
> United Fruit Inc.
> reserved for itself the juiciest,
> the central seaboard of my land,
> America's sweet waist.
> It rebaptized [Bautizó de nuevo] its lands
> the "Banana Republics." (179 [181])

Obviously, the trumpet type was not present at the world's creation and belongs to Isaiah and Revelation rather than to Genesis. Neruda ironically superimposes eschaton on origin, omega on alpha, and implies that the world has been in an eternal state of emergency and war. In Neruda's parody of Scripture, Jehovah creates Eden for humans in natural abundance but not in original innocence. Instead, the absolute covetousness of capitalism takes over immediately, dividing everything among its entities with no remainder. Like some of the Indian messiahs encountered in chapter two, for whom renaming was an act of resistance, the United Fruit Company arrogates to itself the sacerdotal function of baptism. The absolute corruption and covetousness of these origins have as a result the constancy of the millennial trumpet sound. Later we will see how true this has been for Nicaragua historically.

In the first volume of his memoirs, Cardenal mentions reading and translating the Roman poets Catullus, Martial, Propertius, and Juvenal and at the same time scientific books that inspired him to poetry (1999, 81). Polyglossia of this kind, of particular importance in our consideration of *Ovnis*, remains a constant in Cardenal's poetry, which combines the prophetic, political voices of Merton and Neruda with scientific imagery by using the poetic techniques of Ezra Pound, including the latter's rejection of metaphor, his use of collage, and objectivity in his presentation of the world.

Apocalyptic rhetoric came to Cardenal not only from the Bible and from other poets but also out of the politics and culture of the Americas, a theme we have encountered in the Neruda poem. Significantly, the first liberator of Nicaragua, Augusto César Sandino, who had studied Seventh-day Adventism, made use of this rhetoric. Born in 1895, Sandino had seen the first invasion of Nicaragua by U.S. troops in 1912. The purpose of the invasion, following on the model of Panama, was to guarantee a government of *compradores* that would allow U.S. interests to exploit the country's natural resources. Sandino became active politically in the 1920s and began commanding troops to drive out U.S. forces in 1926. He was assassinated on command of the first Anastasio Somoza in 1936. According to Frank Graziano, the epochal violence of World War I had impressed itself on Sandino as the antitype of his scriptural knowledge:

In the context of anti-imperialist nationalism of the 1920s, World War I was given an apocalyptic interpretation by . . . Sandino and his inspirational ideologue, Joaquín Trincado. "One arrives at Armageddon," according to Trincado, because "all the kings and captains and armies of the earth (as told in the Apocalypse) have risen in arms, and there have been all sorts of plagues." Absent from this scenario was only "a great earthquake" that would "abolish borders and landmarks," and private property with them, in order to inaugurate the "redemptive commune." . . . In February 1931 this upbeat millennialism was boosted by the "Light and Truth" manifesto that Sandino presented to troops combating the "blond beasts," meaning United States Marines, who were occupying Nicaragua. "Many times you will have heard of a Last Judgment of the world," and by this "should be understood the destruction of injustice on the earth and the reign of the Spirit of Light and Truth, that is, Love." Sandino continued: "You will also have heard that this twentieth century, that is, the Century of Enlightenment, is the epoch for which the Last Judgment of the world is prophesied." (Graziano 1999, 23)

As Graziano's *Millennial New World* demonstrates, such apocalyptic rhetoric can be found in most Latin American nations at one point or another. What changes from epoch to epoch and from one historical situation to another is who the Beast or Gog and Magog might be. In this case, as in Neruda, Gog and Magog are not the Spanish but the United States. This polyglossic layering of apocalyptic imagery over political discourse is undoubtedly one source of Cardenal's thematics. As he once declared, "I was not drawn to Marxism by reading Marx, but by reading the gospel. . . . I am a Marxist who believes in God, follows Christ, and is a revolutionary for the sake of His kingdom" (Cabestrero 1983, 32). The religious commune of Solentiname brought all of these things together.

In Solentiname, Cardenal worked with native peoples and through them came to realize that Nicaragua's ability to free itself from U.S. domination would not necessarily liberate them. Hence, after the successful 1979 revolution, which put Sandinistas into power, Cardenal declared that the goal of the revolutionary government was nothing less than the creation of a "new race" (Lynch 1991, 25). As culture minister of the Sandinista government of Nicaragua, Cardenal used his poetic talents to create propaganda jingles such as "Maíz es nuestra raíz" [Corn is our roots] that valorize native achievements. He also publicly affirmed Indians' rights to be ethnically different and not subject to discrimination. However, as Charles Hale points out, Cardenal's simultaneous eulogy of Indian peoples and public promulgation of *mestizaje* logically conflict with one another:

Cardenal's eulogies of pre-Columbian civilizations and the assertion that their values could form the basis for a new Nicaraguan nationalism . . . cannot be equated with state-sponsored *indigenismo* in Latin America because [they were] designed in conjunction with a program of wide-reaching social and economic reforms in a country where over 90 percent of the population is Mestizo. Yet Cardenal sent an ambiguous message to the Miskitu and other minority peoples. While recognizing the Miskitu contribution to Nicaragua's cultural diversity, he stopped decidedly short of fully recognizing "Miskituness" as a political identity distinct from that of Nicaraguan Mestizo. The thrust of his message, rather, was to erase this distinction altogether. To be a Nicaraguan Mestizo now meant having Indian roots, celebrating survivals from this Indian past, and actively making use of them to construct a revolutionary future. (Hale 1994, 92)

These contradictions had political results, as some Miskitu committed to armed rebellion against the Sandinista regime. Significantly, none of the poems in *Ovnis* takes the Miskitu as its subject.

Cardenal's "new race," we may assume, will replace the neo-Europeans currently in charge. The principles of this mestizo race had been elaborated at several points in Latin America's intellectual history, most notably in José Vasconcelos's *La raza cósmica* [The Cosmic Race, 1925]. In this context, it is interesting to note Louis Farrakhan's vision of a flying wheel over Tepoztlán, Mexico, on September 17, 1985, which took the leader of the Nation of Islam aboard. Farrakhan's UFO experience, like that of many abductees, imparted an apocalyptic message. His "cosmic race" is the rehabilitated African of the New World, who has thrown off the yoke of Christianity laid on by the Europeans and assumed his "original" religion of Islam. Tepoztlán is a site associated with Quetzalcóatl, the Aztecs' cultural hero. (Cardenal mentions it in an *Ovnis* poem titled "Quetzalcóatl.") Farrakhan's vision, on the other hand, is an adaptation of the Mother Plane seen and described by the founder of the Nation of Islam, Elijah Muhammad:

> The present wheel-shaped plane known as the Mother of Planes, is one-half mile by a half mile and is the largest mechanical man-made object in the sky. It is a small human planet made for the purpose of destroying the present world of the enemies of Allah. . . . The small circular-made planes called flying saucers, which are so much talked of being seen, could be from this Mother Plane. This is only one of the things in store for the white man's evil world. (Muhammad 1992, 291)

Accordingly, inside the spaceship, Farrakhan received the message that President Ronald Reagan was planning war. In the near term, Farrakhan's vision predicted the U.S. bombing of Libya. In the longer term, it referred both to the missile defense initiative that some feel is really aimed at protecting the world against UFO invasion and to the ongoing "war" of neo-Europeans against people of color (see Lieb 1998, 198–229). Significantly, Farrakhan experienced an exact repetition of this vision during a conference with Native Americans near Taos, New Mexico.

Latin America has seen its share of this kind of revolution, attempts at reverting to native values and technologies by eliminating those of the Europeans. Farrakhan's apocalypse is of the United States preparing to use its technological might to crush a people of color (the Libyans), while the larger vision of the Nation of Islam involves a more sophisticated technology that will eliminate white domination entirely. More common, however, are what Cardenal might call mestizo strategies and what Frank Graziano calls "strategic borrowing":

> The elements borrowed from the conquerors were integrated, disengaging from their source and shedding their foreign associations as they became components of indigenous culture, itself transformed in the process. The complementary internal selections privileged those myths, rituals, and tutelary deities that endorsed the nativist agenda, and these too were reformed or adapted under the pressures of colonization and liberation. (Graziano 1999, 95)

In Cardenal's writing the UFO concept becomes, as we will see, an example of strategic borrowing.

Golden UFOs

Los ovnis de oro was published in Mexico City in 1988. A bilingual edition, with a different ordering of the poems, was published in 1992 and is the source of the citations in this chapter. Each and every poem in this volume centers on a First Nation of the Americas, some in their present conditions (such as the Kuna), others in their historical configurations (such as the Aztec, Maya, and Sioux). Of the twenty-one poems in the collection, nine had previously appeared in Cardenal's *Homenaje a los indios americanos* [Homage to the American Indians; 1969]. While the earlier book has received a modicum of critical attention, *Ovnis* has been virtually ignored, perhaps because it was seen as a reedition of previously published material. In its scope and dedication to the recovery (or ventriloquizing) of Native American voices, *Ovnis* finds no precedent in American letters. It attempts to reverse the transculturation that has been going on in the Americas since 1492 by making its neo-European reader think in the terms given by native cultures. Of course, nothing written in Spanish can be considered a wholesale reconstruction of Native viewpoints. What emerges, as I have already pointed out about Cardenal's poetry, is a world of polyglossia. The poems were composed over a span of many years, from 1955 to 1988. Robert Pring-Mill feels that, while the later volume places greater emphasis on the Indians' present-day situation, both books are examples of "The Poetry of Useful Prophecy" (Pring-Mill 1992, 71). Prophecy and indigenous traditions are two themes that link Cardenal's poetic efforts to ufology: We have prophecy as a product of UFO experience in the case of Elijah Muhammad and Louis Farrakhan, who inherit the association from Ezekiel, and we have seen concern with native cultures in John Mack's account of interviews with UFO experiencers and in the Star Knowledge group.

In an interview with his English translator, published in English as part of the introduction to *Los ovnis de oro* (and in Spanish in Salmon 1990–1991), Cardenal explained the relationship between UFOs and indigenous cultures:

> I have the extensive poem about the Kuna Indians where it is told that a long time ago the Indians said their mythological hero or demigod had come down from the sky to the earth on a golden cloud, and today they say on a golden flying saucer, on a golden UFO. I like this and decided to use it as the title for the book. It could also be the first, but I put it last and I like the name, that mixture which there is between the archaic and the modern. . . . The part about an unidentified flying object is contemporary, while gold sounds archaic, doesn't it? It's not a metal for extraterrestrial beings, for an unidentified flying object, all of that. It's not an appropriate metal for it. It's a contemporary metal, not one for indigenous cultures, for history, not for those Indians. (Cardenal 1992, xxv; Salmon 1990–1991, 200)

Let us consider Cardenal's seemingly off-hand comment that "Los ovnis de oro" could be either the last poem or also the first of the collection, followed immediately by his explanation that the title of the poem is an oxymoron that modifies the contemporary

(UFOs) with the archaic (golden). The last poem of *Ovnis* could also be considered the first one if the collection were arranged in a circle—the outline of a flying saucer. The interchangeability of first and last provides an important clue for understanding the link between ufology and prophecy. One thinks, first of all, of the biblical allusions to the last becoming first or also being first. Jesus used this phrase several times, for example, Matthew 19:30: "Many that are first shall be last; and the last shall be first" (cf. also Mark 9:35). As noted earlier, Cardenal claims that reading the Gospels made him political, and these are among Jesus's most political statements, in which he proclaims a revolution that will replace those at the top with those at the bottom. Indeed, this revolution forms the core of the "utter transformation" of society Cohn speaks of. Native Americans are first in order of arrival in the Americas, last in social position, wealth, and technology, but become first again in Cardenal's eulogy of their cultures. Even more relevant, however, is Christ's self-description in Revelation 1:1: "I am the Alpha and Omega, the beginning and the ending, saith the Lord, which is, and which was, and which is to come, the Almighty." This is a statement not of duration but of the simultaneity of events in mythical time and in prophecy. The prophetic word is simultaneously history, commentary on the present, and prediction. Thus UFOs are both the latest technology and the earliest prophecy of Ezekiel.

Accordingly, *Ovnis* shows a fascination for cyclical methods of counting time that see the future coming to meet the past rather than running away from it. In the poem "Mayapán," Cardenal takes time to explain one such chronology, the Mayan *katun*:

> But time is circular [redondo] it repeats itself
> past present future are the same
> revolutions of the sun
> > revolutions of the moon
> synodic revolutions of the planets
> and history also revolutions
> They repeat themselves
> And the priests
> > keeping track
> > > calculating
> the revolutions
> And every 260 years (a Year of years)
> history repeats itself. The katuns repeat themselves
> Past katuns are those of the future
> history and prophecy are the same (1992, 349 [348])

One of the thirteen *katun*s was counted every twenty years. Each *katun* had its own character and was associated with a particular deity who was said to "govern" it. At the end of 260 years the counting repeated itself, thereby implying a similarity of history. Hence, the beginning of a new *katun* allowed for prophecy that was also a link to the past: "The *katun* count brought together religion and science, government and economics, faith in the future and bondage to the eventful past" (*Book of the Jaguar Priest*, ed. Makemson, 1951, 160). This notion of time is Mayan, but in "The Lost

Cities" Cardenal's use of free indirect discourse makes it seem as though the poet wants his readers to accept it as their own:

> Past and future suffused their songs.
> They counted past and future with the same katuns
> because they believed time repeats itself
> as they saw the rotation of the stars repeat itself.
> But the time they worshipped stopped suddenly.
> But will the past katuns ever come back? (1992, 331 [330])

The identity of past and future relates to ufology in the following way: Ufology links myth with science. Gods, one of humankind's oldest ideas, are recast as astronauts. The furthest developments of science, those that allow for space travel, are envisioned as the origins either of human life on this planet or of humans' earliest notions of a higher being. Arthur C. Clarke and Stanley Kubrick's film, *2001: A Space Odyssey*, provides a popular version of this linkage. In that vision, a mysterious henge arrives from outer space and inspires early hominids to invent tools. Its rediscovery on the moon sets off the odyssey, which ends with a single astronaut evolving to a higher stage of existence. In real life, UFO religions believe that their space counterparts are here to save us from our own technology, which we have developed but do not know how to control. Present technology disturbs and destroys earth and life, while the imagined technology of the future restores the equilibrium.

The Kuna's substitution of UFO for cloud seems inevitable, but in fact this movement from a natural to a cultural image needs explanation. Is the UFO, as Michael Lieb argues, "a product of the impulse to 'technologize' the ineffable?" (1998, 156). As the section on millennial movements points out, the confrontation with superior technology can provoke a millennial outbreak. In the case of the Kuna, their appropriation of the UFO into their own mythic system may have been a response to the perceived threat to their way of life from a technological culture. More likely, however, it was an attempt to make their own story more meaningful by appropriating the power of UFOs. Later we will see that the Kuna have a long tradition of borrowing images supplied by Europeans—no less than do Europeans of borrowing images of Kuna and other native peoples.

In the preface to his collection, Cardenal also confesses the seemingly oxymoronic qualities of the epithet that gave the title to his collection. The oxymoron has the function of uniting past with present, postmodern with archaic. It thus stands for the overall intention of the collection and for its task of prophecy. Paul W. Borgeson has shown how Cardenal's *Homenaje* moves "from history to prophecy by means of myth, which the two have in common" (1984, 179). Cardenal undoubtedly intends the "we" of the poet-prophets in "Cantares mexicanos VII" to include himself:

> We poets come [Venimos los poetas] from the interior of Tula.
> We who search for the occult.
> We who perceive what is secret. . .
> Dreamers of songs. (1992, 211 [210])

The poet searches out that which is hidden. In Cardenal's case, this is the "first," or alpha, the lost history of the Americas before the Europeans came, the very history of the Toltecs, whose poets speak here.

In a poem dedicated to the "last" of a tribe, the few dozen remaining members of the Yaruro, living in Venezuela, Cardenal lays out, in all seriousness, the basis for a belief in UFOs. The Yaruros have been driven to the edge of extinction by the loss of their land to whites. Their religion has become one devoted exclusively to death and the afterlife, when they will rejoin each other in the presence of their goddess, Kuma. At night the poet stretches out in a hammock and stargazes:

> I thought of the plains without ranches in the Land of Kuma.
>> The fact that the earth is part of the skies.
>>> (We are the sky for every other planet
>>> which looks at us in the starry night)
>> In the Milky Way there is no central body,
>>> it is a kind of republic
>> where the movements of the members
>> are regulated by combined gravitational forces
>> of all the members of the stellar population.
>>> The republic of the skies.
>>> (It is not a monarchy.)
>> And conscience [la conciencia] in countless points of the universe!
>>> A common universe [Un universo común].
>> The certainty of not being alone in the cosmos. (ibid., 91 [90])

A couple of translation issues point to ambiguities in the original: In Spanish, "la conciencia" can mean either conscience or consciousness, and I myself find the latter meaning more compelling here despite the moral valence of the former. By itself, "a common universe" would be a plain or ordinary universe, but the presence of terms such as "republic" and "monarchy" suggest the translation "shared universe." Similar thoughts on life "out there" can be found throughout another Cardenal volume, the *Cosmic Canticle* (1993), which even more explicitly takes on the task of weaving religious and scientific discourses together. In that volume Cardenal speculates on life on other planets in terms such as the following: "Gazing at this starry sky so utterly silent / and yet populated with millions of civilizations" (ibid., 44) and "Still no travelers have arrived from other solar systems / Will there be selfishness in the other systems too? (ibid., 253).

On the margins of the neo-European state of Venezuela, the Yaruro lead their miserable existence on the verge of extinction. Aware of the precariousness of their culture, their thoughts focus on death and transcendence, an afterlife in the Land of Kuma. There are no ranches (i.e., no fences) on the plains of heaven. In the last part of the poem, quoted earlier, Cardenal layers his own neo-European voice over that of the Indians, rewording their eschatology in the language of relativity. Astronomical discoveries have moved European cosmology from an earth-centered to a heliocentric view of the universe and finally to one in which, since the universe has no limits, there is also no center, no "monarchy." The equal applicability of natural laws to all bodies, regardless of provenance, and the segmentation of time into equal periods not governed by gods but in absolute equivalence with each other, creates a democracy, a republic of the universe.

It is no accident that the successive theories of geocentric, heliocentric, and relativistic universe have accompanied an ever-increasing democratization of society. We live in an increasingly flat world. Science's discovery of the basic building blocks of life and its invention of a reasonable scenario for their synthesis from elements through natural processes has allowed the assumption that these compounds have been created and have given rise elsewhere in the universe to other life, to other consciousness that could be watching us. The remaining step to arrive at a ufological theology is to overcome the enormous distances separating the "[consciousness] in countless points of the universe" from each other. The goddess Kuma disappears from Cardenal's thoughts as he lies in his hammock, watching the stars. Nor does she return in the poem's last lines. Has she ceded her place, in Cardenal's mind, to the conceptual discourse of relativity and the Big Bang? Are the two modes of thinking, mythical and scientific, first and last, to be thought of as compatible or as disjunctive? If Cardenal were to translate his cosmology into Yaruro, reversing the process we see in the poem, would they accept the doctrine as their own?

We arrive then at the beginning, the title poem of the collection. One finds that the phrase "golden UFOs" does not occur in the body of that poem, only in its title. The poem, "Los ovnis de oro," is a travel narrative that recounts Cardenal's visit to the Kuna, who live on islands off the coast of Panama. The fascination of this native people for Cardenal lies in their simultaneous tenacity in preserving their culture through almost five hundred years of European occupation of Panama, in their primitive communism, and in their refusal to allow capitalist inroads into the islands. Cardenal's visit to the Kuna showed him a possible world of harmony and justice and might even have provided him with a practical model for his own projects, such as the founding of Solentiname (Pring-Mill 1992, 61). The literature on the Kuna (whose name is also spelled "Cuna") is extensive and includes accounts by adventurers (Marsh 1934), missionaries (Keeler 1956), and anthropologists (Taussig 1993).

In "Los ovnis de oro," descriptions of the islands' natural beauty and the life forms found there alternate with direct quotations from the Kuna themselves, who recount their history and religion. Cardenal also inserts conversations with other Europeans concerning the Indians:

> Turpana had told me in Panama:
> There you will find what you like
>   a Socialist society.
> The traditional here is revolutionary
> I tell him now in the sand facing the reef.
> Turpana had studied at the Sorbonne.
> And he tells me now facing the green water:
> Before they said Ibeorgun came in a cloud of gold,
>   now in a flying saucer of gold [en un platillo volador de oro].
> But it is not that they believed this to have really happened.
> (Cardenal 1992, 23 [22])

The passage is one of mediation and a confusion of discourses. The allusion to flying saucers comes not from a Kuna but from an outsider, Turpana, who has studied at the Sorbonne. As if preparing the themes of UFOs and millennium, Cardenal posits the historical and cultural Möbius strip in the clearest possible terms: Tradition *is* revolution. Turpana then makes a comparison seemingly straight out of Carl G. Jung: The arrival of the cultural hero Ibeorgun remains more or less the same, whether he is seen as arriving on a cloud of gold or in a flying saucer made of the same material. In Jung's terms (which gave the title to his book about them), UFOs are "modern myths of things seen in the skies." "Now in a flying saucer of gold" raises multiple questions. First of all, exactly what Kuna word or phrase has been translated as "flying saucer"? Is the Kuna term a calque from Spanish (or English), or has the Spanish translator (Turpana?) domesticated the term for his readers? Second, have the Kuna revised their myth because they have converted to ufology or simply as an act of translation because they wish to make their cosmology more understandable to the non-Kuna?

Turpana's next statement confuses the issue even further as he notes that the Kuna tell their primal myth with full awareness of its fictitious nature:

> Ethnologists do not know this.
> That [the Kuna] did not believe this to have really happened.
> They see heaven as a city of light, pure light.
>   That is why they say of gold,
>   gold means light.
> Or that Ibeorgun did not have a mother,
>   it means his ideas are eternal. (ibid., 25 [24])

This statement reverses the position of anthropologist and subject. Anthropology's premise is that observation of a culture from the outside will yield truths not evident in the culture's own discourse about itself. Turpana's words imply that the Kuna carry out on their own myths an allegorical reading more typically done by an anthropologist. The anthropologist becomes more of a true believer in the myth than the Kuna themselves, who take a distanced position from their own stories. Overall, this brief passage weaves at least three voices together (Cardenal's, Turpana's, and the Kuna's) as it subverts the accepted distinctions between inside and outside, tradition and revolution.

However, if the meaning of the Kuna myth remains the same—that of becoming human—then what meaning should be assigned to the change from cloud to UFO in the story of Ibeorgun? The change points more clearly to millennial thought than if there had been no "original" myth at all since a natural image has been replaced by a technological one. In the same way, Cardenal's early poem, "Apocalipsis," technologized the angels and the breaking of the seals in Revelation, attempting to save the Christian myth of divine redemption before a vision of technology that threatened to overcome it. On the other hand, the phrase used, "platillo volador de oro" (the equivalent of "golden flying saucer") domesticates the image as opposed to the more technical "ovni" ("objecto volador no identificado," a literal translation of "unidentified flying object"). Indeed, "flying saucer" is a somewhat dismissive term that gives the Kuna's reshaping of their myth the hint of an ironic dismissal of Christian salvationist schemes. The Kuna may be rejecting the suddenism of millennium in favor of an eternal recurrence of the same.

We have now entered a dizzying series of mimeses or reflections of one culture upon another, for which no better analysis exists than Michael Taussig's study of the Kuna (or rather of the Kuna and their contexts, which includes the ethnographic literature on them), *Mimesis and Alterity* (1993). Taussig's starting point is the theme of sympathetic magic, the making of images in order to capture the power of the Other. Ibeorgun's main contribution to the Kuna was to teach them how to make *uchus*, wooden idols that work medicine by capturing the spirit of what is represented. Hence, like Prometheus, Ibeorgun is a bringer of technology, and so it makes sense that his vehicle would be upgraded to the latest technological marvel.

But there is more. The Kuna have made *uchus* of spirits as diverse as General MacArthur and Uncle Sam and habitually make them of whites. Such representations of the Other, Taussig argues, are different in medium but not in function from those of, say, the *conquistadores*, who created images of the Indians as barbarians and cannibals, thus giving to the Spanish invaders the power to war against and enslave natives in barbarous fashion. We have seen, as well, how Ahab makes Moby-Dick into an *uchu* in the opposite mode in an attempt to break through the wall of being (the "pasteboard mask") onto the plane of spirit. It is worth quoting at length Taussig's analysis of an Igbo image similar to the Kuna *uchus*, called "white man from the ground." (The Igbo, also spelled "Ibo," are a people of present-day Nigeria.) Besides the color of the statue—which indeed shows a white man seeming to sprout out of the ground—other identifiers include his spectacles and pith helmet:

> For the white man, to read this face means facing himself as Others read him, and
> the "natives' point of view" can never substitute for the fact that now the native is
> the white man himself, and that suddenly, woefully, it dawns that the natives' point
> of view is endless and myriad. The white man as viewer is here virtually forced
> to interrogate himself, to interrogate the Other in and partially constitutive of his
> many and conflicting selves, and as yet we have few ground rules for how such an
> interrogation should or might proceed. Such is the effect of the reflection, an after-
> image of an after-image receding to a limitless horizon. (ibid., 238)

The Kuna appropriation of the flying saucer image may be an *uchu*; so, too, however, may be Cardenal's retranslation of their myth back into a millennial framework, taking Kuna prophecy as the foundation for his own. As Taussig argues, this sort of borrowing is engaged in by most, if not all, cultures. This dialectic applies to the whole of the *Ovnis* collection, where Cardenal simultaneously uses his poetry to frame Indian viewpoints in a European language and then ventriloquizes those perspectives to legitimate his critiques of the dominant culture. Who is empowering whom?

Now we see why the title of the poem "Los ovnis de oro" never appears in its text and why it is "mistakenly" rendered in the plural given that Ibeorgun uses only one "flying saucer." In this game of alterity and mimesis, the title is Cardenal's *uchu* of the Kuna myth, indeed of the Kuna people, as a phantasmagoria of both primitive communism and primitive millennialism. Cardenal attempts to capture Kuna power by producing an image of their image of technology as salvation. His is the viewpoint of a neo-European seeking prophetic signs of the end of a reign of injustice. The title is a fetish, a plea, a prophecy, and a myth of origins rather than a report on what the reader will find in the poem. The first (or last) title of the collection, "Los ovnis de oro," may refer to all of the Indian cultures treated in its various poems. Each appears to Cardenal as a golden flying saucer, bringing enlightenment not from beyond the earth but from before history. Positive transformation will be wrought not by a technology so advanced that it negates the negativity of the present situation but by the constitution of a just society that keeps technology from becoming alien and inhuman. For images of such societies Cardenal turns to the distant past, the apparent alpha of human culture in the Americas, and links it at strategic points with the omega of ufology.

While the revolutionary and religious sincerity of Cardenal's millennial writings is palpable, so too is his realization of history, injustice, and scientific complexity, which impedes the participatory fervor of his poetry without however turning it into reflective dissonance. As a poet of the nuclear age Cardenal shares this problematic with the North American Bob Dylan, whose calls to millennium are the topic of the next chapter.

The Old, Millennial America:
Bob Dylan and the Traditions

When I first ran across those words they almost made
me dizzy. "The old free America"—the idea, the words
themselves, seemed all but natural, coded in the inevitable
betrayals that stem from the infinite idealism of American
democracy. . . . As I listened to [Harry] Smith's [*Anthology of American Folk Music*] with [Bob Dylan's] basement
tapes playing before or after, the phrase rolled over. The old,
weird America is what one finds here.

—Greil Marcus, *Invisible Republic: Bob Dylan's* Basement Tapes

$\mathbf{I}$n his analysis of Bob Dylan's (1941–) album titled *Basement Tapes*, Greil Marcus
notes the tapes' proximity to the collection that had so much to do with the "folksong
revival," the *Anthology of American Folk Music* (1952), compiled and annotated by
the legendary Harry Smith. Smith's old, weird America is also the "old, millennial
America" as represented by at least two stunning examples: Blind Willie Johnson's
"John the Revelator" and F. W. McGee's "Fifty Miles of Elbow Room." These songs,
like many others on the album, have seen numerous versions in every format from
country to rock. They are the signifier, the tip of the iceberg, of the Americas' apocalyptic, archetypal imagination.

No other recording artist of widespread renown has tapped into those reimagined
roots to the extent Bob Dylan has. Dylan the musical innovator depends upon Dylan
the musical archivist, who is enabled by the technologies of recording and transmis-
sion. In a familiar dialectic, new technologies allow for the first time a panoramic look
backward at the heterogeneous, "weird" roots of American musical culture. Dylan
represents, then, something unique: a millionaire purveyor of capitalist popular culture with a consistent though often subliminal message of the end of the world. Hence,
I trump Marcus's own rewording of Kenneth Rexroth (who was trying to express the
vision of America evoked by Carl Sandburg with the phrase "the old, free America")
with my own: The former New World is now the old, millennial America. As we will
see, it is populated by artist-prophets such as Johnson, McGee, Blind Willie McTell,
the Carter Family, and Woody Guthrie, whose work has shaped Dylan's own, yet from
which he also feels distanced and condemned to inauthenticity.

Moreover, Dylan's songs are a prime example of the hybridity of American apocalyptic thought, starting with his adoption of an English Welsh pen name that obscures the Jewishness of his birth name, Robert Zimmerman. Dylan/Zimmerman has invoked millennium throughout his career, including times when he was seen as a nihilistic radical of the counterculture. Furthermore, the technology of recording, radio, television, and other media has meant a broader diffusion of this imagery among the general public than at any previous time in history. In this chapter, however, I show that each musical idiom that Dylan has chosen to deliver his message, together with his tendency to mix popular cultural imagery with that drawn from the Bible, has deflected and obscured this eschatological message. He was mistaken for "just another" Mick Jagger or John Lennon. Instead, he is another Melville. At the same time, the very eclecticism of Dylan's sources distances him from any single tradition, and his career has seen every possible take on the theme of millennium from postmodern pastiche to testifying gospel.

Since 1961 Bob Dylan's millennialist language and the themes in his work have been couched in different genres and have addressed their audience indirectly or directly, depending upon the particular mode of Dylan's writing at the time. The origins of Dylan's obsession with eschatechnologies remains something of a mystery. Raised in Hibbing in the heart of the Minnesota iron range, Dylan came from a solidly middle-class family in an area of the country hardly known as a hotbed of mysticism. Stephen Pickering, who has consistently argued for Dylan's association with Jewish mysticism and prophecy, notes that the Agudath Achim Synagogue in Hibbing, where Dylan conducted his bar mitzvah, leaned toward orthodox (1975, 19). He also mentions Dylan's several trips to Israel, his studies with Jewish teachers, and his sending of his children to religious Jewish summer camps. The allusions to the Bible in Dylan's lyrics are obvious enough and I will intensively analyze some of them later on. On the other hand, in his (partial) autobiography, called *Chronicles*, Dylan mentions, on facing pages, both the Holocaust and that his most vivid memory of elementary school was preparing for nuclear attack and hearing of the possibility that Russian paratroopers might one day drop out of the sky over his hometown (2004, 28–30). In high school he formed a rock 'n' roll band and later returned to the genre as one mode of his musical development. In the meantime, Dylan had been drawn to folk music—such as could be heard in the Harry Smith anthology—as a voice of authenticity analogous to what he had found in the *Torah*.

The lack of harmonic sophistication in Dylan's music derived from the same sources as did most of his apocalyptic imagery (i.e., from his experience of liturgical music and his interest in blues and pentatonic-scale folk music, which does not use functional harmony). His disregard of functional harmony in much of his early work contradicted his insistence that the determining influence on his style had been that of Woody Guthrie, whose music derived largely from the country style made popular by the Carter Family. Although the young Dylan idolized Guthrie, he appropriated Guthrie's persona more than his musical style. As Greil Marcus points out in *Invisible Republic* (1996), Harry Smith's *Anthology of American Folksong* was undoubtedly a source of Dylan's primitivism. Smith's choices for the discs—less than ten percent of his huge private collection—aimed at the eccentric and occult side of American music. Recording technology had delivered a range of materials to Dylan that he would shape and mold into a new "folk-rock" style that reached an unprecedentedly wide segment of the market. Dylan became, like Guthrie, a singer-songwriter who used popular music to deliver political and social messages. The complex relationship between master and epigone conforms to the differences between the political folksong movement of the 1930s, of which Guthrie was a part, and the genre's more commercialized development in the early 1960s. Bill Malone has described the conscious appropriation of the traditional ballad to leftist politics in the thirties:

> Through the 1920s amid the depression years there was a conscious effort on the part of leftists to make traditional southern ballad singing into a kind of official working class music: Southern rural songs and melodies were not only introduced to the North, they also acquired radical and intellectual connotations which they have never really lost. The folk, and their music, were glorified during the depression as they had not been since the days of Andrew Jackson. . . . The thirties saw the emergence, therefore, of that musical phenomenon which has flourished so strongly in the sixties: "urban folk music." (1968, 106)

The second folk movement, in which Dylan took part, was not originally a political movement but the reaction to a stagnancy in music and culture. As Jerome Rodnitsky puts it, "Folksingers quietly invaded the musical vacuum on college campuses in the late 1950s. While Jazz had become increasingly complex and abstract, rock 'n' roll had steadily become nonsensical and meaningless. The folk ballad, however, was extremely communicative and intelligible" (1976, 12). Dramatic presentation of human passions and superb narrative construction account for the popularity of ballads such as "The Unquiet Grave," "The Cruel Mother," and "Massy Groves." Dylan wanted both the communicative, message-oriented ballad form and the emotional lyricism of blues and rock 'n' roll. His use of both traditions reflected a position outside of either, a position from which to examine each tradition in terms of the other. This split, artistically resolved in the act of examining it, characterizes the originality of the "twin" apocalyptic songs "A Hard Rain's a-Gonna Fall" and "Talkin' World War III Blues" found on Dylan's second album.

Ballad of the Apocalypse

Dylan took the talking blues format from Woody Guthrie, whose career, persona, and even appearance the younger singer emulated at the start of his career. Talking blues is a kind of broadside, the underlying musical riffs providing background to madrigal rhymes that comment on whatever issues the singer sees as relevant. Dylan had already used the form a number of times for his own pieces and brought it to perfection in "Talkin' World War III Blues." Dylan's narrative begins when he reports his dream—that he had survived World War III—to his doctor. (The framing of the song as a dream allows it to resonate with "Bob Dylan's Dream" on the same album, which in turn alludes to "Last Night I Had the Strangest Dream," an antiwar folksong.) The doctor refers Dylan to a psychiatrist, which begins the theme of technological nightmare, a Foucauldian manipulation of the individual by various technologies of the self:

> I said, "Hold it, Doc, a World War passed through my brain"
> He said, "Nurse, get your pad, this boy's insane"
> He grabbed my arm, I said "Ouch!"
> As I landed on the psychiatric couch (2004, 64)

The doctor and his nurse reappear as functionaries of the "final solution" several years later in "Desolation Row":

> Dr. Filth, he keeps his world
> Inside of a leather cup
> But all his sexless patients
> They're trying to blow it up
> Now his nurse, some local loser
> She's in charge of the cyanide hole
> And she also keeps the cards that read:
> "Have Mercy on His Soul." (ibid., 182)

For all the seeming protest against medical-psychiatric regimes, Dylan proceeds to recount his dream in such a way as to fit the Freudian paradigm perfectly:

> I was down in the sewer with some little lover
> When I peeked out from a manhole cover
> Wondering who turned the lights on (ibid., 64)

Dylan is the underground man here; sex is, in good 1950s' style, "dirty" and relegated to the "subconscious," which is represented by the sewer. Furthermore, there is the typical dream situation of finding oneself in an embarrassing situation, such as being naked in public. Finally, the scene expresses an infantile megalomania that one's individual actions can bring about profound changes in the world, an illusion that both thrills and petrifies with guilt. After encountering several survivors, Dylan returns to the sexual thematic, ostensibly with another woman he encounters:

> "Let's go and play Adam and Eve"
> I took her by the hand and my heart it was thumpin'
> When she said, "Hey man, you crazy or sumpin'
> You see what happened last time they started" (ibid.)

The vision of a new Adam and Eve to populate the New Jerusalem is common to many apocalypses. Hawthorne had titled one of his satires on Millerism "The New Adam and Eve" (1982). In his dream, Dylan reveals a relationship between absolute aggression, as in nuclear war, and absolute horniness, leaving it unclear as to whether the fulfillment of desire causes cataclysm or remedies it.

The postnuclear scene is painted along the lines of survivalist paranoia, with everyone living for themselves and driving off all others around them so as to maintain their own scarce resources. (Stephen King's *The Stand* [1990], to give one example, describes a similarly ghostlike Manhattan without Dylan's humor.)

Dylan sublimates his frustrated desires for human contact into an urge for technology. He finds and manages to drive a Cadillac ("Good car to drive—after a war"), he tries to play the radio and his record player, and he finally calls up the operator "just to hear a voice of some kind." What he gets, of course, is the recording of the operator, which repeats itself over and over, each time giving the exact moment of mass death: "When you hear the beep it will be three o'clock. / She said that for over an hour and I hung up." The rapidity of catastrophic change, which is one of the basic features of millennium, contrasts here with the slow and repetitive nature of comprehension. This play between different aspects and perceptions of time is incorporated into the very structure of "Hard Rain." The repetition of the operator recalls that of the song itself, as something to be played over and over again without change, reminding us that the failure of communication and lack of human intimacy attributed to technology applies as well to the recording medium Dylan uses to get his message across.

Also common to both pieces is the oneiric flavor of the narration—explicitly mentioned in this song, implicit in "Hard Rain," and indistinguishable from poetic-prophetic vision. At the end of the song, the psychiatrist claims to have the same dream, except he of course was the one walking around with no one else. The dream spreads like a virus:

> Well, now time has passed and now it seems
> Everybody's having them dreams
> Everybody sees themselves
> Walkin' around with no one else (2004, 65)

The last line is Dylan's proposed solution: "I'll let you be in my dream if I can be in yours." The ideas of communication and copresence in a dream world contrast sharply with the nonpresence and mutual hostility that technology has created: Dylan has replaced the premillennial script of nuclear catastrophe with a postmillennial vision—albeit an ironic and conditional one—of shared vision. This sharing of vision, it turns out, lies at the heart of this comic song's tragic twin, "Hard Rain."

As opposed to the talking blues format, "Hard Rain" chooses the traditional ballad as its raw material. One can immediately see the relationship by comparing Dylan's opening stanza with that of the ballad "Lord Randall":

> "What leave you your true love, Lord Randall, my son?
> What leave you your true love, my handsome young man?"
> "A rope for to hang her; mother, make my bed soon,
> For I'm weary with hunting and I want to lie down."
> "Lord Randall" (Bronson 1959, vol. 1, 217)

> Oh, what'll you do now, my blue-eyed son?
> Oh, what'll you do now, my darling young one?
> I'm a-goin' back out 'fore the rain starts a-fallin'
> And it's a hard rain's a-gonna fall.
> "A Hard Rain's a-Gonna Fall" (Dylan, 2004, 60)

Heard one after the other as given here, these two stanzas, the first from a traditional ballad and the second by Dylan, would make the American songwriter seem
merely an imitator of the Anglo-American ballad tradition. But, in fact, a whole other
world and a tradition foreign to the ballad are hidden in the ellipses after "fallin'."
Through musical and textual bricolage Dylan has created a new kind of song that I
call the apocalyptic ballad. Dylan's rewrite brings into the ballad structure the theme
of apocalypse and a different role for the narrator of the ballad, which makes that
apocalypse self-referential. Self-reference begins, however, with the polysemy of the
title, "Hard Rain."

Whereas the title of "Lord Randall" serves merely to identify the song's protagonist and hence point to its overwhelmingly worldly interest, the phrase "hard
rain" is thematic, encompassing three important and interrelated areas elaborated
in the song's text: politics, religion, and art. The song's first critical interpretation,
expounded in Nat Hentoff's liner notes to *The Freewheelin' Bob Dylan* (1963), was
purely political. Hentoff, one of the period's most influential music critics, proclaimed
the song to be Dylan's response to the Cuban missile crisis of October 1962, when the
world seemingly stood on the brink of nuclear war. For many listeners, then, "Hard
Rain" instantly became the mimesis of a narrowly avoided war that had revealed to
Americans their perilous position on the edge of catastrophe. In that sense, as mentioned, it becomes the twin of "Talkin' World War III Blues."

In fact, however, the song was written before the political event, and, unlike
"Talkin' World War III Blues," it contains no graphic or realistic references to nuclear
war. Furthermore, such a "protest" motive for the song's writing does little to explain
its meaning, its continued presence in Dylan's repertoire, or its enduring power as a
work of art, including for those who know nothing of its supposed origin. Nuclear
devastation is just one technologized antitype among many for the pouring out of the
vials of destruction. Finally, the song's imagery does not remain at the purely political level but continually shifts between the sacred and the profane. The title, "A Hard
Rain's a-Gonna Fall," superimposes the political with the archetypal: "Hard rain"
refers at once to radioactive fallout, to the Flood of Genesis, and conceivably also to
the vials that are poured out upon the earth in Revelation: "And I heard a great voice
out of the temple saying to the seven angels, Go your ways, and pour out the vials of
the wrath of God upon the earth" (Rev. 16:1).

The singer reports that he has seen "a white ladder all covered with water." This
image recalls the ladder Jacob saw in a dream, which angels used in order to ascend
into heaven and come down to earth (Genesis 28:11–22). It symbolizes God's promise to populate the earth with Jacob's descendants.[1] The ladder is now empty and
useless, inundated by the Flood. In linking the Flood with Jacob's ladder and the
vials of Revelation, Dylan invokes apocalypse as yet another version of the familiar
biblical cycle: human beings' covenant with God; our breaking of the covenant;
and God's subsequent punishment of humankind. There is little one can say about a
white ladder on the political level. For a listener starting from Hentoff's liner notes,
nuclear war, stripped of its political context, becomes during the song's unfolding
a mere signifier of the beginning of Tribulation—that is, a perceptible component
that allows the listener to imagine the unimaginable. Dylan's nuclear apocalyptic
thus follows a pattern described by R. W. B. Lewis as typical of modern American

apocalypses and certainly applicable, for example, to the verse of Thomas Merton and Ernesto Cardenal: "The [atom] bomb, when it has been mentioned at all in our imaginative literature, has usually been taken as a symptom and an instrument: the inevitable product of the diseased energies of mankind, and the physical force that can bring about that grand conflagration which mankind has long been striving to deserve" (1965, 184). The question of whether "Hard Rain" is about nuclear war partakes of another, larger question concerning the overall functioning of the song's possible worlds. I argue that the real mimesis in "Hard Rain" is the depiction of the singer as creator of images and cultural hero.

Dylan's speeding up of the tempo of imagery also makes it resemble Revelation's redundant hyperactivity. Betsy Bowden describes "Hard Rain" as "a Child ballad being run through a projector too fast" (1982, 18) and claims that such intensification is appropriate for a description of nuclear attack. Using a strikingly similar metaphor, Michael Gray notes that the effectiveness of the supposedly "cohesive moral theme" of "Hard Rain" depends upon the "pictures rolling past . . . without opportunity of recall" (1972, 160). However, the issue is not how to describe nuclear attack but rather how to use it as a signifier of apocalypse. Dylan has transformed the ballad genre in order to transmit a message that does not "fit" within ballad form. Beneath the "surface" of overt political protest runs a deeper current of religious vision, just as the song's apparent preservation of the ballad form in its appropriation of "Lord Randall" in fact transcends that form.

Dylan has converted the narrative structure of "Lord Randall" into a vehicle for a far different kind of vision. To begin with, the questions in each stanza of "Hard Rain" do not lead the listener, as in "Lord Randall," to construct a sequence of events that occurred before their narration. The revealed *histoire* of "Lord Randall" is that he has been poisoned by his lover and will soon die. This information is revealed incrementally through the question-and-answer format that Dylan adopts. The verbs "see," "hear," and "meet," which are the heart of the questions in the middle stanzas of "Hard Rain," are verbs of sense rather than of action as in "Lord Randall." Each question asks not for events but instead for the perceptions delivered by a particular sense: "What did you see, my blue-eyed son? What did you hear . . .? Who did you meet . . .?" They serve only to organize the enumeration of the singer's visions, which apparently cannot be organized as a narrative. Indeed, even the different senses are not clearly separated from each other. Synæsthesia is often used to contradict our normal sensory ordering of the world: "I saw ten thousand talkers whose tongues were all broken"; "Heard one person starve, I heard many people laughin'." This is not the hard-nosed, realistic world of the ballad.

The extra length of Dylan's stanza is caused by lines inserted between the four lines modeled on "Lord Randall." The actual stanza excerpted earlier thus runs as follows:

> Oh, what'll you do now, my blue-eyed son?
> Oh, what'll you do now, my darling young one?
> *I'm a-goin' back out 'fore the rain starts a-fallin'*
> *I'll walk to the depths of the deepest black forest,*
> *Where the people are many and their hands are all empty,*

> *Where the pellets of poison are flooding their waters,*
> *Where the home in the valley meets the damp dirty prison,*
> *Where the executioner's face is always well hidden,*
> *Where hunger is ugly, where souls are forgotten,*
> *Where black is the color, where none is the number,*
> *And I'll tell it and think it and speak it and breathe it,*
> *And reflect it from the mountain so all souls can see it,*
> *Then I'll stand on the ocean until I start sinkin'*
> *But I'll know my song well before I start singin'*
> And it's a hard rain's a-gonna fall. (2004, 60; emphasis added)

The number of these inserted, often anaphoric lines (italicized in the preceding stanza) is not constant: The first stanza has five; the second and third have seven; the fourth has six; and the fifth, twelve. This variation imparts to the song a feeling of indeterminacy and incompleteness, as though any one of the stanzas could be prolonged indefinitely, in strict contradiction to ballad tradition, where stanzaic structure never varies. The arrangement of Dylan's stanza points toward the infinite, whereas the ballad stanza doubles back upon itself, holding both character and listener to a concrete here and now. In addition, the ordering of the lines is random since the individual images never show any chronological relation to each other. This randomness and lack of chronology make this part of the stanza antinarrational and hence alien to ballad tradition. The reason for the absence of narrative is that the song's central lines belong to a different musical tradition, that of litany, in which, as Gray points out, moral rather than narrative coherence is at stake.

Thus, in contradistinction to most ballads' impulse to tell a coherent story with objective or "epic" distance, narrative in "Hard Rain" is sacrificed to indeterminate and highly personal imagery. The structural tension between ballad and litany is mirrored by a conflict between the ballad's public or archetypal symbolism and the complex, hermetic imagery shared by Revelation and modern poetry (e.g., Arthur Rimbaud, Dylan Thomas, and others). "I saw a room full of men with their hammers a-bleedin'" and "I saw a black branch with blood that kept drippin'," while they sound as if they were drawn from a ballad—or from the Stith-Thompson index of motifs—do not yield up the secret of their meaning beyond a feeling of impending disaster. Even images borrowed directly from the Bible are revised into a more personal idiom: The archetypal flood becomes an oxymoronic "hard rain," while the symbol of Jacob's ladder is distorted by being superimposed on the image of the Flood, as mentioned earlier.

The first stanza has identified the singer as a *poeta vates*, a John the Revelator, who has made a supernatural or catabatic journey and lived to tell about it. The next three stanzas relate his visions. In the final stanza, the singer's function changes to that of prophet, even of savior, as the "decisive action" of ballad tradition is transformed into the act of singing itself—that third, self-referential meaning of "hard rain." The third stanza returns us to the temporal realm, then, but only inasmuch as it is constituted by performance. It is only in the final stanza, where it becomes obvious that singer and visionary are one, that for the first time a narrative begins to form, a narrative given in the future tense and responding to the question "What'll you do now?" Even this narrative (and the answer to the interlocutor's last question) is suspended in favor of a short series of descriptive metaphors beginning with "where." Here again one notes the absence of any reference to nuclear holocaust or geopolitical concerns. Lines such as "where the people are many and their hands are all empty, / Where the pellets of poison are flooding their waters, / Where the home in the valley meets the damp dirty prison" are rather metonyms for problems of hunger, poverty, environmental disaster, and social injustice. Once the actual narrative begins, it presents the song's most complex problems in interpretation. The prophet will "tell it and think it and speak it and breathe it." To what does the pronoun "it" refer since it has no antecedent? It is perhaps multivalent: "It" refers to the rain, to the apocalypse, to the Bible, and, most centrally, to the song itself as we apprehend in the paradoxical deferral conveyed by "its" final line. The critics who have read "until I start sinkin'" as indicating the death of the singer have neglected the grammar of the sentence: The sinking occurs in a subordinate clause that opens with "until," which suspends the time of its action. The sentence says not that the singer will drown but that he will stand on the ocean until . . . what?

Not until the bomb drops but until he loses faith. The idea of standing on water is a reference to Christ's fisherman, Peter, who walked on the water as long as his faith held him up: "But when he saw the wind boisterous, he was afraid; and beginning to sink, he cried, saying, Lord, save me. And immediately Jesus stretched forth his hand, and caught him, saying unto him, O thou of little faith, why didst thou doubt?" (Matthew 14:30–31). Peter, Christ's favorite and his betrayer, is a more interesting and ambiguous role for the singer than that of Jesus, as Dylan here invokes faith through an example of its failure. The story of Peter also encapsulates this song's split textual and musical structure into a single, brief parable. And like those opposing structures, Peter's story reveals two kinds of time, sacred and profane. Peter's faith places him within sacred time, where the inevitable physical laws, dependent upon the passage of profane time, are suspended. The end of his faith, like the end of the song, means release back into a world where history can come to an end and where souls can indeed sink and be forgotten.

Dylan also plays with time in the line "I'll know my song well before I start singin'." In that final line, listeners are confronted with the fact that the real song has not yet begun. They must ask themselves what further knowledge is needed and what differences there would be between "Hard Rain" and the imagined song of songs. On one level, Dylan is here referring to his own "Hard Rain" as noise, as the tuning up before the real playing. However, this paradox—that the song we are hearing is not the real song—also makes sense both within Jewish mystical tradition, where God's real name is forever hidden behind a screen of false names and the one pure language is palpable only in the interstices of human tongues, and within the millennial tradition, which can remain vital only because the eschaton that it predicts never arrives. Most people are forced to choose between millennium as a real catastrophe occurring in fixable historical time (the Lutheran position) and as an infinitely repeatable occurrence within each person's soul (the Augustinian interpretation). Artists, however, may synthesize rather than choose, just as they may synthesize tradition and noise, ballad and litany. But did Dylan ever get to "know his song well"?

The Desolate City

The synthesis of musical and textual structures I have been calling an "apocalyptic ballad" is fragile and unique, and Dylan never again achieved the precise balancing act of "Hard Rain." The theme of redemption through art broached in "Hard Rain" should have been fair warning to Dylan's fans (many of whom came out of the overtly political period of folk music) that he was in the business of vision rather than of politics. As George Monteiro puts it, as the 1960s wore on, Dylan "discovered that apocalyptic imagery said more about an individual's soul than about what happens to the physical world" (1974, 165). An interesting contrast with "Hard Rain" is the song "Desolation Row," on Dylan's 1965 album, *Highway 61 Revisited* (2004, 181–83). When I first heard this song in 1970, I thought that Dylan was using "desolation" in its etymological sense, indicating the solitude of the soul in opposition to the clutter of the material world. However, the biblical sense of the term was probably uppermost in Dylan's mind, for numerous Old Testament prophets use the word to describe the Lord's vengeance, which will make of Jerusalem a "desolation." Indeed, since "Desolation Row" fits well into Bercovitch's genre of the "American Jeremiad," we need only look at Jeremiah to find frequent examples:

> The peaceful meadows will be laid waste
> because of the fierce anger of the LORD.
> Like a lion he will leave his lair,
> and their land will become desolate
> because of the sword of the oppressor
> and because of the LORD's fierce anger. (25:37–41)

The term occurs twice in Revelation as a clear allusion to Jeremiah and the other prophets. The beast sets upon the whore of Babylon (i.e., Rome) and "shall make her desolate and naked" (17:16), the opposite of the woman clothed in the sun. The same idea is repeated more explicitly at 18:19. In all of these texts, to point out the obvious, desolation is the Lord's punishment for a people's loss of faith.

There is also the "row" part of the epithet, an inversion of the concept of the New Jerusalem: Whereas the latter shows three dimensions and is foursquare, Desolation Row is one dimensional; whereas Jerusalem, because divine, represents the ultimate form of human society, Desolation Row, run by the common denominator of the human, is completely antisocial; and whereas in the New Jerusalem "God shall wipe away all tears from their eyes; and there shall be no more death, neither sorrow, nor crying, neither shall there be any more pain" (Rev. 21:4), each and every stanza of "Desolation Row" shows the unremitting cruelty of man to man. "They're selling postcards of the hanging" are the first words we hear, and it goes downhill from there. (For many years these lines also remained opaque to me until I learned more about the history of lynching in the United States and how the circulation of postcards of these hangings became part of the celebration and maintenance of racism.)

"Desolation Row" is thus Dylan's answer to the American millennial project. The distinction between divine covenant and human degenerateness is invoked again in stanzas such as the following:

> Now Ophelia, she's 'neath the window
> For her I feel so afraid
> On her twenty-second birthday
> She already is an old maid
> To her, death is quite romantic
> She wears an iron vest
> Her profession's her religion
> Her sin is her lifelessness
> And though her eyes are fixed upon
> Noah's great rainbow
> She spends her time peeking
> Into Desolation Row (2004, 182)

The rainbow is that set by God in the sky after Noah leaves the ark. It is a sign of the new heaven and the new earth. Therefore, Noah's (and Ophelia's) glimpse of God's new covenant provides the type for John's vision of the New Jerusalem. One could think of this as an indirect reference to "Hard Rain" since Noah's rainbow appears at the end of the great flood brought on by heavy rains. Similar to Jacob's ladder, the rainbow symbolizes humans' covenant with God and our ability to understand divine intentions for the earth and for human history: "Whenever the rainbow appears in the clouds, I will see it and remember the everlasting covenant between God and all living creatures of every kind on the earth" (Genesis 9:16). In a disturbing double vision, however, reinforced by the paronomasia that links "rainbow" with "row," Ophelia somehow focuses on both the rainbow and Desolation Row.

Dylan wrote these lines just a few years after James Baldwin had published a memoir titled *The Fire Next Time*, the title drawn from a gospel text: "God gave Noah the rainbow sign / No more water, the fire next time!" (1963, 105). Baldwin's text features not a Christian millennium but Elijah Muhammad's predictions of divine cataclysm that will sweep white people from power. Baldwin comments that the desolation's "emotional tone is as familiar to me as my own skin; it is but another way of saying that *sinners shall be bound in Hell a thousand years*" (ibid., 67). The greatest sin of whites, according to Baldwin, is the lifelessness they have created and propagated on their own subalterns and the rest of the world as the only life worth living: Ophelia's life of sterility and madness.

As in "Hard Rain," Dylan refers in the final stanza of this song to its genesis and to the singer's position vis-à-vis society:

> Yes, I received your letter yesterday
> (About the time the doorknob broke)
> When you asked how I was doing

Was that some kind of joke?
All these people that you mention
Yes, I know them, they're quite lame
I had to rearrange their faces
And give them all another name.
Right now I can't read too good
Don't send me no more letters no.
Not unless you mail them from Desolation Row. (2004, 183)

It is tempting to take the acquaintances' lameness literally, the "can't read too good" as a kind of blindness, and to contrast these conditions with the healing to take place in the New Jerusalem, where every tear shall be wiped away. Rather than "going back out" as does the *poeta vates*, this singer breaks the doorknob and rejects correspondence, indicating his total isolation from the community to which he sings. Isolation/desolation leads to detached narrative, with little dialog and no interaction between the singer and the world he describes. Rearranging and renaming are evocative descriptions of Dylan's technique in "Desolation Row," which is, as we have seen with Ophelia, to manipulate and juxtapose cultural symbols so as to either renew their meaning or expose them as clichés. On the other end of the equation, there is a striking contrast between this singer and the one in "Hard Rain." The source of his art is not vision but re-vision and the deconstruction of accepted values. Rearranging faces and giving new names is precisely Dylan's technique on this and many other songs, an extension of typology into the profane. An example are the lines "All except for Cain and Abel / And the Hunchback of Notre Dame / Everybody is making love / Or else expecting rain" (ibid., 205). Cain and Abel are the biblical type for human quarreling and self-destruction, while the hunchback is the Romantic type for the outcast or outlaw. They are joined at the hip by a disjunctive "and," and by their mutual ignorance of the rain, which represents God's wrath.

Thus, whereas "Hard Rain" presented apocalypse as a creative act that lifted the singer out of narrative and its concomitant time frame, "Desolation Row" moves inexorably toward its end as the largely disparate images become more and more gruesome. Indeed, literature itself appears headed toward destruction:

Praise be to Nero's Neptune
The *Titanic* sails at dawn
And everybody's shouting
"Which Side Are You On?"
And Ezra Pound and T. S. Eliot
Fighting in the captain's tower
While calypso singers laugh at them
And fishermen hold flowers. (ibid., 183)

Here Dylan parodies tradition in several of its senses, from the "high" art of writers such as Eliot and Pound to the more popular forms of political song and calypso. The capitalization of "Which Side Are You On" indicates that it is an allusion to the famous song by Florence Reece, which became a hymn for striking mine-workers and was often sung by urban folksingers, most notably Pete Seeger. At the same time, however, the call to take up sides, to be for or against, alludes to the chiliastic vision of the end times. Thus, "Desolation Row" rejects both political and "high" art as not only useless but in fact as part of the coming catastrophe. The alternative is the solipsism that the final stanza adumbrates as a kind of coda. The rather colorless tune to "Desolation Row" does not "fit" the words and seems ironic; the tune is functionally harmonic, indeed romantic, with a second guitar playing arpeggios in the background: elevator music on the descent into hell, to be bound there, as James Baldwin reminds us, for a thousand years.

It is tempting to read the contrast between these two very different visions of millennium as representative of the contrast between the civil rights movement and the Vietnam protests and as the contrast between the "we can change the world" of 1962 and "tune in, turn on, drop out" of 1966.

Joker and Thief

In July 1966 a motorcycle accident caused Dylan to disappear from public view. From conversations with Dylan's brother, journalist Toby Thompson (2008) concluded that Dylan had not been seriously injured in the accident and that the reasons for his seclusion were psychological and professional rather than medical. The country-flavored album, *John Wesley Harding*, which represented Dylan's return to the public eye in 1968, is a self-portrait and a reflection on the two earlier phases of his career, folk and rock. Its Western theme (Harding was a Wild-West outlaw) and country-tinged music seem far from the apocalyptic mentality Dylan had left behind when he retired from the public eye. It was in a sense his most musically conservative album to date, released in a year when the young people influenced by his music—most famously, the radical "Weatherman" group that allegedly took its name from a line of "Subterranean Homesick Blues"—were becoming more radical than ever before. Only one song on the album, "All along the Watchtower," invokes apocalypse, but it is one of Dylan's best-known, most covered, and most interpreted works and became a hit first for Jimi Hendrix a year after Dylan's album appeared. Furthermore, the figure of the joker would surface again many years later in the song "Jokerman" (discussed later).

"Watchtower" presents the singer's two opposing images—joker and thief—that are an extension of Ophelia's double vision of salvation and damnation and also characterize the first two stages of Dylan's career. Moreover, it represents a return to the blending of ballad and Bible examined in "Hard Rain":

> "There must be some way out of here," said the joker to the thief,
> "There's too much confusion, I can't get no relief.
> Businessmen, they drink my wine, plowmen dig my earth,
> None of them along the line know what any of it is worth."
>
> "No reason to get excited," the thief, he kindly spoke,
> "There are many here among us who feel that life is but a joke.

But you and I, we've been through that, and this is not our fate,
So let us not talk falsely now, the hour is getting late." (2004, 224)

The possibilities for interpreting these types of joker and thief recall the polysemy of the phrase "hard rain." They are the two men who were crucified alongside Christ, both of whom were thieves but only one of whom mocked, while the other placed his wager on salvation, asking Jesus to remember him (Luke 23:39–43). Christians think of the thief's salvation as the preservation of his immortal soul; at the time, however, the issue was the coming end of the world, which would destroy Jerusalem, and being on the correct side in the final battle. The desperation of the first line seems to invoke this situation *in extremis*. The joker and the thief also represent two sides of Dylan's art engaged in a moral dialog and, as we have seen, a fight in the captain's tower: the political and the poetical; the striving for a historical millennium and the acceptance of primordial chaos. The thief also alludes to the title figure of the album, an outlaw of the American West. Dylan reinvents the vicious John Wesley Hardin (the added "g" is a hypercorrection of Dylan's, who probably first heard of "John Hardy" through the famous Carter Family song included in the Harry Smith anthology) as a "friend to the poor," who was "never known / to hurt an honest man" (2004, 221). But inasmuch as Harding becomes a self-referential figure, aspects of the joker, that is, of indeterminacy and play, creep into the portrayal.

In "Watchtower," too, this aspect of indeterminacy and "confusion" is the thief's domain, not the joker's. The joker's most striking aspect is his inability to laugh. Indeed, the first words he speaks, "There must be some way out of here," are stolen from the language of desperados rather than clowns. In a similar surprise, the joker's concern is entirely with profit and loss as he speaks of his economic exploitation. Conversely, it is the thief who refers to life as a joke, who is kind and relaxed, and who demands honesty but nevertheless invokes millennium and tribulation with his observation that "the hour is getting late." A flash forward to two songs from Dylan's so-called Christian period may provide clues for yet another identification of these two figures. In the song "When He Returns," a straightforward and unambiguous apocalyptic hymn, Dylan sings the line "For like a thief in the night, He'll replace wrong with right / When He returns" (ibid., 417). Dylan alludes here to Christ's words that he will return suddenly and without warning: "Remember therefore how thou hast received and heard, and hold fast, and repent. If therefore thou shalt not watch, I will come on thee as a thief, and thou shalt not know what hour I will come upon thee" (Rev. 3:3); and "Behold, I come as a thief" (Rev. 15:15). This makes sense of the thief speaking kindly, of admonishing not to talk falsely, of knowing that the hour is getting late, and so on.

This, then, is a minicatechism, an exchange between faith and unbelief, between religion and politics in the context of an impending cataclysm. In the last stanza, our vista suddenly widens like a camera craning back from a close-up to a wide-angle, and the claustrophobia of the first line is reversed as we see the two speakers on horseback approaching a city:

All along the watchtower, princes kept the view
While all the women came and went, barefoot servants, too.

> Outside in the distance a wildcat did growl
> Two riders were approaching, the wind began to howl (2004, 224)

There is a curious division in the final stanza in the printed lyrics, as though it represented the temple veil rent in two by the earthquake at Christ's death. Nearly every image in this final stanza derives from Isaiah's prophecy of the fall of Babylon. As befits a ballad, Dylan's narrative is dry and unemotional, his singing uninflected. The anguish felt by the prophet Isaiah as he predicts catastrophe has been transferred to the joker. The vision is also given as dialog in the Old Testament source, though the interlocutors are not specified:

> Prepare the table,
> watch in the watchtower,
> eat, drink: arise, ye princes,
> and anoint the shield . . .
> And he cried,
> A lion:
> My lord, I stand continually upon the watchtower in the daytime,
> and I am set in my ward whole nights:
> And behold, here cometh a chariot of men,
> with a couple of horsemen.
> And he answered and said,
> Babylon is fallen, is fallen. (Isaiah 21:5, 8–9)

John the Revelator, in turn, takes this motif of the fall of Babylon into Revelation 14:8: "And there followed another angel, saying, Babylon is fallen, is fallen, that great city, because she made all nations drink of the wine of the wrath of her fornication." The message is repeated in 18:2–3:

> And he cried mightily with a strong voice, saying,
> Babylon the great is fallen, is fallen,
> and is become the habitation of devils,
> and the hold of every foul spirit,
> and a cage of every unclean and hateful bird.
> For all nations have drunk
> of the wine of the wrath of her fornication,
> and the kings of the earth have committed fornication with her,
> and the merchants of the earth are waxed
> rich through the abundance of her delicacies.

This, it would seem, Dylan has rewritten as "businessmen they drink my wine. Plowmen dig my earth," identifying the joker with the angel who cries mightily—with a supersonic voice, as Cardenal would put it.

Isaiah's Babylon is indeed Babylon, the dominant imperial power during the years of Israel's existence as a state (mostly as two states). Much later, around the end of the first century ce, John refers to Rome as the antitype of Babylon, the present imperial power and persecutor of Christians. The references to trade and abundance leave little doubt on this point. Millennia later, David Koresh applied them to the United States. When asked how he knew that America (and not, for example, Yugoslavia) was intended as the antitype for Babylon, he responded that "nobody has merchandise in Yugoslavia that makes all the nations of the earth drunk" (Newport 2006, 222). In chapter seven we will see Bob Marley's similar use of Babylon as type, though with a broader and more complex set of allegorical associations. Unlike LaHaye and Jenkins, who for some reason cannot think of the United States as a new version of Rome but must have their Antichrist construct a New Babylon in the Middle East, in the dark years of the Vietnam war Dylan must have identified the United States with Babylon.

In reshaping this text, Dylan has Americanized the image of the lion—which apparently does not correspond to the Hebrew and has been eliminated from the Revised Standard Version—into that of a wildcat. John takes up the lion again as well; it is a symbol for Jesus in Revelation 5:5: "And one of the elders saith unto me, Weep not: behold, the Lion of the tribe of Judah, the Root of David, hath prevailed to open the book, and to loose the seven seals thereof." Isaiah's vision of Babylon destroyed by a great army, for which the chariot and horsemen are synecdoches, has been replaced by the more subtle invasion of chaos and anomie we have seen in the two riders and in the earlier "Desolation Row." The dialog between these two figures contrasts sharply with the silence of the city and its rigid hierarchization, which, this song suggests, will help speed its fall—details that refer us forward to the New Testament meaning of "Babylon."

However, the disturbing effect of this song derives not so much from its prediction of cataclysm as from the seemingly insurmountable distance between the riders and the city they are approaching. For like "Hard Rain" and unlike "Desolation Row," this song invokes a curious deferral. Time here is cyclical. Both Paul Williams and Michael Gray have noticed the extraordinary difference wrought by the unexpected placement of the final stanza. Williams even likens the song's narrative structure to that of a Möbius strip:

> [The song's] ends have been twisted, and taped together. In another universe, Dylan would begin, "All along the watchtower, princes kept the view. . . . Two riders were approaching, the wind began to howl." The second and third verses would then be conversation between the two riders, the Joker and the Thief; and "let us not talk falsely now" would close the song with comfort.
>
> Because indeed, "There must be some way out of here"—what more natural reaction, caught on a Möbius strip? (1969, 76)

Dylan has changed the linear narrative of the ballad into a cycle that moves from eschatology into the deeper mythic stratum of repetition. Jerusalem is never entered, and Babylon never falls. The joker and the thief and all they stand for are condemned to an eternal recurrence of the same. They are trapped before the city gates, just as we are trapped in perpetual nostalgia in a history never able to turn the corner on millennium. After all, "watching," as Jeffrey Kaplan points out, "is what millenarians do best" (1997, 217). When pressed in this fashion, the song veers into reflective dissonance, not least because its musical texture lacks the pure irony of "Desolation Row." If "Hard Rain" presented us with a song not yet sung, "Watchtower" represents a song from which there is no exit. This change parallels the shift in political climate that surrounded Dylan and which may have been a factor in driving him into hiding: When a violent revolutionary cell like the Weathermen inspires itself in your lyrics, you may fear that this violence could be unleashed against yourself. The hope of the early 1960s had given way to bitterness and protest, largely over the Vietnam War. The dialectic between "inside" and "outside" in this song had a special resonance for listeners in 1968, when the chaotic Democratic convention took place in Chicago and the nation's attention was split between the political princes trying to preserve their power and hierarchy on the inside and the jokers and thieves being beaten and teargassed on the outside.

As in "Hard Rain," the endlessness of "Watchtower" is historical and also reflects the peculiar way in which music depends on iterability to convey meaning. Whereas harmonic music (like most narrative) moves through increasing tension to cadential resolution, this song merely repeats the same chords (A minor-G-F-G) over and over as an ostinato. The lack of a tonal center for the song causes the final harmonica solo (the howling of the wind, one supposes) to end on an arbitrary note. Silence follows—but not closure. Dylan found release from his vision ten years later by bracketing it under the rubric of Old Testament, which would find fulfillment in the New. Trapped in history, Dylan found a temporary exit by converting to Christianity and by moving from apocalyptic ballad to apocalyptic gospel song.

From Ballad to Gospel

"Born-again Bob" he was called between 1979 and 1983, when Dylan began attending fundamentalist Christian Bible classes and turning the studied scriptures into what can be described only as gospel music, that is, music whose use-value is the production of religious exaltation. In the first of these "Christian" albums, *Slow Train Coming* of 1979, the engaged singer of "Hard Rain" returned, but his persona had changed from prophet to preacher. The dialog between believer and nonbeliever rehearsed in "Watchtower" has also returned, but the allusions are now mainly to the New Testament. "When He Returns," the final song on *Slow Train Coming*, exhibits a musical structure strikingly different from those previously considered: Here the piano (the only accompanying instrument) opens the song with a repeated sequence of four simple chords: subdominant, tonic, first inversion of the tonic, and dominant. This banal sequence sets down the song's harmonic structure like the foundations of a building. This particular sequence is also called a "church cadence" because it is often used for hymns. Most of the other lines of the song end with this same cadence, thus expressing the persistence of this vision and anchoring the song as firmly in traditional hymnody as its words hark back to the eschatological beginnings of Christianity.

For example, the first stanza of the text presents the millennial message with utter simplicity:

> The iron hand it ain't no match for the iron rod,
> The strongest wall will crumble and fall to a mighty God.
> For all those who have eyes and all those who have ears

It is only He who can reduce me to tears.
Don't you cry and don't you die and don't you burn
For like a thief in the night, He'll replace wrong with right
When He returns. (2004, 417)

A simple listing of the nouns in this text could serve as a primer of biblical typology: the iron rod, the wall, the thief in the night, and so on. The simplicity of Dylan's text returns us to the moment of eschatological anticipation of Paul and the other early Christians. The series of three commands is both plain and mysterious. "Don't you cry," for example can be seen as oscillating between the profane world of popular song and the many injunctions of the prophets to "weep not."

Yet Dylan has not lost his tendency to stamp typology with his unique style. In the first line, for example, the iron rod recalls Revelation 19:13, 15: "He was clothed with a vesture dipped in blood: and his name is called the Word of God. . . . And out of his mouth goeth a sharp sword, that with it he should smite the nations; and he shall rule them with a rod of iron." This iron rod, the symbol of spiritual and, more significant, scriptural power or the power of *logos* is contrasted with the iron hand of secular misrule, that rigid and hierarchical system that characterized the city in "Watchtower." (The phrase "iron hand" does not occur in the Bible.) In the second stanza, the metaphor given by Christ of entering at the narrow gate contrasts with that of truth as an arrow, a favorite of Dylan since the early "Restless Farewell": "Truth is an arrow and the gate is narrow that it passes through." This clouds the theology somewhat since originally it is people or souls who are supposed to be entering at the narrow gate, not truth as an abstract concept. In the third stanza, a typological invocation of Golgotha as "blood-stained ground" is followed by the startling command to "take off your mask": "Surrender your crown on this blood-stained ground, take off your mask." The concept of "mask" does not occur in the Bible but is frequently found both in Dylan's work and in critical assessments of his career as the assumption of a series of personae (*persona* is the Latin term for "mask"). The command to surrender one's crown implies that some of these personae have been caught up in the pursuit of wealth and power.

The song's rhetorical structure balances dialog (this time between singer and audience, as in the commands mentioned earlier) with narrative. As in "Hard Rain," this narration is fragmented, but the numerous allusions make it possible for a listener to fill in the gaps, particularly due to the relatively unproblematic links to the longer, more complete text of the Bible. The first couplet of each of the first two stanzas is grounded in biblical quotation. The first stanza describes Christ's triumph over the forces of evil, which initiates the millennium. In the second stanza, in which truth and the possibility of knowledge are at stake, the central lines are rhetorical questions that pinpoint the spiritual struggle occurring within the singer. In the third and final stanza, the same kinds of question are asked, but this time they are directed at the listener. Accordingly, the first couplet of the final stanza no longer narrates: It exhorts. This shift is balanced by the return to objectivity in the final couplet: "Of every earthly plan that be known to man He is unconcerned / He's got plans of his own to set up His throne when He returns" (*Lyrics* [2004] reproduces this text as three lines, but the musical structure does not differ from the previous two stanzas).

Furthermore, it is the last line of each stanza that contains the direct reference to millennium:

> For like a thief in the night, He'll replace wrong with right, when He returns. . . .
> There'll be no peace . . . the war won't cease, until He returns. . . .
> He's got plans of his own to set up His throne when He returns. (ibid., 417)

Dylan explores three different aspects of premillennial expectations in these three lines. In the first, there is the (un)predictability of the return, which, it should be clear by now, has been an important dividing line between different approaches to the eschaton. The second line refers to the violence and conflict of Armageddon, echoing the first line's binary opposition between wrong and right. The third ending echoes the first, with the mystery of "plans of his own" (i.e., unknown to humans). The internal rhymes of the first two endings echo this binarism. Besides the shifting areas of millennium these lines explore, they also convey a single, unified message: that the Second Coming will be in glory and that the Messiah's power will be absolute.

Jokerman

The 1983 album *Infidels* is generally acknowledged to represent the turning point away from Dylan's overtly Christian phase. Unlike the previous three albums, *Infidels* contained not a single song that could be called doctrinal or even exhortatory. Two songs from this recording session, one the "hit" of the album and another Dylan's most famous unreleased (bootleg) piece, address the theme of millennium from very different angles as though addressing different types of listeners. Furthermore, one takes as its subject a joker, the other one of the greatest thefts of human history: American slavery.

"Jokerman," with which the album opens, is more symbolic and intertextual in nature. Its title figure may refer to other joker figures in Dylan's lyrics, most prominently to the thief's interlocutor in "All along the Watchtower." This reminder brings with it the hint (confirmed in other passages such as "shedding off one more layer of skin") that this song also deals with issues of a divided self. Equally valid are the reminders of Dylan's interest in tarot, where the Fool represents the zero card. Often the Fool is shown with a small companion animal at his heels, and this may explain that Jokerman rests in the fields "with a small dog licking [his] face." On the other hand, many of the song's verses are drawn from the Bible. The song focuses on the ambiguous title figure, moving in its final verses into scenes of "tribulation" and culminating apparently in the rise of Antichrist. In fact, the song's last three stanzas roughly follow the plot structure of Revelation. First, things are getting very bad:

> Well, the rifleman's stalking the sick and the lame
> Preacherman seeks the same, who'll get there first is uncertain
> Nightsticks and water cannons, tear gas, padlocks
> Molotov cocktails and rocks behind every curtain

> False-hearted judges dying in the webs that they spin
> Only a matter of time 'til night comes steppin' in. (2004, 464)

This is an entirely secular, political list of catastrophes—in fact, the parallel between rifleman and preacherman would seem to discount religion as just another hypocritical institution seeking victims (although one could also see it as a chase-movie kind of race, where we are in suspense as to whether the victim can be saved). It is extraordinary how many different areas of human experience Dylan fits into this one stanza—from religion through politics and to the legal system. One also notes the allusion to the popular television series of Dylan's youth, *The Rifleman*, starring Chuck Connors. The hero of that series was a defender of truth, justice, and the disadvantaged; that he now stalks the weak indicates the deterioration of values that apocalyptic discourse always addresses. Also typical is the reference to the irreversibility or incorrigibility of the worsening depravity: It's "only a matter of time" until the end. The following stanza seems to report the birth of Antichrist:

> It's a shadowy world
> Skies are slippery gray
> A woman just gave birth to a prince today and dressed him in scarlet (ibid., 464)

The imagery comes from Revelation 17:3–5, where John sees:

> a woman sit[ting] upon a scarlet coloured beast, full of names of blasphemy, having seven heads and ten horns. And the woman was arrayed in purple and scarlet colour, and decked with gold and precious stones and pearls, having a golden cup in her hand full of abominations and filthiness of her fornication; And upon her forehead was a name written: MYSTERY BABYLON THE GREAT, THE MOTHER OF HARLOTS AND ABOMINATIONS OF THE EARTH.

Dylan saves the term "harlot" for the end of the stanza, which seems to describe metonymically the world's taking the mark of the Beast (the described child, who grows up to carry out the following actions, is probably the false prophet who preaches in the name of the Beast; in popular tradition he is frequently identified with Antichrist):

> He'll put the priests in his pocket, put the blade to the heat
> Take the motherless children off the street and place them at the feet of a harlot.
> Oh, Jokerman, you know what he wants
> Oh, Jokerman, you don't show any response (2004, 464)

"Motherless children" is not only a direct reference to actual children but also an allusion to the song of that title, made famous by the Carter Family and known to nearly every folksinger. After categorizing the affective deprivations that motherless children suffer ("Sister will do the best she can / [But] so many things a sister can't understand"), the song offers a solution: "Jesus will be like a mother to you, when your mother is dead." Hence, the Beast/false prophet's apparent concern with their welfare fits in with the script of Antichrist, who pretends to be the Messiah. Indeed, it may be that in real life we also cannot tell the harlot from the woman clothed in the sun.

Jokerman's lack of response to evil would seem to be a negative characteristic. However, as Skylar Burris (2005) points out, typologically the phrase recalls Christ's silence before his accusers. Indeed, those who argue for Jokerman as the Antichrist have this issue to overcome because Antichrist is in fact known for his glibness. Antichrist always responds and always does so in a way that leads the world into greater and greater chaos. Larry Yudelson (1999), who, like Stephen Pickering, has a clear agenda of highlighting the Jewish strain in Dylan's lyrics, suggests King David as the point of reference and through David to Dylan himself as a political poet and leader. The problem with univocal readings of this kind is that they simply pile up references in the hope that frequency of allusion will settle the matter. However, the way that allusions and quotations are played off against each other in the song does not encourage such a procedure. The best readings are those such as Michael Gray's and Aidan Day's, which focus on the song's contradictions and ambiguities as the very heart of its meaning: "Bob Dylan . . . opens 'Jokerman' with this fusing of allusions to a unique embodiment of the power of faith and a unique embodiment of the legitimacy of doubt. Thinking of Christ, he is also glancing into the mirror of Ecclesiastes" (Gray 2000, 483). If one could summarize Gray's reading of the song, it is that the major theme is heroism not in a laudatory sense but in that of a parsing or an analysis of heroism—and especially of the messiah as hero. That would include not only Christ but of course also Dylan himself, who was thrust unwillingly into the role of prophet:

> [Dylan] accommodates both the Jungian notion and the Judeo-Christian one, by using the superhero figure not only to measure his own fallibility and immaturity but to look, too, at whether he feels that Christ himself might not be a risible figure in the superhero mould while being the son of God [and] savior of the world—himself a figure of fundamental duality. (ibid., 495)

Indeed, were it not for the song's apocalyptic ending, we might decide that it is more about heroes and heroism (including their apparent opposites) than anything else. Hercules ("You were born with a snake in both of your fists"), Hurricane Carter ("While a hurricane was blowing"), David ("Michelangelo indeed could have carved out your features"), the Fool as mentioned, Jesus Christ as mentioned, martyrs ("[you're a] friend to the martyr"), and Dylan himself ("Manipulator of crowds, you're a dream twister" and "dance to the nightingale tune") are among the heroes and cultural heroes the song refers to. Yet, in the end, the "Hero with a Thousand Faces" approach to millennium seems to be a rejection of the messianic role: In his "shadowy world" Jokerman does not "show any response."

If Gray is correct, then the explanation for Dylan's leaving "Jokerman's" twin, "Blind Willie McTell," off the album may have been its extreme contrast with the former song. "I know no one can sing the blues like Blind Willie McTell" is the one-line chorus to every verse (ibid., 478). Here, finally, is an "I" that risks an opinion, "shows a response," in contrast to the constant accusatory "you's" of "Jokerman." Rather than dancing to a nightingale tune, McTell sings a blues. Indeed, the music of this bootleg classic (which is not blues) is slow and somber compared to the driving, bouncy rhythms of "Jokerman." There are fewer melodic leaps, and Dylan keeps his voice in a lower register. Yet, the repeated "oh" sounds in "know no one" remind us of the drawn-out "Oh, oh, oh, Jokerman!" (on the latter, Dylan sings the "oh's" as a single, swooping-and-diving word). McTell is one of those blues martyrs to whom Jokerman is a friend: "I've traveled through East Texas / Where many martyrs fell." Dylan accurately identifies the region as a matrix of blues culture. The geography of a possible United States here is a typically Dylanesque composite, as it is throughout the song—Willie McTell (1901–1959) worked mainly in Atlanta and is a prime representative of the so-called Piedmont style of blues.

Anyone versed in the blues will recognize Dylan's choice of McTell to be paradigmatic rather than a personal confession. Though certainly one of the greats, McTell is known more for his guitar prowess than for his voice. Though his "Statesboro Blues" became a much-covered folk-rock classic, his work in general does not have the foundational quality of a Charlie Patton, Robert Johnson, Bessie Smith, or Howlin' Wolf—none of whose names provides the same rhyming opportunities that McTell's does. Taken literally and nonidiomatically, of course, the phrase about McTell is true enough. No singer sings like any other singer, especially in roots music. But of course we do not hear the literal meaning of the words but rather their idiomatic message that Blind Willie McTell must be the greatest blues singer of all time, a meaning that, I believe, blues aficionados would have trouble accepting.

In actuality, McTell is the antitype for another, more archetypal Blind Willie: Blind Willie Johnson (1897–1945), who was born in East Texas—reportedly in Marlin, just a short distance from Waco—and whose voice on "John the Revelator," "Motherless Children" (vastly different from the Carters' version) and other pieces carries the burden of suffering and history that Dylan attributes to McTell's. (Interestingly, Blind Willie McTell was one of the few sources of information about Johnson, having toured with him from Maine to Mobile.) Adherents of the D. H. Lawrence reading of millennialism would appreciate the (unsubstantiated) stories that circulated about Johnson: His blindness had been caused by his own mother throwing lye in his face after a beating by his father, who would hang a tin cup around his son's neck to rake in the nickels and dimes from his guitar playing. Surely this, at least, unlike Dylan's own middle-class background, is an indisputably Nietzschean scenario, the pain and violence converted by art into religious ecstasy. Johnson recorded his thirty sides in New Orleans between 1927 and 1930, which perhaps accounts for Dylan's use of the city in the "McTell" song, as we will see later. Dylan certainly knew Johnson's songs intimately, having adapted one of them into "In My Time of Dying" on his first album.

Not only is "Blind Willie McTell" not a blues piece, but its lyrics, which mercilessly open the wounds of U.S. history, bear little resemblance to anything McTell would allow to pass his lips. Dylan frequently literalizes idioms in this way, but at the same time in this instance he is applying yet another, symbolic layer that reveals itself only in the course of the song. The second stanza describes a tent show, the third gives an archetypal list of American slavery's abuses and catastrophes (the cracking of the whip, the "tribes a-moaning," the undertaker, the burning plantations), and the next an antebellum scene worthy of *Gone with the Wind*:

> There's a woman by the river
> With some fine young handsome man
> He's dressed up like a squire
> Bootlegged whiskey in his hand
> There's a chain gang on the highway
> I can hear them rebels yell
> And I know no one can sing the blues
> Like Blind Willie McTell (2004, 478)

It becomes apparent that these seemingly incoherent mental images—their incongruity with each other, though all have the same "cause," as it were, namely slavery, is part of the message—are invoked in the "I" who hears McTell sing. It even seems that the rhythm of the chain gang and the rebel yell infuse the timbre of McTell's voice or the particular shaping of his blue notes. Willie McTell's ability to evoke these painful images of truth and power is what makes him unique. Dylan even reminds us of da Cunha's excoriation of Brazil's slavish imitation of European manners with his observation that the young man is "dressed up like a squire." He in fact cannot be a squire because that designation is an English legal one—it denotes the right to wear a sword—that was not imported into any of the American colonies. The performative aspect of squirehood here stands for America's striving to be European.

The images confirm and explain the striking observation that "I" makes at the song's beginning:

> Seen the arrow on the doorpost
> Saying, "This land is condemned
> All the way from New Orleans
> To Jerusalem." (ibid.)

The arrow on the doorpost seems to conflate Exodus 12, the origin of Passover in the sign drawn in lamb's blood on the Hebrews' doorposts, made in order for the Lord to spare their firstborn while striking dead those of the impious Egyptians, with the "truth-as-arrow" motif we have seen in "When He Returns." (An arrow cannot literally "say" anything.) The allusion to Exodus is at the same time an allusion to the centuries-old tradition of African Americans identifying themselves with the Hebrews. Given the two geographical points mentioned, we assume that the arrow must point roughly east or west, and if we keep this in mind when hearing the line about the martyrs of East Texas, west would be the direction. In either case, land does not stretch across the ocean to Jerusalem, so we are forced either to think of Jerusalem as symbolic and as relocated to the Americas or, like the Mormons and others, to posit two Jerusalems, one in the Old World and one in the New. (The Mormons placed the American Jerusalem in Jackson County, Missouri.) The blanket statement returns at the end of the song: "But power and greed and corruptible seed / Seem to be all that there is" (ibid.). In contrast to Jokerman's Hero of a Thousand Faces, this song posits no heroes at all. It supplements the mythology and scripture of the former with U.S. history, in particular with the legacy of slavery, which has delivered a present situation of such potent contradictions that it paralyzes action.

Out of those contradictions the blues itself was born, a transcendent, hybrid artistic genre brought forth from slavery and its aftermath. Born out of African Americans taking their guitars to church, as we can hear in Blind Willie Johnson, the blues is a genre erupting out of the old, millennial America, one of whose Armageddons was fought over slavery. As in "Hard Rain," to sing of the tragedy of history in this genre is the worthiest of actions. To know of someone else's singing is a close second. Hence, Dylan reports in the ultimate verse line that he is only "gazing out the window / Of the St. James Hotel," invoking active martyrdom from the inside, as it were. As in "Hard Rain" and "Desolation Row," the song ends with a focus on the singer's own power of vision—or lack thereof. The St. James Hotel is another composite image, one that combines Elvis Presley's "Heartbreak Hotel," the well-known folksong "St. James Infirmary," which, like this song, is saturated with blues idiom without belonging to the genre, and the apostle James who fell asleep while Jesus prayed in Gethsemane but later was the first apostle to be martyred, bringing us back to the initial stanza.

Both "Jokerman" and "Blind Willie McTell" build to climaxes, both are apocalyptic, and, like "Hard Rain" (and unlike "The Hour When the Ship Comes In" or "When He Returns"), both depict tribulation with no millennium in sight. The millennial aspects of "Blind Willie McTell" are far subtler than those of "Jokerman," but in the end Dylan seems to see in McTell the type of true prophet or messiah of which Jokerman is a mere shadow. The two songs' self-referential aspects then dictated that "McTell" be relegated to shadow status in Dylan's overall recording career, in a sort of anxiety of authenticity. In any case, the two songs heard one after the other show the continuation of the dialectic in Dylan's work between scripture and history, prophecy and ballad, joker and thief. In some sense the most successful typological poetry in U.S. history, Dylan's lyric escapes the participatory side of the spectrum through its proliferation of antitypes drawn from the most disparate realms from the Bible to television, thus demonstrating a reflective dissonance not so much about millennial defeat as about millennial discourse in an age of mass media. The constant imagery of the eschaton in his work does not serve to focus and define American origins; rather, it reveals them as scattered, dispersed, contradictory, and immanent. The suggestion in "Blind Willie McTell" that race belongs to the millennial equation in the Americas points us toward the topic of the next chapter.

The DNA of the Lamb: The Race for the End (Times) in American Millennial Fiction

We in America shall arrive, before any other part of the world, at the creation of a new race fashioned out of the treasures of all the previous ones: The final race, the cosmic race [la raza cósmica].

—José Vasconcelos, *La raza cósmica*

You're a man of the mountains, you can walk on the clouds,
Manipulator of crowds, you're a dream-twister.
You're going to Sodom and Gomorrah
But what do you care? Ain't nobody there would want to
marry your sister.

—Bob Dylan, "Jokerman"

My daughter is too demure
To marry a bandit
She is much too genteel
For you to have with my blessing.

[Ma fille est bien trop tranquille
Pour avoir un bandit
Elle est bien trop gentille
Pour vous sans contredit]

—Louis Riel, *Poésies de jeunesse*

There is a millennial dimension to José Vasconcelos's proposal that the race of the future will be openly miscegenated, of mixed blood and—in the terminology of this chapter—that people's differences in DNA will become random. Vasconcelos, a prominent political figure during and following the Mexican Revolution—he was responsible for commissioning many of the public murals of José Orozco and others—acquired some of his schooling in Eagle Pass, Texas, where he experienced the differential treatment of Anglos and Mexicans firsthand. His response to racism and to the upheavals of the Mexican Revolution was one of the most optimistic and ecumenical visions of evolutionary racial harmony ever published in the Americas, *The Cosmic Race* (*La raza cósmica*). The Dylan quote deflates the (false?) messiah Jokerman's various eschatechnologies with a brutal example of racial stereotyping: an allusion to the cliché about "I wouldn't want one marrying my sister (or daughter)." Since the residents of Sodom and Gomorrah hold this attitude, one may conjecture that their rejection of the Messiah on racial grounds is one of the major sins that will lead to their being zapped by God. (On the other hand, as we have seen in the previous chapter, Dylan's ambiguous treatment of the messiah complicates the divide between belief and apostasy.)

We may compare Dylan's sarcasm with the anguish of Louis Riel, who sees his own Métis status equated with that of a bandit. That designation refers not to crimes committed but to the general outlaw status of the Métis living beyond the boundaries of civilization, a place from which they can never return due to the impurity of their DNA and their dark skin. The stanza is free indirect discourse: Riel tells his own ethnicity to himself through the language of another. The mother of the girl he is in love with (Julie-Marie Guerdon of Montréal, whom Riel met while a seminary student there) and in whose mouth he puts these words is Dylan's Sodomite, the antithesis of the true believer. A similar story of foiled love appears in the life of Marcus Garvey, who at fourteen was friends with the daughter of a white missionary; she was forced to break off correspondence with him on her return to England, in her words, because he was a "nigger" (Erskine 2005, 31). Both Riel and Garvey responded by tying the bloodlines of their peoples—Métis and Afro-Jamaicans, respectively—to those of people living in other places in the world—the Middle East and Africa, respectively—in order to grant them dignity and to define their role in the eschaton, which becomes their point of origin.[1] Riel would later repeat the lesson he apparently learned from his first love. During the second rebellion he wrote the following in his diary:

> The white man stumbles; his two feet slowly slide to the wrong side. He cannot stand up; he is effaced little by little; he gradually disappears; he vanishes—because his heart only has room for evil. To be more precise, he has no heart. When I speak of *white* men, I do not mean *brown* men. (1976, 82; emphasis added)

These epigraphs epitomize the racial divide of American millennialism: an ecumenical view in which the condition of establishing the New Jerusalem is the erasure of racial differences versus a sectarian viewpoint in which race is the very issue that sets off Armageddon. For some writers of the Americas, then, millennium consists of a mixing and harmonization of races, while for others the final battle is for the maintenance of racial purity. There is a third position, which, like the latter, sees racial conflict or domination as the essential evil of the Americas but nevertheless prophesies a positive solution when imbalances are redressed. In terms of this chapter's title, then, and in the language of Revelation, what exactly is the DNA content of the blood of the lamb? Is it the neutral, one-size-fits-all genetic material that Vasconcelos implies, so that washing in the blood removes racial difference? Or, as in some of the darker visions we encounter later, is the washing selective in nature, so that the lamb's blood matches that of the chosen ones?

Blood Types and Antitypes

In this chapter I examine the eschatechnologies of racial division and combination in the Americas. The substitution of "DNA" for "blood" in the title acts as a metaphor for the continuing presence of technology—DNA is the technologized term for "blood" in many racialized millennial fictions. Blood has been the token of inherited characteristics for much of human history; only recently has it been replaced first by genes and then by DNA as a signifier for the inheritance of traits. By the 2002 end-date of this book's title, DNA and genes had entered the debate about racial categorization and the question of whether race "exists," based on findings that large blocks of genetic material, called *haplotypes*, correlate with both geographic location of ancestry and racial self-identification. Neil Risch and others (2002) published an article in an online journal, *Genome Biology*, that called for the use of five racial categories. Obviously, "[s]ociologists, bioethicists, and anthropologists worry that the genetic data could be manipulated to give an air of biological credence to ethnic stereotypes, to revive discredited racial classifications, and even to fuel bogus claims of fundamental genetic differences between groups" (Rotman 2003, 42). It is not my intention in this chapter to intervene in this debate or to critique the scientific use of DNA. I am using DNA as a countersymbol to that of blood, which has been used for millennia to depict the relative closeness of groups of people but is reversed in the symbol of being washed in the blood of the lamb.

In Revelation 7:14 John sees a great multitude standing before the throne, holding palm branches in their hands. When he asks who they are, one of the elders answers him: "These are the ones who have survived the time of great distress; they have washed their robes and made them white in the blood of the Lamb." Using blood, one of the most staining natural substances known, to wash clothes presents a striking image. The meaning of washing in blood, according to Richard Bauckham, is that these have elected martyrdom and "share in the Lamb's victory by means of sacrificial death like his" (1993, 228). Most commentators have understood 7:14 to refer to the lamb's redemption of Christians from sin. This means that the army of the elect, with the Messiah and Michael at its head, conquers through passivity and suffering.

Needless to say, washing in the blood of a lamb was never part of standard Christian practice. Water was enough. Thin, pure, it cleansed one of sin. Thick, sticky, weighty blood ties one to the earth and to one's ancestors and family. Yet the idea of being washed in the blood of the lamb, splashed by the blood of martyrs, quickly arose and has persisted. It probably owes something to older rituals, in which blood was the perfect armor for "fechando o corpo" [literally "closing the body"] against enemy action or for tying one's fate to the spirit of one's familiar. In the *Kingdom of This World* (Carpentier 1957), the new prince of Haiti sacrifices bulls as a counterimage to the sacrifice of a pig by Bouckman and his fellow revolutionaries who

smear their lips with its blood. Blood's coagulation symbolizes the bonding necessary for apocalyptic community. Blood surfaces frequently in apocalyptic literature
in a gamut of contexts from the literal to the symbolic to the metonymic, where it
becomes synonymous with race. The role of blood in the building of community
signals that apocalypse guarantees the forging of racial purity. Just as the apocalyptic
scheme posits opposing forces of absolute good and evil, the racial scheme posits
opposing races of absolute purity and impurity.

As the ultimate discriminant, the last technology for sorting and grouping,
DNA reverses the reversal of Revelation. Such conflicts and tensions are characteristic of the fictions examined in this chapter. The earlier chapters of this book
have disclosed that, from the first European incursions into the New World, race has
been a factor in the construction of various eschatological schemata. To review one
example, it was important to some that the Native Americans be considered descendents of one of the tribes of Israel. Unlike many other millennial scripts, that based
on Revelation is ecumenical in the sense that it is aimed at "seven churches" in different parts of the world that include different languages and ethnic groups. On the
other hand, U.S. history has resulted in the racializing of political and social issues
to the extent that many of the 59 percent—according to a *Time* magazine poll (Gibbs
2002, 43)—who believe that the prophecies of Revelation will come true probably
do not see the New Jerusalem as a rainbow coalition. This chapter examines literary
texts that specifically construct their end-time scenarios around racial conflict or
racial coming-together.

As a counterimage to the blood of the lamb, blood appears again voluminously
in Revelation's "grapes of wrath," as it is pressed out of sinful mortals:

> The angel who has power over fire . . . called with a loud voice to him who had the
> sharp sickle, "Put in your sickle, and gather the clusters of the vine of the earth,
> for its grapes are ripe." So the angel swung his sickle on the earth and gathered
> the vintage of the earth, and threw it into the great wine press of the wrath of God;
> and the wine press was trodden outside the city, and blood flowed from the wine
> press, as high as a horse's bridle, for one thousand six hundred stadia. (Revelation
> 14:18–20)

Only at the end of this passage, when the wine receives the name of blood, is it
clear that these are unrepentant sinners and unbelievers who are being squashed. The
image surprises because of the generally positive assessment of harvest elsewhere
in the Bible. What does it mean that the grapes are "ripe," again an image that is
generally used positively? In any case, millennial fictions of the Americas have been
eager to portray this harvest of blood and to link the image to race. Here, as elsewhere, *Left Behind* takes the route of absolute literalism: When He returns, Christ
zaps the armies of the Antichrist right and left, making them bleed to create the rivers
described in Revelation: "Their blood poured from them in great waves, combining
to make a river that quickly became a swamp" (LaHaye and Jenkins, *Glorious Appearing* 249).

Racialized apocalypses depict three different kinds of possible worlds: In one,
Tribulation is the beginning of openly racial warfare; in another, it is the end of
race war, with the last race(s) becoming first; and the inhabitants of a third take

an ecumenical approach, providing images of a rainbow coalition departing from Babylon and constructing the New Jerusalem. Authors of works in the first category are generally members of the dominant race (in the examples adduced, white North Americans), and their fictions indulge in "blaming the victim" on a cosmic scale. Authors of works in the second two categories have a variety of origins. Of course, some works are ambiguous or self-contradictory, but in general, one can delineate the natural and social laws of these three worlds, and the fictions that take place on them are virtually interchangeable. I discuss them in the order given.

Tribulation as Race War

The very title of Arthur Henry's novel *Nicholas Blood, Candidate* makes it a prime candidate for analysis. Published in 1890 (hence a close cousin of *Caesar's Column*), it is largely a defense of racial apartheid and the disenfranchisement of African Americans. The novel takes place in Memphis "just before the great negro riots in Tennessee" (4). The reference is apparently to the Memphis riots of May 1–2, 1866. Thomas Judd arrives from the North to buy timberland from Judge. Nicholas Blood is a candidate for the city council of Memphis. The mulatto is called "Blood" because "he knew neither father nor mother—because of the streaks in his eyes and the ferociousness of his disposition" (ibid., 28). Judd and Judge go visit Philander Matthews, a philanthropist. The first name obviously reflects the love of all men and all races, while his last name perhaps refers to the Evangelist and hence to the ecumenical basis of Christianity. The name of his interlocutor, "Judge," might then refer to the idea of discrimination and punishment, of separating the sheep from the goats. When Judge deplores the Negro vote, Matthews responds: "It is the will of God; this is your punishment. Why did you bring them here?" (ibid., 59). Judge asks, "[W]ill it be possible for two distinct races, which must always remain as distinct as black and white, to live together on the same soil, and build together a commonwealth?" (ibid., 62). Matthews responds that yes, it will, and points to several upstanding Africans. Judge reveals that they are illegitimate mulattoes. Then Judge takes Judd through the streets, where they watch the blacks gambling, drinking, and whoring. Judd knocks down a surly African, and a mob follows them until Nicholas Blood pops up to quiet them down.

The next evening Judd, disabused, goes to the Episcopal church meeting. There he reencounters his childhood sweetheart, Annie, who of course has blossomed into a beautiful young woman. Judd then goes to a black church, giving the author a chance to minstrel some set pieces of Negro preaching and hymning. This church scene parallels that in *Caesar's Column*. In *Caesar's Column*, religion is faulted for having lost its evangelical fervor and become completely tolerant; in Henry's novel, it is faulted for having become sectarian and racialized. In terms that remind us of Ahab or the Counselor, Blood is described as a messiah figure:

> A crushing will, so fiendish and brutal as to impress even those sordid minds among which he moved as uncanny and frightful, dwelt always behind his formidable face. It was this and the mystery which he threw about himself, his unknown origin, a

certain defined belief that the devil had a hand in it, his dogged persistence, his horrible cruelty, his spirit of revenge that marked his enemy with a seal of death. (ibid., 127)

Blood rapes Annie, who has come to the black area of town to comfort her wet nurse, who is in the throes of death. Judd saves her, but the romance between them is endangered by the insult to her. Judd visits a plantation, whose owner is not in favor of separation and says he gets along fine with the blacks. As Judd walks from plantation back to town, he sees numerous blacks heading for Memphis. "It was seventy-two hours before election day, and the restless negroes throughout all that portion of Tennessee were moving at night toward Memphis" (ibid., 159).

These "Negroes" riot on the eve of election but not on election day, on which Judge emerges triumphant. That night Nicholas Blood enters the winner's house and slits the throats of Judge and his wife. Annie awakens Judd, who throws Blood downstairs, takes Annie to the river, and tries to swim across it with Annie on his back. The story ends there, with the last chapter describing how blacks are setting fire to all of Memphis: houses, cotton bales, and barges. "A sound arose, composed of cries of hate and terror, oaths, coarse laughter and the clamor of despair. It was a banquet of blood. Mingling with the sound of revelry rose the wails of butchered victims" (ibid., 194). The author does not specify the DNA of the blood being spilled. Since the novel ends in (literal) "white flight" from the city, readers are likely to presume that African Americans are massacring whites. History tells us otherwise.

There are several versions of the origins of the Memphis riots of 1866, but most agree that the fuel for the fire was racial tension, especially resentment by former confederates of the freedmen. There were no political leadership issues involved, though the result of the disturbance was to speed Radical Reconstruction, which eventually led to political leadership by blacks. The vast majority of the "butchered victims" were African American (forty-six to two white), and the five rape victims wholly so. Clearly one aspect of Henry's fiction is to reverse the historical record and "blame the victims" of these riots; second, by making the potential election of a black mayor—unthinkable in 1866—the exciting cause of the riots, he condenses the actual ones with the present Southern white grievances against their political disempowerment. However, in my reading more is going on, namely that the story of this public violence cannot be told without inserting it into America's favorite story: the end of the world.

In *Caesar's Column*, published in the same year as Henry's novel, blood also becomes associated with race, and listening to its call helps determine the fate of the world. An intermediate use of the term appears when the men discuss Estella Washington's use of the knife to ward off the Jewish Prince Cabano's henchman, essentially defending herself against rape by someone not of her own Anglo-Saxon race: " 'How she rose to the occasion!' 'Yes,' [Gabriel] said, 'that was blood'" (Donnelly 1890, 88). Washington's name aligns her bloodlines with those of the father of the American nation (her genealogy gives her as descended from Lawrence Washington, George's brother), and it is this combative blood and racial pride that cause her to aggressively defend her honor. The racial solidarity shown here contrasts with its general disruption by a classism exacerbated by technological capitalism: "There is no doubt that if the ruling classes had been willing to recognize these natural leaders [of the proletariat] as men of the same race, blood, tongue, and capacity as themselves, and had reached down to them a kindly and helping hand, there might have been long since a coming together of the two great divisions of society" (ibid., 72). Here racial unity is held out as a prospect for overcoming class divisions that the author predicted would exacerbate themselves. Rather than try to elevate their white brothers and sisters in the lower classes, the ruling elite has sold out to a Jewish cabal of financiers. The infectious agent goes beyond a set of ideas or even money into the very genetic makeup of the ruling class in a strangely literalized metaphor of blood: "The task which Hannibal attempted, so disastrously, to subject the Latin and mixed-Gothic races of Europe to the domination of the Semitic blood, as represented in the merchant-city of Carthage, has been successfully accomplished in these latter days by the cousins of the Phoenicians, the Israelites" (ibid., 101).

Although their assumptions of the impossibility of racial peace converge, *Caesar's Column* and *The Turner Diaries* (Pierce 1980) differ significantly from each other in their depictions of the racial alliances against whites. In *Caesar's Column* it is the Hebrew race that will be warred against with the help of the blacks. Southern blacks are members of the conspiracy to revolt "to a man. Their former masters have kept them in a state of savagery, instead of civilizing them; and the result is that they are as barbarous and bloodthirsty as their ancestors were when brought from Africa, and fit subjects for such a terrible organization" (Donnelly 1890, 126–27). This racist and denigrating portrayal also offers redemption in the sense that African Americans will eventually be on the winning side. Jews, fulfilling their ancient destiny as the "race" that condemned Christ, will find only damnation. The title of Gerald Winrod's book, *The Jewish Assault on Christianity*, made it clear that Jews were Satan's main tool in the battle against Christ (see Fuller 1966, 138–45). The problems of contaminated blood and bloodlines denied can be erased only in a bloodbath, whose details are recounted in chapter four.

In the *Turner Diaries*, on the other hand, African Americans join forces with Jews and liberals to create the "Jewish-liberal-democratic-egalitarian plague" (1980, 42). The book documents a series of "final solutions" for all nonwhites, ranging from hand-to-hand combat, to the deliberate sinking of passenger ships, to nuclear war:

> The blood flowed ankle-deep in the streets of many of Europe's great cities momentarily, as the race traitors, the offspring of generations of dysgenic breeding, and hordes of *Gastarbeiter* met a common fate. . . .
> The Organization resorted to a combination of chemical, biological, and radiological means, on an enormous scale, to deal with the problem [of eliminating Chinese infantry pouring into Europe]. . . . Thus was the Great Eastern Waste created. (ibid., 209–10)

Supposedly written in 2099, the book celebrates one hundred years of the New Era, when the dark-skinned and (worse still) hybridous of the world have been eliminated in favor of the "Aryans." This racial hatred becomes absolutely necessary in order to sustain the narrative's believability because the conspirators never come together as a group—that is, the white race is made far more real and tangible by the enumeration of its enemies than by self-description. As in Atwood's *Handmaid's Tale* (2004), the ideal of conspiratorial unity is exposed as a mirage because there is no final coming together of the hordes of blonde beasts. The two portraits can be symmetrical inversions of one another, grounded in a single white supremacist viewpoint. Whereas *Caesar's Column* allows blacks to be ambiguously on the (temporarily) winning side and to join in the slaughter of the wealthy, Turner allows whites to be ambiguously on the losing side. Any white caught fraternizing with blacks—professors at liberal universities all fall under this category—immediately becomes Africanized ("niggerized," to recall Jim Jones's term) and a candidate for elimination.

The racial composition of salvation conflicts with other principles for the formation of community, notably the sharing of texts and of interpretations, of what Jean-François Lyotard (1984) calls "master narratives"—where the word "master" takes on its political sense. The loss of such narratives can be said to fuel the need for alternative, apocalyptic inventions. *The Turner Diaries* offers a striking example of this process. Christianity is rejected as a possible master narrative. Indeed, it no longer functions as such even for the "mixed bag" of people who call themselves Christians:

> The Christians are a mixed bag. Some of them are among our most devoted and courageous members. Their hatred of the System is based on—in addition to the reasons the rest of us have—their recognition of the System's role in undermining and perverting Christendom. But all the ones who are still affiliated with major churches are against us. (Pierce 1980, 64)

Pierce does not specify further characteristics of these sympathetic Christians. The vision of a bankrupt Christianity is found as well in *Caesar's Column* and to some extent in LeVar Burton's *Aftermath* (1997) and in the *Left Behind* (LaHaye 1995) series.

In *The Turner Diaries*, Earl Turner lambastes the white middle class for whom he is sacrificing everything and that he hopes to save. He cannot understand "why we should take chances and knock ourselves out to save such brainwashed scum from the fate they richly deserve" (Pierce 1980, 152). After all, "Slavery is the just and proper state for a people who have grown as soft, self-indulgent, careless, credulous, and befuddled as we have" (ibid., 33). The evil System has succeeded in creating a network of economic dependence that people cannot do without: "As long as the government is able to keep the economy somehow gasping and wheezing along, the people can be conditioned to accept any outrage" (ibid., 6). This inertia explains the logarithmic growth of destruction in the book: From his early guerilla activities in the East, Turner is transferred to California, where the Organization is larger and has several military bases on its side. Africans and Asians are exiled from California in a huge convoy. In ongoing race wars, hand-to-hand fighting escalates into the total collapse of government and worldwide nuclear war, which finally brings about the desired "White world" (ibid., 210). The millennial violence and destruction thus seem proportional to the lack of enthusiasm of those to be transformed. The four horsemen have become evolutionary gatekeepers who weed out those racially unfit to move humankind forward—not only those who are not white but also all those too weak to fight for survival:

> In Detroit the practice was first established (and it was later adopted elsewhere) of providing any able-bodied White male who sought admittance to the Organization's

enclave with one hot meal and a bayonet or other edged weapon. His forehead was then marked with an indelible dye, and he was turned out and could be readmitted permanently only by bringing back the head of a freshly killed Black or other non-White. This practice assured that precious food would not be wasted on those who would not or could not add to the Organization's fighting strength, but it took a terrible toll of the weaker and more decadent White elements. (ibid., 206–207)

This is the Darwinian version of the division of the Elect from the Preterit. It proceeds from the viewpoint not only that racial essentialism is valid but also that minds cannot be changed and that there is no procedure of replacing stony hearts with ones of flesh.

Earl Turner is interrogated by his own commanders to ascertain his loyalty. When he wakes up from this interrogation, he is allowed to read "the Book":

What I had read—it amounted to a book of about 400 typed pages—had lifted me out of this world, out of my day-to-day existence as an underground fighter for the Organization, and it had taken me to the top of a high mountain from which I could see the whole world, with all its nations and tribes and races, spread out before me. And I could see the ages spread out before me too, from the steaming, primordial swamps of a hundred million years ago to the unlimited possibilities which the centuries and the millennia ahead hold for us. . . . For the first time I understand the deepest meaning of what we are doing. . . . We are truly the instruments of God in the fulfillment of His Grand Design. (ibid., 71)

Here, finally, is a true master narrative. Someone has written an enormously powerful work of literature that holds its techie reader enthralled for four hours—leaving sandwiches uneaten and coffee undrunk. Substituted for the food was the Book itself, as when the angel gives John the book to eat in Revelation. Here the order of bitterness and sweetness is reversed, as Turner's acidic personal recriminations cited earlier are recuperated into a vision of the destiny of humankind. One of the *Turner Diaries'* many fictitious footnotes then intervenes and gives the Book a pedigree: "It is obvious that Turner is referring to the Book. We know from other evidence that it was written approximately ten years before the Record of Martyrs, in which it is mentioned—i.e., probably sometime in 9 BNE or 1990, according to the old chronology. . . . [W]e may have here the only extant reference to the original copy of the Book!" (ibid.). Earl Turner reveals nothing specific about the Book's contents—one suspects that it mixes Herbert Spencer with Adolf Hitler (whose birthdate replaces Christ's as the fulcrum of world history). Just as the "little book" John eats in the middle of his vision contains the vision itself, so too this reference within *The Turner Diaries* seems to point to the novel itself. It is prophetic since *The Turner Diaries*, leaving the realm of fiction to shape reality, has become the "sacred text" of a number of antigovernment hate groups, most famously of the smallest group of all, Timothy McVeigh and his coconspirators, discussed below.

That an American new religion—yet another—is being created is confirmed by Turner's death—in a suicide bombing flight (with a warhead) into the Pentagon—being celebrated on the Day of Martyrs, and the mission being a kind of extreme hazing for acceptance into the holy Order (ibid., 211). These passages clearly make the

Book a substitute for the Bible as a foundational text for the new society. There is, for example, its name which is a lack of name: "Book" simply backtranslates the Greek "biblios" into Anglo-Saxon. The Book, like the Bible, seems to have no author. Both texts have the purpose of making readers aware of their role in the "grand design" of millennium. Both texts found movements that change the course of human history, and consequently each becomes the subject of intense textual criticism and archaeology, perhaps parodied by Atwood at the end of the *Handmaid's Tale* (2004). The fragmentary and highly subjective recordings of Offred are subjected not to worshipful praise but to scrutiny and ironization. The last sentence of Atwood's novel is "Are there any questions?" (ibid., 395).

In Pierce's novel, the last sentence summarizes Turner's posthumous greatness: "[Turner] helped greatly to assure that his race would survive and prosper, that the Organization would achieve its worldwide political and military goals, and that the Order would spread its wise and benevolent rule over the earth for all time to come" (1980, 211). In fact, according to its form, *The Handmaid's Tale* could have been called *The Handmaid's Diaries*, and both texts use the diary form to normatize their possible worlds through the mimesis of subjectivities that resonate with their readers. *The Turner Diaries* eschew a specific theological grounding of racial hatred in favor of the time-honored literary device of *empathy*: Readers will be persuaded simply by the facticity that an Earl Turner can exist, can be disgusted with everything and everyone around him, and can be convinced and enlightened by the Book. The Book exists for the reader because Turner does. It is hard to overestimate the power of the diary form in conveying such empathy. Turner exposes his race hatred in hundreds of offhand ways without ever arguing for it in abstract or theoretical language. He does not have to; the apparently unmotivated hatred "proves" the depth and ubiquity of its justifications in a process Jürgen Habermas (1989) has dubbed the "publication of the private." The Book simply alludes to the fact that someone has made the argument, even if we will never know what the argument actually is.

Aside from the Bible itself, *The Turner Diaries* (Pierce 1980) may be the only millennial fiction to have actually been used by Americans as a blueprint for action in history. Timothy McVeigh, the "Oklahoma City bomber," sold the book at gun shows, quoted it to friends and coconspirators like Terry Nichols, and sent clippings from it to his sister. The novel was introduced as "exhibit one" by the prosecution at McVeigh's trial. The truck bomb that Turner and friends construct and explode at the FBI building (ibid., 38–44) greatly resembles McVeigh and Nichols's weapon of mass destruction, which was detonated on April 19, 1995. Mark Hamm, author of one of the standard accounts of McVeigh's actions, dismisses *The Turner Diaries* as "a well-known terrorism manual" (1997, 145), but I have shown that such a quick reading does not tell the whole story or explain the book's extraordinary influence on its readers. Hamm describes the moment that McVeigh, Earl Turner-like, first became absorbed in his Book:

> One day, as McVeigh was thumbing through the mail-order section of a survivalist magazine, he came across an advertisement for *The Turner Diaries*. McVeigh ordered the book and awaited its arrival with great anticipation. When after several weeks it arrived at Fort Riley, an excited McVeigh said to his roommate, "I've been trying to

get this book forever!" The warrior had found a new obsession. "He took the book to the field and read it for three weeks," recalled [infantryman William Dilly, McVeigh's roommate]. "He said it was really wild and tried to get me to read it."

No doubt of crucial interest to McVeigh was the central motif of *The Turner Diaries*: the usurpation of the Second Amendment via the Cohen Act. (ibid., 144)

Indeed, Earl Turner's first diary entry records his trip to bury guns "in an eight-foot deep pit . . . in the woods of western Pennsylvania" (Pierce 1980, 2) immediately after the Cohen Act forbids private ownership of guns and ammunition. (He keeps one handgun and is arrested in the gun raids of 1989, a foundational incident for the subversive Organization.) The naming of the antigun legislation after a recognizably Jewish senator is not incidental.

McVeigh's actions, it would seem, resulted from a combination of the millennial fiction of *The Turner Diaries* with the millennial reality of Waco—McVeigh traveled there twice in order to protest the ATF and FBI violence against Koresh's sect. A third ingredient was McVeigh's long-standing interest in firepower and weaponry, culminating in the training and encouragement in killing he received in the first Gulf War. These various ingredients were cooked by heavy doses of crystal methamphetamine to create the perfect terrorist.

While Pierce's novel is unimaginative and factual, McVeigh seems interpretable only through other texts since he had very little to say about his own motives. Typically, his final statement before execution was yet another literary text, a poem written by someone else, "Invictus" by Thomas Henley. The often-repeated story that McVeigh believed the army had implanted a computer chip in his buttock is perhaps symbolic of the status of his mind as a textual nexus. "Hard" technology is a phantasmagoria of the "soft" technology of literature. Like the Counselor of Euclides da Cunha, McVeigh was a shadow that projected itself into history, manipulated this time not by the masses but by literature and the horrors of war.

And the Last Race Shall Be First

The texts discussed earlier, which see Armageddon as race war all have, not coincidentally, white men as their authors. They exhibit the Lawrentian view of millennium as *ressentiment* and therefore must first carry out the rhetorical move of convincing readers that the millennial race has been oppressed by historical events and that whites stand at the tipping point of subjugation and eventual extermination. Another set of millennial fictions begins from a more realistic viewpoint on racial inequality in the Americas, arguing their millennial violence as extrapolations from present conditions.

Leslie Marmon Silko, of mixed heritage, is generally identified (and self-identifies) as a Native American writer. Silko's relentlessly prophetic *Almanac of the Dead* (1991) displaces biblical prophetic texts by indigenous ones. The novel is a sprawling, syncretistic accounting of the end of American civilization. Its characters represent a diverse population—whites, Native Americans, Mexicans, and African Americans all play a role, but they mostly share a complete lack of direction in a world without morals. The almanac that inspires the title of the novel is a fragmentary Mesoamerican notebook, smuggled north by fugitive slaves and currently being deciphered by the character Lecha. The language of the text is hybrid, a mixture of Mayan writing systems, Spanish, and Latin. Lecha's mother, Yoeme, had given the materials to her sister, Zeta—the last letter of the Spanish alphabet and hence symbolic of the eschaton—emphasizing that the notebook of the snakes was the key to understanding the rest. There, the snake gives the prophecy of the end of the world: *"What I have told you has always been true. What I have to tell you now is that / this world is about to end"* (ibid., 135). There is a self-referential aspect to the novel's title, a correspondence between the writing that Lecha is working so feverishly to decode and Silko's own prophecies concerning the end times.

Silko's world ends both with a bang—Marxist revolution and assassination in Mexico—and with a whimper, as human communication fails entirely and the protagonists go about their business, which usually involves cannibalizing or vampirizing others. Eventually, we are to infer, the ebbing of white culture will combine with waves of human migration from Mexico and armed revolution à la Chiapas to return the Americas to a state closer to pre-European utopia. The Americas, whose fundamental shaping was through their native peoples, will shed superficial European civilization like a snake sheds its skin. Literature will play an important role in this process, as Lecha's almanac tells us:

> One day a story will arrive in your town. There will always be disagreement over direction—whether the story came from the southwest or the southeast. The story may arrive with a stranger, a traveler thrown out of his home country months ago. Or the story may be brought by an old friend, perhaps the parrot trader. But after you hear the story, you and the others prepare by the new moon to rise up against the slave masters. (ibid., 578)

This scene parallels the end of Sherman Alexie's *Indian Killer*, in which a ghost dancer moves through the American landscape:

> The killer sings and dances for hours, days. Other Indians arrive and quickly learn the song. A dozen Indians, then hundreds, and more, all learning the same song, the exact dance. The killer dances and will not tire. The killer knows this dance is over five hundred years old. . . . With this mask, with this mystery, the killer can dance forever. (1996, 420)

Silko's novel shares with *The Turner Diaries* the idea that the current state of affairs cannot get any worse and must soon end in cataclysm or utter chaos. It is, however, less conspiratorial at both ends: It takes capitalism at its face value of giving absolute freedom to consume, pollute, and destroy oneself. There is no system to fight against and hence also no organization to focus resistance but only a multiplicity of amoral acts that gradually contribute to the end; similarly, no single movement or individual will bring about the overthrow of white culture. The novel's walking "dead" protagonists equate to the wooden people of the *Popol Vuh*, who have no minds or souls. These are one of the gods' early attempts to create humans—other inferior materials include mud and animals. The wooden figures are destroyed when nature itself rises up against them. They are thus also meant to represent the degeneration of humans at the end of their cycle, as the old world is destroyed and a new one created. Silko reproduces the essence of the cataclysm in a syncretistic prayer, the "Ritual of the Four World Quarters," which the shamans of a Mexican village sell to the

> great inter-American market for "Inca secrets" and "Aztec magic." European descendants on American soil anxiously purchased indigenous cures for their dark nights of the soul on the continents where Christianity had repeatedly violated its own canons, and only the Indians could still see the Blessed Virgin among the December roses, her skin color and clothing Native American, not European. (ibid., 478)

The quote describes the Virgin of Guadalupe, who according to tradition appeared in a series of visions to an Indian, Juan Diego, from December 9 to December 12, 1531, and asked that a temple be built in her honor. In one of Diego's visits to the bishop to relate his vision, the Virgin's image miraculously appeared on his *tilma* [cloak] of agave-fiber cloth, and this image became the central focus of her worship. It is housed in a hermetically sealed frame in the basilica in Mexico City and reproduced in countless Mexican and Mexican American households (not to mention stores, offices, schools, cemeteries, buses, and taxis). Scholars consider her origins to lie in the syncretization of the Aztec fertility and earth goddess, Tonantzín. To respond to the diverse market, the sorcerers countersyncretize by placing a Christian invocation at the head of what for the most part has been taken straight from the *Popol Vuh*:

> Jesus, Mary, St. Joseph! Holy Trinity!
> All the saints, and all the souls of the living and dead! . . .
> These wooden figures had no minds or souls.
> They did not remember their Creator. . . .
> Burning pine-pitch rains from the sky.
> Death Macaw gouges their eyes
> Death Jaguar devours their flesh
> Death Crocodile breaks and mangles their nerves
> and bones and crumbles them to dust. (ibid., 479–80)

The snake is Coatlicue, mother goddess of the Aztecs. Similarly, the hero twins Hunahpú and Xbalanqué are alluded to at the end of the novel, when a Laguna Indian named Sterling runs into an image of a stone snake: "The snake was looking south, in the direction from which the twin brothers and the people would come" (ibid., 763). South is toward Mexico, where overpopulation, underemployment, and Yankee exploitation combine to produce Marxist revolution. The twin brothers become characters in the story, the Indians Tacho and El Feo, but these are antitypes for the hero twins, who defeat the Lords of Xibalba, the House of Death.

Silko also incorporates elements of the Ghost Dance prophecy through a minor character, Weasel Tail. A former lawyer turned traditional healer, Weasel Tail prophesies at the Holistic Healers convention in Tucson, in a canned speech that has made him famous and rich. He quotes from Wovoka's supposed letter to General Grant: "You are hated / You are not wanted here / Go away, / Go back where you come from. / You white people are cursed!" (ibid., 721). (Historically, no such letter exists.) Weasel Tail notes that Wovoka's prophecies are finally coming true one hundred years after he uttered them. For example, the buffalo are indeed returning: " 'Have the spirits let us down? Listen to the prophecies! Next to thirty thousand years, five hundred years look like nothing. The buffalo are returning. They roam off federal land in Montana and Wyoming. Fences can't hold them' " (ibid., 725). By extension, the prophecy's remaining stages will undoubtedly be fulfilled as well: The whites will perish, and the land will return to the Indians. Given his many counterfactual statements, interpreting Weasel Tail's prophecies is not a straightforward task, and in the end such a process must resemble a reading of the symbolism of Revelation: The text exists for readers to make their own meanings. The point of prophecy is not to recount a factual future but to spur readers to self-reflection and self-awareness.

This coming to self-awareness, as we have seen in the figure of Lecha, includes the acceptance of nonwhite martyrs of the lamb. LeVar Burton, famous for his role as Kunta Kinte in the *Roots* television series, writes in the preface to his novel, *Aftermath*, that he has always loved reading science fiction but was disappointed by the absence of characters "of African descent or other people of color" (Burton 1997, vii). *Aftermath* shares with the other fictions discussed here an acceptance of standard racial typology and a definition of tribulation as racial warfare. As in Silko's text, Native American spirituality is seen as the successor to previous dominant religions and as the transfer of an earth abused almost unto death by neo-Europeans to those who can deal with it in a healthier way.

Burton makes two technologically oriented African Americans the coprotagonists of his story. The first, Dr. Rene Reynolds, has invented a device, the Neuro-Enhancer, which allows cancer (and other) patients to cure themselves through intense mental concentration. Leon Cane, the second protagonist, worked for NASA until he exposed the environmental damage that missile launches were causing. He was scapegoated and his house firebombed, killing his wife and daughter. When Reynolds is kidnapped by an evil white scientist who fears that Reynolds's invention will eat into his profits, she sends out mental distress signals that are picked up by Cane, Jacob Fire Cloud (an Indian spiritual leader), and a young white girl named Amy, who has lost her mother. The three converge on Chicago to rescue Reynolds and her device. Amy is adopted by a Hispanic man whom Jacob had forced at gunpoint to drive him to Chicago. Leon goes on to fight the Skinners, who kill blacks for their skin and organs. Jacob returns to where thousands are assembled in tents to receive his words of prophecy. His vision quest had been for the White Buffalo Woman, a messiah figure, who in this case was the black, Rene Reynolds. This dialectical creation of a hybrid messiah, both white and black as dreamed into being by the red, contrasts with the medical hybridization that drives the narrative.

The most evil men of this possible world—the doctor and an unnamed man who tries to rape Amy—are both "Zebras," whites with skin grafts that replace tissue damaged by the excessive ultraviolet light. Since the grafting operation is expensive, Zebras tend to be wealthy; furthermore, the expense of the operations is reduced by the employment of the Skinner subclass to obtain skin and organs illegally. Burton's image of *mestizaje* thus differs radically from Vasconcelos's: The human body becomes like most contemporary American cities, a patchwork of various segregated colors. Skin is to be mixed—but not blood. The former is an act of purely medical technology, whose purpose is to preserve the white race in spite of its Darwinian comparative disadvantage; the latter represents the more difficult technologies of self and language that, in this set of texts at least, are dysfunctional. Furthermore, skin is obtained for these grafts not by donation and payment but by "Skinners," who slaughter and carve up blacks, an image that combines the horrors of slavery, lynching, the Holocaust, and organ trafficking. Not coincidentally, the only white "hero" of the book is a young child who is adopted by a Hispanic couple. The racial profiles of the refugees camped near Jacob Fire Cloud's hut to seek "cures for their illness: medicines for their oozing sores, magic for their blindness and withered limbs" (ibid., 86) are not identified. The essential overturning of stereotype is achieved by making black characters the masters of eschatechnology; other stereotypes remain true to form: the exploitative, ultracapitalistic whites; the spiritual Native Americans; the family-oriented Hispanics; and so forth.

Racial difference is essentialized in the teaching Jacob Fire Cloud received from the elders on the Pine Ridge Indian Reservation. First of all, the races of the world are reduced to four and identified by their skin color. Each is given a particular element to guard linked to a specific technology: To the yellow race goes guardianship of the air; to the black race guardianship of the water; to the red race guardianship of the earth; and to the white race guardianship of fire. "It was also in their hearts. Like fire, the white man had moved across the face of the earth, never still, consuming all that lay in his path" (ibid., 32). This teaching is in substantial conformity with the "real" beliefs of the Star Knowledge UFO group, discussed in chapter five. Jacob undergoes a vision quest and sees that the White Buffalo Woman, who had taught the Lakota how to pray, has returned to save the earth by bringing the four races together. "The White Buffalo Woman has returned, only this time she was black" (ibid., 69).

The novel's vision overlaps with that of *The Turner Diaries* in several respects. The events occur in the year 2019, following a three-year race war that resembles Pierce's in eerie ways. In Burton's *Aftermath*, the race war, which precedes the plot events, is set off first by the assassination of the first African American president of the United States and then an enormous earthquake. Both books report cannibalization, in which the only differences are between who consumes whom and the degree of technology involved in the process. Finally, Pierce's written "Book" parallels Jacob's orally transmitted vision.

Right Behind

We arrive at the third type of vision of the eschaton, in which the races work in harmony to defeat Antichrist and construct the New Jerusalem. I discuss two textual clusters in this context: the *Left Behind* series by Timothy LaHaye and Jerry B. Jenkins, and the lyric of Rastafari, with special attention to that of Bob Marley. Both works present an ecumenical millennialism but contrast strongly with one another in many other ways.

From 1992 to 2004 LaHaye and Jenkins published twelve novels in their series, which basically follows the plotline of Revelation with a strong admixture from Daniel. Antichrist rules for seven years, controlling the entire globe except for a small band of true believers, the Tribulation Force, who are picked off and become martyrs one by one until Armageddon and the Glorious Appearing of Christ (the last two titles of the series), who destroys Antichrist and his minions and carries out the final judgment. A complete plot summary or even listing here of all of the titles (which can be found in the bibliography to this study) would be tedious. As of 2002, the flagship novel had sold a reported 7 million copies, while the newest volume published that year, *The Remnant*, had an initial print run of 2.75 million copies (Gibbs 2002, 44–45). Beyond the series itself, there are two feature films (see Corcoran [2002] and Sarin [2000]), a version with high school students as heroes, a graphic novel version, and prequels and parallels. (A complete overview can be found at the official website, www.leftbehind. com.) At a Millennial Studies Conference I attended at Boston University, an interesting debate erupted over whether the popularity of the *Left Behind* series was a sign of the increasing seriousness of evangelical and dispensationalist thought in the United States or a sign of its waning since it can now be trivialized in fictional treatments. The answer may well be "neither." A distinguishing feature of the series is its dispensationalist reading of the eschaton, so my analysis begins with an explanation of this particular form of premillenarianism.

In the course of the nineteenth century, John Nelson Darby and others of the Prophecy movement formulated new tenets concerning the literal accuracy of the Bible and arrived at the premillennial conclusion that "Christ's kingdom, far from being realized in this age or in the natural development of humanity, lay wholly in the future, was totally supernatural in origin, and discontinuous with the history of this era" (Marsden 1980, 51). A cornerstone of the dispensationalist premillenarians was Daniel 9:24–27, where "Seventy weeks of years are decreed concerning your people and your holy city, to finish the transgression, to put an end to sin, and to atone for iniquity." Even 490 years could not possibly cover history since the writing of Daniel or the history of the Christian church. Therefore, 483 years (sixty-nine weeks of years) were said to lie between the writing of Daniel and Christ's death and resurrection. The remaining seven years lay still in the future, thereby making human history since 33 CE a hiatus in prophecy. This interpretation placed an emphasis upon the recognition of current events as signs, such as the rising of both Antichrist (a religious leader) and the Beast (a political leader) and the return of Jews to Israel. The biggest sign of all was to be the Rapture, the taking up of all living true believers into heaven before the beginning of the Tribulation. Paul's letter to the Thessalonians gives the strongest hint of this event: "For the Lord Himself will descend from heaven with a shout, with the voice of an archangel, and with the trumpet of God. And the dead in Christ will rise first. Then we who are alive and remain shall be caught up together with them in the clouds to meet the Lord in the air. And thus we shall always be with the Lord" (1 Thessalonians 4:16–17). Paul does not specify what happens to the nonbelievers, but we can imagine it is not pretty: LaHaye and Jenkins take on the dirty job of depicting their fate.

Tim LaHaye's nonfictional interpretive work on Revelation summarizes the psychodynamics of this fiction:

> In all probability most of the present generation will go into the Tribulation.
>   The great exception to that is the Church of Jesus Christ. If you are a member of the body of Christ—that is, if you have personally invited Jesus Christ into your heart—you will not go into the Tribulation. . . . Your acceptance or rejection of Jesus

Christ determines your relation to that time of great misery and heartache. If you accept Jesus Christ, you will be raptured out before it begins. (1999, 140)

The book quoted from (*Revelation Unveiled*) was published in 1999, allowing a specific reference for the "present generation." In the novel, those left behind confront their own preterit natures and become believers. A tripartite division forms between: (1) those who side with the Antichrist, Nicolae Carpathia, as his lust for power transforms the United Nations into the tyrannical Global Community; (2) observant Jews, who resist the Antichrist by adhering to their religion; and (3) believing Christians, a globalized group that includes some prominent Jewish converts. The Christians confess their pre-Rapture unbelief to each other in evangelical fashion, which confessions, strangely enough, almost never involve having done anything evil or gone over to the dark side but merely having stood on the sidelines. Far more prominently, their anomie and fear of commitment has kept them from being raptured, and they must now make up for this *lapsus* with great courage against overwhelming odds.

Dispensationalism, literalism, and overt eschatechnologism are key characteristics that distinguish LaHaye and Jenkins's fictional approach to millennium. The literal conception of the Rapture makes for a dramatic opening scene: Rayford, the eventual patriarch of the underground Christian movement, is piloting a commercial passenger plane across the Atlantic to London. Hattie, the stewardess, makes a discovery in the middle of the night: "A whole bunch of people, just gone!" . . . Their shoes, their socks, their clothes, everything was left behind. These people are gone!" (LaHaye and Jenkins 1995, 16). It is not clear how a literalist interpretation manages to ignore the first part of Paul's pronouncement, which says that Jesus's return will precede the Rapture, but from the point of view of fiction, the introspection provoked by the mysterious disappearances is superior to the unambiguous return.

Rayford returns the plane to Chicago, though to little purpose. All kinds of personnel have disappeared—those who have let Jesus in and been raptured, we are led to understand—causing various immediate disasters. For example, bus and taxi drivers have been raptured up in the middle of their runs, leading to crashes and deaths. At home, Rayford discovers the coffee burned and the Christian radio station still on. His wife and son are gone, leaving Rayford to commune with the relics and impressions they left behind:

He approached the bed, knowing what he would find. The indented pillow, the wrinkled covers. He could smell her, though he knew the bed would be cold. He carefully peeled back the blankets and sheet to reveal her locket, which carried a picture of him. Her flannel nightgown, the one he always kidded her about and which she wore only when he was not home, evidenced her now departed form. (ibid., 75)

Steele then goes to his church, the one that had helped his wife find Jesus but that he had avoided because its members had interrogated him about what God was doing in his life. Most of the church, as well as its pastor, have disappeared, but the assistant pastor, Bruce Barnes, has been left behind. Barnes, Steele, the Jewish scholar Tsion Ben-Judah, and a few others form the Tribulation Force, which battles Nicolae Carpathia throughout the remaining volumes.

There is no more ecumenical and integrationist work of millennial fiction than the *Left Behind* series. With plodding deliberateness, the authors have found characters from a variety of ethnic groups and nations and brought them together in the Tribulation Force. However, the very constructedness of the gathering makes certain omissions and asymmetries all the more apparent, one of the most prominent of which is the "default" mode that whites are never named as such, whereas minority status is always pointed to explicitly. Floyd Charles, an African American, is a doctor who is working in a hospital that the Global Community eventually takes over. He eventually becomes part of the resistance and dies of poison intended by the Antichrist for his former lover. Hannah Palemoon is Native American. David Hassid is an Israeli who becomes a mole in the New Babylon constructed by the Antichrist. Abdullah Smith ("Smitty") is from Jordan; Al B. ("Albie") is from Al Basrah. China contributes Ming Toy and her brother, Chang Wong, as characters, adding to "Li Ng, the Asian girl on Channel 7 news" (ibid., 64), who lives on Rayford's street and is raptured with her whole family. Only Chinese and Koreans (represented by Ree Woo) seem prone to true belief, no doubt reflecting the relatively high numbers of converts to Christianity in those countries; Indians, Japanese, Malaysians, and so on remain invisible to the fictional events. Ominously, a potentate of Antichrist wears a "jet-black-and-silver kimono" (LaHaye and Jenkins 2003, 291). Greece, whose connection to the New Testament is obvious enough, contributes several characters and becomes the scene of endless operations and rescues. (Basically, the plot is spun out, and material that could have fit into four or five volumes is expanded to twelve by having Tribulation Force members execute daredevil missions that get them captured, thus calling for another rescue mission, and so forth.)

Two Israeli Jews play crucial roles in the text: Tsion Ben-Judah is a former rabbinical scholar whose research has led to the discovery that Jesus Christ is the Messiah whom the Jews await. Chaim Rosenzweig—"pale for an Israeli" (LaHaye and Jenkins 2001, 13)—is a botanist who has discovered a technology for making Israel's deserts productive. One of the few dynamic characters in the text, he is at first entirely sympathetic to Nicolae Carpathia and the Global Community but is slowly brought around to recognize him as the Antichrist and to become a believer. In *Assassins* (2000) he shoots Carpathia (who resurrects himself), and in *Desecration* (2001) he assumes the role of Micah and prophesies against Carpathia. Other Israeli Jews are saved by the Tribulation Force, which transports them out of Israel to a stronghold in Petra, where they survive on manna and are impervious to Global Community's attack. Curiously, no American-based Jews are portrayed, either as believers or as allies of Antichrist. According to the rules of the game, of course, only Jews who convert to Christianity, for which Tsion is the model, can become an object of narrative interest. In its literalist reading of the Bible, the novel absolutely upholds the racial-religious divide between Jews, who are God's chosen people, and Christians, who are His adopted children. What the Jews have been chosen for, however, is conversion and witnessing of the Glorious Appearing (the title of the last novel in the series). Religious Jews who resist Carpathia but do not accept Christ are placed at His left hand at the end of the series, along with all of the other nonbelievers—the "goats"—and dumped into a yawning chasm (LaHaye and Jenkins 2004, 380). The characters themselves seem uncomfortable with this particular eschatechnology: "Despite every horror [Rayford] had witnessed during the Tribulation and the Glorious Appearing, the death and eternal punishment of millions all at once overwhelmed everything else. . . . It hit Rayford that all who were left were believers, worshipers of Christ, and that he was among those who would populate the Millennium" (ibid., 381–82).[2]

It's nothing personal, of course. The text is merely following the dispensationalist script. In fact, dispensationalism can be said to allow Jews a more exalted position in the eschatological scheme than does mainstream Christianity, which regards God's covenant with Israel as completely superseded by the one with the church. Dispensationalists, on the other hand, believe that Israel still has a special role to play in God's plan:

> In the next dispensation, the millennium, Israel will return to its position as God's first nation and will assume a leading role in the kingdom, the very same role the Jews would have played had they accepted Jesus in his first coming. Thus, although dispensationlists have recognized the Jews to be God's chosen nation and have anticipated a great future for that nation, they have also expressed a certain amount of bitterness concerning the Jewish refusal to accept Jesus, which caused the delay in the advancement of the ages and the materialization of the kingdom. (Ariel 1991, 17)

Left Behind is only the most prominent and successful of a host of eschatological treatises and novels set in the Middle East (see Boyer 2002). Sure enough, Israel and New Babylon seem to be the only two countries with a functioning government as the vials are poured out, and virtually all of the crucial events of the fiction (e.g., the assassination of Carpathia, the desecration of the temple, the construction of a safe haven in Petra) take place in the former country. The end-time events of *Left Behind* are triggered by Russia's unprovoked attack on Israel, a scenario taken seriously by many during the Cold War.

As noted earlier, two converted Jews are among the most important characters of the series. However, the "bitterness" is evident in the annihilation of millions of observant Jews by Christ himself. In that last novel, all of the world's people are miraculously transported to the Valley of Jehosophat in Israel. They are described—shades of LeVar Burton—as "white and black and red and yellow" (LaHaye and Jenkins 2004, 130). Like a cabinet of the U.S. government, this palette of characters of different origins in the end mostly serves to emphasize the Anglo-Saxons who remain in the real leadership positions, fulfilling Beveridge's (1968) dictum of bringing order where chaos reigns: Rayford Steele and his daughter, Chloe; Cameron "Buck" Williams; Mac McCullum, George Sebastian, and so forth. There is also a gender-based division of labor: Hannah and Leah Rose are nurses, while Hassid and Chang are computer geniuses, and most of the other men are pilots or military men of some kind. Chloe shows herself to be a master organizer, but her desire to be taking part in the action leads to her constantly disobey orders and put herself at risk. Moreover, unlike the manly George Sebastian, who frees himself when captured by Antichrist's forces, Chloe must always be rescued by others. (Her final, senseless escapade ends in her capture, interrogation, and eventual martyrdom by guillotine in *Armageddon* [2003].)

Hispanics gain major roles only in the latter novels of the series, and other Latins fare even more poorly. Why is the only Mexican on the Tribulation Force named "Razor"? The answer, bizarrely, involves a little snowmobiling accident he had with razor wire: "First time on. In Minnesota. Not exactly like Mexico, you know?" (ibid., 184). The false prophet of the Antichrist is named Leon Fortunato. India's complete absence from this globalized novel can be explained by examining Pat Robertson's *End of the Age* (1995), which, though not dispensationalist, shares many of its plotlines and events with *Left Behind*, including the Jews' special role. Like LaHaye and Jenkins, Robertson builds a rainbow coalition of believers, including an African American, a Chicano family (far more with it than is Razor), and an Asian American. Robertson's Antichrist, Mark Beaulieu, realizes his destiny as a Peace Corps volunteer in India, where he receives enlightenment from a statue of Shiva and Kali. He then studies "the secrets of the ascended masters" (ibid., 169) with guru Raj Baba. Shiva guides Beaulieu through a series of political triumphs until he takes over as U.S. president after a comet hits the earth and eventually as the leader of the ironically named "Union for Peace." In his first presidential address, Beaulieu opens his right hand "in the universal sign for peace. On his palm was a bright red dot. Those who watched saw the dot glow intensely bright. They were transfixed by its hypnotic power" (ibid., 260). The dot is the mark of Vishnu, interpreted by John Edwards (descended, yes, from Jonathan Edwards, the famous preacher of the Great Awakening) as "a symbol of a third eye—a spiritual eye" (ibid., 272) and hence of a demon that inhabits Beaulieu and speaks through his mouth. Indian, Iranian, and central Asian troops are massed by the Union for Peace at Armageddon for the final battle. Clearly, readers of Robertson's novel are to understand Hinduism—not Islam—to be the religion of Antichrist. In *Left Behind*, on the other hand, this role seems to fall to Catholicism.

Peter Mathews, a former Catholic cardinal from Cincinnati, seizes the opportunity to become the pontifex maximus of the Enigma Babylon One World Faith—the only legal religion once Carpathia takes control of the world. His assumed title of Peter II continues the Catholic tradition of naming popes, and the new title indicates that he is the pope of popes. Hence, the One World Faith begins as a kind of super-Catholicism—in fact, it is headquartered in the Vatican. Our first view of Mathews when he is interviewed by Buck Williams shows him drinking his morning champagne as a pick-me-up, while dropping broad hints that he has been named pontifex maximus (LaHaye and Jenkins 1996, 269–71). He plots against Carpathia and is destroyed by the ten potentates "in fulfillment of the scriptures." Mathews's seamless transition from Catholic to Enigmatic seems calculated to show the identity of the two religions, which would explain the absence of characters who might also have believed in Christ but through that form of religion. No Catholic character assumes a leadership role in Tribulation Force.

However, it is not so much Catholic doctrine that makes it unappealing as the church's size and reach, which inevitably bring with them a lack of evangelistic spirit and a lackadaisical surveillance of the true spiritual balance of parishioners. Second, the global reach and organization of Catholicism make it a kind of shadow of the United Nations itself, which the series shows to be a mere tool of Antichrist. Methodists, Episcopalians, and others do not fare much better on this score. A logical fallacy is put in the mouth of a Rastafarian leader about to hand the keys to the kingdom over to the One World Faith: "'Some religions saw many disappear [in the Rapture]. Some saw very few. Many saw none. But the fact that many were left from each proves that none was better than the other. We will be tolerant of all, believing that the best of us remain'" (ibid., 276).

Since much of this is wrong—in fact, the best have disappeared and the worst remain—we assume that all of it is wrong and thus that religious tolerance too is not only wrong but a tool to be used by Antichrist as well (at least in the preliminary stages; eventually, when he raises himself from the dead following his assassination, Carpathia makes himself the unique object of worship). When churchgoing is mentioned, as it frequently is in the believers' stories, denominations are never named, and the impression is of small, local churches. At one point Mathews makes it explicit: "The religious Jews and the fundamentalist Christians are the only factions who have not brought themselves into step with Enigma Babylon Faith" (LaHaye and Jenkins 2000, 225). The ecumenical nature of the faith and its reading of the Rapture as the disappearance of the wicked rather than of the righteous form equal bases of the false doctrine of Enigma Babylon Faith or, in its later evolution, Carpathianism.

In short, while *Left Behind* explicitly seems to integrate and internationalize the team of the elect, it actually reproduces ethnic divides that have historically been associated with one Christian denomination or another. In fact, it indirectly tells the standard millennial story we have been hearing since John Winthrop. A small group of the elect, a "communitie in perill," recognizes the truth of things and sets itself apart under the leadership of a few outstanding white men. Evil comes from Europe and multilateralism. In the numerological tradition of William Miller and others, God has a plan that trumps historical fact and rational causality and in which North Americans play a big role—in converting Jews, for example.

That plan raises Carpathia to the position of Antichrist and allows him to rule the world for seven years, during which he becomes the one and only source of evil on earth. (That is to say, the only issues quickly become those of loyalty or disloyalty to Carpathia's Global Community, who controls it, and how it can be used to control others.) The inequality, injustice, racism, sexism, and economic deprivation that most of us can see as part of our daily lives—and some of which Jesus saw and spoke out against—are neither shown nor mentioned but are replaced (rather than compounded, as would happen in real life) by the machinations of Carpathia and the disaster-movie effects as the seven seals are broken. The Rapture is triggered neither by political events nor by the degradation of individual souls in the world but simply because it was always planned for that date. This disjunction between God's plan and humans' planning is of course an old theme (and has been discussed elsewhere in this book), but this fiction drives its paradoxical nature to the extreme by never questioning it. The best example of this paradox is the epigraph that begins this book: "Rayford had cast his lot with God *and* the miracle of technology" (LaHaye and Jenkins 2001, 1; emphasis added).

Besides belief, the other great leveler and ecumenical motivator in this text is technology. With the exception of the main prophet, Tsion Ben-Judah, Buck and Chloe (the novel's major love interest, who also exhibit technical and organizational skills), and George Sebastian, whose main contribution lies in his military training, every other leader of the Tribulation Force has extensive scientific or technical skills. There are so many pilots, starting with Rayford, that one wonders how any were left for the Antichrist. (Apparently no competent techies were left him either, as the Tribulation Force's moles hack and bug everywhere with impunity.) Tribulation Force members are continually shown as superior technicians to the Global Community operatives, but whenever the latter can mount a superior show of force, God intervenes to foil their attempt. Shortly after the Rapture, we hear the following about the state of the world: "People checked the graves of loved ones to see if their corpses had disappeared, and unscrupulous types pretended to do the same while looking for valuables that might have been buried with the wealthy. It had become an ugly world overnight" (LaHaye and Jenkins 1995, 207). *Had become*? The age-old problem of theodicy is invoked here, as God seems to cause evil. The "theology" of the series succumbs to a suffocating self-reflexivity as the only matters discussed concern the correct interpretations of prophetic texts, rarely matters of ethics or morality. Jesus's core teachings, such as the parables, make no appearance. Only John 14, the teaching that no one comes to God except through Jesus as the Son, matters. It is as though the Bible's only purpose were to predict its own fulfillment in the modern world.

The last disaster of the series is the casting of nonbelievers, who line up on the left hand of Christ, into a chasm that opens to swallow them. Before that, Christ had descended from heaven and killed millions of baddies with the divine *logos*, crushing out the grapes of wrath. The gory scenario recalls Nat Turner, whose confession contains the following:

> I had a vision—and I saw white spirits and black spirits engaged in battle, and the sun was darkened—the thunder rolled in the Heavens, and blood flowed in streams. . . . I discovered drops of blood on the corn as though it were dew from heaven . . . and I then found on the leaves in the woods hieroglyphic characters, and numbers, with the forms of men in different attitudes, portrayed in blood, and representing the figures I had seen before in the heavens. And now the Holy Ghost had revealed itself to me, and made plain the miracles it had shown me—For as the blood of Christ had been shed on this earth, and had ascended to heaven for the salvation of sinners, and was now returning to earth again in the form of dew—and as the leaves on the trees bore the impression of the figures I had seen in the heavens, it was plain to me that the Saviour was about to lay down the yoke he had borne for the sins of men, and the great day of judgment was at hand. (Turner and Gray 1996, 46–47)

Turner first sees the blood of sinning mortals, then the blood of Christ, which prepares him to execute the final, bloody judgment in which as much white and as little black blood as possible is to be spilled. There is a cycle or weather pattern of blood, resembling the water cycle, in which it is shed into the earth and returns to the sky, from which it falls again as rain or condenses as dew. The preservation of such cycles may ground practices of blood sacrifice. Such visions tend to confirm D. H. Lawrence's reading of Revelation as an expression of *ressentiment*. And yet Turner's vision is the product of an individual in the classic position of revitalization, the other of those who belong to the dominant race and class, whose Antichrist represents not a real enemy but a phantasmagoria of globalization and its technologies, which multiply contact with the myriad Others of the world, who have heterogenous beliefs and practices. Thus, the central theme of *Left Behind* may in fact be that of seizing these technologies and using them solely for evangelization.

Ras Tafari Is the Messiah, and Bob Marley His Prophet

It is appropriate to conclude both this chapter and this book with an examination of the Rastafarian songs of Bob Marley, which bring us full circle in three ways: first, because they represent most clearly the reversal of the Columbian trajectory, which becomes, at the same time, a rejection of hybridity in favor of a (supposedly) "roots" Africanism; second, because, in a postmodern period noted for its ironic relation to apocalypse, they represent a literature completely instrumentalized by the millennial project; finally, because they are the most ambivalent of all of the literary treatments of race and millennium, thereby allowing us to experience hope or despair according to our own predilections. (Curiously, the only other text featured here that sees Africa as Zion or at least as a safe zone after conflagration is *Caesar's Column*. The opposite view is provided by Sterling's *Islands in the Net*.) Marley's "postcolonial sufferin'," to use Grant Farred's (2003) epithet, was over a historically tangled, racially and religiously complex Jamaica, whose pain mirrored Marley's own birth from a white father—a plantation overseer who soon decamped—and a black mother. A progressive series of ideological adoptions of father figures took place, culminating in Haile Selassie, emperor of Ethiopia, acclaimed as the Messiah by the Rastafarians. Selassie, whose personal name was Ras Ta Fari, thus replaces Christ in the Holy Trinity. "If your mother forsake you, your father forsake you, then Rasta will take you." So goes the saying in the streets of Trenchtown, the Kingston, Jamaica, slum where Marley spent his teenage years. Traditionally, "coloreds" like Marley have tended to despise Africans and attempted to climb in society by cooperating with whites. Marley, faced with a choice no less monumental than that of the earthbound of *Left Behind*, chose Africa.

The chiliastic representation of the world as a war between good and evil, which began in Zoroastrianism and became a central element of millennialism, appears in Rastafari and in Marley's lyrics as "Babylon" ("Africa, unite, / 'Cause we're moving right out of Babylon"; Marley 1992, 9) versus "Zion" ("Jah sitteth in Mount Zion and rules all creation"; ibid., 94). Both terms are multiply allegorical: On the most concrete level, the former is present-day, "skinocratic" Jamaica, while the latter is Ethiopia. Moving up a level, Babylon is the world created by white colonialism, while Zion is the world of the African patriarchs described in the Bible. A key component of Rastafari is the belief that translations of the Bible have deleted most of the references to Africans that it originally contained. This view derives in part from the Afrocentric politico-theological program of Marcus Garvey, who "insisted that African Jamaicans should see God and view life through the spectacles of Ethiopia" (Erskine 2005, 33). At the most comprehensive level, however, Babylon can be understood simply to be the world as it presently exists, with its racial and class divisions, while Zion is a world of unity, so that the journey out of one into the other becomes a decolonizing of the mind. The aim of reggae, as Marley practiced it, was to "chant down Babylon": "Hear the voice of the Rasta Man say: / Babylon your throne gone down. . . . Hear the angel of the seven seals say: / Babylon your throne gone down" (Marley 2007).

Other binary oppositions that ground Marley's political lyrics are war vs. peace and oppression vs. freedom. Marley's lyrics are not the only Rasta poetry to project this thematic. Benjamin Zephaniah's "Can't Keep a Good Dread Down," for example, claims that "the Seven Seals is I" and ends with the injunction "Alpha is here wid us, / so stop praying to polluted air / and give rasta your trust" (Darren Middleton 2000, 260–61). In Revelation 1:8 Jesus calls himself the "Alpha and Omega." The poem is an example of Rastafari's creation theology, which brings God down from heaven and makes God part of the earth.

On the surface and read in certain ways, Marley's self-styled "rebel music" seems to call for violent revolution, symbolized in "I Shot the Sheriff" (Marley 1992, 64) and "Small Axe" (ibid., 151). Stephen King and Richard Jensen argue that "Marley's use of the 'war' metaphor indicates that he issues threats and prescribes violent acts to end oppression in the world" (1995, 33). However, "chanting down Babylon" also takes the form of positive approaches to racial unity, for which the song "One Love" is perhaps the most prominent example. "One love, one heart, one song. Let's get together and feel all right." In Noel Erskine's reading, this song, like so many of Marley's, "is one of exodus, people leaving oppressive traditions and histories and moving to their father's land. The basis of this hope is love, One Love rooted and grounded in God because this love provides hope for the 'hopeless sinner'" (Erskine 2005, 182). The song exudes millennial types, such as Armageddon, the Second Coming, and the Last Judgment:

> Let's get together to fight this Holy Armageddon. (One love.)
> So when the Man comes there will be no, no doom. (One song.)
> Have pity on those whose chances grow thinner
> There ain't no hiding place from the Father of Creation. (Marley 1992, 147)

Performance renders each phrase into Rastafarian speech: Marley's pronunciation, "Armagiddyon," emphasizes that this is not a literal and bloody confrontation, as literalist texts like *Left Behind* would have it, but a spiritual battle for the decolonization of the mind. Rastafari replaces Jesus in the divine trinity with a black Messiah, identified as Haile Selassie—the man who will come to judge the living and the dead. "No hiding place" derives from Revelation 6:17–18:

> And the kings of the earth, and the great men, and the rich men, and the chief captains, and the mighty men, and every bondman, and every free man, *hid* themselves in the dens and in the rocks of the mountains; And said to the mountains and rocks, Fall on us, and *hide us* from the face of him that sitteth on the throne, and from the wrath of the Lamb: For the great day of his wrath is come; and who shall be able to stand? (emphasis added)

Finally, J. Richard Middleton's reading of "One Love" as revealing "the power of a creation theology to sustain hope" (2000, 191) is supported in the epithet for God as "Father of Creation." At the request of representatives of the two main Jamaican political parties, who were fighting each other in the streets, Marley performed this and other songs at the "One Love Peace Concert" in Jamaica's National Stadium on April 21, 1978. Marley called the leaders of the rival political factions, Edward Seaga and Michael Manley, onstage and had them clasp hands while he chanted "Peace, love, Jah." It was an extraordinary moment as a member of the hybridous underclass held Jamaica's political destiny in his hand and voice, and a truly millennial reversal of first and last revealed itself. At this moment, reggae's worldwide commercial success had been completely instrumentalized in bringing about a performative millennium.[3]

Beyond the fact that this millennium was perhaps of 1000 seconds rather than years, as the political factions continued to battle each other, Carolyn Cooper (2005) points out that "One Love" is more ambiguous than its anthemization would indicate, as in the following lyrics:

> There is one question I'd really love to ask. (One heart.)
> Is there a place for the hopeless sinner
> Who has hurt all mankind just to save his own? (Marley 1992, 147)

Listeners seem to have forgotten the song's questioning aspects in favor of its anthemlike call to unity. "What about it?" asks Cooper. "That's the question. Is it possible? How does one accommodate 'the hopeless sinner' in the discourse of 'one love'? That is the challenge. Peace and love require justice" (2005, 222). Cooper has deconstructed the myth of Bob Marley as peaceful saint. This myth participates in the repeated pattern of millennial rebellion in the Americas: A group or an individual originally in the minority and considered dangerous by the authorities—the Puritans by the Church of England or Roger Williams by the Puritans themselves—when not eliminated eventually finds acceptance and becomes normalized. The Jamaican Tourist Board has adopted "One Love" for its advertising campaigns, thus stripping it of its disturbing questions, and the establishment canonizes Bob Marley in opposition to the newest "Rude Boys." This reversal of fortunes in millennial discourse, from prophetic protest to upholder of the status quo, has a familiar ring. In the context of this chapter, the question (whose answer may vary a great deal among listeners) concerns the racial harmony or antagonism that Marley's participatory lyrics provoke. We may confront here the opposite interpretive dilemma from that of *Left Behind*: Marley's may be a discourse that on the surface seems to address one race but which at a deeper level addresses a divine plan that is more ecumenical. Such, at any rate, is the note of hope on which I rest the argument of this chapter and this book. I, for one, having looked back on the mass murder and racial triumphalism of *Nicholas Blood* and the *Turner Diaries*, am willing to wager on the ambiguities of Marley's violence and racial reconciliation.

Conclusion

Iraq: Very Interesting—Did You Know?

1. The garden of Eden was in Iraq.
2. Mesopotamia, which is now Iraq, was the cradle of civilization!
3. Noah built the ark in Iraq.
4. The Tower of Babel was in Iraq.
5. Abraham was from Ur, which is in southern Iraq!
6. Isaac's wife, Rebekah, is from Nahor, which is in Iraq.
7. Jacob met Rachel in Iraq.
8. Jonah preached in Nineveh, which is in Iraq.
9. Assyria, which is in Iraq, conquered the ten tribes of Israel.
10. Amos cried out in Iraq!
11. Babylon, which is in Iraq, destroyed Jerusalem.
12. Daniel was in the lion's den in Iraq!
13. The three Hebrew children were in the fire in Iraq (Jesus had been in Iraq also as the fourth person in the fiery furnace!)
14. Belshazzar, the king of Babylon, saw the "writing on the wall" in Iraq.
15. Nebuchadnezzar, king of Babylon, carried the Jews captive into Iraq.
16. Ezekiel preached in Iraq.
17. The Wise Men were from Iraq.
18. Peter preached in Iraq.
19. The "Empire of Man" described in Revelation is called Babylon, which was a city in Iraq!

No other nation, except Israel, has more history and prophecy associated with it than Iraq.

The preceding list is from an e-mail circulated in 2005, supposedly through the internal e-mail systems of one or more U.S. government agencies.[1] The technology of electronic mail systems and websites creates an enormous Millerite tent meeting in that it allows prophecy and millennial discourse to be spread in personalized fashion—"Did *you* know?"—to a greater extent and at lower direct cost to the sender than was previously possible. (Tsion Ben-Judah's main weapon in *Left Behind* is his website, whereas the Global Community relies on the "cool" medium of television.) On the other hand, the technology of e-mail complicates the possibility of ruse and deception, false address and false agency, inherent in all writing. The e-mail could be a fiction, invented and circulated either as a parody or as an ironic protest against the neocon philosophy of the Bush regime that helped justify both the Iraq war and an iron allegiance to Israel's position in its dealing with Palestinians and other Arabs, a loyalty and interest strongly represented in the fictions and website of the *Left Behind* series, among others.

On the other hand, truth (especially when it is created by myth) is stranger than fiction. In an August 13, 2006, radio interview with BBC World Service, Richard Armey, former majority leader in the U.S. House of Representatives, affirmed not only his own conviction in the truth of the coming Tribulation, including its relation to events in the Middle East, but also his belief that President Bush held the same views. The context for the interview was the Hezbollah-Israel-Lebanon conflict, as well as a previous BBC report on an American group that collects funds specifically for the Israeli war effort under the religious imperative that war is a sign of the *eschaton*. Armey denied that U.S. policy would ever seek to encourage conflict in order to help trigger the Tribulation: Such things will happen on God's time, not ours. But of course, this supposed restraint in not actively helping to bring about war does not speak to the increased bias that eschatology brings to U.S. foreign policy, nor does it explain how a society can uphold the ideals of a secular society and vigorously prosecute the separation of church and state and at the same time conduct itself in the world as though it were battling the Antichrist. Furthermore, Armey leads an army of believers: "For millions of Americans . . . the Bush administration's go-it-alone foreign policy, hands-off attitude toward the Israeli-Palestinian conflict and . . . war on Iraq are not simply actions in the national self-interest or an extension of the war on terrorism, but part of an unfolding divine plan" (Boyer 2002, 313). Indeed, adds Walter Mead:

> The return of the Jews to the Holy Land, their extraordinary victories over larger Arab armies, and even the rising tide of hatred that threatens Jews in Israel and abroad strengthen not only the evangelical commitment to Israel but also the position of evangelical religion in American life. The story of modern Jewry reads like a book in the Bible. . . . The extraordinary events of modern Jewish history are held up by evangelicals as proof that God exists and acts in history. Add to this the psychological consequences of nuclear weapons, and many evangelicals begin to feel that they are living in a world like the world of the Bible. That U.S. foreign policy now centers on defending the country against the threat of mass terrorism involving, potentially, weapons of apocalyptic horror wielded by anti-Christian fanatics waging a religious war motivated by hatred of Israel only reinforces the claims of evangelical religion. (2006, 43)

For the true premillennial believers, what's bad is good: Conflict in the Middle East is not only about oil and geopolitics but also about the *eschaton*, so "bring it on." Whether prophecy really played a role in Bush's foreign policy and whether the writer of the e-mail, as it appears, really believes in the *eschaton* are far less relevant than the way this e-mail epigraph calls for readers competent in the syntax and grammar of the Bible and of prophecy. It represents *in nuce* the topic of representation explored in this book, including the function of literature as an eschatechnology that is positioned not only to encourage and map the end of the world but also to question, interpret, and doubt the end of history in acts of reflective dissonance.

The text implies a sublimation of war from a means of achieving economic, political, or even national ends into an instrument of ultimate, universal teleology. The United States has graven this particular eschatechnology into its national psyche: The Civil War (1861–1865) is the locus of departure for this melding of evangelism and conquest. Premillennialists found a confirmation of their beliefs in the Armageddon of battle between North and South. At the same time, however, the battles were fought by human armies. According to James Moorehead, the military outcome meant that, from then on, in the opinion of many, America's millennial mission would be carried out by an army rather than by divine plan or divine word:

> In spite of their awareness that the Apocalypse foretold wars, calamity, and judgment, the previous generation had usually spoken of a spiritual process—at least in America—by which the saeculum would be claimed for God: tract and Bible distribution, voluntary reform associations, and missionaries would evangelize the world until the millennium dawned. These activities remained, of course, crucial instruments in the building of the Kingdom; but after the federal war effort became a battle at Armageddon, the weapons of the saints were hopelessly confounded with the military power of the nation. (1978, 80)

They have remained confounded ever since. The United States became one of the few nations in history to adopt the position that its national wars, waged on other peoples, are for the losers' improvement. While public attention focuses on the frightening but limited violence of a Jonestown or a Waco, hundreds of thousands of lives are lost in wars fought to fulfill a mission that is millennial at its core.

I began this book prior to the turn of 2000, having noticed that most of the Y2K panic was a secularized form of millennial countdown. I soldiered on as 9/11 took the place of Y2K and reintroduced a religious dimension to Armageddon, as noted earlier. Now, however, as I revise for publication, Iraq and the Middle East seem to have been recognized as endless quagmires rather than the end of the world, and global warming has climbed the ladder to become the *eschaton*'s central symbol. (Osama bin Laden conveniently added global warming to the list of evils brought on the world by the United States in a September 2007 videotape.) The aptly titled 2004 Hollywood film, *The Day after Tomorrow*, features as its hero a climatologist (Dennis Quaid) who must find a way to save the world from its weather woes.

It's always something.

To the occulted, semiofficial position on eschatechnology adumbrated earlier are opposed myriad hybridized movements in the Americas, some of which—Canudos, Nat Turner, Red River, Wounded Knee—have entered into this study in the form of their literary representations and provocations. Such movements also envision themselves as working toward a Land without Evil but with its architectural and social engineering based upon community values that are disappearing rapidly under the crushing weight of capitalist reality.

These two instrumentalizations of millennium vary in their representational strategies but otherwise share more than we might think. Both, for example, contribute to the construction of American nations as imagined communities, to use Benedict Anderson's (1991) phrase. The millennial roots of exceptionalism freight American national discourses with typological destinies, as noted earlier, while oppositional movements such as Red River and Canudos eventually become canonized as central events of national histories. The style of representation differs between dominant and subversive, but the problem of linking past, present, and future is addressed on either level by typological cyclicality. Cairns Craig, glossing Benedict Anderson, defines this paradox of "national time" as that "the nation both acknowledges in its form that we live in fact only in the present moment, cut off from the past and the future, while giving us the comfort of believing we belong to something which appears to be eternal. . . . [I]t is the 'magic' of nations to 'forge' a relation of past to future through the present and thus to conceal the brutal truth of our limited lives" (2007, 21). Anderson believes that national time, "homogeneous, empty time" (ibid., 26) necessarily substitutes sacred, cyclical time, but an examination of millennial discourse shows that, in the Americas, this substitution was not complete. Instead, phrases such as "manifest destiny" link past, present, and future in the fullness of *kairos*. Simultaneous reading of newspapers or novels, as Anderson posits, will not do the trick: The variety and vehemence of representations examined in this study provide the counterexample. We Americans need to tell ourselves the myth of the end in order to feel whole and original.

Having inherited millennialism from Europe and the Near East, the Americas are now a prime locus for its exportation to the rest of the world. In the twenty-first century, processes of capitalism and globalization emanating largely from the United States continue their history of destroying value systems and disintegrating communities around the world, producing movements analogous to those discussed in the previous pages but with the difference that current technologies of transport and communication allow such movements to be born globalized and multilingual. Sarin gas attacks in the Tokyo subway in June 1995 revealed the Aum Shinrikyo cult to the world. Buddhist at its core, this movement has no central religious text and incorporates elements of Hinduism (its primary deity is Shiva), Taoism, and (increasingly as it felt itself persecuted by the government and betrayed by renegade members) the book of Revelation. Aum's path from relative optimism to being yet another "world-destroying cult" was proportional to its increasing rage against the lack of values of present-day Japan.

It was not until I visited Beijing in 2004 that I understood the Falun Gong, which I had vaguely become aware of as a revitalization movement in China. The group had piqued my interest as I stood in line outside the Chinese Consulate in New York City to pick up my visa and saw several of them doing their traditional *qigong* exercises across the street. Their silent persistence puzzled me. Inside, the consulate offered various leaflets that explained that human rights were being protected in China, no matter what Falun Gong had to say on the matter. I came to understand Falun Gong a little bit not because I quizzed locals about it or interviewed members but because in Beijing I saw for myself the complete and sudden collapse under capitalism of not one but two value systems: "traditional" and communist. I walked through rubble-strewn areas that seemed like war zones but were actually the result of the government's clearing out traditional *wu tongs* in favor of modern housing. This modern housing consists of the alienating, multistory boxes I was familiar with from New York, São Paulo, and Frankfurt. Riding through Beijing was a hallucinatory experience, the precession of advertising for Western companies erasing much of the identity the city might have once had. From communism to capitalism without an intervening stage of democracy. From Mao to McDonalds.

It is at such moments that revitalization movements arise in order to return to people—usually the most disenfranchised—the values they have seen destroyed. Selected values, practices, and narratives of the culture in question are combined with those derived from technology or imported scripts to create a vision for the future commonly called "millennium." In the case of Falun Gong, the old values are the movements and exercises called *qigong*, the new ones an interest in UFOs and a critique of communism. At my university, the local chapter's website includes an interpretation of the book of Revelation. Since millennial movements counter the values that dominate a particular period, they eventually draw the negative attention of regimes and are destroyed.

Several methods have been implemented for getting rid of millennial thinking, for making it anodyne and throwing it onto the trash pile of human thought. Rationalism and Enlightenment emphasize gradualism, carefully explain that the time frame chosen for apocalypse is arbitrary, and tell us all not to worry. This, in essence, was Stephen Jay Gould's mission and method in his aptly titled *Questioning the Millennium: A Rationalist's Guide to a Precisely Arbitrary Countdown* (1997). In order to cure those hypnotized by numerical rhetoric, Gould learnedly discoursed on the origins of the Western calendar, on the fact that the year 2000 was arbitrarily chosen, and on the additional fact that 2001 is really the beginning of the millennium. We rationalists already know that, however, just as we know that, within the framework of geological or astronomical time, every process on earth belongs to gradualism rather than to suddenism; the irrationalists neither know nor care. Millennialists will always find a way to reconcile cognitive dissonance. In the opinion of some, a part of everyone's mind needs to imagine an end of the world, and there is not much we can do about people allowing this thought pattern to take the upper hand under special circumstances. For Robert J. Lifton, "End-of-the-world imagery is something fundamental at the far reaches of the human mind, and I think [it] can be understood as a delicate cutting edge in the balance or imbalance between the struggle against disintegration, on the one hand, and the struggle toward renewal and restitution on the other. . . . [S]chizophrenia has relevance for all end-of-the-world imagery" (1987, 39). The murder of the world is the murder of the soul writ large.

Beyond rationalism, another option is to expose the self-interest and hypocrisy behind millennial thinking. In D. H. Lawrence's famous analysis, the apocalypse remains the most compelling expression of the will to power of the weak, helpless, and oppressed: "Revelation . . . is the revelation of the undying will-to-power in man, and its sanctification, its final triumph" (1982, 11). Lawrence clearly takes his orientation from Nietzschean thought, with its distinction between aristocratic and slave types.

Aristocrats, Lawrence argues, identify with Jesus and the Gospel. Love, gentleness, and unselfishness are harder to achieve and require more energy than Revelation's hatred and violence, always the favorites of the slave type. Revelation shows what has actually happened:

> The weak and pseudo-humble are going to wipe all worldly power, glory and riches off the face of the earth, and then they, the truly weak, are going to reign. It will be a millennium of pseudo-humble saints, and gruesome to contemplate. But it is what religion stands for today: down with all strong, free life, let the weak triumph, let the pseudo-humble reign. . . . This is the spirit of society today, religious and political. (ibid., 9)

It is worth examining the contradiction or dialectic of this passage. It posits a present state that is the culmination of Revelation (a postmillennial situation) and yet attempts to explain the persistence of apocalypse through that. It depicts the society of Lawrence's day as a dystopic millennium. It also represses those parts of Revelation that are loving and gentle, such as the depiction of the New Jerusalem and the healing of nations: "And he shewed me a pure river of water of life, clear as crystal, proceeding out of the throne of God and of the Lamb. In the midst of the street of it, and on either side of the river, was there the tree of life, which bare twelve manner of fruits, and yielded her fruit every month: and the leaves of the tree were for the healing of the nations. And there shall be no more curse" (22:1–5).

The conflicting imagery and moods of Revelation show that, like the grammar and vocabulary of a language, apocalypse cannot ultimately be judged as simply negative or simply positive, essential or superfluous. In concluding his rhetorical study of apocalyptic texts, such as those by Hal Lindsey and Billy Graham, Barry Brummett reaches this conclusion:

> The reader may be looking for a summary judgment as to whether apocalyptic rhetoric in general is a "good" or "bad" thing. No such judgment would be appropriate, any more than it would be for other fundamental, recurring genres in Western thought and culture, such as comedy or tragedy. . . . It may well be that "single-issue" rhetoric, just like single-issue politics, is the most dangerous and that attention to and balance among a multitude of discourses is necessary for mental, political, social, and discursive "health." (1991, 172)

Embracing multitudes, too, are the possible millennial worlds of literature examined in this book, which range from the abject ressentiment of *The Turner Diaries* to the transcendent resistance of Ernesto Cardenal and Bob Marley. In this view, not apocalypse as such but the exclusive or morbid focus on apocalypse is bad, as in the single-issue politics of *Left Behind*. Moreover, the removal of the apocalyptic dimension from Western discourse would be at least as bad as its presence in view of the fact that it would upset a balance between various kinds of discourses.

At its outer edges, millennialism becomes secular and progressive or hieratic and hermetic, respectively. Within these margins, it becomes subject to the reflective dissonances of literary representation analyzed in the foregoing. Its name becomes legion, and the messiah always comes in us, its readers and interpreters.

NOTES

Introduction

1. For the sake of consistency, throughout this book I use the term "millennial" rather than its synonym, "millenarian," as Noble does in the above quote. Though I consider the two versions synonymous, I find the former adjective being usually used for literary works ("millennial fiction" but never a "millenarian novel"), whereas the latter is more commonly used for political movements. I have left the term unchanged when it occurs in citations.

2. A study with a similar limitation is Douglas Robinson's *American Apocalypses* (1985), where "American" refers to the United States. In contrast, Jorge Cañizares-Esguerra's *Puritan Conquistadors* (2006), which I read after the present book was in production, is thoroughly comparative and contains much discussion of millennial literature and iconography in the Americas of the colonial period. Cañizares-Esguerra's overall goal, however, is to examine more broadly the "Iberianizing of the Atlantic."

3. I use the terms "Indian," "Native American," "First Nations," and "indigenous" interchangeably to designate the original inhabitants of the Americas; similarly, I use "black" and "African (American)" as synonyms. I do so principally because the sources for this study employ a range of terms for these peoples, and I am translating into English from different languages, each with its own terminology.

4. As detailed more fully in chapter two, I have chosen *hybridity* as the term to describe phenomena also known by terms such as *mestizaje, métissage*, syncretism, and transculturation. On their operation in the Americas see Antonio Cornejo Polar (2004).

5. Science fiction as a literary eschatechnology seems to me worthy of a separate volume, and I have not tried to survey the field for the present one, though I do incidentally treat a few texts considered to belong to the genre, such as *The Handmaid's Tale* [Atwood 1985].

Chapter One

1. Columbus himself used the term *otro mundo* (other world) and always maintained that this "other world" was part of Asia.

2. For a summary of Pay Zumé legends from various sources see Barbara Anne Ganson (1994, 77–84); cf. also Lafaye (1976, 177–207).

3. "Cargo cult" may be a misleading term here and in general. For critiques of the category see, for example, Lamont Lindstrom's *Cargo Cult* (1993) and the volume edited by Holger Jebens (2004) (neither study mentions Brazil). In this vein, European misreadings of Native American religions continue the cycle of millennial (mis)translation; the exact categorization of the movement here is less important than its specific details.

Chapter Two

1. The idea is Mary Douglas's in *Purity and Danger* (1966). Douglas gives shamans rather than messiahs as examples.

2. My discussion of the Friend is indebted to Catherine Keller (1996, 233–37).

3. In fact, Mooney records eleven names in all for Wovoka (1970, 765).

4. Cf., however, Glen Campbell's (1985) analysis of the affective drift in Riel's construction of the Métis as alternatively impedimental, tarnished, and betrayed icons.

5. I have emended Putnam's translation, which at this point takes substantial liberties with da Cunha's meaning. Above all, I have restored da Cunha's intention of making "shadow" the subject of the last sentence rather than "he" (the Counselor), as Putnam would have it. The solecism provides an excellent clue as to the poetic nature of da Cunha's style and his deliberate choice of typological imagery.

Chapter Three

1. Perhaps the first novel by a Native American to describe Wounded Knee, Dallas Chief Eagle's *Winter Count* (1967) devotes very little time and detail to the Ghost Dance. The vision of the dead and the return of the buffalo are not mentioned. In the story, the aspect of the dance emphasized is its provocation of a reaction from the U.S. Army, which results in the Wounded Knee massacre. The main character, wounded by a stray bullet from a Hotchkiss, accepts Christianity at his death.

2. Leopoldo Bernucci (1995, 65–84) has thoroughly documented mutual borrowings between Arinos and Da Cunha, along with conceivable resemblance owing to shared reliance on other sources, without however making an overall assessment of the very different results.

Chapter Four

1. For further examples and contestations of Festinger's hypothesis see *Expecting Armageddon: Essential Readings in Failed Prophecy*, ed. John Stone (2000).

2. Frederick Evans, in his *Autobiography of a Shaker* (1888), quotes Revelations 14:14: "And I looked, and behold a white cloud, and upon the cloud one sat like unto the Son of man, having on his head a golden crown, and in his hand a sharp sickle." He notes (conveniently ignoring the masculine pronouns): "What is so like a man as a woman? Ann Lee was like the Son of Man" (82).

Chapter Six

1. The ladder receives fuller treatment in the pseudepigraphical "Testament of Jacob," where the angel Sariel predicts that the Lord will "pour out his wrath" against Leviathan and Falkon (*The Hidden Bible* 47).

Chapter Seven

1. "Race" in this chapter is taken as the dividing line between one group and another based on perceived inherited characteristics. Hence, I am not overly concerned with the distinction between "race," "ethnic group," "people," and so forth, nor do I mean to imply any positivist basis for racial categories.

2. According to the theology of the novel and presumably of dispensationalism, this judgment of Christ will be followed by another at the end of the millennium: the Great White Throne Judgment. The souls linger in Hades for a thousand years until they are cast into the lake of fire after the second judgment (LaHaye and Jenkins 2004, 369).

3. The song Marley was performing at that moment was not "One Love"; nonetheless, a still of the three men is reproduced with the lyrics to "One Love" in *Songs of Freedom* [1992].

Conclusion

1. I am indebted to Steven W. Thomas, St. John's University, for bringing this text to my attention.

BIBLIOGRAPHY

This bibliography is divided into primary works, which include all creative works and millennial writings, and secondary works, which include scholarly or journalistic studies of millennialism or of specific authors or works in the primary list.

Primary

Alexie, Sherman. *Indian Killer*. New York: Atlantic Monthly Press, 1996.

Ampiés, Martín Martínez de. *Libro del anticristo*. 1494. Ed. Françoise Gilbert. Pamplona: Ediciones Universidad de Navarra, 1999.

Apocalypse de Chiokoyhikoy, chéf des Iroquois, sauvages du Nord de l'Amérique: écrite par lui-même vers l'an de l'ère chrétienne, 1305. Philadelphia [Paris?]: W. Roberdson, 1777.

Arguedas, José Maria. "La agonía de Rasu-Ñiti." *La agonía de Rasu-Ñiti*. Lima: Populibros Peruanos, 1962. 7–17.

———. *Tupac Amaru Kamaq Taytanchisman*. Lima: Salqantay, 1962.

Aridjis, Homero. *El señor de los últimos dias*. Mexico City: Alfaguara, 1994. Trans. Betty Ferber. *The Lord of the Last Days: Visions of the Year 1000*. New York: William Morrow, 1995.

Arinos, Afonso. "Campanha de Canudos (Epílogo da Guerra)." *Obra completa*. Ed. Afrânio Coutinho. Rio de Janeiro: Instituto Nacional do Livro, 1969. 646.

———. *Os jagunços*. 1898. 3d ed. Rio de Janeiro: Philobiblion, 1985.

Arregui, Mario. "Los dos amantes del apocalipsis." *El narrador*. Montevideo: Marcha, 1972. 97–104.

Atwood, Margaret. *The Handmaid's Tale*. New York: Houghton Mifflin, 1985.

Bailey, Paul. *Ghost Dance Messiah*. Tuscon: Westernlore, 1986.

Baldwin, James. *The Fire Next Time*. 1963. Reprint, New York: Modern Library, 1995.

Barbour, L. G. *The End of Time: A Poem of the Future*. New York: Putnam, 1892.

Benício, Manoel. *O rei dos jagunços*. Rio de Janeiro: Jornal do Comércio, 1899.

Beveridge, Albert J. "Our Philippine Policy." *The Meaning of the Times and Other Speeches.* 1908. Reprint, Freeport, N.Y.: Books for Libraries Press, 1968. 58–88.

The Book of the Jaguar Priest. Trans. and ed. Maude Worcester Makemson. New York: Schuman, 1951.

Born in Flames. Dir. Lizzie Borden. Screenplay by Lizzie Borden and Hisa Tayo. First Run Features, 1983.

Brown, Chester. *Louis Riel: A Comic Strip Biography.* Montreal: Drawn and Quarterly, 2003.

Burton, LeVar. *Aftermath.* New York: Aspect-Warner, 1997.

Bush, George. *The Millennium of the Apocalypse,* 2d ed. Salem: Jewett, 1842.

Cairns, Scott. "The End of the World." *The Translation of Babel: Poems.* Athens: University of Georgia Press, 1990. 19–20.

Canário, Eldon. *Os mal-aventurados do Belo Monte.* Aracajú (Sergipe), Brazil: Universidade Tiradentes, 1997.

Cardenal, Ernesto. "Apocalipsis." *Antología.* Santiago, Chile: Editora Santiago, 1967. 75–81.

———. *Canto cósmico.* Managua: Nueva Nicaragua, 1989. Trans. John Lyons. *Cosmic Canticle.* Willimantic, Conn.: Curbstone, 1993.

———. *El evangelio en Solentiname.* 4 vols. Salamanca, Spain: Sigueme, 1975–1977. Trans. Donald D. Walsh. *The Gospel in Solentiname.* 4 vols. Maryknoll, N.Y.: Orbis, 1982.

———. *Homenaje a los indios americanos.* León: Universidad Nacional Autónoma de Nicaragua, 1969. Trans. Monique Altschul and Carlos Altschul. *Homage to the American Indians.* Baltimore: Johns Hopkins University Press, 1973.

———. *Los ovnis de oro: poemas indios* [Golden UFOs: Indian Poems]. Trans. Carlos Altschul and Monique Altschul. Ed. Russell O. Salmon. Bloomington: Indiana University Press, 1992.

———. *Vida perdida: primera parte.* Barcelona: Seix Barral, 1999.

Carpentier, Alejo. "Literatura y revolución (encuestas)." *Casa de las Américas* 51/52 (1968–1969): 125–27.

———. *El reino de este mundo.* 1949. 6th ed. Mexico City: Cia. General de Ediciones, 1973. Trans. Harriet de Onis. *The Kingdom of This World.* New York: Knopf, 1957.

Chief Eagle, Dallas. *Winter Count.* 1967. Lincoln: University of Nebraska Press, 2003.

Codrescu, Andrei. *Messiah: A Novel.* New York: Simon and Schuster, 1999.

Coelho Fontes, Oleone. *A quinta expedição (romance histórico).* 2d ed. Salvador, Brazil: Editora Ponto e Vírgula, 2002.

Columbus, Christopher. *The* Libro de profecías *of Christopher Columbus.* Trans. Delno C. West and August Kling. Gainesville: University of Florida Press, 1991.

———. *Select Letters.* Trans. and ed. R. H. Major. London: Hakluyt Society, 1847.

———. *Textos y documentos completos.* Ed. Consuelo Varela and Juan Gil. Madrid: Alianza Editorial, 1987.

Constantin-Weyer, Maurice. *La bourrasque.* Paris: Rieder, 1925. Trans. anonymous. *The Half-breed.* New York: Macauley, 1930.

Coover, Robert. *The Origin of the Brunists.* New York: Putnam, 1966.

Corcoran, Bill, dir. *Left Behind II: Tribulation Force.* Screenplay John Patus and Paul Lalonde. Cloud Ten Pictures, 2002.

Cortázar, Júlio. "Apocalipsis de Solentiname." *Relatos 4.* Madrid: Alianza, 1985. 12–18. Trans. Gregory Rabassa. "Apocalypse of Solentiname." *We Love Glenda So Much and a Change of Light.* New York: Knopf, 1984.

Cotton, John. *Exposition upon the Thirteenth Chapter of the Revelation.* London, 1655.

———. *The Powring out of the Seven Vials.* London, 1642.

Coulter, John. *The Crime of Louis Riel.* Toronto: Playwrights Co-op, 1976.

———. *The Trial of Louis Riel.* Ottawa: Oberon, 1968.

da Cunha, Euclides. *Os sertões: campanha de Canudos*, 31st. ed. 1902. Rio de Janeiro: Alves, 1982. Trans. Samuel Putnam. *Rebellion in the Backlands*. Chicago: University of Chicago Press, 1944.

D'Alessio, Rafael Henzo. *El apocalipsis según don Quijote*. Buenos Aires: Plus Ultra, 1974.

Däniken, Eric von. *Chariots of the Gods? Unsolved Mysteries of the Past*. Trans. Michael Heron. London: Souvenir, 1969.

Dantas Barreto, Emygdio. *Accidentes da guerra: operações de Canudos*. Porto Alegre, Brazil: R. Strauch, 1905.

———. *Última expedição a Canudos*. Porto Alegre, Brazil: Franco and Irmão, 1898.

del Barco Centenera, Martín. "Canto XX. Como un indio llamado Obera se intitulaba hijo de Dios, y à un hijo suyo, Papa, y à otro Emperador." *La Argentina; o, la conquista espiritual del Rio de la Plata, poema histórico*. Buenos Aires: Imprenta del Estado, 1836. 215–33.

Donnelly, Ignatius. "Address to the People's Party Convention." 1892. Ignatius Donnelly Papers, Minnesota Historical Society. Microfilm roll 102.

[Donnelly, Ignatius]. *Caesar's Column: A Story of the Twentieth Century*. By Edmund Boisgilbert. Chicago: F. J. Schulte, 1890.

Dylan, Bob. *Biograph*. Audiocassettes. Columbia, 1985.

———. *The Bootleg Series* (rare and unreleased), vols. 1–3. Audiocassettes. Columbia, 1991.

———. *Chronicles*, vol. 1. New York: Simon and Schuster, 2004.

———. *The Freewheelin' Bob Dylan*. LP. Columbia, 1963.

———. *Highway 61 Revisited*. LP. Columbia, 1965.

———. *Infidels*. LP. Columbia, 1983.

———. *Lyrics, 1962–2001*. New York: Simon and Schuster, 2004.

———. *Saved*. Audiocassette. Columbia, 1980.

———. *Slow Train Coming*. LP. Columbia, 1979.

Edwards, Jonathan. *Apocalyptic Writings: The Works of Jonathan Edwards*, vol. 5. New Haven, Conn.: Yale University Press, 1977.

Eggleston, Edward. *The End of the World*. New York: Orange Judd, 1872.

The End Is Near! Visions of Apocalypse, Millennium, and Utopia: Works from the American Visionary Art Museum. Los Angeles: Dilettante Press, 1998.

Evans, Frederick W. *Autobiography of a Shaker and Revelation of the Apocalypse*, 2d ed. New York: American News, 1888.

Faid, R. W. *Gorbachev! Has the Real Antichrist Come?* Tulsa: Victory House, 1988.

Freixedo, Salvador. *La amenaza extraterrestre*. Madrid: Bitacor, 1989.

Freneau, Philip, and H. H. Brackenridge. "A Poem, on the Rising Glory of America." London: Crukshank, 1772.

Guedes, Edmundo. "O novo Antônio Conselheiro." *O novo Antônio Conselheiro e outros contos*. Salvador, Brazil: Fundação Biblioteca Nacional, 1997. 13–77.

Hawthorne, Nathaniel. "The Celestial Rail-road." 1843. *Tales and Sketches*, 808–24.

———. "Earth's Holocaust." 1844. *Tales and Sketches*, 887–906.

———. "The Hall of Fantasy." 1843. *Tales and Sketches*, 734–45.

———. "The New Adam and Eve." 1843. *Tales and Sketches*, 746–63.

———. *Tales and Sketches*. Ed. Roy Harvey Pearce. New York: Library of America, 1982.

Henry, Arthur. *Nicholas Blood, Candidate*. New York: Oliver Dodd, 1890.

Hernández, Luisa Josefina. *Apocalipsis cum figuris*. Xalapa, Mexico: UV Editorial, 1982.

Hinostroza, Rodolfo. *Apocalipsis de una noche de verano*. Lima: Instituto Nacional de Cultura, 1988.

Ibañez, Sara de. "Apocalipsis XX." *Poemas escogidos*. Mexico City: Veintinuno, 1974. 137–44.

Ironside, Harry A. *Lectures on the Revelation*. Neptune, N.J.: Loizeaux Bros., 1919.

Johnson, Blind Willie. "John the Revelator." *Anthology of American Folk Music*. Comp. and annotated by Harry Smith. Three LPs. Folkways Records, 1952.

Jurieu, Pierre. *The Accomplishment of the Scripture Prophecies*. London, 1687.

Karr, Mary. "Disappointments of the Apocalypse." *The Devil's Tour*. New York: New Directions, 1986. 18–20.

King, Stephen. *The Stand*. 1978. Rev. ed., New York: Signet, 1990.

Koresh, David. "The Seven Seals of the Book of Revelation." *Why Waco? Cults and the Battle for Religious Freedom in America*. Ed. James D. Tabor and Eugene V. Gallagher. Berkeley: University of California Press, 1993. 191–211.

Lacunza, Manuel. *La venida del Mesías en gloria y majestad*. 1790. Ed. Mario Gongora. Santiago, Chile: Editorial Universitaria, 1969.

LaHaye, Tim. *Revelation Unveiled*. Grand Rapids, Mich.: Zondervan, 1999.

———, and Jerry B. Jenkins. *Apollyon*. Wheaton, Ill.: Tyndale House, 1999.

———. *Armageddon: The Cosmic Battle of the Ages*. Wheaton, Ill.: Tyndale House, 2003.

———. *Assassins*. Wheaton, Ill.: Tyndale House, 2000.

———. *Desecration: Antichrist Takes the Throne*. Wheaton, Ill.: Tyndale House, 2001.

———. *Glorious Appearing: The End of Days*. Wheaton, Ill.: Tyndale House, 2004.

———. *The Indwelling: The Beast Takes Possession*. Wheaton, Ill.: Tyndale House, 2000.

———. *Left Behind: A Novel of the Earth's Last Days*. Wheaton, Ill.: Tyndale House, 1995.

———. *The Mark: The Beast Rules the World*. Wheaton, Ill.: Tyndale House, 2001.

———. *Nicolae: The Rise of Antichrist*. Wheaton, Ill.: Tyndale House, 1997.

———. *The Remnant: On the Brink of Armageddon*. Wheaton, Ill.: Tyndale House, 2002.

———. *Soul Harvest: The World Takes Sides*. Wheaton, Ill.: Tyndale House, 1998.

———. *Tribulation Force: The Continuing Drama of Those Left Behind*. Wheaton, Ill.: Tyndale House, 1996.

Lane, Charles. "Millennial Church." *Dial* 4 (March 1844): 537–40.

Lindsey, Hal. *The Late Great Planet Earth*. Grand Rapids, Mich.: Zondervan, 1970.

———. *The 1980s: Countdown to Armageddon*. New York: Bantam, 1981.

Lutz, Giles A. *The Magnificent Failure*. Garden City, N.Y.: Doubleday, 1967.

MacDonald, Alex. *The End Is Near! Visions of Apocalypse, Millennium, and Utopia*. With contributions by Roger Manley et al. Los Angeles: Dilettante Press, 1998.

Maciel, Antônio Vicente Mendes. *Prédicas aos canudenses e um discurso sobre a República*. 1897. *Antônio Conselheiro e Canudos: revisão histórica*. Ed. José Carlos de Ataliba Nogueira. 2d ed. São Paulo: Editora Nacional, 1978. 47–190.

Marcondes, Ayrton. *As memórias de Frei João Evangelista de Monte Marciano*. São Paulo: Best Seller, 1997.

Marley, Bob. "Rasta Man Chant." http://members.tripod.com/~Herbs_Pirate/burnin.html. Accessed September 12, 2007.

———. *Songs of Freedom*. Milwaukee: Hal Leonard, 1992.

Martorell, Joanot. *Libre del valeros e strenu cavaller Tirant lo Blanch*. 4 vols. Barcelona: Verdaguer, 1873–1905.

Mather, Cotton. *Magnalia Christi americana*. 3 vols. London: Sowle, 1703.

———. "An Authoritative Edition of Cotton Mather's Unpublished Manuscript 'Triparadisus.'" Ed. Reiner Smolinski. 3 vols., PhD diss., Pennsylvania State University, 1987.

Mather, Samuel. *The Figures or Types of the Old Testament, by which Christ and the Heavenly Things of the Gospel were preached and shadowed to the People of God of old*. Dublin, 1683.

McGee, F. W. (and congregation). "Fifty Miles of Elbow Room." *Anthology of American Folk Music*. Compiled and annotated by Harry Smith. Three LPs. Folkways Records, 1952.

McNamee, James. *Them Damn Canadians Hanged Louis Riel! A Novel.* Toronto: Macmillan of Canada, 1971.

Mede, Joseph. *The Key of the Revelation.* London, 1643.

Meehan, Richard L. "Ignatius Donnelly and the End of the World." Palo Alto: Kirribili, 1999. February 4, 2006; http://www.stanford.edu/~meehan/donnelly.

Melville, Herman. *The Confidence-Man: His Masquerade.* 1857. New York: Norton, 2006.

———. *Moby-Dick, or, The White Whale.* 1851. *Herman Melville.* New York: Library of America, 1983. 771–1408.

———. *White-Jacket; or, the World in a Man-of-War.* 1850. Ed. Hennig Cohen. New York: Holt, Rinehart, and Winston, 1967.

Mendieta, Gerónimo de. *Historia eclesiástica indiana.* Ed. Joaquín García Icazbalceta. 4 vols. Mexico City: Salvador Chávez Hayhoe, 1945.

Merton, Thomas. "Figures for an Apocalypse." 1947. In *Collected Poems.* New York: New Directions, 1977. 135–47.

Miller, Walter M. *A Canticle for Leibowitz.* New York: Lippincott, 1960.

Miller, William. *Evidence from Scripture and History of the Second Coming of Christ, about the Year 1843.* Boston: Joshua Himes, 1842. Payson, Ariz.: Leaves-of-Autumn Books, 1994.

"El Mito de Inkarrí." Ed. and trans. François Bourricaud. *Folklore Americano* (Lima) 4(4) (December 1956): 178–87.

Mojtabai, A. G. *Blessed Assurance.* Boston: Houghton Mifflin, 1986.

Morningstar, Ed. "Star Knowledge Conference." November 24, 2002; http://www.angelfire. com/ms/MelchizedekAngel/elk1.html.

Motolinía, Toribio. *Memoriales e historia de los indios de Nueva España.* Ed. Fidel de Lejana. Biblioteca de autores españoles 240. Madrid: Atlas, 1970. 1–199.

Muhammad, Elijah. *Message to the Blackman in America.* 1965. Reprint, Newport News, Va.: United Brothers Communications Systems, 1992.

Napier, John. *A Plaine Discovery of the Whole Revelation of St. John set down in two Treatises: The One Searching and Proving the True Interpretation thereof: The other Applying the same Paraphrasticallie and Historicallie to the Text.* London, 1611.

Neruda, Pablo. "La United Fruit Co." *Canto General I,* 3d. ed. Buenos Aires: Losada, 1955. 181–82. Trans. Jack Schmitt. "United Fruit Co." *Canto General.* Berkeley: University of California Press, 1991. 179.

Novakovich, Josip. "The End." *Salvation and Other Disasters.* St. Paul: Graywolf, 1998. 139–59.

O'Connor, Flannery. *The Complete Stories.* New York: Farrar, Straus, and Giroux, 1971.

———. "Judgment Day." *Complete Stories.* 531–50.

———. "Revelation." *Complete Stories.* 488–509.

Oliveira Falcón, José de. *Canudos, guerra santa no sertão.* Savador, Brazil: BDA-Bahia, 1996.

Panger, Daniel. *Ol' Prophet Nat.* Winston-Salem, N.C.: John F. Blair, 1967.

Parker, Jane Marsh. *The Midnight Cry.* New York: Dodd and Mead, 1886.

Peabody, Elizabeth. "A Glimpse of Christ's Ideal of Society." *Dial* 2 (October 1841): 214–28.

———. "Plan of the West Roxbury Community." *Dial* 2 (January 1842): 361–72.

Pierce, William [Andrew MacDonald]. *The Turner Diaries,* 2d ed. Hillsboro, W.Va.: National Vanguard, 1980.

Raël [Claude Vorilhon]. *Le livre qui dit la vérité: "j'ai rencontré un extra-terrestre."* Clermont-Ferrand, France: L'Édition du Message, 1974. Trans. anon., *Space Aliens Took Me to Their Planet: The Book Which Tells the Truth.* Liechtenstein: L'Edition du Message, 1978.

Reid, Alejandro. *Apocalipsis: 17 visiones, 3 páginas de silencio y 4 epílogos*. Santiago, Chile: Minga, 1984.

Rezende, Sergio, dir. *Guerra de Canudos*. Morena Filmes, 1997.

Richard, Jean-Jules. *Exovide Louis Riel*. Montreal: Les Editions de la Presse, 1972.

Riel, Louis. *The Collected Writings/Les écrits complets*. Ed. George F. G. Stanley. 5 vols. Edmonton: University of Alberta Press, 1985.

———. *The Diaries of Louis Riel*. Ed. Thomas Flanagan. Edmonton: Hurtig, 1976.

———. *Journaux de guerre et de prison*. Ed. Ismène Toussaint. Outremont, Quebec: Stanké, 2005.

———. *Poésies de jeunesse*. Ed. Glen Campbell, Thomas E. Flanagan, and Gilles Martel. St. Boniface, Manitoba: Les Editions du Blé, 1977.

———. *Poésies religieuses et politiques*. Montreal: L'Etendard, 1886.

———. *Selected Poetry of Louis Riel*. Ed. Glen Campbell and trans. Paul Savoie. Toronto: Exile, 1993.

———. *Visions and Revelations of St. Louis the Métis*. Ed. and trans. David Day. Saskatoon: Thistledown], 1997.

Robertson, Pat. *The End of the Age: A Novel*. Dallas: Word, 1995.

Roquebrune, Robert de. *D'un océan à l'autre*. 1924. Reprint, Montreal: Fides, 1958.

Ruiz de Montoya, Antonio. *Catecismo de la lengua guaraní*. Madrid: Diego Diaz de la Carrera, 1640.

———. *Conquista espiritual hecha por los religiosos de la compañía de Jesus en las provincias del Paraguay, Paraná, Uruguay y Tape*. Bilbao, Spain: Corazón de Jesús, 1892.

———. *Tesoro de la lengua Guaraní*. Madrid: Juan Sánchez, 1639.

———. *Vocabulario de la lengua Guaraní*. 2 vols. Ed. Julio Platzmann. Leipzig: Teubner, 1876.

Santos, João Felício dos. *João Abade*. Rio de Janeiro: AGIR, 1958.

Sarin, Vic, dir. *Left Behind: The Movie*. Screenplay Alan B. McElroy and Paul Lalonde. Cloud Ten Pictures, 2000.

"Sevenseals.com." 2007. http://www.sevenseals.com.

Sherwood, Samuel. *The Church's Flight into the Wilderness*. New York: S. Loudon, 1776.

Silko, Leslie Marmon. *Almanac of the Dead*. New York: Simon and Schuster, 1991.

———. *Gardens in the Dunes*. New York: Simon and Schuster, 1999.

Sterling, Bruce. *Islands in the Net*. 1988. New York: Ace, 1989.

Stowe, Harriet Beecher. *Dred: A Tale of the Great Dismal Swamp*. 2 vols. Boston: Phillips-Samson, 1856.

Styron, William. *The Confessions of Nat Turner*. New York: Random House, 1967.

Turner, Nat, and Thomas R. Gray. *The Confessions of Nat Turner, the Leader of the Late Insurrection in Southampton, Va*. 1831. Ed. Kenneth S. Greenburg. Bedford Series in History and Culture. New York: Bedford-St. Martin's, 1996.

Vargas Llosa, Mario. *La guerra del fin del mundo*. Madrid: Seix Barral, 1981. Trans. Helen R. Lane. *The War of the End of the World*. New York: Farrar, Strauss, and Giroux, 1984.

Vasconcelos, José. *The Cosmic Race/La raza cósmica*. 1925. Trans. Didier T. Jaén. Baltimore: Johns Hopkins University Press, 1997.

Veiga, José J. *A casca da serpente*, 4th ed. Rio de Janeiro: Bertrand, 1994.

Vieira, Antônio. "Carta ao Padre André Fernandes." April 29, 1659. *Cartas*. Ed. J. Lúcio d'Azevedo. 3 vols. Coimbra, Portugal: Imprensa da Universidade, 1925. Vol. 1: 488–547.

———. *Clavis prophetarum: chave dos profetas*. *Livro III*. Ed. Arnaldo do Espírito. Lisbon: Biblioteca Nacional, 2000.

———. *Historia do futuro: livro anteprimeyro*. Ed. Maria Leonor Carvalhão Buescu. Lisbon: Casa da Moeda, 1982.

Villaboim Filho, Paschoal. *Canudos*, 2d ed. Rio de Janeiro: Tipo Editor, 1984.

Walcott, Derek. "The Ghost Dance." *Walker and the Ghost Dance*. New York: Farrar, Straus, and Giroux, 2002. 115–246.

"Walk in Jerusalem." Arranged by the Five Blind Boys of Alabama. *I Brought Him with Me.* Compendia Media, 1995.

Walsh, Frederick G. *The Trial of Louis Riel*. Fargo, N.D.: Institute for Regional Studies, 1965.

Whisenant, Edgar C. *On Borrowed Time and 88 Reasons Why the Rapture Will Be in 1988.* Nashville: World Bible Society, 1988.

Whiston, William. *An Essay on the Revelation of Saint John.* Cambridge, UK, 1706.

Wiebe, Rudy. *The Scorched-wood People.* Toronto: McClelland and Stewart, 1977.

Wigglesworth, Michael. "The Day of Doom." 1662. *Colonial American Writing.* Ed. Roy Harvey Pearce. New York: Holt, Rinehart, and Winston, 1962. 233–97.

Wilkins, Mary E. "A New England Prophet." *Harper's Magazine* 89 (1894): 601–12.

Williams, Roger. Letter to Thomas Thorowgood. December 20, 1635. *The Correspondence of Roger Williams.* Ed. Glenn W. LaFantasie. 2 vols. Providence, R.I.: Published for the Rhode Island Historical Society by Brown University Press, 1988. 30–31.

Winthrop, James. *An Attempt to Translate the Prophetic Part of the Apocalypse of Saint John into Familiar Language, by Divesting It of the Metaphors in Which It Is Involved.* Boston: Belknap and Hall, 1794.

———. *A Systematic Arrangement of Several Scriptural Prophecies relating to Antichrist with Their Application to the Course of History.* Boston: Thomas Hall, 1795.

Winthrop, John. "A Modell of Christian Charity." 1630. *Winthrop Papers.* Vol. 2: 1623–1630. Massachusetts Historical Society, 1931.

Secondary

Aberle, David F. "A Note on Relative Deprivation Theory as Applied to Millenarian and Other Cult Movements." Thrupp 209–14.

Adas, Michael. *Prophets of Rebellion: Millenarian Protest Movements against the European Colonial Order.* Chapel Hill: University of North Carolina Press, 1979.

Adolph, Robert. "Apocalypse Then and Now: History, Myth, and the American Imagination." *Canadian Review of American Studies* 18(2) (Summer 1987): 279–86.

Agüero, Oscar Alfredo. *The Millennium among the Tupí-Cocama: A Case of Religious Ethnodynamism in the Peruvian Amazon.* Uppsala: Uppsala Research Reports in Cultural Anthroplogy, 1992.

Ainsa, Fernando. *Génesis del discurso utópico americano.* Ortega and Amor y Vásquez 267–78.

Amanat, Abbas, and Magnus T. Bernhardsson, eds. *Imagining the End: Visions of Apocalypse from the Ancient Middle East to Modern America.* London: I. B. Tauris, 2002.

Anderson, Benedict. *Imagined Communities: Reflections on the Origin and Spread of Nationalism*, rev. ed. New York: Verso, 1991.

Anderson, David D. *Ignatius Donnelly.* Boston: Twayne Publishers, 1980.

Aridjis, Homero. *Apocalipsis con figuras: el hombre milenario.* Mexico City: Taurus, 1997.

Ariel, Yaakov. *On Behalf of Israel: American Fundamentalist Attitudes toward Jews, Judaism, and Zionism, 1865–1945.* Brooklyn: Carlson, 1991.

Armani, Alberto. *Ciudad de Dios y ciudad del sol: el "estado" jesuita de los guaraníes, 1609– 1768.* Mexico City: Fondo de Cultura Económica, 1982.

Arruda, João. *Antônio Conselheiro e a comunidade de Canudos.* Fortaleza, Brazil: RVC, 1996.

———. *Canudos: messianismo e conflito social.* Fortaleza, Brazil: Edições UFC/SECULT, 1993.

Atwood, Margaret. "The Handmaid's Tale and Oryx and Crake in Context." *PMLA* 119(3) (May 2004): 513–17.

Bailey, Paul. *Wovoka: The Indian Messiah.* Los Angeles: Westernlore, 1957.

Barber, Bernard. "Acculturation and Messianic Movements." *American Sociological Review* 6(5) (October 1941): 663–69.

Baritz, Loren. *City on a Hill: A History of Ideas and Myths in America.* New York: John Wiley and Sons, 1964.

Barkun, Michael. *Crucible of the Millennium: The Burned-over District of New York in the 1850s.* Syracuse: Syracuse University Press, 1986.

———. *A Culture of Conspiracy: Apocalyptic Visions in Contemporary America.* Comparative Studies in Religion and Society 15. Berkeley: University of California Press, 2003.

———. *Disaster and the Millennium.* New Haven, Ct.: Yale University Press, 1974.

Barney, Garold D. *Mormons, Indians, and the Ghost Dance Religion of 1890.* Lanham, Md.: University Press of America, 1986.

Bartram, William. *Travels through North and South Carolina, Georgia, East and West Florida, the Cherokee Country.* Philadelphia: James Johnson, 1791.

Batstone, David B. "Jesus, Apocalyptic, and World Transformation." *Theology Today* 49(3) (1992): 383–97.

Bauckham, Richard. *The Climax of Prophecy: Studies on the Book of Revelation.* Edinburgh: T. and T. Clark, 1993.

Baudot, Georges. "Amerindian Image and Utopian Project: Motolinía and Millenarian Discourse." Trans. Donna Buhl LeGrand. In *Amerindian Images and the Legacy of Columbus.* Ed. René Jara and Nicholas Spadaccini. Hispanic Issues 9. Minneapolis: Minnesota University Press, 1992. 375–400.

Baudrillard, Jean. "Hysteresis of the Millennium." Strozier and Flynn 250–62.

Bauer, Ralph. "Millennium's Darker Side: The Missionary Utopias of Franciscan New Spain and Puritan New England." *Finding Colonial America(s): Essays Honoring J. A. Leo Lemay.* Ed. Carla Mulford and David Shields. Newark: University of Delaware Press, 2001.

Bellman, Samuel. "The Apocalypse in Literature." *Costerus* 7 (1973): 13–26.

Bercovitch, Sacvan. *The American Jeremiad.* Madison: University of Wisconsin Press, 1978.

———, ed. *Typology and Early American Literature.* Amherst: University of Massachusetts Press, 1972.

Berger, James. *After the End: Representations of Post-Apocalypse.* Minneapolis: University of Minnesota Press, 1999.

Bergson, Henri. *Le rire.* 1911. Trans. Cloudesley Shovell Henry Brereton and Fred Rothwell. *Laughter: An Essay on the Meaning of the Comic.* New York: MacMillan, 1911.

Berkeley, David S. "*Figurae Futurarum* in *Moby-Dick*." *Bucknell Review* 21(2–3) (Fall–Winter 1973): 108–23.

Bernucci, Leopoldo. *A imitação dos sentidos: prógonos, contemporâneos e epígonos de Euclides da Cunha.* São Paulo: EDUSP/University of Colorado Press, 1995.

Besselaar, José van den. *Antônio Vieira: profecia e polêmica.* Rio de Janeiro: Editora da Universidade do Estado do Rio de Janeiro, 2002.

Bhabha, Homi. *The Location of Culture.* New York: Routledge, 1994.

Biddick, Kathleen. *The Typological Imaginary: Circumcision, Technology, History.* Philadelphia: University of Pennsylvania Press, 2003.

Bloch, Ruth H. *Visionary Republic: Millennial Themes in American Thought, 1756–1800.* New York: Cambridge University Press, 1985.

Bonilla, Luis. *Mitos y creencias sobre el fin del mundo.* Madrid: Escelicer, 1967.

Borgeson, Paul W. *Hacia el hombre nuevo: poesia y pensamiento de Ernesto Cardenal*. London: Tamesis, 1984.

Bowden, Betsy. *Performed Literature: Words and Music by Bob Dylan*. Bloomington: Indiana University Press, 1982.

Bowie, Fiona, ed. *The Coming Deliverer: Millennial Themes in World Religions*. Cardiff: University of Wales Press, 1997.

Boyd, James P. "Messiah Craze and Ghost Dance." *Recent Indian Wars, under the Lead of Sitting Bull, and Other Chiefs; with a Full Account of the Messiah Craze, and Ghost Dances*. Philadelphia, 1891. 175–210.

Boyer, Paul. "The Middle East in Modern American Popular Prophetic Belief." Amanat and Bernhardsson 312–35.

———. *When Time Shall Be No More: Prophecy Belief in American Culture*. Cambridge, Mass.: Harvard University Press, 1992.

———. "When US Foreign Policy Meets Biblical Prophecy." Alternet, February 20, 2003; http://www.alternet.org/story/15221.

Bozeman, John M. "Technological Millenarianism in the United States." Robbins and Palmer 139–58.

Braz, Albert. *The False Traitor: Louis Riel in Canadian Culture*. Toronto: University of Toronto Press, 2003.

Brodhead, Richard H. "Millennium, Prophecy, and the Energies of Social Transformation: The Case of Nat Turner." Amanat and Bernhardsson 212–33.

Bronson, Bertrand H. *The Traditional Tunes of the Child Ballads*. 4 vols. Princeton, N.J.: Princeton University Press, 1959.

Brooke, John L. *The Refiner's Fire: The Making of Mormon Cosmology, 1644–1844*. New York: Cambridge University Press, 1994.

Brumm, Ursula. *American Thought and Religious Typology*. New Brunswick, N.J.: Rutgers University Press, 1970.

Brummett, Barry. *Contemporary Apocalyptic Rhetoric*. Westport, Conn.: Praeger, 1991.

———. "Premillennial Apocalyptic as a Rhetorical Genre." *Critical Questions: Invention, Creativity, and the Criticism of Discourse and Media*. Ed. William L. Nothstine, Carole Blair, and Gary A. Copeland. New York: St. Martin's, 1994. 286–300.

Buarque de Holanda, Sérgio. *Visão do paraíso: os motivos edênicos no descobrimento e colonização do Brasil*. Rio de Janeiro: José Olympio, 1959.

Bubandt, Nils. "Violence and Millenarian Modernity in Eastern Indonesia." Jebens 92–116.

Bull, Malcolm, ed. *Apocalypse Theory and the Ends of the World*. Oxford, UK: Blackwell, 1995.

Burridge, Kenelm. *New Heaven, New Earth: A Study of Millenarian Activities*. New York: Schocken, 1969.

Burris, Skylar Hamilton. "Bob Dylan's Jokerman and the Bible: Using the Bible as a Key to Unlock the Meaning of Bob Dylan's 'Jokerman.'" *Bible Allusion in Bob Dylan's Lyrics*. 1999. December 2, 2005; http://www.literatureclassics.com/ancientpaths/jokerman.html.

Cabestrero, Teófilo. *Ministers of God, Ministers of the People: Testimonies of Faith from Nicaragua*. Trans. Robert R. Barr. Maryknoll, N.Y.: Orbis, 1983.

Câmara Cascudo, Luís da. *Cinco livros do povo brasileiro: introdução ao estudo da novelística no Brasil*. Rio de Janeiro: José Olympio, 1953.

Campbell, Glen. "Dithyramb and Diatribe: The Polysemic Perception of the Métis in Louis Riel's Poetry." *Canadian Ethnic Studies* 17 (1985): 1–10.

Campbell, Joseph. *The Hero with a Thousand Faces*. 1949. 2nd ed. Princeton: Princeton University Press, 1972.

Cañizares-Esguerra, Jorge. *Puritan Conquistadors: Iberianizing the Atlantic 1550–1700*. Stanford: Stanford University Press, 2006.

Carrasco, Davíd. *Quetzalcóatl and the Irony of Empire: Myths and Prophecies in the Aztec Tradition*. Chicago: University of Chicago Press, 1992.

Castro-Klaren, Sara. "Dancing and the Sacred in the Andes: From the Taqui-Oncoy to Rasu-Ñiti." *Dispositio* 14 (1989): 169–86.

Chacon, Vamireh. *Deus é brasileiro: o imaginário do messianismo político no Brasil*. Rio de Janeiro: Civilização Brasileira, 1990.

Chamberlin, E. R. *Antichrist and the Millennium*. New York: Dutton, 1975.

Chambers, Ross. *Room for Maneuver: Reading (the) Oppositional (in) Narrative*. Chicago: University of Chicago Press, 1991.

Chaves, Julio César. *Tupac Amaru*. Buenos Aires: Editorial Asunción, 1973.

Cherry, Conrad. *God's New Israel: Religious Interpretation of American Destiny*. Englewood Cliffs, N.J.: Prentice-Hall, 1971.

Chiampi, Irlemar. "Historia y mitologismo en *El reino de este mundo*." *Cuadernos Hispano-americanos* (July–August 2004): 51–60.

Chidester, David. *Salvation and Suicide: An Interpretation of Jim Jones, the Peoples Temple, and Jonestown*. Bloomington: Indiana University Press, 1988.

Cirqueira Galo, Antero de. Letter to the Barão de Canudos. March 19, 1897. In *Canudos: Cartas para o barão*. Ed. Consuelo Novais Sampaio. São Paulo: EDUSP, 1999. 158–61.

Clastres, Hélène. *The Land-without-Evil: Tupí-Guaraní Prophetism*. Trans. Jacqeuline Grenez Brovender. Urbana: University of Illinois Press, 1995.

Cloud, John. "Meet the Prophet: How an Evangelist and Conservative Prophet Turned Prophecy into a Fiction Juggernaut." *Time* (July 1, 2002): 50–53.

Cohen, Thomas. "Millenarian Themes in the Writings of Antônio Vieira." Levine, *Messianism* 23–46.

Cohn, Norman. *Cosmos, Chaos, and the World to Come: The Ancient Roots of Apocalyptic Faith*. New Haven, Conn.: Yale University Press, 1993.

———. *Pursuit of the Millennium: Revolutionary Millenarians and Mystical Anarchists of the Middle Ages*, rev. ed. New York: Oxford University Press, 1970.

"O Contestado: cinco anos e vinte mil mortos." *O Estado de São Paulo*, November 19, 1972, folios 7 and 8; November 26, 1972, folios 10 and 11.

Cook, David. *Contemporary Muslim Apocalyptic Literature*. Syracuse, N.Y.: Syracuse University Press, 2005.

Cook, Jonathan A. "New Heavens, Poor Old Earth: Satirical Apocalypse in Hawthorne's *Mosses from an Old Manse*." *ESQ* 39(4) (1993): 208–51.

———. *Satirical Apocalypse: An Anatomy of Melville's* The Confidence Man. Westport, Conn.: Greenwood, 1996.

Cooper, Carolyn. "'More Fire': Chanting Down Babylon from Bob Marley to Capleton.'" Reiss 215–36.

Cornejo Polar, Antonio. "Mestizaje, Transculturation, Heterogeneity." In *The Latin American Cultural Studies Reader*. Ed. Ana del Sarto, Alicia Ríos, and Abril Trigo. Durham, N.C.: Duke University Press, 2004. 116–19.

Craig, Cairns. "Benedict Anderson's Fictional Communities." Ed. Alistair McCleery and Benjamin A. Brabon. *The Influence of Benedict Anderson*. Edinburgh: Merchiston, 2007. 21–40.

Cro, Stelio. "Las reducciones jesuíticas en la encrucijada de dos utopías." Étienvre 41–56.

Cross, Whitney R. *The Burned-Over District: The Social and Intellectual History of Enthusiastic Religion in Western New York, 1800–1850*. New York: Harper and Row, 1950.

Cunninghame Graham, Robert B. *A Brazilian Mystic: Being the Life and Miracles of Antonio Conselheiro*. 1920. Reprint, New York: Dial, 1925.

————. *A Vanished Arcadia: Being Some Account of the Jesuits in Paraguay, 1607–1767.* 1901. Reprint, New York: Dial, 1924.

Danker, Donald F., ed. "The Wounded Knee Interviews of Eli S. Ricker." *Nebraska History* 62(2) (1981): 151–243.

Davidson, James A. *The Logic of Millennial Thought.* New Haven, Conn.: Yale University Press, 1977.

Davis, Mary Kemp. *Nat Turner before the Bar of Judgment: Fictional Treatments of the Southampton Slave Insurrection.* Baton Rouge: Louisiana State University Press, 1999.

Davis, Thomas M. "The Traditions of Puritan Typology." Bercovitch, *Typology* 11–45.

Dawes, Kwame. "Forging a Distinctive Sensibility: Babylon by Bus." Reiss 201–14.

Dawson, John David. *Christian Figural Reading and the Fashioning of Identity.* Berkeley: University of California Press, 2002.

Dawson, Lorne L. *Comprehending Cults: The Sociology of New Religious Movements.* New York: Oxford University Press, 1998.

Day, Aidan. *Jokerman: Reading the Lyrics of Bob Dylan.* New York: Basil Blackwell, 1988.

de Grandis, Rita. "The Neo-postcolonial Condition of the Work of Art." *José María Arguedas: Reconsiderations for Latin American Cultural Studies.* Ed. Ciro A. Sandoval and Sandra M. Boschetto-Sandoval. Ohio University Center for International Studies Monographs, Latin American Series 29. Athens: Ohio University Press, 1998. 53–69.

Della Cava, Ralph. "Brazilian Messianism and National Institutions: A Reappraisal of Canudos and Joaseiro." *Hispanic American Historical Review* 48(3) (1968): 410–25.

Dellamora, Richard, ed. *Postmodern Apocalypse: Theory and Cultural Practice at the End.* Philadelphia: University of Pennsylvania Press, 1995.

DeMallie, Raymond J. "The Lakota Ghost Dance: An Ethnohistorical Account." *Pacific Historical Review* 51(4) (1982): 385–405.

Derrida, Jacques. "Of an Apocalyptic Tone Recently Adopted in Philosophy." Trans. John P. Leavey Jr. *Semeia* 23 (1982): 63–97.

Desroche, Henri. "Les messianismes et la catégorie de l'échec." *Cahiers Internationaux de Sociologie* 35 (1963): 61–84.

————. *Les Shakers américains: D'un néo-christianisme à un présocialisme?* Paris: Minuit, 1955. Trans. and ed. John K. Savacool. *The American Shakers: From Neo-Christianity to Presocialism.* Amherst: University of Massachusetts Press, 1971.

Diacon, Todd A. *Millenarian Vision, Capitalist Reality: Brazil's Contestado Rebellion, 1912– 1916.* Durham, N.C.: Duke University Press, 1991.

————. "Peasants, Prophets, and the Power of a Millenarian Vision in Twentieth-century Brazil." *Comparative Studies in Society and History* 32(3) (1990): 488–514.

Doan, Ruth Alden. *The Miller Heresy, Millennialism, and American Culture.* Philadelphia: Temple University Press, 1987.

Dolezel, Lubomír. *Heterocosmica: Fiction and Possible Worlds.* Baltimore: Johns Hopkins University Press, 1998.

Dorsinfang-Smets, Annie. "Fins du monde en Amérique précolombienne." *Eschatologie et cosmologie.* Ed. Armand Abel et al. Annales du Centre d'Etude des Religions 3. Brussels: Les Editions de l'Institut de Sociologie, 1969. 73–87.

Douglas, Mary. *Purity and Danger: An Analysis of Concepts of Pollution and Taboo.* New York: Praeger, 1966.

Durham, Lord. *An Abridgement of "Report on the Affairs of British North America."* Ed. G. M. Craig. Toronto: McClelland and Stewart, 1963.

Dussel, Enrique. "A Nahuatl Interpretation of the Conquest: From the 'Parousia' of the Gods to the 'Invasion.'" *Latin American Identity and Constructions of Difference.* Ed. Amaryll Chanady. Hispanic Issues, vol. 10. Minneapolis: University of Minnesota Press, 1994. 104–29.

Duviols, Pierre. *La lutte contre les religions autocthones dans le Pérou colonial : "L'extirpation de l'idolâtrie" entre 1532 et 1660.* Travaux de l'Institut Français d'Etudes Andines 13. Paris: Ophrys, 1971.

Eastman, Elaine Goodale. "The Ghost Dance War and Wounded Knee Massacre of 1890–91." *Nebraska History* 26(1) (1945): 26–42.

Eichler, Margrit. "Charismatic and Ideological Leadership in Secular and Religious Millenarian Movements: A Sociological Study." PhD diss., Duke University, 1971.

Erickson, Sandra S. Fernandes, and Glenn W. Erickson. "Cunningham Graham's Plagiarism of da Cunha's *Os sertões* and Its Role in Vargas Llosa's *La guerra del fin del mundo.*" *Luso-Brazilian Review* 29(2) (Winter 1992): 67–85.

Erskine, Noel Leo. *From Garvey to Marley: Rastafari Theology.* Gainesville: University Press of Florida, 2005.

Étienvre, Jean-Pierre, ed. *Las utopías en el mundo hispánico/Les utopies dans le monde hispanique.* Madrid: Casa de Velásquez, 1990.

Facó, Rui. *Cangaceiros e fanáticos,* 2d. ed. Rio de Janeiro: Civilização Brasileira, 1963.

Farred, Grant. "Bob Marley: Postcolonial Sufferer." *What's My Name? Black Vernacular Intellectuals.* Minneapolis: University of Minnesota Press, 2003. 215–74.

Faubion, James D. *The Shadows and Lights of Waco: Millennialism Today.* Princeton, N.J.: Princeton University Press, 2001.

"Fear of Y2K Catastrophe Creates Survivalist Culture. Hoosiers Worried That Computer-driven World Will Be Crippled Are Preparing for the Worst." *Indianapolis Star* (January 17, 1999), A01ff.

Fekete, John. "Williams, Raymond." *The Johns Hopkins Guide to Literary Theory and Criticism.* Ed. Michael Groden and Martin Kreiswirth. Baltimore: Johns Hopkins University Press, 1994.

Fernández, Miguel Ángel. *La Jerusalén indiana: Los conventos-fortaleza mexicanos del siglo XVI.* Mexico City: Smurfit Cartón y Papel de México, 1992.

Festinger, Leon. *A Theory of Cognitive Dissonance.* Evanston, IL: Row, Peterson, 1957.

———. *When Prophecy Fails: A Social and Psychological Study of a Modern Group That Predicted the Destruction of the World.* 1956. Reprint, New York: Harper and Row, 1964.

Fiddes, Paul S. *The Promised End: Eschatology in Theology and Literature.* Malden, Mass.: Blackwell, 2000.

Flanagan, Thomas. *Louis "David" Riel, Prophet of the New World,* rev. ed. Toronto: University of Toronto Press, 1996.

Fletcher, Alice C. "The Indian Messiah." *Journal of American Folklore* 4 (1891): 57–60.

Fuller, John G. *The Interrupted Journey: Two Lost Hours "Aboard a Flying Saucer."* New York: Dial, 1966.

Fuller, Robert. *Naming the Antichrist: The History of an American Obsession.* New York: Oxford University Press, 1995.

Gálvez, Lucía. *Guaraníes y jesuitas: De la tierra sin mal al paraíso.* Buenos Aires: Sudamericana, 1995.

Ganson, Barbara Anne. "Better Not Take My Manioc: Guarani Religion, Society, and Politics in the Jesuit Missions of Paraguay, 1500–1800." PhD diss., University of Texas, 1994.

Garavaglia, J. C. "I gesuiti del Paraguay: utopia e realtà." *Rivista storica italiana* 93(2) (1981): 269–314.

Gibbs, Nancy. "Apocalypse Now." *Time* (July 1, 2002): 40–48.

Gilmore, Michael T. "Melville's Apocalypse: American Millennialism and *Moby-Dick.*" *ESQ* 21(3) (1975): 154–61.

Gilsdorf, Joy. *The Puritan Apocalypse.* New York: Garland, 1989.

Glissant, Edouard. "Creolization in the Making of the Americas." Hyatt and Nettleford 268–75.

Goldman, Marlene. *Rewriting Apocalypse in Canadian Fiction*. Montreal: McGill-Queen's University Press, 2005.

González-Echevarría, Roberto. *Alejo Carpentier: The Pilgrim at Home*. Ithaca, N.Y.: Cornell University Press, 1977.

Gossai, Hemchand, and Nathaniel Samuel Murrell, eds. *Religion, Culture, and Tradition in the Caribbean*. New York: St. Martin's Press, 2000.

Gould, Stephen Jay. *Questioning the Millennium: A Rationalist's Guide to a Precisely Arbitrary Countdown*. New York: Harmony Books, 1997.

Gray, Michael. *Song and Dance Man: The Art of Bob Dylan*. New York: Dutton, 1972.

———. *Song and Dance Man III: The Art of Bob Dylan*. New York: Continuum, 2000.

Graziano, Frank. *The Millennial New World*. New York: Oxford University Press, 1999.

Grinnell, George Bird. "The Messiah Superstition." *Journal of American Folklore* 4 (1891): 61–68.

Habermas, Jürgen. *Strukturwandel der Öffentlichkeit: Untersuchungen zu einer Kategorie der bürgerlichen Gesellschaft*, 2d ed. Frankfurt am Main: Suhrkamp, 1990. Trans. Thomas Burger and Frederick Lawrence, *Structural Transformations of the Public Sphere: An Inquiry into a Category of Bourgeois Society*. Cambridge: MIT Press, 1989.

Hale, Charles R. *Resistance and Contradiction: Miskitu Indians and the Nicaraguan State, 1894–1987*. Stanford: Stanford University Press, 1994.

Hamm, Mark S. *Apocalypse in Oklahoma City: Waco and Ruby Ridge Revenged*. Boston: Northeastern University Press, 1997.

Hardy, Friedhelm. "Despair and Hope of the Defeated: Andean Messianism." *Religious Studies* 11 (1975): 257–64.

Hathorn, Ramon, and Patrick Holland, eds. *Images of Louis Riel in Canadian Culture*. Lewiston, N.Y.: Edwin Mellen, 1992.

Haubert, Maxime. "Indiens et jésuites au Paraguay: Rencontre de deux messianismes." *Archives de Sociologie des Religions* 27 (1969): 119–33.

———. *Índios e jesuítas no tempo das missões: séculos XVII–XVIII*. São Paulo: Companhia das Letras/Círculo do Livro, 1990.

Hawthorne, Nathaniel. *Letters 1813–1843*. Ed. Thomas Woodson, L. Neal Smith, and Norman Holmes Pearson. Columbus: Ohio State University Press, 1984.

Heard, Alex. *Apocalypse Pretty Soon: Travels in End-time America*. New York: Doubleday, 1999.

Heidegger, Martin. *The Question concerning Technology and Other Essays*. Trans. William Lovitt. New York: Garland, 1977.

Herbert, T. Walter, Jr. *Moby-Dick and Calvinism: A World Dismantled*. New Brunswick, N.J.: Rutgers University Press, 1977.

Hittman, Michael. "The 1870 Ghost Dance at the Walker River Reservation: A Reconstruction." *Ethnohistory* 20(3) (Summer 1973): 247–78.

———. *Wovoka and the Ghost Dance*, expanded ed. Ed. Don Lynch. Lincoln: University of Nebraska Press, 1990.

Hoffmann, Charles. *The Depression of the Nineties*. Westport, Conn.: Greenwood, 1970.

Hoffman, Daniel. *Form and Fable in American Fiction*. New York: Oxford University Press, 1965.

Howell, Luisa J. "Elementos de la tradición judeo-cristiana en El reino de este mundo." *Diaspora: Journal of the Annual Afro-Hispanic Literature and Culture Conference* 10 (2000): 117–25.

Hoyer, Mark T. *Dancing Ghosts: Native American and Christian Syncretism in Mary Austin's Work*. Reno: University of Nevada Press, 1998.

———. "Prophecy in a New West: Mary Austin and the Ghost Dance Religion." *Western American Literature* 30(3) (November 1995): 235–55.

Hutcheon, Linda. *Irony's Edge: The Theory and Politics of Irony*. New York: Routledge, 1994.

Hyatt, Vera Lawrence, and Rex Nettleford, eds. *Race, Discourse, and the Origin of the Americas: A New World View*. Washington, D.C.: Smithsonian Institution Press, 1995.

Hyde, George E. *A Sioux Chronicle*. Norman, Okla.: University of Oklahoma Press 1956.

James, C. L. R. *Mariners, Renegades and Castaways: The Story of Herman Melville and the World We Live In*. London: Allison and Busby, 1985.

Jameson, Fredric. *Postmodernism; Or, the Logic of Late Capitalism*. Durham, N.C.: Duke University Press, 1991.

Jebens, Holger, ed. *Cargo, Cult, and Culture Critique*. Honolulu: University of Hawaii Press, 2004.

Johnstone, Richard. "The Rise of Faction." *Quadrant* 29(4) (April 1985): 76–78.

Jordán, María V. "The Empire of the Future and the Chosen People: Father Antônio Vieira and the Prophetic Tradition in the Hispanic World." *Luso-Brazilian Review* 40(1) (Summer 2003): 45–58.

"The Judgment Day Will Hold Him Liable." Anonymous review of *Moby-Dick*. *The Independent* (New York), November 20, 1851. *Critical Essays on Moby-Dick*. Ed. Brian Higgins and Hershel Parker. New York: Hall, 1992. 56–57.

Jung, Carl Gustav. *A Modern Myth of Things Seen in the Skies*. Princeton, N.J.: Princeton University Press, 1978.

———. *Psychology and Religion*. 1938. Reprint, New Haven, Conn.: Yale, 1966.

Kadir, Djelal. *Columbus and the Ends of the Earth: Europe's Prophetic Rhetoric as Conquering Ideology*. Berkeley: University of California Press, 1992.

Kant, Immanuel. *Kritik der Urteilskraft*. 1790. *Critique of Judgment*. Trans. Werner S. Pluhar. Indianapolis: Hackett, 1987.

Kaplan, Jeffrey. *Radical Religion in America: Millenarian Movements from the Far Right to the Children of Noah*. Syracuse, N.Y.: Syracuse University Press, 1997.

Keeler, Clyde E. *Land of the Moon-children: The Primitive San Blas Culture in Flux*. Athens: University of Georgia Press, 1956.

Keep, Christopher. "An Absolute Acceleration: Apocalypticism and the War Machines of Waco." Dellamora 262–73.

Keith, W. J. "Apocalyptic Imaginations: Notes on Atwood's *The Handmaid's Tale* and Findley's *Not Wanted on the Voyage*." *Essays on Canadian Writing* 35 (1987): 123–34.

Keller, Catherine. *Apocalypse Now and Then: A Feminist Guide to the End of the World*. Boston: Beacon, 1996.

———. "The Breast, the Apocalypse, and the Colonial Journey." *The Year 2000: Essays on the End*. Ed. Charles B. Strozier and Michael Flynn. New York: New York University Press, 1997. 42–58.

Kermode, Frank. "Apocalypse and the Modern." *Visions of Apocalypse: End or Rebirth?* Ed. Saul Friedländer, Gerald Holton, Eugene Skolnikoff, and Leo Marx. New York: Holmes and Meier, 1985. 84–106.

———. *The Sense of an Ending: Studies in the Theory of Fiction*. New York: Oxford University Press, 1967.

King, Stephen, and Richard J. Jensen. "Bob Marley's 'Redemption Song': The Rhetoric of Reggae and Rastafarianism." *Journal of Popular Culture* 29(3) (Winter 1995): 17–36.

Klooss, Wolfgang. *Geschichte und Mythos in der Literatur Kanadas: Die englischsprachige Métis und Riel-Rezeption*: Heidelberg: Carl Winter, 1989.

Kramer, Michael P. "New English Typology and the Jewish Question." *Sacvan Bercovitch and the Puritan Imagination*. Ed. Michael Schuldiner. Lewiston, N.Y.: Edwin Mellen, 1992. 97–124.

Krauze, Enrique. "Perú y Vargas Llosa: vidas variopintas." *Vuelta* 17(199) (June 1993): 17–20.

Kucich, John J. "The Politics of Heaven: *The Ghost Dance, The Gates Ajar*, and *Captain Stormfield.*" *Spectral America: Phantoms and the National Imagination*. Ed. Jeffrey Andrew Weinstock. Madison: University of Wisconsin/Popular Press, 2004. 101–23.

Kumar, Krishan. *Utopianism*. Minneapolis: University of Minnesota Press, 1991.

———, and Stephen Bann. *Utopias and the Millennium*. London: Reaktion Books, 1993.

Labarre, Weston. *The Ghost Dance: The Origins of Religion*. New York: Doubleday, 1970.

LaFargue, Paul. "Der Jesuitenstaat in Paraguay." *Vorläufer des neueren Sozialismus*. 3 vols. Berlin: Dietz and Vorwärts, 1922. 139–72.

Lafaye, Jacques. *Quetzalcóatl and Guadalupe: The Formation of Mexican National Consciousness 1531–1813*. Trans. Benjamin Keen. Chicago: University of Chicago Press, 1976.

Lamy, Philip. "Ufology." Landes, *Encyclopedia* 410–13.

Landa Ábrego, María Elena. *Juan Gersón, tlacuilo*. Puebla, Mexico: Gobierno del Estado de Puebla, 1992.

Landes, Richard, ed. *The Encyclopedia of Millennialism and Millennial Movements*. New York: Routledge, 2000.

———. *Relics, Apocalypse, and the Deceits of History*. Cambridge, Mass.: Harvard University Press, 1995.

Lara, Jaime. *City, Temple, Stage: Eschatological Architecture and Liturgical Theatrics in New Spain*. South Bend, Ind.: University of Notre Dame Press, 2004.

Laternari, Vittorio. *Les mouvements religieux des peuples opprimés*. Paris: Maspéro, 1962. Trans. Lisa Gergo. *The Religions of the Oppressed: A Study of Modern Messianic Cults*. New York: Knopf, 1963.

Lawrence, D. H. *Apocalypse*. New York: Viking, 1982.

Leverenz, David. "Historicizing Hell in Hawthorne's Tales." *New Essays on Hawthorne's Major Tales*. Ed. Millicent Bell. New York: Cambridge University Press, 1993. 101–32.

Levine, Robert M. *Messianism and Millenarianism in the Luso-Brazilian World*. Special issue of *Luso-Brazilian Review* 28(1) (1991): 1–151.

———. "Mud-hut Jerusalem: Canudos Revisited." *Hispanic American Historical Review* 68(3) (1988): 41–91.

———. *Vale of Tears: Revisiting the Canudos Massacre in Northeastern Brazil, 1893–1897*. Berkeley: University of California Press, 1992.

———. *The World out of Which Canudos Came*. Special issue of *Luso-Brazilian Review* 30(2) (1993): 1–116.

Levy, Steven, and Katie Hafner. "The Day the World Crashes." *Newsweek* (June 2, 1997): 52–59.

Lewicki, Zbigniew. *The Bang and the Whimper: Apocalypse and Entropy in American Literature*. Westport, Conn.: Greenwood, 1984.

Lewis, James R., ed. *The Gods Have Landed: New Religions from Other Worlds*. Albany, N.Y.: SUNY Press, 1995.

Lewis, R. W. B. "Days of Wrath and Laughter." *Trials of the Word: Essays in American Literature and the Humanistic Tradition*. New Haven, Conn.: Yale University Press, 1965. 184–235.

Lieb, Michael. *Children of Ezekiel: Aliens, UFOs, the Crisis of Race, and the Advent of End Time*. Durham, N.C.: Duke University Press, 1998.

Lifton, Robert J. "The Image of the 'End of the World': A Psychohistorical View." *Facing Apocalypse*. Ed. Valerie Andrews, Robert Bosnak, and Karen Walter Goodwin. Dallas: Spring, 1987. 26–48.

———. *Destroying the World to Save It: Aum Shinrikyo, Apocalyptic Violence, and the New Global Terrorism*. New York: Henry Holt, 1999.

Lindstrom, Lamont. *Cargo Cult: Strange Stories of Desire from Melanesia and Beyond*. Honolulu: University of Hawaii Press, 1993.

Lockhart, James. *The Nahuas after the Conquest: A Social and Cultural History of the Indians of Central Mexico, Sixteenth through Eighteenth Centuries*. Stanford: Stanford University Press, 1992.

Lynch, Edward A. *Religion and Politics in Latin America: Liberation Theology and Christian Democracy*. New York: Praeger, 1991.

Lyotard, Jean-François. *The Postmodern Condition: A Report on Knowledge*. Trans. Geoff Bennington and Brian Massumi. Minnesota: University of Minnesota Press, 1984.

Mack, John E. *Abduction: Human Encounters with Aliens*. New York: Scribner's, 1994.

———. *Passport to the Cosmos: Human Transformation and Alien Encounters*. New York: Random House, 1999.

Madden, Lori. "The Canudos War in History." Levine, *World* 6–22.

Malone, Bill C. *Country Music U.S.A.: A Fifty-year History*. Austin: University of Texas Press, 1968.

Mani, Lakshmi. "The Apocalypse in Cooper, Hawthorne, and Melville." PhD diss., McGill University, 1972.

Marcus, Greil. *Invisible Republic: Bob Dylan's* Basement Tapes. New York: Henry Holt, 1996.

Marsden, George M. *Fundamentalism and American Culture: The Shaping of Twentieth-century Evangelism, 1870–1925*. New York: Oxford University Press, 1980.

Marsh, Richard Oglesby. *White Indians of Darien*. New York: Putnam, 1934.

Martel, Gilles. *Le méssianisme de Louis Riel*. Waterloo, Ontario: Wilfrid Laurier University Press, 1984.

Martin, Luther H., and Patrick H. Hutton. *Technologies of the Self: A Seminar with Michel Foucault*. Amherst: University of Massachusetts Press, 1988.

Marx, Leo. *The Machine in the Garden: Technology and the Pastoral Ideal in America*. New York: Oxford University Press, 1964.

———. "*Moby-Dick* as an American Apocalypse." *Extracts: An Occasional Newsletter* 26 (1976): 3.

Mathews, Donald G. *Religion in the Old South*. Chicago: University of Chicago Press, 1977.

May, John R. *Toward a New Earth: Apocalypse in the American Novel*. South Bend, Ind.: University of Notre Dame Press, 1972.

McArthur, Benjamin. "Millennial Fevers." *Reviews in American History* 24(3) (1996): 369–82.

McGinn, Bernard. *Anti-Christ: Two Thousand Years of the Human Fascination with Evil*. New York: HarperCollins, 1994.

Mead, Walter Russell. "Evangelicals and Foreign Policy." *Foreign Affairs* 85(5) (September–October 2006): 24–44.

Mélia, Bartomeu. *El Guaraní conquistado y reducido: ensayos de etnohistoria*. Asunción, Paraguay: Centro de Estudios Antropológicos de la Universidad Católica, 1986.

Métraux, Alfred. *Migrations historiques des Tupi-Guaraní*. Paris: Maisonneuve Frères, n.d.

Middlekauff, Robert. *The Mathers: Three Generations of Puritan Intellectuals, 1596–1728*. New York: Oxford University Press, 1971.

Middleton, Darren J. N. "Riddim Wise and Scripture Smart: Interview and Interpretation with Ras Benjamin Zephaniah." Gossai and Murrell 257–70.

Middleton, J. Richard. "Identity and Subversion in Babylon: Strategies for 'Resisting against the System' in the Music of Bob Marley and the Wailers." Gossai and Murrell 181–208.

Milhou, Alain. *Colón y su mentalidad mesiánica en el ambiente franciscanista español.* Valladolid, Spain: Casa-Museo de Colón, 1983.

———. "El concepto de 'destrucción' en el evangelio milenario franciscano." *Actas del II Congreso Internacional sobre los Franciscanos en el Nuevo Mundo.* Madrid: Deimos, 1987. 297–315.

Miller, Perry. "The End of the World." *Errand into the Wilderness,* 2d ed. New York: Harper, 1964. 217–39.

Millones, Luis. *Mesianismo e idolatría en los Andes centrales.* Cuadernos Simón Rodríguez 15. Buenos Aires: Biblos, 1989.

Moniz, Edmondo. *A guerra social de Canudos.* São Paulo: Civilização Brasileiro, 1978.

Monteiro, George. "Dylan in the Sixties." *South Atlantic Quarterly* 73 (1974): 160–72.

Montenegro, Abelardo. *Antônio Conselheiro.* Fortaleza, Brazil: Batista Fontenelle, 1954.

Montgomery, Maxine. *The Apocalypse in African-American Fiction.* Gainesville: University Press of Florida, 1996.

Mooney, James. *The Ghost-dance Religion and the Sioux Outbreak of 1890.* Chicago: University of Chicago Press, 1970.

Moorehead, James H. *American Apocalypse: Yankee Protestants and the Civil War 1860–1869.* New Haven, Conn.: Yale University Press, 1978.

———.*World without End: Mainstream American Protestant Visions of the Last Things, 1880–1925.* Bloomington: Indiana University Press, 1999.

Moreno Cebrían, Alfredo. *Túpac Amaru: el cacique inca que rebeló los Andes.* Mexico City: Iberoamericana, 1988.

Morisset, Jean. "Louis Riel, écrivain des Amériques." Hathorn and Holland 397–408.

Moses, L. G., and Margaret C. Szasz. "My Father, Have Pity on Me: Indian Revitalization Movements of the Late Nineteenth Century." *Journal of the West* 23 (January 1984): 5–15.

Muratori, Ludovico Antonio. *Relation des missions du Paraguay.* Trans. F. E. de Lourmel. Paris: La Découverte/Maspero, 1983.

Murrell, Nathaniel Samuel, and Burchell K. Taylor. "Rastafari's Messianic Ideology and Caribbean Theology of Liberation." *Chanting Down Babylon: The Rastafari Reader.* Ed. Nathaniel Samuel Murrell, William David Spencer, and Adrian Anthony McFarlane. Philadelphia: Temple University Press, 1998. 390–411.

Newport, Kenneth G. *The Branch Davidians of Waco: The History and Beliefs of an Apocalyptic Sect.* New York: Oxford University Press, 2006.

Nichol, Francis D. *The Midnight Cry: A Defense of the Character and Conduct of William Miller and the Millerites, Who Mistakenly Believed that the Second Coming of Christ Would Take Place in the Year 1844.* Brushton, N.Y.: TEACH Services, 2000.

Nimuendajú, Curt. *The Tukuna.* Ed. R. Lowie. American Archaeology and Ethnology 45. Berkeley: University of California Press, 1952.

Noble, David F. *The Religion of Technology: The Divinity of Man and the Spirit of Invention.* New York: Penguin, 1999.

Nogueira, José Carlos de Ataliba. *Antônio Conselheiro e Canudos: revisão histórica,* 2d ed. São Paulo: Editora Nacional, 1978.

Nogueira Galvão, Walnice. "*Rebellion in the Backlands*: Landscape with Figures." Trans. Shoshanna Lurie. *Portuguese Literary and Cultural Studies* 4/5 (Spring–Fall 2001): 149–56.

Nye, David. *America as Second Creation: Technology and Narratives of New Beginnings.* Cambridge, Mass.: MIT Press, 2003.

Obenzinger, Hilton. *American Palestine: Melville, Twain, and the Holy Land Mania.* Princeton, N.J.: Princeton University Press, 1999.

O'Leary, Stephen D. *Arguing the Apocalypse: A Theory of Millennial Rhetoric.* New York: Oxford University Press, 1994.

Oliveira, Franklin de. *Euclydes: A espada e a letra.* Rio de Janeiro: Paz e Terra, 1983.

Olson, Charles. *Call Me Ishmael.* San Francisco: City Lights, 1947.

Ortega, Julio, and José Amor y Vásquez, eds. *Conquista y contraconquista: la escritura del Nuevo Mundo: Actas del XXVIII Congreso del Instituto Internacional de Literatura Iberoamericana.* Mexico City: Colegio de México; Providence, R.I.: Brown University, 1994.

Ossio Acuña, Juan M., ed. *Ideologia mesiánica del mundo andino.* Lima: Ignacio Prado Pastor, 1973.

———. *Las paradojas del Perú oficial.* Lima: Pontificia Universidad Católica del Perú, 1994.

Ostwalt, Conrad E. "Hollywood and Armageddon: Apocalyptic Themes in Recent Cinematic Presentation." In *Screening the Sacred: Religion, Myth, and Ideology in Popular American Film.* Ed. Joel W. Martin and Conrad E. Ostwalt. Boulder, Colo.: Westview, 1995. 55–63.

Otten, Alexandre. *"Só deus é grande": A mensagem religiosa do Antônio Conselheiro.* São Paulo: Loyola, 1990.

Painter, Nell Irvin. *Sojourner Truth: A Life, a Symbol.* New York: Norton, 1996.

Palmer, Susan J. *Aliens Adored: Raël's UFO Religion.* New Brunswick, N.J.: Rutgers University Press, 2004.

———. "Woman as World Savior: The Feminization of the Millennium in New Religious Movements." Robbins and Palmer 159–71.

Patrides, C. A., and Joseph Wittreich, eds. *The Apocalypse in English Renaissance Thought and Literature.* Ithaca, N.Y.: Cornell University Press, 1984.

Pease, Franklin. "Un movimiento mesiánico en Lircay, Huancavélica (1811)." *Revista del Museu Nacional* (Lima) 40 (1974): 221–52.

Peixoto, Demerval. *Campanha do Contestado.* 3 vols. Curitiba, Brazil: Fundação Cultural, 1995.

Pereira de Queiroz, Maria Isaura. *Images messianiques du Brésil.* Sondeos 87. Cuernavaca, Mexico: Centro Intercultural de Documentación, 1972.

———. "L'influence du milieu social interne sur les mouvements messianiques brésiliens." *Archives de Sociologie des Religions* 5 (January–June 1958): 3–30.

———. "Messiahs in Brazil." *Past and Present* 31 (July 1965): 62–86.

———. "On Materials for a History of Studies of Crisis Cults." *Current Anthropology* 12 (1971): 387–90.

Pessar, Patricia R. *From Fanatics to Folk: Brazilian Millenarianism and Popular Culture.* Durham, N.C.: Duke University Press, 2004.

———. "Revolution, Salvation, Extermination: The Future of Millenarianism in Brazil." *Southern Anthropological Society Proceedings* 13. Ed. Susan Abbot and John Van Willigen. Athens: University of Georgia Press, 1980. 95–113.

———. "Unmasking the Politics of Religion: The Case of Brazilian Millenarianism." *Journal of Latin American Lore* 7(2) (1981): 255–78.

Peters, Ted. "Exo-theology: Speculations on Extraterrestrial Life." James Lewis 187–206.

Phelan, John L. *The Millennial Kingdom of the Franciscans in the New World: A Study of the Writings of Gerónimo de Mendieta (1525–1604).* Berkeley: University of California Press, 1970.

Pickering, Stephen. *Bob Dylan Approximately: A Portrait of the Jewish Poet in Search of God.* New York: McKay, 1975.

Pinto, Luis Fernando. "A personalidade carismática de Antônio Conselheiro: aspectos psicanalíticos." *Revista da FAEEBA* 4 (1995): 23–53.

Powell, Timothy B. *Ruthless Democracy: The Multicultural Interpretation of the American Renaissance.* Princeton, N.J.: Princeton University Press, 2000.

Pring-Mill, Robert. "Cardenal's Treatment of Amerindian Cultures in *Homenaje a los indios americanos*." *Renaissance and Modern Studies* 35 (1992): 52–74.

Rama, Angel. "La guerra del fin del mundo: una obra maestra del fanatismo artístico." *Eco: Revista de la Cultura de Occidente* 40(6) (April 1982): 600–40.

"Red, White, Blue, and Brimstone: New World Literature and the American Millennium." Online catalog of an exhibit of the University Libraries of Virginia, November 15, 1999–April 28, 2000. http://www.lib.virginia.edu/small/exhibits/brimstone.

Reid, R. F. "Apocalypticism and Typology: Rhetorical Dimensions of a Symbolic Reality." *Quarterly Journal of Speech* 69 (1983): 229–48.

Reiss, Timothy J., ed. *Music, Writing, and Cultural Unity in the Caribbean.* Trenton, N.J.: Africa World Press, 2005.

Reiter, Frederick J. *They Built Utopia: The Jesuit Missions in Paraguay 1610–1768.* Scripta Humanistica 116. Potomac, Md.: Scripta Humanistica, 1995.

Ribeiro, René. "Messianic Movements in Brazil." *Luso-Brazilian Review* 29(2) (Summer 1992): 71–81.

Richard, Pablo. *Apocalypse: A People's Commentary on the Book of Revelation.* Maryknoll, N.Y.: Orbis, 1995.

Risch, Neil, Esteban Burchard, Elad Ziv, and Hua Tang. "Categorizing of Humans in Biomedical Research: Genes, Race, and Disease." *Genome Biology* 3(7) (2002). http://genomebiology.com/2002/3/7/comment/2007.

Robbins, Thomas, and Susan J. Palmer, eds. *Millennium, Messiahs, and Mayhem: Contemporary Apocalyptic Movements.* New York: Routledge, 1997.

Robinson, Douglas. *American Apocalypses: The Image of the End of the World in American Literature.* Baltimore: Johns Hopkins University Press, 1985.

Rodnitsky, Jerome L. *Minstrels of the Dawn.* Chicago: Nelson-Hall, 1976.

Rotman, David. "Genes, Medicine, and the New Race Debate." *Technology Review* 106(5) (June 2003): 40–51.

Ruby, Robert H., and John A. Brown. *Dreamer-prophets of the Columbia Plateau: Smohalla and Skolaskin.* Norman: University of Oklahoma Press, 1989.

Saínz de Medrano, Luis. "Tensiones utópicas en la literatura hispanoamericana del siglo XX." Étienvre 291–300.

Sakai, Naoki. *Translation and Subjectivity: On "Japan" and Cultural Nationalism.* Minneapolis: University of Minnesota Press, 1997.

Saliba, John I. "Religious Dimensions of UFO Phenomena." James Lewis 15–64.

Salmon, Russel O. Introduction. Cardenal, *Los ovnis de oro* 9–35.

———. "El proceso poético: entrevista con Ernesto Cardenal." *Inti* 32–33 (Fall–Spring 1990–1991): 189–200.

Sandeen, Ernest R. *The Roots of Fundamentalism: British and American Millenarianism.* Chicago: University of Chicago Press, 1970.

Schaden, Egon. "Kulturwandel und Messianismus bei den Indianern Brasiliens." *Studien-Jahrbuch* (São Paulo) 19 (1971): 9–20.

Scharnhorst, Gary. "Images of the Millerites in American Literature." *American Quarterly* 32 (1980): 19–36.

Schulz, Elizabeth A. *Unpainted to the Last: Moby-Dick and Twentieth-century American Art.* Lawrence: University Press of Kansas, 1995.

Serra, Ana. "La revolución como simulacro en *El reino de este mundo* y *El siglo de las luces* de Alejo Carpentier." *Romance Language Annual* 7 (1995): 621–25.

Sheffield, Marcus L. "Melville's Puritan Imagination." *Prospects* 25 (2000): 69–114.

Shih, Shu-Mei: "Global Literature and the Technologies of Recognition." *PMLA* 119:1 (Jan. 2004): 16–30.

Skidmore, Thomas E. *Black into White: Race and Nationality in Brazilian Thought.* Durham, N.C.: Duke University Press, 1993.

Sokoloff, Naomi B. "The Discourse of Contradiction: Metaphor, Metonymy and *El reino de este mundo.*" *Modern Language Studies* 16(2) (Spring 1986): 39–53.

Souza Martins, José de. *Os camponeses e a política no Brasil.* Petrópolis, Brazil: Vozes, 1981.

Stavans, Ilan. "Two Peruvians: How a Novelist and a Theorist Came to Represent Peru's Divided Soul." *Transition* 61 (1993): 18–39.

St. Clair, Michael. *Millenarian Movements in Historical Context.* New York: Garland, 1992.

Stein, Stephen J. "American Millennial Visions: Towards Construction of a New Architectonic of American Apocalypticism." Amanat and Bernhardsson 187–211.

———. "Transatlantic Extensions: Apocalyptic in Early New England." Patrides and Wittreich 266–98.

Stern, Steve J. *Peru's Indian Peoples and the Challenge of Spanish Conquest: Huamanga to 1640.* Madison: University of Wisconsin Press, 1982.

Stiegler, Brian. "Peruvian Political Metafiction." PhD diss, Pennsylvania State University, 1998.

Stoll, David. *Is Latin America Turning Protestant? The Politics of Evangelical Growth.* Berkeley: University of California Press, 1990.

Stone, Albert E. *The Return of Nat Turner: History, Literature, and Cultural Politics in Sixties America.* Athens: University of Georgia Press, 1992.

Stone, John R., ed. *Expecting Armageddon: Essential Readings in Failed Prophecy.* New York: Routledge, 2000.

Strozier, Charles B. *Apocalypse: On the Psychology of Fundamentalism in America.* Boston: Beacon, 1994.

———, and Michael Flynn, eds. *The Year 2000: Essays on the End.* New York: New York University Press, 1997.

Sundquist, Eric J. *To Wake the Nations: Race in the Making of American Literature.* Cambridge, Mass.: Harvard University Press, 1993.

"Survivalist Plans Built around Y2K." *Sunday Gazette Mail* (Charleston, S.C.) (November 29, 1998), 7Bff.

Sweet, Leonard I. "Christopher Columbus and the Millennial Vision of the New World." *Catholic Historical Review* 72 (July 1986): 369–82.

———. "Millennialism in America." *Theological Studies* 40 (1979): 510–31.

Tabor, James D., and Eugene V. Gallagher. *Why Waco? Cults and the Battle for Religious Freedom in America.* Berkeley: University of California Press, 1995.

Taussig, Michael. *Mimesis and Alterity: A Particular History of the Senses.* New York: Routledge, 1993.

Thompson, Damian. *The End of Time: Faith and Fear in the Shadow of the Millennium.* London: Sinclair-Stevenson, 1996.

Thompson, Keith. *Angels and Aliens: UFOs and the Mythic Imagination.* Reading, Mass.: Addison Wesley, 1991.

Thompson, Leonard. *The Book of Revelation: Apocalypse and Empire.* New York: Oxford University Press, 1990.

Thompson, Toby. *Positively Main Street: Bob Dylan's Minnesota*, rev. ed. Minneapolis: University of Minnesota Press, 2008.

Thoreau, Henry David. *Walden*. 1854. Ed. Walter Harding. Boston: Houghton Mifflin, 1995.

Thrupp, Sylvia L., ed. *Millennial Dreams in Action: Essays in Comparative Study*. The Hague: Mouton, 1962.

Tolkin, Michael. "Something Wicked This Way Comes." *Village Voice* (December 5, 1995): 13–19.

Toon, Peter. *Puritans, the Millennium and the Future of Israel: Puritan Eschatology 1600–1660*. Cambridge, Mass.: Harvard University Press, 1970.

Tuveson, Ernest Lee. *Redeemer Nation: The Idea of America's Millennial Role*. Chicago: University of Chicago Press, 1968.

"2000 Reasons to Take Stock." *Pittsburgh Post Gazette* (February 6, 1999), B-1ff.

Ueda, Reed T. "Economic and Technological Evil in the Modern Apocalypse: Donnelly's *Caesar's Column* and *The Golden Bottle*." *Journal of Popular Culture* 14 (1980): 1–9.

Underwood, Grant. *The Millenarian World of Early Mormonism*. Chicago: University of Illinois Press, 1999.

Valente, Valdemar. "Antônio Conselheiro e o Sebastianismo de Canudos." *Misticismo e região*. Recife: IJNPS, 1963. 89–103.

Vargas Llosa, Mario. *A Fish in the Water: A Memoir*. Trans. Helen Lane. New York: Farrar, Straus, and Giroux, 1994.

———. "El precio de ser moderno." Ossio Acuña, *Paradojas* 13–18.

———. *La utopia arcáica: Jose Maria Arguedas y las ficciones del indigenismo*. Mexico: Fondo de Cultura Económica, 1996.

———. *A Writer's Reality*. Ed. Myron F. Lichtblau. Syracuse, N.Y.: Syracuse University Press, 1991.

Versényi, Adam. *Theatre in Latin America: Religion, Politics, and Culture from Cortés to the 1980s*. New York: Cambridge University Press, 1999.

Villa, Marco Antônio. *Canudos: o povo da terra*. São Paulo: Ática, 1995.

Vinhas de Queiroz, Maurício. "Cargo Cult na Amazônia: Observações sobre o milenarismo tukuna." *América Latina* (Rio de Janeiro) 6 (1963): 43–61.

Wadding, Luke. *Annales minorum seu trium ordinum A. S. Francisco institutorum*, 3d ed. Vol. 16. Florence: Quaracchi, 1931.

Waggoner, Hyatt H. *Hawthorne: A Critical Study*, rev. ed. Cambridge, Mass.: Harvard-Belknap, 1963.

Wallace, Anthony F. C. "Revitalization Movements." *American Anthropologist* 58 (1956): 264–81.

Wallace, Wilson D. *Messiahs, Christian and Pagan*. Boston: Gorham, 1918.

———. *Messiahs: Their Role in Civilization*. Washington, D.C.: American Council of Public Affairs, 1943.

Wallis, Wilson D. "Socio-cultural Sources of Messiahs." *Religion, Society, and the Individual*. Ed. J. Milton Yinger. New York: Macmillan, 1957. 578–86.

Washington, Paul. "The Breaking of Knowledge: Utopia, Apocalypse and the New World." *Antithesis* 6(1) (1992): 97–104.

Wasserman, Renata R. Mautner. "Mario Vargas Llosa, Euclides da Cunha, and the Strategy of Intertextuality." *PMLA* 108(3) (1993): 460–73.

Watts, Pauline Moffitt. "Prophecy and Discovery: On the Spiritual Origins of Christopher Columbus' Enterprise of the Indies." *American Historical Review* 90 (1985): 73–102.

Weber, Eugen. *Apocalypses: Prophecies, Cults, and Millennial Beliefs through the Ages*. Cambridge, Mass.: Harvard University Press, 1999.

Weber, Timothy P. *Living in the Shadow of the Second Coming: American Premillenarianism, 1875–1982*. Chicago: University of Chicago Press, 1987.

Werner, Eric. *The Sacred Bridge*. New York: Columbia University Press, 1959.

Wessinger, Catherine, ed. *Millennialism, Persecution, and Violence: Historical Cases*. Syracuse, N.Y.: Syracuse University Press, 2000.

Whitman, Walt. "Matters in the South West." *Brooklyn Eagle* (May 6, 1846).

Williams, Paul. *Outlaw Blues*. New York: Dutton, 1969.

Wilson, Bryan R. *Magic and the Millennium: A Sociological Study of Religious Movements of Protest among Tribal and Third-world Peoples*. London: Heinemann, 1973.

Wojcik, Daniel. "Apocalyptic and Millenarian Aspects of American UFOism." *UFO Religions*. Ed. Christopher Partridge. New York: Routledge, 2003. 274–300.

Young, Robert J. C. *Colonial Desire: Hybridity in Theory, Culture, and Race*. New York: Routledge, 1995.

Yudelson, Larry. "Jokerman." *Dylan and the Jews*. October 9, 1999; http://www.well.com/user/yudel/Jokerman.html.

Zamora, Lois P., ed. *The Apocalyptic Vision in America: Interdisciplinary Essays on Myth and Culture*. Bowling Green, Ohio: Bowling Green University Popular Press, 1982.

———. *Writing the Apocalypse: Historical Vision in Contemporary U.S. and Latin American Fiction*. New York: Cambridge University Press, 1987.

Zarzara, Alonso. *Apo Capac Huayna, Jesús Sacramentado: mito, utopía, y milenarismo en el pensamiento de Juan Santos Atahualpa*. Lima: CAAAP, 1989.

———. "La conquista y la utopía según Atahualpa." Ortega and Amor y Vásquez 91–106.

Ziff, Larzer. *The American 1890s: Life and Times of a Lost Generation*. New York: Viking, 1966.

INDEX